"At long last! We finally have a scholarly volume of work that critically and efficaciously examines the multiple crossovers between tourism, migration, and exile. This remarkable collection of chapters provides an endless buffet of theoretically rich and empirically inspiring insights into diverse human mobilities and their implications for tourism. Crucial concepts, including migration, belonging, identity, existential fluidity, imaginaries, exclusion and inclusion, and many others, are skillfully interpreted through the lenses of mobilities, diasporas, migrations, refugees, and exiles. I congratulate Natalia Bloch and Kathleen M. Adams for putting together this consequential tome, which is global in its reach and appeal. This masterpiece belongs on the desk of every social scientist who has interests in tourism, migration, exile, and all other manifestations of human mobility."

Dallen J. Timothy, *Professor and Senior Sustainability Scientist,*
Arizona State University

"One of the most important developments in the study of mobilities over the last quarter century has been a growing willingness by scholars to consider the intersections between different forms of (im)mobility. Natalia Bloch and Kathleen M. Adams's edited volume constitutes a major contribution to this effort. This diverse collection of ethnographic case studies demonstrates the dynamic productiveness of addressing the overlaps and interplays between tourism, migration, and exile rather than treating these mobilities as investigative siloes. It will be a significant resource in both research and teaching."

Vered Amit, *Professor Emerita of Anthropology,*
Concordia University Montreal

"This collection constitutes an important step towards the integration of the study of mobilities. In a series of ethnographic case studies of tourists, migrants, exiles, refugees, returnees, and volunteers, the volume provides a framework for the systematic study of the great variety of personal mobility phenomena in different parts of the contemporary world. The insights of the authors and editors constitute a step forward towards the formulation of a systematic comparative approach to mobilities."

Erik Cohen, *Department of Sociology and Anthropology, Hebrew University of Jerusalem*

"Tourist, migrant, traveler, refugee: too often we take for granted what these terms mean and to whom they should be applied. This collection's lucid, thought-provoking chapters trenchantly challenge such simplistic categorizations, using the fine-grained lens of ethnography to reveal how mobilities overlap, intersect, and blur in lived experience – despite deep-rooted systems of governance, finance, representation, and scholarship that keep them conceptually distinct. Addressing a dazzling range of geographical settings, populations, motivations, and outcomes, this wonderfully coherent yet notably interdisciplinary volume will be a landmark work, prompting serious reflection and debate."

Dr. Naomi Leite, *Reader in Anthropology, SOAS, University of London*

INTERSECTIONS OF TOURISM, MIGRATION, AND EXILE

This book challenges the classic – and often tacit – compartmentalization of tourism, migration, and refugee studies by exploring the intersections of these forms of spatial mobility: each prompts distinctive images and moral reactions, yet they often intertwine, overlap, and influence one another.

Tourism, migration, and exile evoke widely varying policies, diverse popular reactions, and contrasting imagery. What are the ramifications of these siloed conceptions for people on the move? To what extent do gender, class, ethnic, and racial global inequalities shape moral discourses surrounding people's movements? This book presents 12 predominantly ethnographic case studies from around the world, and a pandemic-focused conclusion, that address these issues. In recounting and juxtaposing stories of refugees' and migrants' returns, marriage migrants, voluntourists, migrant retirees, migrant tourism workers and entrepreneurs, mobile investors and professionals, and refugees pursuing educational mobility, this book cultivates more nuanced insights into intersecting forms of mobility. Ultimately, this work promises to foster not only empathy but also greater resolve for forging trails toward mobility justice.

This accessibly written volume will be essential to scholars and students in critical migration, tourism, and refugee studies, including anthropologists, sociologists, human geographers, and researchers in political science and cultural studies. The book will also be of interest to non-academic professionals and general readers interested in contemporary mobilities.

Natalia Bloch is an Anthropologist and Associate Professor in the Institute of Anthropology and Ethnology, Adam Mickiewicz University in Poznań, Poland. She specializes in the anthropology of mobility in the postcolonial context. She conducted research in Tibetan refugee settlements and among mobile workers and entrepreneurs of the informal tourism sector in India. She is the author of the book

Encounters across Difference. Tourism and Overcoming Subalternity in India (2021). Her articles have appeared, among others, in *Critique of Anthropology*, *Annals of Tourism Research*, *Journal of Refugee Studies*, *Critical Asian Studies*, and *Transfers. Interdisciplinary Journal of Mobility Studies*.

Kathleen M. Adams is an Anthropologist, Professorial Research Associate at SOAS, University of London, and Professor Emerita at Loyola University Chicago. Her specializations include the politics of tourism and heritage, museums, arts, public interest anthropology, and the nexus of tourism and homeland migrant visits in Indonesia. She has authored five books, including two award-winning volumes, *Art as Politics: Re-crafting Identities, Tourism and Power in Tana Toraja, Indonesia* (2006) and *The Ethnography of Tourism* (2019, coedited). Her articles have appeared in various journals, such as *Annals of Tourism Research*, *Tourism Geographies*, *Museum Worlds*, *International Journal of Heritage Studies*, and *American Ethnologist*.

INTERSECTIONS OF TOURISM, MIGRATION, AND EXILE

*Edited by Natalia Bloch
Kathleen M. Adams*

Cover image: Michał Sita

First published 2023
by Routledge
4 Park Square, Milton Park, Abingdon, Oxon OX14 4RN

and by Routledge
605 Third Avenue, New York, NY 10158

Routledge is an imprint of the Taylor & Francis Group, an informa business

OR

© 2023 selection and editorial matter, Natalia Bloch and Kathleen M. Adams; individual chapters, the contributors

The right of Natalia Bloch and Kathleen M. Adams to be identified as the authors of the editorial material, and of the authors for their individual chapters, has been asserted in accordance with sections 77 and 78 of the Copyright, Designs and Patents Act 1988.

With the exception of Chapter 2, no part of this book may be reprinted or reproduced or utilised in any form or by any electronic, mechanical, or other means, now known or hereafter invented, including photocopying and recording, or in any information storage or retrieval system, without permission in writing from the publishers.

Chapter 2 of this book is available for free in PDF format as Open Access from the individual product page at www.routledge.com. It has been made available under a Creative Commons Attribution-Non Commercial-No Derivatives 4.0 license.

Trademark notice: Product or corporate names may be trademarks or registered trademarks, and are used only for identification and explanation without intent to infringe.

British Library Cataloguing-in-Publication Data
A catalogue record for this book is available from the British Library

ISBN: 978-1-032-02279-6 (hbk)
ISBN: 978-1-032-02280-2 (pbk)
ISBN: 978-1-003-18268-9 (ebk)

DOI: 10.4324/9781003182689

Typeset in Bembo
by Apex CoVantage, LLC

CONTENTS

List of Figures	*ix*
List of Tables	*x*
Foreword	*xi*
Mimi Sheller	
Acknowledgments	*xiv*
List of Contributors	*xv*

Problematizing Siloed Mobilities: Tourism, Migration, Exile   1
Kathleen M. Adams and Natalia Bloch

1   Temporality and the Intersection of Tourism and
Migration: Mobilities Between Cuba and Denmark   31
Nadine T. Fernandez

2   Migrant, Tourist, Cuban: Identification and Belonging in
Return Visits to Cuba   45
Valerio Simoni

3   Diasporic Im/mobilities: Migrants, Returnees, Deportees,
Expats, Tourists, and Beyond in the Vietnamese Homeland   60
Long T. Bui

4   Student Migration as an Escape from Protracted Exile: The
Case of Young Sahrawi Refugees   78
Rita Reis

viii Contents

5 The Intersections Between Tourism and Exile: Justice
Tourism in Bethlehem, Palestine 94
Rami K. Isaac

6 Crafting Activists from Tourists: Volunteer Engagement
During the "Refugee Crisis" in Serbia 112
Robert Rydzewski

7 Panama's Temporary Migrants in the Tourism Era 130
Carla Guerrón Montero

8 Intersections of Tourism, Cross–border Marriage,
and Retirement Migration in Thailand 148
Kosita Butratana, Alexander Trupp and Karl Husa

9 The Tourist, the Migrant, and the Anthropologist:
A Problematic Encounter Within European Cities 170
Francesco Vietti

10 In and out of Brazil: Overlapping Mobilities in the
Capoeira Archipelago 187
Lauren Miller Griffith

11 Intersections of Professional Mobility and Tourism Among
Swedish Physicians and Researchers 201
*Magnus Öhlander, Katarzyna Wolanik Boström
and Helena Pettersson*

12 Mobility Through Investment: Economics, Tourism, or
Lifestyle Migration? Narratives of Chinese and Brazilian
Golden Visa Holders in Portugal 217
Maria de Fátima Amante and Irene Rodrigues

13 Pandemic Postscript: Tourism, Migration, and Exile 238
Stephanie Malia Hom

Index 252

FIGURES

1.1	People of Cuban origin in Denmark	37
1.2	International tourism – numbers of arrivals in Cuba in 1995–2018	38
7.1	Afro-Antillean migrants on Colon Island, 19th century	132
7.2	Map of Panama	135
7.3	Marta in Providencia	140

TABLES

5.1	Most frequently used words	100
8.1	Reasons for migration to Thailand	156
8.2	Aspects of visiting family and relatives in Thailand	162
12.1	GV grantees by country of origin, October 2012 to May 2021	218

FOREWORD

In these times of pandemic disruptions to travel, hardening migration and border policies, and roiling climate emergencies troubling our entire planet, the burning questions of human and other species' (dis)placements press upon all other issues. The fractious and fragmented temporalities of moving and dwelling are at the forefront of social and ecological thought. In the face of inexorable climate mobilities, multispecies extinctions, viral outbreaks, political violence and wars driving exile, skyrocketing inflation, logistics breakdowns, and economic recessions, many are asking: Where can we stay or where can we go? How can we stay and how can we go? Shall we stay or shall we go?

Even so, in the midst of these existential crises, things may be weirdly calm and business as usual also continues. People go back to workplaces (which some never left); tourists go off on vacations (while others indulge in local staycations); families make decisions about where to move or how to stay in touch across distances; hopeful migrants climb into boats and cross deserts; and many people continue to find new ways to combine work, travel, migration, and international opportunities such as education or entrepreneurship. Birds and animals migrate; plants reproduce; tides come and go. Life goes on.

While the study of tourism mobilities, migrant mobilities, and experiences of exile and return has animated many debates about belonging and mobility in the contemporary world, it still remains a challenge to think about them simultaneously. Yet especially now this is a necessity in the emergent worlds of (re)mixed and mixed up (im)mobilities. And our theories, methodologies, and epistemological questions must forge new pathways to understand the current context.

This volume brings together sensitive investigations of multidimensional human mobilities and multilayered representations of complex (im)mobilities. One of the great outcomes of this book, like much satisfying ethnography, is to disrupt taken-for-granted dichotomies and dualistic thinking with more subtle hybrid models

xii Foreword

and braided forms of understanding. In drawing our attention to the many ways in which tourism, migration, and exile are not just entangled subjects but are intrinsically co-present flickering identities within diverse performances of travel, the authors dislodge settled categories and the assumptions we bring to them: home and away, consumption and production, citizen and foreigner, self and other, belonging and estrangement, danger and safety, and the local and the global.

Many of the contributions also hint at some ways for building more ethical relations of mobility and mobilizing research for greater mobility justice. All human mobilities, whether we like it or not, are governed by highly unequal mobility regimes and legal regimes (borders, visas, passports, temporary work permits, citizenship laws, racialized discrimination, data collection, surveillance, mobile tracking, vaccine cards, etc.). Such mobility regimes differentiate these subject positions of the tourist, the migrant, and the exile and diffract the spaces of mobility into splintered channels and systems of rule. Yet as the field of mobilities research shows us, these mobile subjects are also always interrelated with each other in multiple obvious and not-so-obvious ways. It is the complexity of these possible entanglements – and their implications for mobility justice – that this book compellingly conveys, delving into unexamined places with new optics and research approaches.

In the studies presented here, we encounter complex mixtures of expatriates, exiles, deported refugees, and diasporic return tourists, for example, in return mobilities to Viet Nam (Bui) or the subtly hyphenated practices of pilgrimage, educational travel, migration, and "visiting friends and relatives" tourism in the *capoeira* communities of practice around the world (Griffith). Tourism, migration, and exile all rely on the creation of "imagined archipelagoes" of different kinds (places where one desires to travel, places where one visits for a while, places where one anchors nostalgic memories or dreamed of futures), as well as more dystopian archipelagoes (places where one gets stuck, places to which one can never return, places where one cannot get a visa, and places one was forced to flee in terror). Yet the tourist archipelagoes, the migrant archipelagoes, and the archipelagoes of exile are overlapping and mutually constitutive.

Whether in physical places of transiting, waiting, and dwelling, or in imagined representational spaces of belonging, alienation, and nostalgia, the stories of the tourist, the migrant, and the exile appear together, confront each other, transform each other, and get wrapped into individual experiences of multi-mobilities. New stories and physical experiences can also be intentionally produced. Other chapters focus on the active intersectional practices of co-production and public pedagogy such as "justice tourism" in Palestine (Isaac) or "responsible tourism" in the European *Migrantour* (Vietti). Both seek to "radicalize" tourism not only by juxtaposing the politics of migration and displacement with the tourist's experience of freedom of mobility but also by building relations of learning and active engagement between oppressed groups suffering domination and those who seek out cross-cultural understanding of the places they visit or even their own homes.

At the heart of these inquiries are also questions of the mobilities of the ethnographer, the researcher, the academic, and the writer. What are our obligations to others and to the places through which we travel or stop traveling? Can dreams of liberation, justice, and healing still motivate our research travels or are we just business travelers becoming tourists? How does the diversification of higher education allow for the emergence of new mobile subjects who can practice ethical tourism/research/mobilities in ways that can respond to the demands of these times? These are questions for anthropology, global education, and academia as a whole. And in asking these questions, we can perhaps radicalize not only tourism but also radicalize ourselves, our methodologies, and our multidimensional travels through the world, or better yet in relation to the world(s) of others.

Mimi Sheller
Dean of The Global School, Worcester Polytechnic Institute

ACKNOWLEDGMENTS

This volume emerged from a co-organized panel presented at the 2019 International Union of Anthropological and Ethnological Sciences. The Congress, *World Solidarities*, was held at the Adam Mickiewicz University in Poznań, Poland: We thank both these institutions for creating a fertile venue in which to germinate the ideas at the core of this book. Our appreciation also goes to Bobby Luthra Sinha who served as a discussant for the panel. In addition, we extend our heartfelt thanks to Uma Kothari and Nelson Graburn for their suggestions, feedback, and encouragement. We also wish to express our gratitude to our editor at Routledge, Faye Leerink, for seeing the promise of this volume, for her patience with pandemic-induced delays, and for her impressive professionalism. Our thanks are also due to the rest of the staff at Routledge, Prati Priyanka, Spandana P.B. and others, who skillfully shepherded us through the publishing process, as well as our indexer, Kamila Grześkowiak.

Natalia would like to thank the co-editor of this book, Kathleen M. Adams, for her encouragement and constant support. It was a great pleasure to work with such a prominent anthropologist. She also thanks her colleagues in the Institute of Anthropology and Ethnology at the Adam Mickiewicz University in Poznań for creating an inspiring working environment. Last but not least, her heartfelt gratitude goes, as always, to her family, especially her partner and fellow anthropologist, Łukasz Kaczmarek, their son Leonard, and her parents, Marianna and Stanisław Bloch for their love and support.

Kathleen conveys her heartfelt appreciation to her co-editor, Natalia Bloch: Her intellectual curiosity, tireless work ethic, and good humor made it a genuine delight to work together on this project. She also thanks the Little Engines/Unicorns writing group for their support: They made the months spent in front of her laptop a little less isolating. She also offers her gratitude to Don LeBuhn, Kelly Halligan, and J.J. for enabling her to spend time in an inspiring setting replete with unforgettable vineyard walks (and the most wonderful canine companion) during the most intensive phase of manuscript preparation. Finally, her deepest debt of gratitude is to her family, especially her husband, Peter Sanchez, who saw to it that manuscript preparation did not crowd out tennis and hikes in the redwoods.

CONTRIBUTORS

Kathleen M. Adams is a Cultural Anthropologist, Professorial Research Associate at SOAS, University of London, and Professor Emerita at Loyola University Chicago. Her specializations include the politics of tourism and heritage, museums, arts, public interest anthropology, and the nexus of tourism and homeland migrant visits in Indonesia. She has authored five books, including two award-winning volumes, *Art as Politics: Re-crafting Identities, Tourism and Power in Tana Toraja, Indonesia* (2006) and *The Ethnography of Tourism* (2019, coedited). Her articles have appeared in various journals, such as *Annals of Tourism Research, Tourism Geographies, Museum Worlds, International Journal of Heritage Studies,* and *American Ethnologist.*

Maria de Fátima Amante is an Anthropologist, Associate Professor, and Head of the Anthropology Department at the School of Social and Political Sciences (ISCSP), University of Lisbon. She teaches several courses on migration. Her specializations include topics in political anthropology such as images and practices of the State, borders, mobility, and migration issues. Her current research interests are in mobility regimes, which she examines through the case of the Golden Visas policy in Portugal, focusing on Brazilian investors. She has published in several peer-reviewed journals, including the *Journal of Ethnic and Migration Studies* and the *Journal of Borderland Studies.*

Natalia Bloch is an Anthropologist and Associate Professor in the Institute of Anthropology and Ethnology, Adam Mickiewicz University in Poznań, Poland. She specializes in the anthropology of mobility in the postcolonial context. She conducted research in Tibetan refugee settlements and among mobile workers and entrepreneurs of the informal tourism sector in India. She is the author of the book *Encounters across Difference. Tourism and Overcoming Subalternity in India* (2021). Her articles have appeared, among others, in *Critique of Anthropology, Annals of Tourism*

xvi Contributors

Research, Journal of Refugee Studies, Critical Asian Studies, and *Transfers Interdisciplinary Journal of Mobility Studies.*

Long T. Bui is an Associate Professor at the University of California, Irvine, in the Department of Global and International Studies. His book, *Returns of War: South Vietnam and the Price of Refugee Memory* (2018), reframes the legacy of the Republic of Vietnam (South Vietnam) through a multidisciplinary approach that includes ethnography, oral history, literary memoirs, and archival research to understand how individuals and groups today remember this figure of loss. His second book is *Model Machines: A History of the Asian as Automaton* (2022).

Kosita Butratana has a Master's degree in Educational Psychology and Guidance from Chiang Mai University, Thailand, worked as an independent certified tourist guide, and was a lecturer at Suan Dusit Rajabhat University (Hua Hin Campus). She has conducted fieldwork for various projects related to tourism and migration in Southeast Asia and is currently a doctoral student at the Department of Geography and Regional Research at the University of Vienna, Austria, working on Thai marriage migration.

Nadine T. Fernandez is a Cultural Anthropologist and Professor in the Social Science and Public Affairs Department at SUNY Empire State College. Her research on race and gender relations in Cuba and Cuban marriage migration takes an intersectional perspective on transnational migration and tourism. Her publications include *Revolutionizing Romance: Interracial Couples in Contemporary Cuba* (2010); a co-edited (with Christian Groes) book *Intimate Mobilities: Sexual Economies, Marriage and Migration in a Disparate World* (2018); a co-edited (with Katie Nelson) open-access textbook *Gendered Lives: Global Issues* (2022); and several book chapters and journal articles.

Lauren Miller Griffith, Ph.D., is an Associate Professor of Anthropology at Texas Tech University. She studies performance and tourism in Latin America and the USA. Her most recent book (forthcoming from the University of Illinois Press) focuses on the relationship between capoeira and social justice and is titled *Graceful Resistance: How Capoeiristas Use Their Art for Activism and Community Engagement.* She is also the author of *In Search of Legitimacy: How Outsiders Become Part of the Afro-Brazilian Capoeira Tradition* (2016) and co-author of *Apprenticeship Pilgrimage* (with Jonathan S. Marion), which was published in 2018.

Carla Guerrón Montero is a Cultural and Applied Anthropologist, and Professor of Anthropology at the University of Delaware, United States, with joint appointments in Africana Studies, Latin American and Iberian Studies, and Women and Gender Studies. Her specializations include the anthropological study of tourism, cuisine, gender, and race in the Latin American African Diaspora. She is the author of *From Temporary Migrants to Permanent Attractions: Tourism, Cultural Heritage,* and

Afro-Antillean Identities in Panama (2020), co-editor of the award-winning book *Why the World Needs Anthropologists* (Routledge, 2021), and author of numerous book chapters and peer-reviewed journal articles in English, Spanish, and Portuguese.

Stephanie Malia Hom is an Associate Professor of Transnational Italian Studies at UC Santa Barbara and co-founder of the UC Berkeley Tourism Studies Working Group. She is the author of *Empire's Mobius Strip: Historical Echoes in Italy's Crisis of Migration and Detention* (2019) and *The Beautiful Country: Tourism and the Impossible State of Destination Italy* (2015). She also co-edited the volume *Italian Mobilities* (Routledge, 2016) and a special issue of California Italian Studies (2019) on "Borderless Italy." She writes and lectures on Italy and the Mediterranean, mobility studies, colonialism and imperialism, migration and detention, and tourism history and practice.

Karl Husa is an Associate Professor (ret.) at the Department of Geography and Regional Research at the University of Vienna, Austria. Until 2016, he was Head of the Southeast Asia Research Group at the Department and acted as Deputy ASEA-UNINET representative of the University of Vienna. Since 2010, he has also acted as an affiliate researcher at Suan Dusit University and as a visiting professor at the Research Institute for Languages and Cultures of Asia at Mahidol University in Thailand, most recently in 2022. His main research areas are demography, population geography, and human migration, with a regional focus on Southeast Asia.

Rami K. Isaac, born in Palestine, holds a Ph.D. in Spatial Sciences from the University of Groningen, in the Netherlands. He is currently a Senior Lecturer in tourism at Breda University of Applied Sciences in the Netherlands. In addition, he is an Assistant Professor at the Faculty of Tourism and Hotel Management at Bethlehem University, Palestine. His research interests are in tourism development and management, critical theory, and political aspects of tourism. He co-edited several books and published book chapters and numerous articles on tourism and political (in)stability, occupation, tourism, and war, dark (heritage) tourism, and transformational tourism.

Magnus Öhlander is a Professor in European Ethnology at the Department of Ethnology, History of Religions and Gender Studies, Stockholm University, Sweden. He has done research about elderly care, ideas about racism in Swedish public debate, the discourse on immigrant patients in health care, Polish-born physicians working in Sweden, internationalization and knowledge transfer in the field of medicine, and internationalization among scholars in the Humanities. His latest research interests focus on nurses migrating to Sweden to work. He has also written about culture theory and ethnographic methods and teaches European ethnology, diversity studies, and culture theory.

Helena Pettersson is an Associate Professor in Ethnology at the Department of Culture and Media Studies, Umeå University, Sweden. Over the past decade,

xviii Contributors

her research has been focused on highly skilled migration, international mobility, and knowledge production in the academy, parallel with science and technology studies and gender studies. Currently, she is also working on the topic of the cognitive and cultural understandings of curiosity. She is Departmental Deputy Chair and Head of Research, as well as Elected Member of the Royal Skyttean Academy of Letters & Science.

Rita Reis is a Ph.D. candidate in Social Anthropology at the Institute of Social Sciences, University of Lisbon. Through the case of Sahrawi refugees, Reis' research focuses on contexts of refugees and forced migrations, with special emphasis on youths' perspectives. Her research project focuses on Sahrawi student mobilities from refugee camps to Algiers (Algeria) and Badajoz (Spain). By analyzing the subjective and moral dimensions of prolonged forced migrations, her research aims to understand the notions of normality/exception and future perspectives.

Irene Rodrigues, Ph.D. in Anthropology (2013, ICS, Universidade de Lisboa), is an Assistant Professor in Anthropology at ISCSP, University of Lisbon. Since 2002, she has been engaged in several research projects on Chinese migration. She is the co-editor of the book *The Presence of China and the Chinese Diaspora in Portugal and Portuguese-Speaking Territories* (2021), co-author of the documentary on Chinese migrants in Portugal *We the Chinese* (2013), and has authored several articles and book chapters.

Robert Rydzewski defended his Ph.D. in Anthropology and Cultural Studies at Adam Mickiewicz University in Poznań, Poland, in 2020. He is Assistant Professor at Adam Mickiewicz University in Poznań and Postdoctoral Researcher at the Centre for Southeast European Studies at the University of Graz. Currently, he is working on a monograph on the migratory Balkan route in South-Eastern Europe. In cooperation with pro-migrant activists, he also runs a project on partnerships between pro-refugee grassroots groups and formal entities in Poland.

Valerio Simoni is a Senior Research Fellow at the Department of Anthropology and Sociology and the Global Migration Centre, Geneva Graduate Institute, Switzerland, and Research Associate at the Centre for Research in Anthropology, Portugal. Drawing on long-term ethnographic research in Cuba and Spain and focusing on situations marked by cross-border mobilities, notably international tourism and migration, his work addresses processes of social transformation with a special interest in the study of ethics, intimacy, economic practice, and the politics of belonging and community formation. He is the author of the award-winning monograph *Tourism and Informal Encounters in Cuba* (2016).

Contributors **xix**

Alexander Trupp is the Associate Dean for Research and Postgraduate Studies cum Associate Professor at the School of Hospitality and Service Management, Sunway University, Malaysia. He is also the acting head of the Asia Pacific Centre for Hospitality Research and editor-in-chief of the Austrian Journal of South-East Asian Studies. Prior to joining Sunway University, Alexander worked at the University of Vienna (Austria), Mahidol University (Thailand), and the University of the South Pacific (Fiji). His research is nested in the fields of tourism geography, mobilities, and sustainable tourism, with a regional focus on Southeast Asia and the Pacific Islands.

Francesco Vietti is an Anthropologist and Assistant Professor at the University of Turin, Italy. His main research topics are mobility, heritage, and intercultural education. In the last decade, he has conducted fieldwork in Eastern Europe and the Balkans and has recently turned to focus his interest on the Mediterranean small islands that experience significant flows both of tourists and migrants. From 2009 to 2019, he was the Scientific Coordinator of the European project "Migrantour. Intercultural Urban Routes." Since 2019, he has been coordinating the summer school "Mobility and Heritage in the Mediterranean" (University of Milan Bicocca and University of Malta).

Katarzyna Wolanik Boström is an Associate Professor in Ethnology in the Department of Culture and Media Studies, Umeå University, Sweden. Her research interests include narrativity, life stories, highly skilled mobility, and professional learning. Her Ph.D. thesis analyzed how Polish professionals narrated their life stories after the fall of communism. Her other research projects have focused on international mobility among medical personnel, the practices of "internationalization" among Swedish Humanities scholars, and autobiographic storytelling.

PROBLEMATIZING SILOED MOBILITIES

Tourism, Migration, Exile

Kathleen M. Adams and Natalia Bloch

Roughly three hours by car from Mexico City nestled in the arid hills of the Central Mexican highlands lies Parque EcoAlberto, a three-thousand-acre resort and eco-adventure destination collectively owned by the indigenous Hñúhñú community. Here, *capitalinos* (urban Mexicans from the capital) and tourists from farther afield can romp in a sprawling waterpark, soak in natural hot springs, or enjoy zip-lining, rock-climbing, kayaking, camping, and overnight stays in rustic cabins. However, the park's biggest draw is *La Caminata Nocturna*, an interactive "night walk" where, for about US$20, tourists experience a simulated evening of dark play as undocumented migrants. For four moonlight hours, local guides lead small groups of vacationers through rugged desert terrain, winding through craggy hills, forging riverbeds, circumnavigating brambly cacti clumps, and balancing atop imposing walls in simulated attempts to surreptitiously cross the "border" into the United States. Along the way, these groups of make-believe migrants encounter assorted staged threats, ranging from pre-positioned wild beasts to costumed border patrol officers. When sirens or gunshots puncture the nocturnal desert soundscape, the Hñúhñú guides harangue their tourist charges to shut off their lights, move more quickly, or run for cover lest they be captured by *la migra* (immigration patrol). When Hñúhñús masquerading as border patrol agents ultimately capture and interrogate the tourists, the lighter-skinned Mexican tourists from the capital are sometimes singled out and questioned for being "too white to be Mexican" (Hasian, Maldonado and Ono, 2015, p. 319).

Centuries ago, the indigenous Hñúhñús' homeland was in the more fertile Mezquital Valley, but conquest by Aztecs, Spaniards, and other groups forced them to retreat into the region's most arid mountain nooks (Schmidt, 2012, p. 204), effectively rendering them marginalized exiles living on the fringes of their own ancestral lands. The Hñúhñús in this particular craggy hinterland valley had long relied on farming for their livelihood, but much changed with the 1980s

DOI: 10.4324/9781003182689-1

2 Kathleen M. Adams and Natalia Bloch

devastation of Mexico's agricultural base and the subsequent rise of industrial farms that wreaked havoc on small-scale farmers: An estimated 80% of the community has undertaken the dangerous journey north to toil as undocumented farmworkers, construction workers, and truck drivers in the United States (Healy, 2007, par. 9; Walsh, 2019, p. 41). Aiming to curtail out-migration by creating local jobs, the community initiated Parque EcoAlberto in 2004, with financial assistance from the Mexican government. Before the COVID-19 pandemic, *La Caminata Nocturna* employed over 70 Hñúhñús playing roles as masked guides (*coyotes*, who smuggle migrants into the United States for a fee), Border Patrol agents, guards, ranchers, and fellow aspiring migrants (Healy, 2007). Many of these indigenous employees themselves had spent time as undocumented workers in the American Southwest (Hasian et al., 2015, p. 322). Today, most community residents rely on jobs at the eco-resort or on remittances from undocumented migrants for their livelihood (Hasian et al., 2015, p. 322).

In recent years, the Park's *Camina Nocturna* has attracted growing media attention: It has been featured in *The New York Times*, *The Daily Mail*, *Vice*, and the BBC news and has even been the topic of a documentary film,[1] drawing ever more tourists from around the world up until the advent of the COVID-19 pandemic. Although some commentators note the ethically problematic dimensions of tourists play-acting as undocumented migrants,[2] *La Caminata Nocturna*'s founders and its Hñúhñú actors envision the touristic simulation as offering not only a novel source of locally based income but also an opportunity to forge a sense of community and raise awareness of migrants' experiences (Healy, 2007, par. 12). Some scholars aptly herald the park as a "prime example of the complexities of freedom and liberty in the contemporary age of free trade, global markets, diasporas and human migrations" (Hasian et al., 2015, p. 312). For us, the park also poignantly encapsulates the core themes of this book: The intersections of tourism, migration, and exile.

Within the borders of the park, we find descendants of internally displaced persons (IDPs) – many of them returned undocumented migrants – working as performers in a tourist setting. As they reenact sanitized versions of community members' haunting border-crossing experiences, their tourist entourages play at being migrants. The simulations themselves showcase how peoples' varied experiences with mobility are entwined with race, ethnicity, class, politics, and global regimes. Moreover, the park embodies the touristic commercialization of painful, danger-fraught migrant experiences and prompts an array of ethical debates.

Beyond Silos: Decompartmentalizing Tourism, Migration, and Exile

This book aims to challenge the classic – and often taken-for-granted – compartmentalization of tourism, migration, and refugee studies by exploring the intersections of these forms of human spatial mobility. The chapters in this volume offer case studies from around the world examining how tourism, migration, and exile

Problematizing Siloed Mobilities **3**

intertwine, overlap, and influence one another.[3] Such intersections are multidimensional and multidirectional. Migrants and established exiles can be tourists in their home countries (and elsewhere), drawing on economic, social, and cultural capital gained through mobility. While visiting friends and relatives (VFR tourism), tracing ancestral roots (ancestral/roots/diaspora tourism), or traveling via transnational networks, they engage in tourism and leisure activities. Moreover, some return migrants invest in tourism enterprises. Migrant and refugee neighborhoods can also become tourist destinations for both outsiders and other migrants seeking a taste of home, as witnessed in "Chinatowns" worldwide. In addition, refugee communities can attract tourists within the framework of justice tourism, via solidarity tours or as volunteer tourists (who often become activists). Refugee children from the Global South are offered holiday escapes in the Global North, which can sometimes pave paths out of protracted exile. Furthermore, it is not only "locals" but also migrants who work as laborers and entrepreneurs in the tourism sector (at times becoming tourists themselves, using forms of capital acquired through interactions with tourists). Tourism, on the other hand, can stimulate migration. Vacationers develop friendships and romantic relationships with local residents and tourism sector employees, ultimately relocating to their countries of origin and sometimes becoming migrant-tourism entrepreneurs themselves. Additionally, tourism is often an initial step to retirement migration. Finally, in many forms of mobility, the boundaries between migration and tourism are vague, as evidenced in entrepreneurs' and investors' lifestyle migrations and in the mobilities of highly skilled professionals. Thus, while scholars have classically researched and theorized tourism, migration, and exile separately, social reality blurs these seemingly fixed categorical boundaries. As a growing chorus of researchers has begun to observe, people may be migrants/exiles and tourists simultaneously and their status may change over time, sometimes repeatedly; "one set of movements leads to another" (Hall and Tucker, 2004, p. 15; see Levitt and Glick Schiller, 2004). In offering a collection of ethnographic case studies that dismantle and move beyond these deep-seated conceptual boundaries, this book aims to examine mobilities in their mutual constitution and "fluid interdependence" (Sheller and Urry, 2006, p. 212). Rather than circumscribing ourselves within a single mobility silo, we advocate for greater recognition of the variegated and intersecting mobility experiences that shape people's lives and inform their practices.

As many of the chapters in this volume illustrate, different mobilities evoke varying political and popular imagery: some forms of mobility are positively valued, appreciated, and encouraged, while others are demonized and restrained (Glick Schiller and Salazar, 2013, p. 188). Consider, for instance, the semantic valorization of second home owners and long-term tourists from the Global North as "cosmopolitan nomads" versus the typical media representation of migrants from the Global South as "aliens" and "intruders." In a similar vein, highly skilled professionals and business travelers freely traverse nation-states' borders whereas impoverished asylum seekers are pushed back from "fortress Europe."[4] We believe that considering how uneven distributions of power permeate people's movements will prove valuable on several levels. First, such

4 Kathleen M. Adams and Natalia Bloch

examinations promise to sharpen social critiques of how public discourses conceptualize and moralize various forms of mobility, reflecting gender, class, ethnicity, race, and other global inequalities. Second, deconstructing the conceptual foundations of these moral valorizations of people's movements will enable new theoretical insights and, finally (we hope), will also foster empathy with those whose movements are restrained.

Beyond the Trinity of Tourism, Migration, and Exile: Other Intersecting Mobilities

Scholars interested in forms of human mobility and their intersections have highlighted a broad range of movements, far more than the trinity we are spotlighting in this volume (see Clifford, 1997; Salazar, 2017). For instance, we have abundant studies highlighting intersections between pilgrimage or sacred travels and tourism, dating back to the 1970s, when Nelson Graburn (1977) penned his classic treatise on tourism as a sacred journey and Victor and Edith Turner (1978, p. 20) made their much-quoted observation that "a tourist is half a pilgrim if a pilgrim is half a tourist" (e.g., Badone and Roseman, 2004; Cohen, 1992; DiGiovine and Choe, 2020; Eade, 1992; Ebron, 1999; Graburn, 1983; Pfaffenberger, 1983; Smith, 1992; Timothy and Olsen, 2006). We also have studies that spotlight (post)modern forms of nomadism and their intersections with exile, diaspora, or tourism (e.g., Cohen, 1973; Peters, 2006; Richards and Wilson, 2004; D'Andrea, 2009), including a growing array of studies of digital nomads (e.g., Makimoto and Manners, 1997; Richards, 2015; Thompson, 2019). In addition to the pilgrim, the nomad, the exile, and the tourist, a recent special issue of *Social Anthropology* offers individual chapters on two other "key figures" that have animated mobility research theory: the pedestrian and the flaneur (see Salazar, 2017). So why did we select tourism, migration, and exile as our focal points?

While we could have opted to embrace a scattershot approach in this collection, highlighting all these varied and intersecting forms of mobility, we felt that by focusing our lens on tourism, migration, and exile, we could enable richer, more nuanced analyses and foster an opportunity for patterns to surface between the chapters. For us, tourism, migration, and exile have been especially important for structuring people's lives, imaginations, and understandings of their own and others' experiences in the current era.[5] Moreover, as others have argued, migration and tourism are two of the most important social and economic (and we would add cultural) dynamics in society today (Hall and Williams, 2002). We believe this statement also applies to exile/refugees/forcibly displaced people. However, many of the chapters in this book also highlight how other genres of human mobility articulate within their case studies. For instance, Rami K. Isaac (Chapter 5) and Lauren Miller Griffith (Chapter 10) weave the theme of pilgrimage into their respective discussions of justice tourism in Bethlehem and capoeira-oriented mobilities. Also, Rita Reis (Chapter 4) addresses nomadism in her analysis of young Sahrawi refugees' vacation and educational migrations. Moreover, although a growing number of works highlight intersections between tourism and migration or between exile/

diasporas and tourism, very few works address all three forms of mobility together. We believe that dismantling the pernicious dichotomous classifications haunting migration, tourism, and refugee studies will enable us to better understand mobility practices. Spotlighting the intersections of different forms of human spatial mobilities promises to yield fertile grounds for harvesting new insights, including critical insights into the global power relations and inequalities inscribed in various moralizations of specific mobilities.

The Conundrum of Definitions

Offering definitions of the three forms of mobility at the core of this volume carries the risk of reifying the very silos we seek to problematize. The categories of tourism, migration, and exile are, after all, abstractions that cannot possibly capture the multidimensional nature of human mobilities (see Bell and Ward, 2000; Hall and Williams, 2002). Here we briefly sketch some of the classic ways in which these concepts have been defined and indicate the challenges in finding suitable definitions.

Anthropologists have had a notoriously difficult time defining tourism (Nash, 1981; Stronza, 2001). In what is widely hailed as one of the first anthropological volumes dedicated to tourism, *Hosts and guests* (1977[1989]), Valene L. Smith defined the tourist as "a temporarily leisured person who voluntarily visits a place away from home for the purpose of experiencing a change" (1989, p. 2). Yet, the boundaries of this classic definition quickly unravel when one asks questions such as, "what constitutes home?" For instance, how does second home travel fit in (Jaakson, 1986)? This category of mobility – one that straddles the tourism and migration binary – has inspired a number of studies, ranging from examinations of elite, wealthy tourists/(temporary) migrants with second homes (e.g., Hall and Müller, 2004) to more "ordinary" middle-class getaway cottage owners (e.g., Harrison, 2008, 2010). Analyses of second home travel challenge the notion that tourism, by definition, entails leaving a home: rather studies have highlighted the negotiations of home, identity, and place entailed in second home travel (e.g., McIntyre et al., 2006). And what of migrant tourist-workers who combine motivations and practices related to leisure, sightseeing, and paid work (Williams and Hall, 2002, pp. 5, 13; see also Bianchi, 2000). Consider, for instance, Australian and New Zealander backpackers traveling in Europe who supplement their tourism budgets with odd jobs (Mason, 2002), or backpackers from Japan, South Korea, or Taiwan on "working holidays" who are temporarily employed by tourism entrepreneurs from those countries (both first- and second-generation migrants to Australia and New Zealand) who provide services to tourists from their countries of origin (Cooper, 2002). In short, classic definitions of tourism invariably have fuzzy borders that pull us into other travel genres.

The classic definition of migration as production-led mobility is unfounded not only when we reflect on "migrant tourist-workers" and "working holidays"

6 Kathleen M. Adams and Natalia Bloch

but also when we consider migrants engaging in tourism practices, in the form of VFR or homeland tourism (see, e.g., Boyne et al., 2002; Nguyen and King, 1998; Duval, 2003; Ashtar et al., 2017; Din, 2017; Horolets, 2018; Adams, 2019; Moon et al., 2019) as well as other forms of leisure tourism (Dwyer et al., 2014). Moreover, many migrants do not produce but consume, as in the case of retirement migration, both residential and seasonal (e.g., Ono, 2008; Gustafson, 2002; Woube, 2014). Additionally, the time span that seemingly distinguishes migration from tourism – with more permanent migrant mobility and temporary tourist trips – fails to capture the complex nature of current mobilities (see Williams and Hall, 2002, pp. 4–5), if we compare circular migrants (e.g., Skeldon, 2012; Duany, 2002; Deshingkar and Farrington, 2009), business travelers (e.g., Gustafson, 2014; Unger et al., 2016), and highly skilled mobile professionals (e.g., Nowicka, 2007; Baas, 2017) with residential tourists (O'Reilly, 2007). Finally, the voluntary character of migration which is treated as a core distinction between migrants and forcibly displaced people, including refugees, becomes less obvious if we question the very notion of voluntariness (Bakewell, 2021). This is also the case with the classic distinction between migrants' economic motivations and refugees' political motivations. Is it voluntary or forced migration when someone decides to flee their homeland due to being unable to secure a livelihood and provide for their family? And if a poor economic situation in one's country is the result of political circumstances – an authoritarian regime, occupation, or war – can we still talk about purely economic motivations? Is starvation necessary to speak of economic coercion? And what of situations where one can no longer live a dignified life in one's own country?

Moreover, humans are guided by multiple and complex motives, and the labels they use to define themselves are often strategies for maneuvering global mobility regimes (consider Cubans who employ the category of migrants to maintain rights to return visits discussed in Chapters 1 and 2 in this volume or Chinese investors in Portugal who remain silent about their political motivations for mobility featured in Chapter 12). In addition, when defining refugeehood, we encounter a narrow, legal definition of a person who flees persecution and is recognized as a refugee by being granted this status based on the 1951 Geneva Convention relating to the Status of Refugees. However, this definition excludes a number of forcibly displaced peoples (see Malkki's critique, 1995a), such as IDPs, climate refugees, asylum seekers whose claims have been rejected, and those who, for various reasons, decide not to pursue such a status. Thus, as Liisa Malkki rightly points out, "the label 'refugees' connotes a bureaucratic and international humanitarian realm," while " 'exile' connotes a readily aestheticizable realm" (1995a, p. 513), often explored in 20th-century literature (e.g., Said, 1984). In this book, however, we have decided to employ the category of exile in its structural rather than symbolic sense. That is, as a broader, more encompassing term which refers to all those people who are not free (or able) to return to their home countries (drawing on the historical concept of exile as punishment, i.e., the banishment of a person from one's homeland; see Böss, 2006). In other words, when talking about exile, we bear in mind the need to historicize and politicize this category (Malkki, 1995a, p. 514), as Malkki did in her seminal book *Purity and exile. Violence, memory, and national cosmology among Hutu refugees in Tanzania* (1995b).

When discussing the complexities of mobilities, the ground-breaking book *Mobilities* by John Urry (2007), along with Mimi Sheller's and Urry's article "The new mobilities paradigm" (2006), must be mentioned. They postulated a new paradigm for theorizing (im)mobilities which would not only dismantle the conceptual boundaries between different forms of mobilities but also move us beyond the binary conceptualizations of movement and stasis, displacement and emplacement, and fixity and motion. Their work has thus created fertile theoretical terrain for projects such as ours. Finally, an important theoretical framework for this book has been shaped by studies of global mobility regimes that privilege some sets of movements while restraining others, thus creating hierarchies of mobilities and producing inequalities in terms of the right and opportunities to be mobile (see Tesfahuney, 1998; Cunningham, 2004; Shamir, 2005; Gogia, 2006; Turner, 2007; Koslowski, 2011; Glick Schiller and Salazar, 2013).

Multiple Mobilities: Prior Iterations

Although multiple mobilities have been embedded in historical processes for centuries, it is only recently that they have come to be recognized as an undeniable aspect of the human condition (Urry, 2007, p. 35). Clearly, we are not the first scholars to realize that the siloed fields of migration, tourism, and refugee studies have much to gain by engaging in dialogue. Over the past two decades, scholarship problematizing the divisions between tourism and migration has blossomed. C. Michael Hall and Allan M. Williams' edited volume, *Tourism and migration: New relationships between production and consumption* (2002) was the first major book to address the dynamic interplay between tourism and migration, questioning the taken-for-granted binary of production/labor/migration and consumption/leisure/tourism. Path breaking for its time, it was composed of studies by human geographers and scholars of tourism and tourism management and addressed tourism's intersection with labor migration, consumption-led migration, VFR travel, and other forms of tourism-induced mobilities. Our book, published 20 years after this landmark publication, aims to further explore these intersections by addressing newer forms of mobility that have emerged in recent years and adding one more important dimension of mobility, namely, exile.

The intersections between tourism and migration were further explored in the book *Going abroad: Travel, tourism, and migration. Cross-cultural perspectives on mobility* edited by Christine Geoffroy and Richard Sibley (2007) as well as by Peter Burns and Marina Novelli in the edited volume *Tourism and mobilities. Local-global connections* (2008). The authors of the latter argue that the "tourism" category is no longer useful in capturing the complex realities of traveling people as it encompasses various forms of mobile practices. Already in 2003, Karen O'Reilly queried "When is a tourist?" and presented ethnographic accounts of three forms of

8 Kathleen M. Adams and Natalia Bloch

tourism-related migration of British citizens to Spain: retirement migrants, entrepreneurial migrants, and consumption-driven, economically active migrants (O'Reilly, 2003). Fiona Allon, Kay Anderson, and Robyn Bushell demonstrated that "backpackers are not just tourists; they are also frequently students, working holidaymakers, highly skilled professional workers, and even, at times, long-term semi-permanent residents" (2003, p. 73).

Studies of lifestyle/amenity migration also illustrate the blurred boundary between migration and tourism, given that many migrants are not (only) economically motivated: they make their migration choices by weighing factors akin to those considered by tourists when selecting their destinations. Lifestyle migration is thus a form of mobility in which both the quest for a good life and class constitute particularly important fields of inquiry (Moss, 2006; Amit, 2007; Benson and O'Reilly, 2009; Benson and Osbaldiston, 2014; Åkerlund and Sandberg, 2015; Duncan et al., 2016). Lifestyle migration encompasses a range of leisure-oriented mobilities already mentioned in this introduction – residential tourism, retirement migration, and second home tourism – in which "home" and "away" (another often taken-for-granted binary) are deconstructed (Janoschka and Haas, 2014). However, this form of consumption-led mobility can be combined with production, challenging the dichotomy of work and leisure, as in the case of "travel-stimulated entrepreneurial migrants" (Snepenger et al., 1995), "lifestyle entrepreneurs in tourism" (Ateljevic and Doorne, 2000), and the previously discussed "digital nomads" (Makimoto and Manners, 1997). Moreover, not only are these mobilities usually inspired by prior tourist experiences, but lifestyle entrepreneurship often occurs within the tourism sector.

Tourism is not only a leisure activity for tourists but also a workplace and a source of income for migrants, given the sector's many low-skilled and low-paid jobs. A number of studies have explored international and domestic migrant workers and small-scale entrepreneurs in the tourism sector, both formal and informal (e.g., Adams, 1992, 1996; Forshee, 2001, 2002; Bianet Castellanos, 2010; Lenz, 2010), including sexual relations offered to tourists by migrant women (Brennan, 2004; Lindquist, 2008). These migrant workers in the tourism sector challenge the classic notions – and another binary – of "hosts" and "guests" (Griffin, 2017; Bloch, 2020).[6] Studies of this realm address postcolonial and postsocialist disparities, interrogate tourism's emancipatory potential for migrants' well-being and empowerment, or spotlight tourism's capacity for serving as a platform for creating self-representations (Enloe, 1989; Castellanos, 2010; Ghodsee, 2005; Bloch, 2021b). Sometimes, the encounters between migrant tourism service providers and tourists trigger further mobility, i.e., marriage migration, which itself can be economically driven or a lifestyle mobility (see, e.g., Jaisuekun and Sunanta, 2021). In some tourist destinations, migrant workers and working tourists share the same space (Carson et al., 2016). Finally, return migrants challenge the dichotomy of migration and tourism, not only because they often feel or are treated as tourists in their own homeland but also because they sometimes provide services to tourists (Adams and Sandarupa, 2018; Adams, 2019; Pido, 2017). Thus, as Noel Salazar

Problematizing Siloed Mobilities **9**

(2020) notes, tourism without migration would not be the same as it is (if it would be at all), just as migration without tourism be entirely different; for this reason, labor migration and tourism mobilities should be consistently brought together in our analyses. Likewise, writing in broader terms, Erik Cohen and Scott Cohen (2015) called for tourism studies' incorporation into the mobilities paradigm in order to shed new light on how tourism is entangled with other forms of discretionary mobilities and to deconstruct "problematic binary modernist thinking in tourism studies" (2015, p. 157).

Recognition of the importance of exploring the ways in which exile intersects with migration is evident in the establishment of the *Journal of Immigrant & Refugee Studies* in 2002. Its editors declare that "it is unique in its character as it covers both migration and refugee studies,"[7] creating a platform where studies of these two mobilities can be presented together although in most cases they continue to be analyzed separately. Moreover, exiles may become migrants. This is not obvious, given the popular mass media image of refugees as newcomers struggling in temporary camps. However, the majority of the world's forcibly displaced people live in protracted exile (see Aleinikoff, 2015). These are mostly second- and subsequent-generation refugees who see international educational mobility and economic migration as avenues for gaining political agency and/or as pathways for escaping from exile, as has been demonstrated in studies of Sahrawi refugees (Chatty et al., 2010; Farah, 2010; Reis, 2019), Sahrawi and Palestinian refugees (Fiddian-Qasmiyeh, 2015), or Tibetan refugees (Choedup, 2015).

In their edited volume *Coming home? Refugees, migrants and those who stayed behind*, Lynellyn D. Long and Ellen Oxfeld (2004) discuss not only return migrants but also the experiences of returning refugees during both temporary visits and permanent repatriation. Many other studies have addressed the links between established diasporas/subsequent generations of refugees and tourism in the form of diaspora/roots/ancestral tourism (e.g., Butler, 2003; Leite, 2005, 2017; Tie and Seaton, 2013; Marschall, 2017). The landmark volume in this field is *Tourism, diasporas and space* edited by Tim Coles and Dallen J. Timothy (2004a) which discusses the production of diaspora tourism destinations as well as the experiences of diaspora tourists. In addition, Sabine Marschall's edited volume, *Tourism and memories of home. Migrants, displaced people, exiles and diasporic communities* (2017), offers a collection of ethnographic studies from different parts of the world highlighting the tourism-memory nexus in diaspora tourism. Here, the emphasis is on examining how memory underpins the touristic mobility of exiles and migrants who travel to their (often imagined) homelands. The ethnographic monographs exploring this nexus include Shaul Kelner' (2010) volume on political-religious homeland tours organized by the Israeli government to foster Jewish-American youths' attachment to Israel. Other writers have explored how Jewish diaspora tourism is tethered to processing difficult pasts and cultivating new personal identities (e.g., Lehrer, 2013; Feldman, 1995) The intersections between historic exile and diaspora have been also explored with regard to the slave trade and contemporary black diaspora tourism to ancestral homelands (e.g., Holsey, 2008; Bruner, 1996).

Not only do members of diasporas become tourists, but refugees can also transform into tourism sector entrepreneurs, which is an important topic with regard to both urban refugees (i.e., those living outside the camps and not being assisted by humanitarian agencies) and refugee self-reliance (e.g., Portes and Jensen, 1989; Wauters and Lambrecht, 2008; Alrawadieh et al., 2019; Cetin et al., 2022). Also, the cultural capital of refugee groups can be skillfully converted into economic capital via tourism – commodifying refugees' ethnic culture may be a survival strategy in exile, as demonstrated by the case of Tibetan refugees in India (McGuckin, 1997), who have maintained their ability to manage their cultural heritage and its commodification. In contrast, Kayan refugees from Myanmar are denied control of tourism in their villages in Thailand by Thai state agencies that use Kayan "long-neck women" as an icon of ethnic tourism in Thailand (Cole and Eriksson, 2010, pp. 115–117).

Nevertheless, tourism also has the potential to become a platform for recovering refugees' voices – empowering refugees not only economically (as in the studies discussed earlier) but also politically. The history of exile is often subaltern history, unvoiced in the narrative of mainstream tourism shaped by the state and its citizens. However, alternative tours – in the form of solidarity or justice tourism (see Higgins-Desbiolle, 2009) – can bring these stories to light, as demonstrated in studies of tourists visiting Palestinian refugee camps (Isaac, 2010; Kassis et al., 2016), Tibetan refugee settlements (Bloch, 2018, 2021b, pp. 149–157), and refugee camps in Western Sahara (Popović, 2018) or refugees acting as tourist guides in refugee-receiving countries (Burrai et al., 2022).

Since Europe's crisis of receiving refugees in 2015 and 2016,[8] voluntourism in support of asylum seekers has been widely explored (e.g., Chtouris and Miller, 2017; Trihas and Tsilimpokos, 2018; Sandri, 2017; Freedman, 2018) wherein not only do tourists become volunteers – responding to the call "what can tourist do to help?" (Porter, 2015) – but also volunteers become accidental tourists (Paraskevaidis and Andriotis, 2021). In addition, the influence of refugees' presence in the tourism sector in receiving countries – when "refugees and tourists share the same beaches" (Kingsley, 2015) – has been studied, particularly by scholars in economics and tourism management (e.g., İstanbullu Dinçer et al., 2017; Pappas and Papatheodorou, 2017; Tsartas et al., 2020). Moreover, tourism infrastructure – hotels, hostels, guesthouses – is often used to accommodate refugees. This intersection has been documented since the eve of the World War II when Amsterdam's Lloyd Hotel housed Jewish refugees. Other notable examples of tourism infrastructure being repurposed for refugees occurred during the war in Yugoslavia when Dalmatian resorts opened their doors to refugees from Bosnia and during the genocide in Rwanda when Hotel des Milles Collines in Kigali offered refuge to a few hundred Tutsis (Fregonese and Ramadan, 2015). Such actions can constitute revival strategies for hotels experiencing stagnation or survival strategies in periods of tourism decline due to political instability. They can also be acts of solidarity (see, e.g., Manning, 2009). There are also cases where asylum seekers (and grass roots groups working on their behalf) have organized initiatives to occupy hotels, as was the case with the shuttered Hotel City Plaza in Athens which was appropriated as a residence for refugees in 2016 (García Agustín and Jørgensen, 2019).

Finally, of particular interest are the studies that encompass all three forms of mobility. Magdalena Bodzan (2020) offers an ethnographic case study of several culinary initiatives in Warsaw, Poland, which brought together refugees and migrants as cooks and tourists as customers. These initiatives drew on the cultural and refugee capitals of the cooks and involved both capitalizing on their ethnicity and modifying it to mesh with the tourists' tastes (for instance, adapting meals to accommodate vegetarians).

Researching Mobilities: Methods

Given the volume's anthropological origin, the majority of the chapters' authors are anthropologists, although contributors also include human geographers, a scholar in spatial sciences, and a scholar in ethnic studies. Therefore, the chapters' findings emerge primarily from anthropology's hallmark methodology of ethnographic field research (participant observation, informal conversations, autoethnography, activist research, and online ethnography), as well as in-depth unstructured interviews, and semi-structured interviews (Fetterman, 2020; LeCompte and Schensul, 2010; Spradley, 2016). Some chapters also draw on visual and textual content analysis, archival research, and certain quantitative methods (word frequency count and surveys). We believe that qualitative research methods, particularly ethnography, are the best means for gaining insights into people's everyday perceptions and experiences of (im)mobility. This sort of approach, which foregrounds emic perspectives, has much potential to deconstruct the legacy of scholarly and state-imposed conceptual categories. Ethnographic methods, particularly long-term participant observation – living with and partaking in the daily life of the community one seeks to understand for an extended period – inevitably force researchers to reassess their prior understandings.

Long-term participant observation also enables researchers to build trust with individuals who may be hesitant to speak candidly during formal interviews with outsiders (Adams, 2012). This is especially important for research on sensitive topics, such as undocumented migration or tourist destination residents' ambivalence about tourism in their communities. As Stroma Cole observed while researching local understandings of tourism in Eastern Indonesia, "spontaneous, indoor fireside chats were a more successful technique than attempting to carry out questionnaire-based interviews . . . [and] disclosed information on topics that were not openly discussed at other times" (Cole, 2004, pp. 295–296). Moreover, unlike surveys, long-term fieldwork allows us to capture not only frozen moments in time but also dynamic processes and changes.

Anthropologists studying mobilities argue that such fieldwork needs to be mobilized, that is, moved away from synchronic studies of territorially bound culture to enable us to follow people on the move (e.g., Appadurai, 1996; Clifford, 1997; Elliot et al., 2017). Although many scholars researching mobile lives draw on mobile or itinerant ethnography (Schein, 2005, 2002; see also Sheller and Urry, 2006, pp. 217–218), studying mobilities does not always involve movement on the

12 Kathleen M. Adams and Natalia Bloch

researcher's part: sometimes "staying put" turns out to be the most effective way to observe mobilities (Coates, 2017, p. 119). Often scholars combine mobile methods (following our research partners) with ethnographic research rooted in concrete locales. In essence, "a processual, collaborative, and creative ethnographic focus enables anthropologists to document the many ways in which mobility transforms social life, both for 'movers,' 'stayers,' and those in-between" (Salazar et al., 2017, p. 15).

Many of the chapters in this volume draw on the methodology of multi-sited ethnography (Marcus, 1995). George E. Marcus coined this expression to describe the adaptation of "conventional ethnographic research designs to examine the circulation of cultural meanings, objects and identities in diffuse time-space" (1995, p. 96). Although some of the contributors to this volume may not use Marcus' term to describe their data gathering practices, their approaches fit under the broad umbrella of multi-sited ethnography. Ideally suited for learning about the lives, experiences, and meaning-making dynamics of moving peoples, multi-sited ethnography is not limited to simply studying individuals in various geographical locales: it also entails following people, objects, ideas, and meanings through various social and political contexts: tracing the connections between local and global, between offline and online, and between discourses and practices (for instance, by bridging migrants' everyday experiences and the macro workings of mobility regimes).

Paths to This Book

Often, one gleans only small hints of how the volume editors came to the topic at hand, beyond usually via passing mention of an initial conference panel (see endnote 3). Since length constraints prompted us to refrain from contributing our own ethnographic chapters to this volume, we turn to share some of our relevant research findings here, thereby adding two additional Asian regions – India and Indonesia – to those addressed in this volume. In keeping with scholarly recognition of the value of attending to how the personal informs research paths (e.g., Okely and Callaway, 1992; Amit, 2000), we also briefly reference our formative experiences with these intersecting mobilities. In so doing, we nod to calls for greater transparency regarding the ways in which personal backgrounds intersect with and color our research agendas, engagements, and findings.

Both of us, the editors of this book, encountered intersecting mobilities in our anthropological research and personal lives. When she was an undergraduate student from a postsocialist Central European country, Natalia Bloch became a "migrant tourist-worker" at a melon plantation and a vineyard in Valencia in order to earn money to support her desire to travel to Spain. She worked with undocumented migrants from Morocco who dreamed of further migration to France, migrants who rushed to hide in the shed when the Spanish police made periodic unannounced inspections (she noted that they did not check too carefully – presumably they had an arrangement with the vineyard's owner). Later, when she became a PhD student in anthropology, Bloch worked as a tour guide for Polish tourists traveling to India and Nepal (see similar experiences of leading anthropologists of tourism: Bruner, 1995; see also 2005; Smith, 2005). This enabled her to travel to India and conduct her fieldwork in Tibetan refugee settlements before she obtained a PhD research grant. At the close of each tourist season, she sent tourists home and turned to her research. In this way, her interest in the anthropology of tourism was born and comingled with refugee and, subsequently, migration studies.

One of Bloch's field sites was Dharamshala, a refugee settlement in northern India and an informal capital of a Tibetan diaspora that has been turned into a tourist attraction. Dharamshala's attractiveness is used by refugees to gain visibility and promote their political cause via their direct encounters with tourists. In her book *Encounters across difference. Tourism and overcoming subalternity in India* (2021b), Bloch demonstrated that skillfully politicized tourism can both transform tourists into allies in refugees' struggle for self-determination and serve as a platform for recovering refugees' voices. In this form of justice tourism, tourists become recipients and conveyors of the diaspora's political postulates – postulates for which the diaspora is struggling to gain international moral and political support. Creating self-representations and engaging tourists in political activities for the Tibetan cause takes place in Dharamshala in several arenas. These arenas include producing political souvenirs which refer to the "Free Tibet" slogan; creating educational experiences for tourists (for instance, awareness talks, movie screenings, and meetings with former political prisoners); and organizing political reality/solidarity tours around Dharamshala (see also Mahrouse, 2008).

Bloch researched another dimension of the intersections between tourism and forced displacement in Hampi, a village in southern India, located within a UNESCO World Heritage site. Hampi residents experienced eviction and their houses and small tourism businesses were demolished in the name of protecting tangible national heritage in its "splendid isolation" (Herzfeld, 2006, p. 143). The forcibly displaced residents struggled for their own vision of living heritage, as well as their rights to housing, and the benefits accrued from tourism. Their allies in this struggle were, again, tourists who expressed their solidarity in the media, organized online support campaigns, took videos, and crafted petitions for UNESCO and the Indian government to stop evictions, thus developing – as Freya Higgins-Desbiolles (2010, p. 200) calls it – a transnational solidarity-based activism (Bloch, 2016, 2017, 2018).

While researching the informal tourism sector in India, Bloch noticed that many tourism service providers – workers and small-scale entrepreneurs – were not "locals," as it is usually imagined, but migrants (both settled and seasonal, international and domestic), IDPs (from draught-afflicted regions), so-called expats (tourists-turned-migrants from the countries of the Global North) and refugees (both newcomers and second-generation exiles). They all challenge the often taken-for-granted "binary between mobile tourists and place-bound locals" (Salazar, 2012, p. 874). Moreover, these mobile tourism workers also engaged in leisure

14 Kathleen M. Adams and Natalia Bloch

activities, becoming tourists themselves – either by being invited by befriended tourists or using social networks built with other tourism service providers to perform VFR (both in India and abroad). VFR facilitated their leisure mobilities, making them more affordable and thus more accessible.

The informal, heterogeneous character of both tourist destinations where Bloch conducted her ethnographic fieldwork enabled the "hosts" to develop unmediated, close relationships with tourists beyond the service provider–customer framework. For the "hosts," these relationships were a source of alternative social networks that sometimes resulted in marriage migration to the tourists' home countries, usually located in the Global North; Tibetan refugees referred to them as "greener pastures" in the West (see Bloch, 2020). In some cases, these intersections were even more unexpected. For instance, Bloch analyzed the case of Tibetan refugees who – supported financially by befriended international tourists – provided humanitarian aid to other forcibly displaced people, i.e., Indian climate IDPs from draught-afflicted areas who lived in a slum alongside a riverbank in Dharamshala (Bloch, 2021a).

Kathleen M. Adams's path to this volume was fueled by a combination of personal and scholarly factors. Reared in a predominantly immigrant enclave in the touristic city of San Francisco, Adams' mother was a French immigrant and her maternal grandmother had migrated at age 12 from Italy to Paris to toil in the garment industry, relocating again decades later to follow her daughter to California. Like many of her classmates, Adams' early childhood was animated by nostalgic stories of lives in the homeland. For Adams, San Francisco was always "home," but other ancestral homes – Paris and Turin – were ever present in the fabric of family life, enlivened by the aroma of her grandmother's pasta simmering on the stove, the arias of her mother's beloved French operas, and the garden cage of live snails awaiting transformation into *escargot*. These sensory experiences and subsequent familial visits to French and Italian "homelands" fostered Adams' abiding interest in the interplay between mobility and identity.

Adams' fieldwork in Indonesia and the United States has broadly focused on the politics of tourism, heritage, and identity (e.g., Adams, 1984, 1995, 2003, 2011). Her mid-1980s dissertation research on ethnic and artistic change in the context of tourism was based in the Toraja highlands in Indonesia, at a time when anthropologists identified field sites as stationary and bounded (Adams, 1988). Yet, living with a Toraja family in a carving village popular with tourists, Adams saw that mobility beyond the homeland informed their lives (2006, p. 33). It quickly became apparent that tourism was entwined with other forms of mobility: not only did foreign and domestic tourists flow through the village daily but also local guides formed relationships with tourists, sometimes relocating abroad to pursue opportunities presented by these relationships.[9] Likewise, local carvers whose shops catered to tourists participated in workshops and exhibit openings in Bali, Jakarta, and Japan. Moreover, many families had children and other kin who studied or found jobs off-island: villagers with disposable wealth occasionally visited these far-flung relatives and engaged in VFR tourism. In addition, these migrant relatives returned for rituals, vacations, and, sometimes, retirement. Some who acquired foreign language skills while abroad ultimately returned home and found employment in the tourism sector. In short, Adams came to realize that the borders of tourism were fuzzier than the classic scholarship suggested and that the varied human flows across time and space – ethnoscapes in the language of Arjun Appadurai (1986, 1990, 1996) – were interconnected.

Adams's 1988 dissertation and subsequent book (2006) examined how movements of tourists, anthropologists, art dealers, missionaries, and Torajans were entangled with shifting Torajan perceptions of themselves and their arts. In these works, she argued that Torajans were artfully deploying the touristic and anthropological interest in their culture to navigate a better position for themselves in the hierarchy of Indonesian ethnic groups. Her recent research has focused more directly on the intersections between tourism and migration. Some of this research foregrounds the emotional terrain entailed in migrant return visits to the ancestral homeland, visits that combine tourism with familial time (VFR), and demonstrates that returning migrant visitors' somatic, sensory experiences during their travels home serve to reframe their understandings of their current-day identities (2019).

Another dimension of Adams' research examines how entwined forms of mobility (labor, educational, recreational, and cyber) pose new opportunities and challenges for Indonesian families in translocal times. Marjorie Esman (1984), Dallen Timothy (1997), and others have underscored that people draw on "travel and tourism to the 'home country' to (re)assert, reaffirm and perform their heritage" (Coles and Timothy, 2004b, p. 12). Adams argued that it was not solely "heritage" in the generic ethnic sense that is being (re)affirmed via these travels but also culturally specific ideas about the nature of the family. As she demonstrated via the Toraja case, Toraja migrants and their foreign-reared children return to the homeland for funeral rituals and, simultaneously, tourism. While there, they tour not only typical touristic sites but also specific ancestral houses and attend rituals with hundreds of other members of their "house families." For these migrants, tourism becomes an integral dimension of the discovery, exploration, articulation, and, sometimes, rejection of more expansive ancestral house-based notions of the family (Adams, 2015). More broadly, Adams has argued that attending to "local knowledge" can destabilize our entrenched siloed conceptions of tourism and migration and foster more nuanced understandings of mobility dynamics, as illustrated via Toraja practices and the Malay concept of *merantau* (travel for financial and experiential enrichment), a commonly used term in Indonesia and Malaysia which does not map neatly onto the Western siloed categories of tourism and migration (2020; also see Adams, 2016 and Din, 2017).

A Roadmap to This Volume

The studies in this volume draw on original, predominantly ethnographic, research. Each chapter presents a case study that challenges persistent dichotomous classifications (tourists vs. migrants; migrants vs. refugees; voluntary vs. forced migration;

16 Kathleen M. Adams and Natalia Bloch

leisure vs. work; etc.). The work presented here spans the globe. For instance, chapters analyze intersecting and overlapping mobilities between Cuba and Europe; Vietnam and the United States; Sahrawi refugee camps and temporary homes in Western Sahara and Spain; as well as Western countries and Palestinian camps in the Middle East. Additional chapters address intersecting forms of mobility between China, Brazil, and Portugal; Thailand, East Asia, and Europe; Panama and Europe; and along the Balkan route refugees followed during Europe's crisis of receiving refugees. These mobility vectors are multi-directional: from the Global South to the Global North, from the Global North to the Global South, and within these regions. Collectively, the chapters chronicle both short- and long-term mobilities prompted by various motives, desires, and aspirations. These include political, economic, and safety challenges, expulsion, leisure, earning possibilities, educational opportunities, love, marriage, retirement, lifestyle aspirations, career advancement, and investment possibilities.

Chapters 1 and 2 unveil the intersections of migration and tourism by analyzing the stories of Cuban return migrants occupying the status of tourists in their own country and, at times, engaging in the tourism sector as entrepreneurs. On the surface, their motivations to leave Cuba seem to be primarily economic; however, Cuba's economic struggles are tethered to its political regime (and the US embargo); thus, the exile dimension also emerges. Many Cubans leaving the country adopt the status of migrants, rather than refugees, to enable returns. The Cuban state plays with mobility categories by imposing the category of (economic) migrants on those who leave the country unless they migrate to the United States in which case they are automatically considered exiles. Nadine T. Fernandez's chapter focuses on long-term, mobile relationships between Cubans and Danes who move between both (and sometimes additional) countries. Fernandez uses the lens of temporality and the life course perspective to scrutinize the intersections and overlaps between peoples' experiences of tourism and migration and the state policies that control and categorize their movements. She shows how Cuban–Danish couples maneuver these temporal regulations – visas, residencies, permits, and so on – revealing inequalities in terms of people's access to both mobility and residency. Valerio Simoni's chapter also discusses the experiences of Cubans living abroad in Europe during and after their return to Cuba. His chapter spotlights the complex questions of when one is migrant, tourist, or local and who imposes these designations. Simoni examines the potentials and limitations of these categories for evoking different modes of belonging and identification and the emotions involved, when "you are less than a tourist, and less than a Cuban," in the words of one of his research participants. Returnees' mobility and their tourist/migrant/Cuban identifications are grounded in global inequalities across a North–South divide. Returnees are aware of expectations of sharing (i.e., providing material support) and feel exploited, much in the same way (foreign) tourists often feel, which results in "downscaling" family and reconstructing social life, leading to fragmentation and differentiation.

Chapters 3–6 scrutinize how exile intersects with other mobilities, namely, return migration, deportation, VFR tourism, student mobility, solidarity tourism, justice tourism, and volunteer tourism. Long T. Bui discusses the involuntary and voluntary returns of post-war South Vietnamese refugees from the United States, analyzing the categories of repatriated deportees, incarcerated tourists, and retired or working expats. The author juxtaposes cases of Vietnamese exiles sent back to Vietnam by the US government against their will (due to old criminal records or other infractions) with cases of US tourists of Vietnamese origin arrested and expelled by the Vietnamese government. He also addresses voluntary returnees who move to Vietnam either upon retirement or for work, thus transforming from exiles to expats. Here, the blurred boundaries between exile, migrant, and tourist follow the enduring Cold War line, distinguishing a friend from an enemy in a world of global flows of ideas, capital, and bodies. VFR tourism, in this case, is a way for the Vietnamese state to manage refugee/returnee politics. But at the same time, the threat of being banished mitigates such tourism. Rita Reis, in her chapter on young Sahrawi refugees, argues that educational mobility can work as a strategy for escaping protracted exile and pursuing a better future. Via ethnographic stories, Reis shows a typical trajectory for Sahrawi exiled youth from refugee camps to Spain: first participating in the Holidays in Peace program (which offers Sahrawi children an opportunity to spend their summer vacations in Europe), then being fostered by one's Spanish host family, studying abroad, and ultimately becoming an economic migrant. These mobilities are accompanied by flows in the opposite direction – the travels of Spanish host families to the refugee camps within the framework of solidarity tourism. The mobilities she discusses are embedded in a nation-building process that takes place in the diaspora. Rami K. Isaac's chapter explores the intersections between exile and tourism (as well as pilgrimage) through the lens of justice tourism. He examines the motivations, perceptions, and experiences of international tourists attending alternative tours to the Segregation Wall and Palestinian refugee camps in Bethlehem. Justice tourism here plays a similar role to that seen in Bloch's study of Tibetan refugees discussed earlier in this chapter: it offers a platform for subaltern histories of exile and suffering which are not voiced in mainstream tourism. Here, the otherwise silenced voice of Palestinian refugees can be heard by tourists. The author discusses the potential of this form of tourism to create empathy and solidarities between international tourists and Palestinian refugees. Finally, Robert Rydzewski's chapter shows how, during the first crisis of receiving refugees in Europe in 2015–2016, refugee camps, bus and train stations, and informal asylum seekers' settlements in the Balkan route brought together two mobile groups: refugees from the Global South and volunteers from the Global North, the latter resembling tourists in their itinerant volunteerism. Asylum seekers and the voluntourists Rydzewski accompanied in Serbia acted in concert with one another, following each other and responding to each other's needs. However, their movements reflected unequal access to mobility: While the mobility of the former was restricted, the latter enjoyed the privilege of unhampered mobility, moving freely across nation-states' borders. What emerged from encounters between these two mobile groups were new forms of political activity and solidarity based on reciprocity that resulted in challenging the European Union's border regime.

18 Kathleen M. Adams and Natalia Bloch

Intersections between tourism and migration are explored in Chapters 7–10. Carla Guerrón Montero writes about migrants who are workers in the tourism sector, tourists who turn into lifestyle migrants, and diaspora roots tourists in Panama. In particular, she focuses on Afro-Antilleans who since the mid-19th century were treated as "temporary migrants" in Panama until tourism offered them a platform for creating their self-representations and a degree of cultural-political autonomy from the national meta-narrative. At the same time, Panama attracts lifestyle migrants – mostly from the United States – who were once tourists. Guerrón Montero demonstrates how cultural and economic capital gained through interactions with those lifestyle migrants and tourists has the potential to help undocumented "temporary migrants" working in the tourism sector overcome their status-related constraints. She also shows how migrants working in the tourism sector can act as tourists both through VFR and traveling in dwelling. Finally, she indicates an additional dimension of overlapping mobilities, i.e., diasporic Afro-Antilleans visiting Panama as tourists within a framework of roots tourism. In their chapter, Kosita Butratana, Alexander Trupp, and Karl Husa analyze tourism as an impetus for retirement migration and marriage migration in the Thai context. Retired migrants in Thailand are mostly men from Europe, North America, Australia, and some East Asian countries, who often live with a local partner. This is a consumption-led migration that itself blurs the boundaries between migration and tourism with regard to both motivations and destinations. The counter-mobility of retirement migration, with converse selectivity, is the cross-border marriage migration of young Thai women, who often are internal migrants themselves working in the tourism sector. Upon migration, they join the Thai diaspora in the Global North countries which, in turn, propels VFR tourism. Here, VFR tourism does not only mean return visits for leisure but reflects the gender obligations of Thai women toward their family members (especially, the parents). The authors argue that short-term stays for leisure often generate more permanent mobility, i.e., that previous tourism experiences play an important role in the migration decision-making and therefore they should be examined together. Francesco Vietti's chapter explores another dimension of overlaps between migration and tourism. He discusses migrants acting as tourist guides and migrant heritage as a tourist attraction in European cities. His case study offers a critical analysis of the Migrantour project developed in 20 cities in cooperation with anthropologists to highlight migrants' contributions to transforming these cities. As with the case of solidarity tours to Palestinian refugee camps, tourism here offers first- and second-generation migrants a platform for telling their stories about life in their current cities – to both tourists and residents. These encounters between migrants and tourists are aimed at transcending touristic folklorization and trivialization of migrants' otherness. Vietti discusses the categories of "transformative encounters," "traveling-in-dwelling," and "daily multiculturalism" to explore their potential and limitations for living together "in difference." Finally, Lauren Miller Griffith scrutinizes the complex and overlapping mobilities of the transnational capoeira community. North American students travel to Brazil as tourists/pilgrims following

Problematizing Siloed Mobilities **19**

their masters while capoeira teachers move in the opposite direction, engaging in VFR tourism and other "touristy" activities. These movements enable both groups to move up within capoeira's internal hierarchy and sometimes lead to more-or-less permanent migrations. Ultimately, Griffith shifts our gaze from the focus on capoeira's globalization to the movements of people who pursue it and, in so doing, addresses issues of race and class inscribed in these mobilities.

The last two chapters of the book address blurred boundaries between migration and tourism in privileged mobilities. Magnus Öhlander, Katarzyna Wolanik Boström, and Helena Pettersson analyze the international mobility of Swedish scholars and physicians – highly skilled professionals – to problematize the multidimensional practices of their work-related mobility and tourism. The authors demonstrate how tourism imaginaries and opportunities figure into these professionals' travel planning. In this case, professional and tourist gazes, as well as work and tourist moments, overlap to the point that they are sometimes hard to distinguish, converging in a professionals' tourist gaze. Finally, Maria de Fátima Amante and Irene Rodrigues observe how migration and tourism intertwine in the category of foreign investor. Their case study focuses on the motivations and experiences of Chinese and Brazilian Golden Visa holders in Portugal. They also demonstrate how the state strategically deploys the country's tourist attractiveness to entice international investors. However, contrary to the state's aims, these investors are neither super-rich nor absent from the country. For many of them, the opportunity to obtain a Golden Visa to this European Union country is an avenue for pursuing a better life which exceeds the desire to expatriate capital. What a better life means depends on the group under study; for Chinese investors, a less stressful educational environment for their children and cleaner air were key, while for Brazilian Golden Visa holders, a sense of personal security and a less stressful work environment were most significant. Therefore, as the authors argue, these Golden Visa holders might be best understood as lifestyle migrants rather than capital investors. Interestingly, the political dimension can also be detected in this form of mobility – although the mainland Chinese did not express this explicitly, the Brazilians were very vocal about the unstable political and economic situation in their country of origin as well as the banalization of violence that motivated them to relocate to Portugal as investors.

Finally, Stephanie Malia Hom's postscript addresses the varied ways in which the COVID-19 pandemic has altered and "reshuffled" subjective experiences of tourism, migration, and exile. Building on points elaborated in the volume's chapters and interweaving her own cogent analyses of media stories in the COVID-19 era, Hom spotlights the mobility-related paradoxes wrought by the pandemic. She chronicles how the pandemic's rhetoric of contagion was cast onto tourists who found themselves trapped and immobile while vacationing, prompting tourists to adopt vocabularies of limbo, waiting, imprisonment, and uncertainty more typically associated with migrants and refugees. She also observes that the pandemic brought reassessments of earlier associations between mobility and privilege: those of means could choose to shelter in place thereby shielding themselves from the virus, whereas those without "network capital" (Urry, 2007, cited by Hom) – migrant agricultural farmworkers and food workers, in particular – were mobilized as "essential workers" and exposed to the virus (for migrants, staying home means the loss of income and their ability to send remittances). Ultimately, Hom's chapter underscores the importance of considering ethical issues and matters of biopolitics underpinning intersecting forms of mobility in the COVID-19 era. Hom also offers various suggestions for future research directions. As she suggests, scholars interested in the intersections of tourism, migration, and exile in the (post-)pandemic era might want to examine the ethical dimensions of these shifting experiences of mobility. That is, we might ask who gains advantages from "deploying" (im-)mobility and how? How might considering "variegated" mobilities foster new paths toward mobility justice?

In raising these questions, Hom signals our broader hopes for this volume. In recounting, juxtaposing, and analyzing stories of (im-)mobile lives – refugees' and migrants' returns, marriage migrants, voluntourists, migrant retirees, migrant tourism workers and entrepreneurs, mobile investors and professionals, and refugees pursuing educational mobility – the chapters comprising this volume aim to cultivate more nuanced insights into intersecting forms of mobility. Moreover, taken together, they invite reflections on the moral, economic, and cultural dynamics of spatial mobility. It is our hope that these richer understandings will foster not only empathy but also greater resolve for forging trails toward mobility justice.

Notes

1 See *La Caminata* (The Long Walk). Available at: www.newday.com/film/la-caminata.
2 For example, Patrick O'Gilfoil Healy suggests that tourists' activities on *La Caminata Nocternal* can appear "crass, like Marie Antoinette playing peasant on the grounds of Versailles" (2007, par. 12).
3 The idea for this volume was born at the 2019 Congress of the International Union of Anthropological and Ethnological Sciences (IUAES) held at the Adam Mickiewicz University in Poznań, Poland. There, we (the volume editors) co-chaired a panel on "The Intersections of Tourism, Migration, and Exile" which garnered much interest from anthropologists working on mobility-related topics. Three of this book's chapters were presented as part of this panel (Chapters 1, 11, and 12). Additional chapters were subsequently solicited with the aim of creating a broader geographical range of case studies and fostering a more diverse array of contributors (in terms of gender, nationality, ethnicity, and academic seniority).
4 Hilary Cunningham (2004) coined the expression "gated globe" to convey these inequities in access to mobility, drawing on the metaphor of gated communities.
5 It is estimated that in 2019 (just prior to the COVID-19 pandemic), 1.5 billion international tourist arrivals were recorded globally (www.unwto.org/international-tourism-growth-continues-to-outpace-the-economy, accessed on: May 28, 2022). In the same year, the number of international migrants worldwide reached nearly 272 million (www.un.org/en/development/desa/population/migration/publications/migrationreport/docs/InternationalMigration2019_Report.pdf, accessed on: May 28, 2022) and the number of forcibly displaced reached 79.5 million (including 26 million people who were granted refugee status and 45.7 million internally displaced persons; see www.unhcr.org/flagship-reports/globaltrends/globaltrends2019/, accessed on: May 28,

2022). The latter statistics have grown significantly in 2022, due to the Russian invasion of Ukraine. Although difficult to calculate, the numbers for pilgrimages are also high (estimated at 155 million annually in 2011), but they are not that widely distributed around the world. Hindu and Sikh (primarily domestic) pilgrims comprise half the total of pilgrims worldwide. Muslim travels to spiritual sites account for approximately 2.3 million pilgrimages annually (for data on pilgrimages, see: www.arcworld.org/downloads/ARC%20pilgrimage%20statistics%20155m%2011-12-19.pdf, accessed on: May 28, 2022).

6 An early volume that highlighted the "converging interests" of mobile workers and tourists merits mention here, namely, Jill Forshee et al. (1999).

7 www.tandfonline.com/action/journalInformation?show=aimsScope&journalCode=wimm20 (Accessed on: May 13, 2022).

8 See Chapter 6, endnote 1, for an explanation regarding why the crisis of 2015–2016 was not a crisis of refugees but rather a crisis of receiving refugees marked by securitization, border control, and institutional violence (push-backs) or even a crisis of European values (Buchowski, 2017, p. 521). Therefore, we opt to term this phenomenon a "crisis of receiving refugees" (see Bloch, forthcoming).

9 For more on this dynamic elsewhere in Indonesia, see Dahles and Bras (1999).

References

Adams, K.M. (1984) 'Come to Tana Toraja, "Land of the Heavenly Kings": Travel agents as brokers of ethnicity', *Annals of Tourism Research*, 1(3), pp. 469–485.

Adams, K.M. (1988) *Carving a new identity: Ethnic and artistic change in Tana Toraja*. PhD thesis. Washington, DC, University of Washington.

Adams, K.M. (1995) 'Making-up the Toraja? The appropriation of tourism, anthropology and museums for politics in upland Sulawesi (Indonesia)', *Ethnology*, 34(2), pp. 143–153.

Adams, K.M. (2003) 'The politics of heritage in Tana Toraja, Indonesia: Interplaying the local and the global', *Indonesia and the Malay World*, 31(89), pp. 91–107.

Adams, K.M. (2006) *Art as politics: Re-crafting identities, tourism, and power in Tana Toraja, Indonesia*. Honolulu, HI: University of Hawai'i Press.

Adams, K.M. (2011) 'Public interest anthropology, political market squares and re-scripting dominance: From swallows to "race" in San Juan Capistrano, CA', *Journal of Policy Research in Tourism, Leisure and Events*, 3(2), pp. 147–169.

Adams, K.M. (2012) 'Ethnographic methods' in Dwyer, L., Gill, A. and Seetaram, N. (eds.) *Handbook of research methods in tourism*. Cheltenham and Northampton: Edward Elgar Publishing, pp. 339–351.

Adams, K.M. (2015) 'Families, funerals and Facebook: Reimag(in)ing and curating Toraja kin in translocal times', *tRaNS: Trans – Regional and – National Studies of Southeast Asia*, 3(2), pp. 239–266.

Adams, K.M. (2016) 'Tourism and ethnicity in insular Southeast Asia: Eating, praying, loving and beyond', *Asian Journal of Tourism Research*, 1(1), pp. 1–28.

Adams, K.M. (2019) "Being a tourist in (my own) home": Negotiating identities and belonging in Indonesian heritage tourism' in Leite, N.M, Casteñeda, Q. and Adams, K.M. (eds.) *The ethnography of tourism: Edward Bruner and beyond*. Lanham: Lexington Books, pp. 147–165.

Adams, K.M. (2020) 'What Western tourism concepts obscure: Intersections of migration and tourism in Indonesia', *Tourism Geographies*, 23(1), pp. 1–26.

Adams, K.M. and Sandarupa, D. (2018) 'A room with a view: Local knowledge and tourism entrepreneurship in an unlikely Indonesian locale', *Asian Journal of Tourism Research*, 3(1), pp. 1–26.

22 Kathleen M. Adams and Natalia Bloch

Adams, V. (1992) 'Tourism and Sherpas, Nepal: Reconstruction of reciprocity', *Annals of Tourism Research*, 19(3), pp. 534–554.

Adams, V. (1996) *Tigers of the snow and other virtual Sherpas: An ethnography of Himalayan encounters*. Princeton, NJ: Princeton University Press.

Åkerlund, U. and Sandberg, L. (2015) 'Stories of lifestyle mobility: Representing self and place in the search for the "good life"', *Social & Cultural Geography*, 16(3), pp. 351–370.

Aleinikoff, T.A. (2015) *From dependence to self-reliance: Changing the paradigm in protracted refugee situations*. Washington, DC: Migration Policy Institute.

Allon, F., Anderson, K. and Bushell, R. (2003) 'Mutant mobilities: Backpacker tourism in "global" Sydney', *Mobilities*, 3, pp. 73–94.

Alrawadieh, Z., Karayilan, E. and Cetin, G. (2019) 'Understanding the challenges of refugee entrepreneurship in tourism and hospitality', *The Service Industries Journal*, 39(9–10), pp. 717–740.

Amit, V (2000) 'Introduction: Constructing the field' in Amit, V. (ed.) *Constructing the field: Ethnographic fieldwork in the contemporary world*. London and New York: Routledge, pp. 1–18.

Amit, V. (2007) *Going first class: New approaches to privileged travel and movement*. Oxford and New York: Berghahn Books.

Appadurai, A. (1986) *The social life of things: Commodities in cultural perspective*. Cambridge: Cambridge University Press.

Appadurai, A. (1990) 'Disjuncture and difference in the global economy', *Public Culture*, 2(2), pp. 1–24.

Appadurai, A. (1996) *Modernity at large: Cultural dimensions of globalization*. Minneapolis: University of Minnesota Press.

Ashtar, L., Shani, A. and Uriely, N. (2017) 'Blending "home" and "away": Young Israeli migrants as VFR travelers', *Tourism Geographies*, 19(4), pp. 658–672.

Ateljevic, I. and Doorne, S. (2000) 'Staying within the fence': Lifestyle entrepreneurship in Tourism', *Journal of Sustainable Tourism*, 8(5), pp. 378–392.

Baas, M. (2017) 'The mobile middle: Indian skilled migrants in Singapore and the "middling" space between migration categories', *Transitions. Journal of Transient Migration*, 1(1), pp. 47–63.

Badone, E. and Roseman, S.R. (2004) *Intersecting journeys: The anthropology of pilgrimage and tourism*. Urbana and Chicago, IL: University of Illinois Press.

Bakewell, O. (2021) 'Unsettling the boundaries between forced and voluntary migration' in Carmel, E., Lenner, K. and Paul, R. (eds.) *Handbook on the governance and politics of migration*. Cheltenham and Northampton: Edward Elgar Publishing, pp. 124–136.

Bell, M. and Ward, G. (2000) 'Comparing temporary mobility with permanent migration', *Tourism Geographies*, 2(3), pp. 87–107.

Benson, M. and O'Reilly, K. (eds.) (2009) *Lifestyle migration: Expectations, aspirations and experiences*. Farnham: Ashgate.

Benson, M. and Osbaldiston, N. (eds.) (2014) *Understanding lifestyle migration: Theoretical approaches to migration and the quest for a better way of life*. London: Palgrave Macmillan.

Bianchi, R.V. (2000) 'Migrant tourist-workers: Exploring the "contact zones" of post-industrial tourism', *Current Issues in Tourism*, 3(2), pp. 107–187.

Bianet Castellanos, M. (2010) *A return to servitude: Maya migration and the tourist trade in Cancún*. Minnesota, MN: University of Minnesota Press.

Bloch, N. (2016) 'Evicting heritage. Spatial cleansing and cultural legacy at the Hampi UNESCO site in India', *Critical Asian Studies*, 48(4), pp. 556–578.

Bloch, N. (2017) 'Taxonomic panic and the art of "making do" at a heritage site. The case of Hampi UNESCO site, India', *Anthropological Notebooks*, 23(3), pp. 19–44.

Bloch, N. (2018) 'Making tourists engaged by vulnerable communities in India' in Owsianowska, S. and Banaszkiewicz, M. (eds.) *Anthropology of tourism in Central and Eastern Europe. Bridging worlds.* Lanham, MD: Lexington Books, pp. 181–197.

Bloch, N. (2020) 'Beyond a sedentary Other and a mobile tourist. Transgressing mobility categories in the informal tourism sector in India', *Critique of Anthropology*, 40(2), pp. 218–237.

Bloch, N. (2021a) 'Refugees as donors. "Rich" Tibetan refugees, evicted Indian slum dwellers and a smart city', *Journal of Refugee Studies*, 34(2), pp. 1840–1858.

Bloch, N. (2021b) *Encounters across difference. Tourism and overcoming subalternity in India.* Lanham, MD, Boulder, CO, New York and London: Lexington Books.

Bloch, N. (forthcoming) 'Whose crisis? Between Othering and solidarity during the so-called refugee crisis in Europe' in Luthra Sinha, B., Gopal, N.D. and Pandey, A.D. (eds.) *Dark ethnography, state and the vulnerable communities: Is solidarity a threat to nation states?* London and New York: Routledge.

Bodzan, M. (2020) 'Cooking with refugees and migrants. Staging authenticity and traditionality for Warsaw's culinary tourists', *Ethnologia Polona*, 41, pp. 51–67.

Böss, M. (2006) 'Theorising exile' in Böss, M., Gilsenan Nordin, I. and Olinder, B. (eds.) *Re-mapping exile: Realities and metaphors in Irish literature and history.* Aarhus: Aarhus University Press, pp. 15–46.

Boyne, S., Carswell, F. and Hall, D. (2002) 'Reconceptualising VFR tourism. Friends, relatives and migration in a domestic context' in Hall, C.M. and Williams, A.M. (eds.) *Tourism and migration: New relationships between production and consumption.* Dordrecht: Kluwer Academic Publishers, pp. 241–256.

Brennan, D. (2004) *What's love got to do with it? Transnational desires and sex tourism in the Dominican Republic.* Durham, NC: Duke University Press.

Bruner, E.M. (1995) 'The ethnographer/tourist in Indonesia' in Lanfant, M.-F., Allcock, J.B. and Bruner, E.M. (eds.) *International tourism: Identity and change.* London: SAGE, pp. 224–241.

Bruner, E.M. (1996) 'Tourism in Ghana: The representation of slavery and the return of the black diaspora', *American Anthropologist*, 98(2), pp. 290–304.

Bruner, E.M. (2005) *Culture on tour: Ethnographies of travel.* Chicago, IL: University of Chicago Press.

Buchowski, M. (2017) 'A new tide of racism, xenophobia, and islamophobia in Europe: Polish anthropologists swim against the current', *American Anthropologist*, 119(3), pp. 519–523.

Burns, P.M. and Novelli, M. (eds.) (2008) *Tourism and mobilities: Local-global connections.* Wallingford and Cambridge: CABI.

Burrai, E., Buda, D.-M. and Stevenson, E. (2022) 'Tourism and refugee-crisis intersections: Co-creating tour guide experiences in Leeds, England', *Journal of Sustainable Tourism.* https://doi.org/10.1080/09669582.2022.2072851

Butler, R. (2003) 'Relationships between tourism and diasporas: Influences and patterns', *Espac Populations Sociétés*, 2, pp. 317–326.

Carson, D.A., Carson, D.B. and Lundmark, L. (eds.) (2016) *Tourism, mobilities, and development in sparsely populated areas.* London and New York: Routledge.

Castellanos, M.B. (2010) *A return to servitude: Maya migration and the tourist trade in Cancún.* Minnesota, MN: University of Minnesota Press.

Cetin, G., Altinay, L. and Alrawadieh, Z. (2022) 'Entrepreneurial motives, entrepreneurial success and life satisfaction of refugees venturing in tourism and hospitality', *International Journal of Contemporary Hospitality Management*, 34(6), pp. 2227–2249.

Chatty, D., Fiddian-Qasmiyeh, E. and Crivello, G. (2010) 'Identity with/out territory: Sahrawi refugee in transnational space', in Chatty, D. (ed.) *Deterritorialized youth – Sahrawi and Afghan refugees at the margins of the Middle East.* New York: Berghahn Books, pp. 37–84.

24 Kathleen M. Adams and Natalia Bloch

Choedup, N. (2015) *From Tibetan refugees to transmigrants: Negotiating cultural continuity and economic mobility through migration.* PhD thesis. Washington, DC: Washington University. Available at: https://openscholarship.wustl.edu/art_sci_etds/643

Chtouris, S. and Miller, D.S. (2017) 'Refugee flows and volunteers in the current humanitarian crisis in Greece', *Journal of Applied Security Research,* 12(1), pp. 61–77.

Clifford, J. (1997) *Routes: Travel and translation in the late twentieth century.* Cambridge, MA: Harvard University Press.

Coates, J. (2017) 'Idleness as method: Hairdressers and Chinese urban mobility in Tokyo' in Elliot, A., Norum, R. and Salazar, N.B. (eds.) *Methodologies of mobility: Ethnography and experiment.* New York: Berghahn Books, pp. 109–128.

Cohen, E. (1973) 'Nomads from affluence: Notes on the phenomenon of drifter-tourism', *International Journal of Comparative Sociology,* 14(1), pp. 89–103.

Cohen, E. (1992) 'Pilgrimage and tourism: Convergence and divergence', in Morinis, E.A. (ed) *Sacred journeys: The anthropology of pilgrimage.* New York: Greenwood Press, pp. 47–61.

Cohen, E. and Cohen, S. (2015) 'Beyond Eurocentrism in tourism: A paradigm shift to mobilities', *Tourism Recreation Research,* 40(2), pp. 157–168.

Cole, S. (2004) 'Shared benefits: Longitudinal research in Eastern Indonesia' in Phillimore, J. and Goodson, L. (eds) *Qualitative research in tourism: Ontologies, epistemologies and methodologies.* Abingdon: Routledge, pp. 292–310.

Cole, S. and Eriksson, J. (2010) 'Tourism and human rights', in Cole, S. and Morgan, N.J. (eds.) *Tourism and inequality: Problems and prospects.* Wallingford and Cambridge: CABI Publishing, pp. 107–125.

Coles, T. and Timothy, D.J. (eds.) (2004a) *Tourism, diasporas and space.* London and New York: Routledge.

Coles, T. and Timothy, D.J. (2004b) 'My field is the world: Conceptualizing diasporas, travel and tourism' in Coles, T and Timothy, D.J. (eds) Tourism, diasporas and space. London and New York: Routledge, pp. 1–29.

Cooper, M.J. (2002) 'Flexible labour markets, ethnicity and tourism-related migration in Australia and New Zealand' in Hall, C.M. and Williams, A.M. (eds.) *Tourism and migration: New relationships between production and consumption.* Dordrecht: Kluwer Academic Publishers, pp. 73–86.

Cunningham, H. (2004) 'Nations rebound? Crossing borders in a gated globe', *Identities: Global Studies in Culture and Power,* 11(3), pp. 329–350.

D'Andrea, A. (2009) *Global nomads: Techno and New Age as transnational countercultures in Ibiza and Goa.* Abingdon: Routledge.

Dahles, H. and Bras, C.H. (1999) 'Entrepreneurs in romance. Tourism in Indonesia', *Annals of Tourism Research,* 26(2), pp. 267–293.

Deshingkar, P. and Farrington, J. (eds.) (2009) *Circular migration and multilocational livelihood strategies in rural India.* Oxford: Oxford University Press.

DiGiovine, M.A. and Choe, J. (2020) *Pilgrimage beyond the officially sacred: Understanding the geographies of religion and spirituality in sacred travel.* Abingdon: Routledge.

Din, K. (2017) 'Returning home: A reflection on the Malaysian practice of *balik kampung'*, *Asian Journal of Tourism Research,* 2(1), pp. 36–49.

Duany, J. (2002) 'Mobile livelihoods: The sociocultural practices of circular migrant between Puerto Rico and the United States', *The International Migration Review,* 36(2), pp. 355–388.

Duncan, T., Cohen, S.A. and Thulemark, M. (2016) *Lifestyle mobilities. Intersections of travel, leisure and migration.* London and New York: Routledge.

Duval, D. (2003) 'When hosts become guests: Return visits and diasporic identities in a Commonwealth eastern Caribbean community,' *Current Issues in Tourism*, 6(4), pp. 267–308.

Dwyer, L., Seetaram, N., Forsyth, P. and King, B. (2014) 'Is the migration-tourism relationship only about VFR?,' *Annals of Tourism Research*, 46, pp. 130–143.

Eade, J. (1992) 'Pilgrimage and tourism at Lourdes, France', *Annals of Tourism Research*, 19, pp. 18–32.

Ebron, P. (1999) 'Tourists as pilgrims: Commercial fashioning of Trans-Atlantic politics', *American Ethnologist*, 26, pp. 910–932.

Elliot, A., Norum, R. and Salazar, N.B. (eds.) (2017) *Methodologies of mobility: Ethnography and experiment*. New York: Berghahn Books.

Enloe, C. (1989) *Bananas, beaches & bases: Making feminist sense of international politics*. Berkeley, CA and Los Angeles, CA: University of California Press.

Esman, M.R. (1984) 'Tourism as ethnic preservation: The Cajuns of Louisiana', *Annals of Tourism Research*, 11, pp. 451–467.

Farah, R. (2010) ' "Knowledge in the service of the cause": Education and the Sahrawi struggle for self-determination', *Refuge: Canada's Journal on Refugees*, 27(2), pp. 30–41.

Feldman, J. (1995) ' "It is my brothers whom I am seeking": Israeli youths' pilgrimages to Poland of the Shoah', *Jewish Folklore and Ethnology Review*, 17(1–2), pp. 33–37.

Fetterman, D.M. (2020) *Ethnography step-by-step*. Los Angeles, CA: SAGE.

Fiddian-Qasmiyeh, E. (2015) *South-South educational migration, humanitarianism and development – Views from the Caribbean, North Africa and the Middle East*. London: Routledge.

Forshee, J. (2001) *Between the folds: Stories of cloth, lives, and travels from Sumba*. Honolulu, HI: University of Hawai'i Press.

Forshee, J. (2002) 'Pushing the margins: Fabrics from Sumba, traders in Bali, and tourists from everywhere' in Swain, M. and Momsen, J.H. (eds.) *Gender/Tourism/Fun(?)*. Elmsford: Cognizant Communication Corporation, pp. 134–140.

Forshee, J., Fink, C. and Cate, S. (eds.) (1999) *Converging interests: Traders, travelers, and tourists in Southeast Asia*. Berkeley, CA: University of California at Berkeley Center for Southeast Asian Studies.

Freedman, J. (2018) 'Amateur humanitarianism, social solidarity and "volunteer tourism" in the EU refugee "crisis"' in Ahmad, A. and Smith, J. (eds.) *Humanitarian action and ethics*. London: Zed Books, pp. 94–111.

Fregonese, S. and Ramadan, A. (2015) 'Hotel geopolitics: A research agenda', *Geopolitics*, 20(4), pp. 793–813.

García Agustín, Ó. and Jørgensen, M.B. (2019) 'Autonomous solidarity: Hotel City Plaza' in García Agustín, Ó. and Jørgensen, M.B. (eds.) *Solidarity and the 'refugee crisis' in Europe*. Cham: Palgrave Pivot, pp. 49–72.

Ghodsee, K. (2005) *The Red Riviera: Gender, tourism, and postsocialism on the Black Sea*. Durham, NC: Duke University Press.

Geoffroy, C. and Sibley, R. (eds.) (2007) *Going abroad: Travel, tourism, and migration. Cross-cultural perspectives on mobility*. Newcastle upon Tyne: Cambridge Scholars Publishing.

Glick Schiller, N. and Salazar, N.B. (2013) 'Regimes of mobility across the globe', *Journal of Ethnic and Migration Studies*, 39(2), pp. 183–200.

Gogia, N. (2006) 'Unpacking corporeal mobilities: The global voyages of labour and leisure', *Environment and Planning A: Economy and Space*, 38, pp. 359–375.

Graburn, N.H.H. (1983) *To pray, pay and play: The cultural structure of Japanese domestic tourism*. Aix-en-Provence: Centre des Etudes Touristiques.

Graburn, N.H.H. (1989) 'Tourism: The sacred journey' in Smith, V.L. (ed.) *Hosts and guests: The anthropology of tourism*. Philadelphia, PA: University of Pennsylvania Press, pp. 17–32.

Griffin, T. (2017) 'Immigrant hosts and intra-regional travel', *Tourism Geographies*, 19(1), pp. 44–62.

Gustafson, P. (2002) 'Tourism and seasonal retirement migration', *Annals of Tourism Research*, 29(4), pp. 899–918.

Gustafson, P. (2014) 'Business travel from the traveller's perspective: Stress, stimulation and normalization', *Mobilities*, 9(1), pp. 63–83.

Hasian, M.A., Maldonado, J.A. and Ono, K.A. (2015) 'Thanatourism, Caminata Nocturna, and the complex geopolitics of Mexico's Parque EcoAlberto', *Southern Communication Journal*, 80(4), pp. 311–330. https://doi.org/10.1080/1041794X.2015.1043138.

Hall, C.M. and Müller, D.K. (eds.) (2004) *Tourism, mobility and second homes: Between elite landscape and common ground.* Clevedon: Channel View Pubs.

Hall, C.M. and Tucker, H. (eds.) (2004) *Tourism and postcolonialism: Contested discourses, identities and representations.* London and New York: Routledge.

Hall, C.M. and Williams, A.M. (eds.) (2002) *Tourism and migration. New relationships between production and consumption.* Dordrecht: Kluwer Academic Publishers.

Harrison, J. (2008) 'Shifting positions,' *Tourist Studies*, 8(1), pp. 41–60.

Harrison, J. (2010) 'Belonging at the cottage' in Scott, J. and Selwyn, T. (eds.) *Thinking through tourism.* London: Routledge, pp. 71–92.

Healy, P.O. (2007) 'Heads up: Hidalgo, Mexico; Run! Hide! The illegal border crossing experience'. *The New York Times*, Feb. 4. Available at: https://www.nytimes.com/2007/02/04/travel/04HeadsUp.html

Herzfeld, M. (2006) 'Spatial cleansing: Monumental vacuity and the idea of the West', *Journal of Material Culture*, 11(1/2), pp. 127–149.

Higgins-Desbiolles, F. (2009) 'International solidarity movement: A case study in volunteer tourism for justice', *Annals of Leisure Research*, 12(3–4), pp. 333–339.

Higgins-Desbiolles, F. (2010) 'Justifying tourism: Justice through tourism' in Cole, S. and Morgan, N.J. (eds.) *Tourism and inequality: Problems and prospects.* Wallingford and Cambridge: CABI, pp. 195–212.

Holsey, B. (2008) *Routes of remembrance: Refashioning the slave trade in Ghana.* Chicago, IL: University of Chicago Press.

Horolets, A. (2018) 'On holiday? Polish migrants visit their families in Poland' in Ślusarczyk, M., Pustułka, P. and Struzik, J. (eds.) *Contemporary migrant families: Actors and issues.* Newcastle upon Tyne: Cambridge Scholars Publishers, pp. 117–136.

Isaac, R.K. (2010) 'Alternative tourism: New forms of tourism in Bethlehem for the Palestinian tourism industry', *Current Issues in Tourism*, 13(1), pp. 21–36.

İstanbullu Dinçer, F.F., Karayilan, E. and Aydoğan Çifçi, M. (2017) 'Refugee crisis (RC) after the Arab Spring (AS) and its impacts on Turkish tourism industry: The case of Istanbul', *Journal of Tourismology*, 3(1), pp. 2–12.

Jaakson, R. (1986) 'Second-home domestic tourism', *Annals of Tourism Research*, 13(3), pp. 367–391.

Jaisuekun, K. and Sunanta, S. (2021) 'German migrants in Pattaya, Thailand: Gendered mobilities and the blurring boundaries between sex tourism, marriage migration, and lifestyle migration' in Mora, C. and Piper, N. (eds.) *The Palgrave handbook of gender and migration.* London: Palgrave Macmillan, pp. 137–149.

Janoschka, M. and Haas, H. (2014) *Contested spatialities, lifestyle migration and residential tourism.* London and New York: Routledge.

Kassis, R., Solomon, R. and Higgins-Desbiolles, F. (2016) 'Solidarity tourism in Palestine: The Alternative Tourism Group of Palestine as a catalyzing instrument of resistance' in Isaac, R.K., Hall, C.M. and Higgins-Desbiolles, F. (eds) *The politics and power of tourism in Palestine.* London: Routledge, pp. 37–52.

Kelner, S. (2010) *Tours that bind: Diaspora, pilgrimage and Israeli birthright tourism*. New York: NYU Press.

Kingsley, P. (2015) 'Kos: The Greek island where refugees and tourists share the same beaches', *The Guardian*, 5 September. Available at: www.theguardian.com/world/2015/sep/05/refugees-and-holidaymakers-in-kos-patrick-kingsley

Koslowski, R. (ed.) (2011) *Global mobility regimes: A conceptual reframing*. New York: Palgrave Macmillan.

LeCompte, M.D. and Schensul, J.J. (2010) *Designing and conducting ethnographic research: An introduction*. Lanham, MD: AltaMira.

Lehrer, E.T. (2013) *Jewish Poland revisited: Heritage tourism in unquiet places*. Indianopolis, IN: University of Indiana Press.

Leite, N. (2005) 'Travels to an ancestral past: On diasporic tourism, embodied memory, and identity', *Anthropologicas*, 9, pp. 273–304.

Leite, N. (2017) *Unorthodox kin: Portuguese Marranos and the global search for belonging*. Berkeley, CA: University of California Press.

Lenz, R. (2010) '"Hotel Royal" and other spaces of hospitality: Tourists and migrants in the Mediterranean' in Scott, J. and Selwyn, T. (eds.) *Thinking through tourism*. London: Routledge, pp. 209–229.

Levitt, P. and Glick Schiller, N. (2004) 'Conceptualizing simultaneity: A transnational social field perspective on society', *International Migration Review*, 38(3), pp. 1002–1039.

Lindquist, J. (2008) *The anxieties of mobility: Migration and tourism in the Indonesian borderlands*. Honolulu, HI: University of Hawai'i Press.

Long, L.D. and Oxfeld, E. (eds.) (2004) *Coming home? Refugees, migrants and those who stayed behind*. Philadelphia, PA: University of Pennsylvania Press.

Mahrouse, G. (2008) 'Race-conscious transnational activists with cameras: Mediators of compassion', *International Journal of Cultural Studies*, 11(1), pp. 87–105.

Makimoto, T. and Manners, D. (1997) *Digital nomad*. New York: Wiley.

Malkki, L.H. (1995a) 'Refugees and exile: From "refugee studies" to the national order of things', *Annual Review of Anthropology*, 24, pp. 495–523.

Malkki, L.H. (1995b) *Purity and exile. Violence, memory, and national cosmology among Hutu refugees in Tanzania*. Chicago, IL: Chicago University Press.

Manning, P. (2009) 'The hotel/refugee camp Iveria: Symptom, monster, fetish, home' in Assche, K.V., Salukvadze, J. and Shavishvili, N. (eds.) *City culture and city planning in Tbilisi: Where Europe and Asia meet*. Lewiston: Edwin Mellen Press, pp. 319–349.

Marcus, G. (1995) 'Ethnography in/of the world system: The emergence of multi-sited ethnography', *Annual Review of Anthropology*, 24(1), pp. 95–117.

Marschall, S. (2017) *Tourism and memories of home. Migrants, displaced people, exiles and diasporic communities*. Bristol: Channel View Pubs.

Mason, P. (2002) 'The "Big OE": New Zealanders overseas experiences in Britain' in Hall, C.M. and Williams, A.M. (eds.) *Tourism and migration: New relationships between production and consumption*. Dordrecht: Kluwer Academic Publishers, pp. 87–101.

McGuckin, E.A. (1997) *Postcards from Shangri-la: Tourism, Tibetan refugees, and the politics of cultural production*. PhD thesis. New York: New York University.

McIntyre, N. Williams, D. and K. McHugh (eds.) (2006) *Multiple dwelling and tourism: Negotiating place, home and identity*. Wallingford and Cambridge: CABI.

Moon, B.-Y., Yang, S.-H. and Lee, T.J. (2019) 'Married immigrant women's VFR tourism as the way to ethnic minority group acculturation', *Journal of Tourism and Cultural Change*, 17, pp. 544–561.

Moss, L. (2006) *The amenity migrants: Seeking and sustaining mountains and their cultures*. Wallingford and Cambridge: CABI.

Nash, D. (1981) 'Tourism as an anthropological subject', *Current Anthropology*, 22, pp. 461–481.

Nguyen, T.H. and King, B. (1998) 'Migrant homecoming: Viet kieu attitudes towards travelling back to Vietnam,' *Pacific Tourism Review*, 1, pp. 349–361.

Nowicka, M. (2007) 'Mobile locations: Construction of home in a group of mobile transnational professionals', *Global Networks. A Journal of Transnational Affiars*, 7(1), pp. 69–86.

O'Reilly, K. (2003) 'When is a tourist? The articulation of tourism and migration in Spain's Costa del Sol', *Tourist Studies*, 3(3), pp. 301–317.

O'Reilly, K. (2007) 'Emerging tourism futures: Residential tourism and its implications' in Geoffroy, C. and Sibley, R. (eds.) *Going abroad: Travel, tourism, and migration. Cross-cultural perspectives on mobility*. Newcastle upon Tyne: Cambridge Scholars Publishing, pp. 144–157.

Okely, J. and Callaway, H. (eds.) (1992) *Anthropology and autobiography*. London and New York: Routledge.

Ono, M. (2008) 'Long-stay tourism and international retirement migration: Japanese retirees in Malaysia' in Haines, D.W., Minami, M. and Yamashita, S. (eds.) *Transnational migration in East Asia: Japan in a comparative focus*. Osaka: National Museum of Ethnology, pp. 151–162.

Pappas, N. and Papatheodorou, A. (2017) 'Tourism and the refugee crisis in Greece: Perceptions and decision-making of accommodation providers', *Tourism Management*, 63, pp. 31–41.

Paraskevaidis, P. and Andriotis, K. (2021) 'Medical volunteers as accidental tourists: Humanitarianism and the European refugee crisis', *Tourism Recreation Research*. https://doi.org/10.1080/02508281.2021.2011591

Peters, J.D. (2006) 'Exile, nomadism and diaspora: The stakes of mobility in the Western canon', in Morra, J. and Smith, M. (eds.) *Visual culture: Spaces of visual culture*. London: Taylor and Francis, pp. 17–41.

Pfaffenberger, B. (1983) 'Serious pilgrims and frivolous tourists. The chimera of tourism in the pilgrimages of Sri Lanka', *Annals of Tourism Research*, 10(1), pp. 57–74.

Pido, E.J. (2017) *Migrant returns: Manila, development, and transnational connectivity*. Durham, NC: Duke University Press.

Popović, M. (2018) *Tourism in contested regions: A typology of tourists visiting the refugee camps of Western Sahara*. MSc Thesis. Ljubljana: University of Ljubljana.

Porter, L. (2015) 'Refugee crisis: Greece – what can tourists do to help', *Telegraph*, 25 September. Available at: www.telegraph.co.uk/travel/news/refugee-crisis-greece-what-can-tourists-do-to-help/

Portes, A. and Jensen, L. (1989) 'The enclave and the entrants: Patterns of ethnic enterprise in Miami before and after Mariel', *American Sociological Review*, 54(6), pp. 929–949.

Reis, R. (2019) 'Mobilities from the exile: the Sahrawi student migrations', in Rafik Khalil, R.M. and Malit, F.T. (eds) *Recent migrations and refugees in the MENA Region*. London: Transnational Press London, pp. 65–80.

Richards, G. (2015) 'The new global nomads: Youth travel in a globalizing world', *Tourism Recreation Research*, 40, pp. 340–352.

Richards, G. and Wilson, J. (eds.) (2004) *The global nomad: Backpacker travel in theory and practice*. Clevedon: Channel View Publications.

Said, E. (1984) 'Reflections on exile', *Graizta*, 13, pp. 159–172.

Salazar, N.B. (2012) 'Tourism imaginaries. A conceptual approach', *Annals of Tourism Research*, 39(2), pp. 863–882.

Salazar, N.B. (2017) 'Key figures of mobility: An introduction', *Social Anthropology*, 25(1), pp. 5–12.

Salazar, N.B. (2020) 'Labour migration and tourism mobilities: Time to bring sustainability into the debate', *Tourism Geographies*. https://doi.org/10.1080/14616688.2020.1801827

Salazar, N.B., Elliot, A. and Norum, R. (2017) 'Studying mobilities: Theoretical notes and methodological queries' in Elliot, A., Norum, R. and Salazar, N.B. (eds.) *Methodologies of mobility: Ethnography and experiment*. New York: Berghahn Books, pp. 1–24.

Sandri, E. (2017) '"Volunteer humanitarianism": Volunteers and humanitarian aid in the Jungle refugee camp Calais', *Journal of Ethnic and Migration Studies*, 44(1), pp. 65–80.

Schein, L. (1998) 'Forged transnationality and oppositional cosmopolitanism', in Smith, M. and Guarnizo, L. (eds.) *Transnationalism from below*. New Brunswick: Transaction Books, pp. 291–313.

Schein, L. (2002) 'Mapping Hmong media in diasporic space' in Ginsburg, F.D., Abu-Lughod, L. and Larkin, B. (eds.) *Media worlds: Anthropology on new terrains*. Berkeley, CA: University of California Press, pp. 229–244.

Schein, L. (2005) 'Minorities, homelands and methods' in Nyíri, P. and Breidenbach, J. (eds.) *China inside out: Contemporary Chinese nationalism and transnationalism*. Budapest: Central European University Press, pp. 99–140.

Schmidt, E. (2012) 'Citizenship from below: Hñúhñú heritage in a transnational world', *Latino Studies*, 10(1–2), pp. 196–219.

Shamir, R. (2005) 'Without borders? Notes on globalization as a mobility regime', *Sociological Theory*, 23(2), pp. 197–217.

Sheller, M. and Urry, J. (2006) 'The new mobilities paradigm', *Environment and Planning A*, 38(2), pp. 207–226.

Skeldon, R. (2012) 'Going round in circles: Circular migration, poverty alleviation and marginality', *International Migration*, 50(3), pp. 43–60.

Smith, V.L. (ed.) (1977) *Hosts and guests: The anthropology of tourism* (1st edition). Oxford: Blackwell.

Smith, V.L. (ed.) (1989) *Hosts and guests: The anthropology of tourism* (2nd edition). Philadelphia, PA: University of Pennsylvania Press.

Smith, V.L. (1992) 'Pilgrimage and tourism: The quest in guest', *Annals of Tourism Research*, 19, pp. 1–17.

Smith, V.L. (2005) 'Anthropologists in the tourism workplace', *NAPA Bulletin*, 23, pp. 252–269.

Snepenger, D.J., Johnson, J.D. and Rasker, R. (1995) 'Travel-stimulated entrepreneurial migration', *Journal of Travel Research*, 34(1), pp. 40–44.

Spradley, J. (2016) *Participant observation*. Long Grove, IL: Waveland Press.

Stronza, A. (2001) 'Anthropology of tourism: Forging new ground for ecotourism and other alternatives', *Annual Review of Anthropology*, 30, pp. 261–283.

Tesfahuney, M. (1998) 'Mobility, racism and geopolitics', *Political Geography*, 17(5), pp. 499–515.

Thompson, B.Y. (2019) 'The digital nomad lifestyle: (Remote) work/leisure balance, privilege, and constructed community,' *International Journal of the Sociology of Leisure*, 2(1–2), pp. 27–42.

Tie, C. and Seaton, T. (2013) 'Diasporic identity, heritage and "homecoming": How Sarawakian-Chinese feel on tour in Beijing,' *Tourism Analysis*, 18(3), pp. 227–243.

Timothy, D.J. (1997) 'Tourism and the personal heritage experience', *Annals of Tourism Research*, 34(3), pp. 751–754.

Timothy, D.J. and Olsen, D. (eds) (2006) *Tourism, religion and spiritual journeys*. New York and Abingdon: Routledge.

Trihas, N. and Tsilimpokos, K. (2018) 'Refugee crisis and volunteer tourism in Lesvos, Greece', *Journal on Tourism & Sustainability*, 2(1), pp. 42–56.

Tsartas, P., Kyriakaki, A., Stavrinoudis, T., Despotaki, G., Doumi, M., Sarantajou, E. and Tsilimpokos, K. (2020) 'Refugees and tourism: A case study from the islands of Chios and Lesvos, Greece', *Current Issues in Tourism*, 23(11), pp. 1311–1327

Turner, B.S. (2007) 'The enclave society. Towards a sociology of immobility', *European Journal of Social Theory*, 10(2), pp. 287–304.

Turner, V. and Turner, E. (1978) *Image and pilgrimage in Christian culture*. New York: Columbia University Press.

Unger, O., Uriely, N. and Fuchs, G. (2016) 'The business travel experience', *Annals of Tourism Research*, 61, pp. 142–156.

Urry, J. (2007), *Mobilities*. Cambridge: Polity Press.

Walsh, M.D. (2019) 'Partiendo la madre: Borders, thresholds and transnational sites of belonging', *Chiricú Journal: Latina/o Literatures, Arts, and Culture*, 3(2), pp. 41–58.

Wauters, B. and Lambrecht, J. (2008) 'Barriers to refugee entrepreneurship in Belgium: Towards an explanatory model', *Journal of Ethnic and Migration Studies*, 34(6), pp. 895–915.

Williams, A.M. and Hall, C.M. (2002) 'Tourism, migration, circulation and mobility. The contingencies of time and place' in Hall, C.M. and Williams, A.M. (eds.) *Tourism and migration: New relationships between production and consumption*. Dordrecht: Kluwer Academic Publishers, pp. 1–52.

Woube, A. (2014) *Finding one's place: An ethnological study of belonging among Swedish migrants on the Costa del Sol in Spain*. Uppsala: Uppsala University.

1

TEMPORALITY AND THE INTERSECTION OF TOURISM AND MIGRATION

Mobilities Between Cuba and Denmark

Nadine T. Fernandez

Introduction

We are living in what has been called the second age of migration[1] – with a rising percentage of people on the move and settling in other countries. Even as we have been experiencing lockdowns of the COVID-19 pandemic since 2020, many suggest that once the coronavirus is controlled, migration will surge again as it often provides social mobility, rejuvenates economies, and circulates new ideas (Staff, 2020). It has also been said that we are in the age of tourism – with dramatically increasing numbers of people visiting and vacationing in other countries. In fact, tourism has become one of the largest industries in the world generating global export revenues of 1.7 trillion US dollars in 2019 (World Tourism Organization, 2020). These numbers, too, are predicted to rebound as the pandemic wanes. How these categories of tourist and migrant intersect, the focus of this book, is a productive ground for thinking about today's highly mobile world. Fiona Allon et al. (2008) argue that by studying single types of mobility, we often fail to see the connections and relations between mobile forms and groups. The chapters in this book explore some of the many ways these categories overlap and shape each other, providing insights only possible when studying the broad diversity of today's mobilities. I would add that by looking across categories, we also clearly see that mobilities are socially and politically specific, and access to the labels of migrant or tourist and the length of stays each implies are not equally distributed around the world.

Two TED talks address this same issue of a mobile world with a global, multinational, multi-local population that is increasingly becoming the norm in many places. In their presentations, the writers, Pico Iyer and Taiye Selasi, introduce their viewers and listeners to examples of the new global citizens – multiracial and/or multilingual people with binational parents (Iyer, 2013; Selasi, 2014). They were

DOI: 10.4324/9781003182689-2

born in one continent, are educated in another, now work and live in a third, vacation in a fourth, and so on. These writers are questioning some of the same categories this book is exploring, namely, how to understand a mobility that crisscrosses categories, fitting neatly into none of them. Both TED talks, which mainly probe questions of identity, also highlight two central issues that are the key focus of this chapter: (1) An implicit focus on time and (2) the role of the state in facilitating or blocking movement. As foregrounded in the title of her talk, "Don't ask where I'm from, ask where I'm a local," Selasi challenges us to shift our paradigm by not asking about origin, but about familiarity and belonging. Implicitly, this new question counters the idea of a singular, settled, and rooted past and instead asks "where have you spent your time?" In this chapter, I suggest that we use the temporal idea of "length of stay" to examine the intersections, overlaps, and rifts between peoples' lived experiences of tourist/migrant mobilities and the state policies that control and categorize their movements.

The chapter focuses on Cubans and Danes involved in long-term, mobile relationships, all in different stages of the life course. Their cases present diverse multi-local/multinational people whose experiences traverse the categories of migration, exile, and tourism. The couples met in Cuba while their Danish spouse was there on vacation or a short study trip. Some married and moved to Denmark under family reunification. Others are engaged in rhythms and cycles of mobility that reflect different points in the life course, living/working/vacationing part of the year in Cuba and part of the year in Denmark, constantly negotiating a type of semi-permanent residence in both countries. Some of them have now become tourism entrepreneurs operating Airbnbs in Cuba. These Danish–Cubans are both tourists and migrants, and trips between Denmark and Cuba are both leisure and work. Their length of stay in each place dislodges the idea of tourism as short term, and migration as long term, and challenges governments' attempts to control and categorize their mobilities. Where tourism erases boundaries, migration builds walls. The distinction between these concepts is partly an issue of time. Through the lens of temporality, we can see how migration and tourism are deeply connected, and how issues of time are at the heart of states' efforts to control the movement of people. People's abilities to plan movements, travel, stays, and relocations are varyingly constrained by government regulations that are time-based (visas, residencies, permits, etc.). For the state, permanence comes with services, structures, and obligations that are not offered to or required of short-term visitors. However, the line between temporary and permanent is not always so easily defined. The focus on temporality helps us analyze and assess differential access to mobility in ways that reveal inequalities and thus forces us to rethink policy (Bear, 2016). As we will see with the Cuban–Danish couples, maneuvering in and around these rules is easier for some than for others.

This chapter starts with an examination of how time, particularly length of stay, rhythms, and life course have been theorized in mobility, migration, and tourism studies. Then it moves to three cases before closing with some implications for mobility studies. The cases are drawn from ethnographic fieldwork and in-depth,

Time, Length of Stay, Rhythms, and Life Course

Temporalities of mobility are increasingly heterogeneous and dynamic. Shanthi Robertson (2015) argues that modern transportation and communication technologies have led to increased temporal heterogeneity and new modes of temporariness in global migration, creating what some have called "mottled profiles" (Yeoh and Lin, 2013) or "mutant mobilities" (Allon et al., 2008). As Roberton (2015) notes, "migration and mobility more generally might better be seen not as a single act in time, but as a complex and possibly fragmented process across time. Such trajectories are temporal as well as spatial" (Robertson, 2015: 48). Implicit in ideas of migration are boundaries of time and distance which serve to differentiate it from other types of short-term mobilities.

A permanent move to a new and distant location is called "migration," which is distinct from a short trip or a temporary move that characterizes leisure or business travel (Malmberg, 1997 in King et al., 2004). Although as King et al. (2004) note, the temporal "edges" of migration are difficult to define but become relevant to nation-states in regard to issues of "integration and social cohesion: the shorter the time-frame of mobility and 'residence abroad,' the less relevant the question of integration tends to become" (King et al., 2004: 7). However, "integration" itself is an amorphous concept and not something equally relevant for all migrants regardless of their length of stay. For some, integration is an unattainable requirement (e.g., Muslim migrants in Denmark, see Rytter, 2019), but for others, it is neither expected nor attempted (e.g., British retirees in Spain, see Hall and Hardill, 2016). Backpackers, on working holiday visas in Australia, explicitly seek out a kind of "integration." This cadre of young, flexible workers both "travel through place and dwell in place," combining work, leisure, and residence to glean an "authentic" travel experience with the goal of living like a local, not a tourist (Allon et al., 2008, p. 75). These "mutant mobilities" stretch the time span of tourism and shrink that of migration creating a new long-term temporariness in which people may seek to "integrate" into local life or live in parallel societies, in part depending on how mobility intersects with their life course. Melanie Griffiths et al. (2013), in their comprehensive review of time, temporalities, and migration literature, argue that there is an emerging realization in migration studies that length of stay is as central to understanding the migrant experience as gender or nationality.

Tourism, on the other hand, has been defined by its short-term nature – a ritual, with a distinct start and end point. Scholars (Lofgren, 1999; Graburn, 2001) have characterized vacation and leisure travel as a time free from work, regulations, and daily routines. Implicit in this view is a short, time-limited period after which the tourist returns to the quotidian life of work and scheduled responsibilities. Length of stay is also embodied in how the state regulates the movement of people across borders. For example, within Europe, a tourist can enter a Schengen country and stay for a maximum of 90 days in a six-month period. These tourist visas usually do not entitle the traveler to work or access social welfare or benefits that are reserved for permanent residents and citizens.

At a general level, state systems are designed to ensure and serve a fixed population enclosed within territorial boundaries, and controlling and disciplining mobile and nomadic groups has long been the objective of governmental regulations (see Rabinow, 1984, p. 17, in Allon et al., 2008). Today, we see this in the securitization of borders in Europe and the United States, increasingly restrictive family reunification processes, and a rhetoric of fear and hatred toward immigrants and refugees. At the same time, the tourism industry is growing exponentially and national borders, while closed to migrants and refugees, must be open to tourists. At the heart of this tension is the length of stay (locals vs. non-locals, residents vs. visitors) and national status (well-resourced, higher status/Western citizens vs. poorer, lower status/non-Western citizens).

Examining length of stay, we see the contrasting notions of time, objective and subjective, clash. Rhetoricians have long employed two Greek terms for time to contrast its objective and subjective aspects: *chronos* being objective and quantitative and *kairos* being time as subjective and shaped by the actor (Orlikowski and Yates, 2002). For the state, time is objective, existing independently of human action. As an organization, the state operates on "clock time" (*chronos*) which is linear, mechanical, and invariant (Orlikowski and Yates, 2002, p. 686). Visa categories are time-limited, and the assumption is that migrants will settle, and follow a linear, sequenced process toward permanent residency and eventually citizenship. Mobile practices, however, prove these assumptions faulty. Scholars (Cohen and Sirkeci, 2011; Holmes, 2013) have established the often circular, non-regular paths migrants take, and the rhythms of border crossings even for tourists are more complicated than timed tourist visas suggest.

The life course and life events (marriages, birth of children, retirement) shape the length of stay and reveal the subjective aspect of time (*kairos*) which highlights the human, living time of intentions and goals (Orlikowski and Yates, 2002, p. 686). Scholars have used the concept of life course to "emphasize the timing by which individuals make their transitions into and out of various roles and development tasks in relation to 'social time clocks'" (Hareven, 1996, p. 31 in King et al., 2004). This approach focuses on the different responsibilities and positions people take on as they age both in the context of family life and more broadly in society. These "social time clocks" are neither standard nor fixed but instead reflect the subjective aspect of time, *kairos*. Many (Oppermann, 1995; Gibson and Yiannakis, 2002) note the relevance of the life course paradigm for understanding mobilities within tourism as the needs and types of tourism among the young can differ dramatically from those of retirees. Likewise, its application in migration research is also key, as life course considers the individual's and group's decisions about migration and the broader impact of the migration outcomes (King et al., 2004). From Iyer's and Selasi's TED talks, we see how highly mobile lives are increasingly common, with

Temporality and Cuba-Denmark Mobilities **35**

residency and movement patterns crisscrossing the globe as individuals and families transition through various life stages. However, the time it takes to become a "local" (*kairos* time) often confronts the restrictions of states' definitions of legalized belonging (*chronos* time).

Some "migration" is short, and some "tourism" is repeated or prolonged. In both cases, many of these temporalities are to some extent shaped by national policies controlling residency and border crossings and the relative status of an individual's passport/citizenship. As we will see in the following cases, people's life paths (*kairos*) maneuver through and around these constraints (*chronos*). The temporal complexity of Cuban–Danish couples' experiences weaves between the categories of tourist and migrant, revealing a much more multi-directional and jagged process than either term suggests as their trajectories travel across time, both *kairos* and *chronos*.

Case 1: Bettina and Alberto

The Cuban–Danish couple, Bettina and Alberto, have leapfrogged from the world of tourism to migration, and then back to tourism, nurturing their relationship and their lives in the interstices of state-imposed, time-limited immigration categories. Bettina arrives in Havana for a one-month vacation during her gap – year between finishing high school and starting university. In the first two weeks there, she meets a young Cuban man, Alberto, who escorts her around for the rest of the trip and with whom she falls in love. Once Bettina's vacation is over, she returns to Copenhagen, where she works and saves up money for a return trip to Cuba to see Alberto. She repeats this process several times – over the next two years, and each trip is time-limited by her 30-day Cuban tourist visa (renewable once). Their fledgling relationship not only is structured by the time constraints of Cuban tourism regulations but also has a flexible time frame, shaped by a young person without the responsibilities of family or career.

When Bettina is 22, the long-distance relationship which they have maintained for two years becomes more and more expensive and untenable. The couple, still very much in love, wants to spend more time together than the short tourist visas allow. As Alberto recalls:

> The relationship got more serious . . . she came [to Cuba] two, three, like five times. I couldn't come here [to Denmark], like she could [to Cuba]. Because she had the freedom to travel to Cuba [and I didn't].

If Alberto had been Danish, at this stage in the life course, they would have moved in together and let the relationship develop. However, in a bi-national relationship, this is not possible, so while not quite certain of their long-term future, they decide to marry. They are accelerating their courtship and a life course decision that more commonly might have occurred much later (if at all). Bettina's circular mobility

36 Nadine T. Fernandez

and her connection to Alberto over the past two years have made her more than a "tourist" in Cuba (despite her short-term visa status).

The couple marries in Havana, and Bettina begins the bureaucratic process to get Alberto into Denmark under family reunification regulations. Denmark has one of the most restrictive family reunification policies in Europe which many scholars have critiqued (Schmidt, 2011; Rytter, 2012; Fernandez, 2013; Eggebø and Brekke, 2019). One of the requirements for family reunification with a non-European spouse is that both spouses be at least 24 years old, which Bettina is not. So, the couple moves instead to Malmö, Sweden – a short train ride from Copenhagen. Here the supposedly linear migration process to Denmark is disrupted and decelerates, as the couple's life in Denmark is on hold until Bettina turns 24. The process of arranging for papers for Alberto's Danish residency that might have taken six months is now nearly two-year long. The couple, and especially Alberto, is in a kind of a "liminal" stage akin to that in tourism (Graburn, 2001). Bettina recounts:

> When we moved to Sweden, it was very stressful. It's difficult to live in a place knowing that you will not stay, and that you didn't move there voluntarily.

Bettina is commuting back and forth to Copenhagen where she is enrolled at university, and Alberto must remain in Malmö. Though he has a Swedish work permit, he is unable to find work and is unwilling to learn Swedish since his final destination will be Denmark. While the Swedish authorities treat them as "settled" (or in the process of becoming settled), they see their mobility as on hold, in a period of stasis.

Their mobility has thus moved from tourism toward migration, but it is by no means a continuous trajectory. They have been living too long in Sweden to be considered tourists, but they will not settle there, so they are not exactly migrants, nor do they think of themselves as locals. Their long-term temporariness places them between categories. Finally, after Bettina's 24th birthday, the couple moves to Copenhagen, and their trajectory moves forward more predictably, as Alberto begins Danish classes, gains legal permission to work in Denmark, and ultimately obtains his residency permit through family reunification. While his path is more what one would now expect from a "migrant," the couple's mobility is far from over.

In the earlier quote, Alberto observes that it is Bettina who has the freedom to visit him in Cuba; he cannot visit her. The Cuban state has also shaped their movements in time due to the tight control the state has over the mobility of its citizens. In Cuba, as in other socialist states, loyalty to the regime was expected, and abandoning the country was seen as treasonous. Since 1959 when Fidel Castro came to power, Cuba has been a country of emigration with more than 30,000 people leaving annually, mostly to the United States. The US government, with its Cold War politics and strident anti-communism, continues to categorize arriving Cubans as political refugees. Their exile status opens doors to the United States and simultaneously closes doors to Cuba. While the "official" grounds for leaving have to be political, people's actual motivations are often much more nuanced, encompassing economic, personal, and familial considerations. For Alberto, this anachronistic Cold War context meant that he still required an "exit permit" to leave Cuba (*la tarjeta blanca* was eliminated in 2013), even though his destination was Denmark.

However, Alberto's emigration via marriage granted him privileges not available to those labeled "exiles" (namely, those in the United States). His leaving was not a political statement against the regime, but a matter of love and family – a marriage. Since this was the case, he was eligible for a "permit to reside abroad" (PRE – *permiso de residencia en al exterior*), allowing Cubans who marry (non-US) foreigners to live permanently abroad (not in the United States) and retain their residency rights in Cuba. With the PRE, Alberto could own property in Cuba, inherit from his family, and return to Cuba for up to six months (extendable up to 12 months) without requesting additional permissions. However, because he is living abroad, the Cuban state still places temporal restrictions on his trips to Cuba, not dissimilar from those placed on tourists.

From the mid-1990s, tourism exploded in Cuba and the number of Cubans leaving via marriage to a foreigner also rose, demonstrating the intersection of these two types of mobilities (tourism and marriage migration). This new path of migration for Cubans was an unforeseen outcome of the expansion of the tourism industry on the island. Figure 1.1 shows the steady increase in Cubans living in Denmark starting in the mid-1990s. This rise parallels the growth of tourism in Cuba which also accelerated in the mid-1990s as shown in Figure 1.2.

This increased type of marriage migration has brought on new business opportunities for Cubans living abroad in Europe (see also Simoni, this book). Bettina and Alberto, with financial capital from her parents, invest in purchasing an apartment in Havana across the street from Alberto's family. With the help of his siblings who still live in Cuba, they have been renting the apartment as a *casa particular* for the last several years. Paying a special annual tax to officially register the apartment

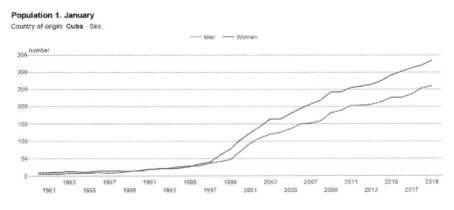

FIGURE 1.1 People of Cuban origin in Denmark

Source: Statistics Denmark, www.statbank.dk/FOLK2

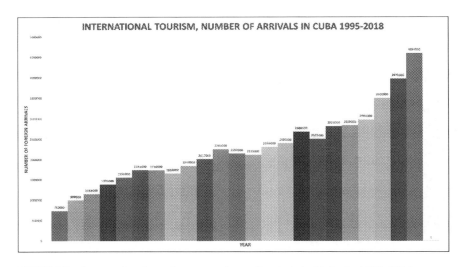

FIGURE 1.2 International tourism – numbers of arrivals in Cuba in 1995–2018

Source: World Bank, CC BY 4.0, https://databank.worldbank.org/source/world-development-indicators#advancedDownloadOptions

with the Cuban government, they are permitted to rent it out to foreign tourists and list it on the Airbnb website. Scandinavian and other European guests enjoy the *casa particular* – exotically located with views of the seaside promenade (the *Malecón*) and of crumbling, but picturesque, Old Havana. The guests find the space comfortably familiar with the same bed linens, shower curtains, and dishes they have in their own households (thanks to IKEA). The Scandinavian-style furnishings which Bettina and Alberto brought to Havana from Denmark make guests feel "at home" in Cuba.

Alberto, Bettina, and their young son regularly visit Cuba. While their stays are, by Cuban policy, time-limited, they have been there too often and too long to be "tourists" – even if Bettina continues to enter Cuba on a tourist visa. Furthermore, these trips are never just about leisure, as they also involve maintaining, improving, and monitoring the Airbnb apartment. Alberto is in contact on a regular basis (nearly daily) with his family regarding the flat and the other services his family provides to their guests (meals, laundry, transportation, guided tours, etc.). The apartment has given his family in Cuba a new income stream (though it fluctuates with the tourism season). The profits from the apartment are divided. When the apartment is rented, his family in Havana receives a monthly payment to cover their labor, supplies, and cleaning, while another portion of the profits is set aside for larger repairs and improvements. In addition, his family earns income from additional services they offer the guests such as meals, tours, and transportation. As of now, the apartment generates only a sporadic supplementary income for Bettina and Alberto, who maintain their household through work in Denmark (she as an office manager and he in the service industry).

The couple's networks in Copenhagen helped to launch the *casa particular* business in Cuba. Early guests were often connected to Bettina's (and her family's) social circles. After several years, they are now Airbnb "super hosts" and have over 500 reviews for their apartment. Their mobility between Cuba and Denmark now intersects the tourist-migrant categories in new ways, and Alberto has come to see Havana with new eyes, namely, those of his tourist guests. He has learned to see Havana as a tourist in his own home (Adams, 2019).

Case 2: Myladi and Mikkel

In 2000, Mikkel, then 37, decided to take a year off from his teaching job in the Copenhagen suburbs and move to Cuba to study music. He had been to Cuba twice before in the mid-1990s and had such negative experiences he vowed never to return. There for three months as a tourist in 1997, he felt plagued by all the Cubans who tried to get something from him. In his view, all his interactions with Cubans were instrumental – people would befriend him just to get his money or offer to marry him to leave the country (Simoni, 2014). Frustrated by his lack of Spanish and exhausted by the constant requests, he was happy to return to teaching music in Denmark. But in 2000, he felt life had become stale; he was single and needed a change. At this point in his life course, he decided to take a sabbatical year partially funded by the teacher's union and moved to Cuba for a year and enrolled in music classes. He stated:

> I began studying percussion there . . . But at the same time, I was very interested in getting deeper and deeper into the Cuban society because I wanted to understand everything. Why people were so critical [of Cuba] on the one hand, and on the other hand they were very, very proud [of their country]. There were so many contradictions and I wanted to find out more.

During the year, he became involved with a Cuban woman, who, as it turned out, wanted to leave the country. He took her to Denmark for a 3-month trip. During their time in Denmark, they broke up, and she immediately married another Danish man, so she could remain in Denmark. Though completely disillusioned by this experience, Mikkel still decided to quit his teaching job in Denmark and return to Cuba. In Cuba, he again enrolled in music classes and began studying Spanish as well.

From here, his life trajectory unfolds, less directed by deliberate decisions, but more by coincidence and circumstance. Enrolling in music classes, Mikkel obtains a student visa. He pays the school a monthly tuition fee of 100 US, and this grants him a "student" status recognized by Cuban immigration authorities. He manages to keep extending this temporary visa status for more than seven years. Laughing, he recounts the day he went to Cuban immigration for his usual renewal:

> Finally, they also told me "No, you are not doing a doctoral degree . . . You are only supposed to have this type of visa 12–18 months!" [but I knew]

several foreign students, you know, that had been "studying" in Cuba for many, many years.

At this point, Mikkel has been in a several-year-long relationship with Myladi, a black Cuban woman 13 years his junior, who worked as a nurse. In 2005, their child was born, and as the father of a Cuban child, Mikkel was able to obtain residency in Cuba (renewable every five years).

Myladi was employed in the healthcare field, so she could not easily get permission to leave Cuba and travel to Denmark. The couple eventually married, and today, Mikkel "commutes" back and forth between Denmark and Cuba. He feels it is not uncommon in Cuba for spouses to be regularly separated for work, so they have just accepted this way of living. Now, his trips out of Cuba can be no longer than three months at a time, or he will lose residency rights in Cuba. As the cycle continues, the couple benefits from the relatively high wages in Denmark (where Mikkel works night shifts at a residential social service institution) and the relatively low cost of living in Cuba. Mikkel remains in Denmark long enough each year to maintain his benefits there (though he was not certain what exactly he would lose if he did not return to Denmark regularly). His temporariness in both countries disrupts the "settled" idea implicit in residency. Apart from the financial aspects of the trips to Denmark, he also feels the need to be there annually. He comments that "I feel a big need to come back to my own culture, talk to friends, and family." I asked how he decided that he wanted to live in Cuba. Interestingly, he responded:

No, I never decided that. It was just coincidence. The way my relationship developed, then she was pregnant, and we had a child, and suddenly I realized that life changed a lot. Having a child and moving away from the tourist area [of Havana]. I would say before [the first years in Havana living in a touristy area] it was . . . I was always ready to leave, you know? Because I always had these times where I felt like, no, I can't take it anymore and I want to leave, and things like that. Now, I don't think that much about "oh, I want to leave [Cuba]," anymore, like that. I really enjoy life today compared to how it was before [in Denmark and living in tourist area in Havana], I know what I want. I enjoy coming back [to Cuba] every time, you know, really, I really enjoy it . . . Now I have a child, you know, it's just, I have a family . . . It's just my life now. It changes a lot of things. Certainly, because, I even think, I have a much better cultural understanding too. And having this apartment where we are living now, in a place where we like to stay, with good neighbors, a good neighborhood, and things like that. And where there are not a lot of tourists and so the people are very different [in this neighborhood]. Another thing, I think also having a child meant that suddenly people realized that I wasn't going to leave just like all the others. So it's made me integrate much more now . . . But it's all just coincidence, I would say. There was no big decision. It's just coincidence that makes my life.

In Cuba, he works as a freelancer with Danish tourist groups, providing information and contacts, and offering introductory talks to the tourists and translation services to Danish tour operators. Having had both negative and very positive relationships with Cubans, he tries to listen and offer advice to Danish tourists who are overwhelmed by the cultural differences they encounter on the island. His long-term stays in Cuba, as well as his annual trips to Denmark, make him an ideal culture broker for these short-term tourists. Major life course events (his relationship and having a child) deeply influenced his mobility patterns. Mikkel was able to extend his "temporariness" in Cuba as a student, yet return regularly to Denmark to work as if he were permanently there. The "coincidence" that he feels shapes his life is, of course, profoundly rooted in the relatively privileged status of being from a wealthy Western country which gives him a mobility not available to all.

Case 3: Ingrid and Juan Antonio

Ingrid first went to Cuba on a two-week vacation with her now ex-husband in 1999. Over the next five years, she returned repeatedly to take Spanish classes. It was through Inez, a teacher at the language school, that she met her Cuban husband in 2005. Inez held a birthday celebration which Ingrid attended and there she met Juan Antonio, Inez's brother. Both were in their late 50s, and Ingrid, a divorced woman, was happy for his companionship and enjoyed being part of his lively extended family who lived in a leafy suburb of Havana. After an intense correspondence and recurring trips (usually two months in duration), the romance continued. They decided to marry in 2007 because Ingrid could not legally stay with Juan Antonio in his house in Cuba on her tourist visa. At the time, tourists (defined as those on a tourist visa) could only reside in hotels or in private homes officially registered as *casas particulares*. However, once they were married, she could stay in his house legally as a family member. Their decision to marry, a central life course event, was accelerated by the Cuban state's restrictions on where and how long she could stay in Cuba on a tourist visa. Now she enters Cuba on a family visa which allows her to stay three months with extensions possible for up to 11 months.

Juan Antonio, a retired office manager, who has adult children and grandchildren in Cuba from a previous marriage, and an adult daughter in the United States, was never interested in moving permanently to Denmark, nor could Ingrid imagine living long term in Cuba. Likewise, on the Danish side, it was not possible for Juan Antonio to stay in Denmark for six months as a tourist. Ingrid recounted: "I thought he could stay here [in Denmark] six months each year as a tourist. Before people could do this, have a three-month tourist visa and renew it once for three more months. I thought this was still possible, but no." Juan Antonio added: "I never had plans to live here. The idea always was that we'd travel, six months here, six months there. But we were obligated to get residency here [in Denmark]." Ingrid continued: "residency, just to stay three more months here [in Denmark]. It's crazy!"

42 Nadine T. Fernandez

Their idea of a cyclical mobility between the two countries was only possible if Juan Antonio obtained permanent residency through family reunification in Denmark, a long, expensive, and complicated procedure. After a lot of paperwork, time, and money, this is what they did. In 2007, Juan Antonio received what he called "the famous yellow card," the Danish health insurance card which serves as an ID for all Danish citizens and people with permanent residency (equivalent to a US Social Security card). The card gives access to everything from healthcare to public libraries. Juan Antonio concluded: "So, I've been here four years now!" He paused and then added with a smile: "Well, physically I've been here only two." The couples' travel rhythm both conforms to but also goes against the grain of the idea of permanent residency that the "famous yellow card" implies. At this stage of their life course, they chose (and had the resources) to comply with both states and pursue their desired lifestyle in the spaces between the resident and the tourist.

The summer and fall months they spend in Denmark where they live very frugally in Ingrid's tiny summer house. While in Denmark, Ingrid continues to do short-term consulting work which provides enough income to support their bi-national lifestyle. Permanently settling in either country was not appealing to them, and their temporariness was distinctly seasonal, like retiree snowbirds found around the world. While they are locals in both cities (Havana and Copenhagen), they are neither fully migrants nor fully tourists in either place.

Conclusions

In examining the intersections of migration and tourism, these three cases bring to the fore the implicit and often overlooked centrality of time. These couples experience human, living time (*kairos*) as they move through the life course marking time through life events such as forming new relationships, having children, divorcing, and retiring. The focus on life course underlines the centrality of relationships, children, and families in migration decisions. In these examples, the categories of tourist and migrant serve as umbrella terms for a variety of mobilities of very different durations and cyclical repetitions. In all the cases, mobility shifts between tourism and migration, but not in a unidirectional or seamless flow. Their life course events (in *kairos* time) are accelerated, paused, and restarted in an uneven circulation that intersects and disrupts the ideas of migrants and tourists. They move, dwell, belong, and become "locals" in two places; spending significant time in both countries. The temporal complexity of border and status crossings forces us to rethink the categories of migrants and tourists, blurring the edges between these types of mobilities.

In each case, however, the couples' "social time clocks" measured in *kairos* time clash with the states' migration policies and visa categories measured in *chronos* time. By accelerating marriages, forcing mobilities and separations after visas expire, and/or insisting on settlement procedures toward citizenship, the couples' life course events were profoundly affected by state migration policies. The role of the states in defining categories of mobile populations (migrants vs. tourists) and then facilitating or obstructing movement is undeniable. However, in each of these cases, one partner came from Denmark, a wealthy country whose citizens hold a high-status European Union passport. The political and financial resources at the Danish partners' disposal allowed them to strategically take advantage of opportunities to maneuver in the interstices of both states' regulations. In all instances, this position of relative privilege granted them the ability to achieve a certain "time sovereignty" (Cwerner, 2001). Mikkel can pursue self-development and an unconventional life by extending his student visa in Cuba for years by paying a small monthly tuition fee. Juan Antonio and Ingrid can be semi-permanent residents in two countries as they had the resources to conform to residency rules in both places which were costly endeavors. Bettina and Alberto also relied on financial capital from their Danish family to insert themselves into the tourist market as entrepreneurs in Havana.

Nevertheless, no passport, regardless of whether it was from a richer or poorer country, could facilitate mobility during the COVID-19 pandemic. In unprecedented peace-time actions, many nation-states around the world closed their borders to nearly all travelers (tourists and migrants alike). Bettina and Alberto were particularly hard-hit, as their Airbnb apartment in Havana stood empty for nearly a year as tourism in Cuba came grinding to a halt. All of these bi-national couples were forced to stay put, as states imposed a new kind of immobility, pausing their previously mobile lives. While this pandemic situation will certainly be temporary, it brings into sharp focus the power of the state to permit and foster (or suspend) the global lifestyles we sometimes take for granted. While we may ask, as writer Taiye Salesi suggests, where these couples are locals, we must recognize that their answers would certainly need to account for how their trajectories span both time and space within states' constraints.

Note

1   The 19th century is often regarded as the first age of migration.

References

Adams, K.M. (2019) 'Being a tourist in my (own) home: Negotiating identity between tourism and migration in Indonesia' in Leite, N.M., Castañeda, Q.E. and Adams, K.M. (eds.) *The ethnography of tourism: Edward Bruner and beyond*. Lanham, MD: Lexington Books, pp. 147–165.

Allon, F., Anderson, K. and Bushell, R. (2008) 'Mutant mobilities: Backpacker tourism in "global" Sydney', *Mobilities*, 3, pp. 73–94.

Bear, L. (2016) 'Time as technique', *Annual Review of Anthropology*, 45, pp. 487–502.

Cohen, J.H. and Sirkeci, I. (2011) *Cultures of migration: The global nature of contemporary mobility*. Austin, TX: University of Texas Press.

Cwerner, S.B. (2001) 'The times of migration', *Journal of Ethnic & Migration Studies*, 27, pp. 7–36.

Eggebø, H. and Brekke, J.P. (2019) 'Family migration and integration: The need for a new research agenda', *Nordic Journal of Migration Research*, 9(4), pp. 425–444.

Fernandez, N.T. (2013) 'Moral boundaries and national borders: Cuban marriage migration to Denmark', *Identities: Global Studies in Power and Culture*, 20(3), pp. 270–287.

Gibson, H. and Yiannakis, A. (2002) 'Tourist roles: Needs and the lifecourse', *Annals of Tourism Research*, 29(2), pp. 358–383.

Graburn, N.H.H. (2001) 'Tourism as ritual: A general theory of tourism' in Smith, V.L. and Brent, M. (eds.) *Hosts and guests revisited: Tourism issues of the 21st century*. New York: Cognizant Communications, pp. 42–52.

Griffiths, M., Rogers, A. and Anderson, B. (2013) *Migration, time and temporalities: Review and prospect*. Oxford: University of Oxford.

Hall, K. and Hardill, I. (2016) 'Retirement migration, the "other" story: Caring for frail elderly British citizens in Spain', *Ageing and Society*, 36(3), pp. 562–585.

Hareven, T.K. (1996) 'Life course' in Birren, J.E. (ed.) *Encyclopedia of gerontology*. San Diego, CA: Academic Press, pp. 31–40.

Holmes, S. (2013) *Fresh fruit, broken bodies: Migrant farmworkers in the United States*. Berkeley, CA: University of California Press.

Iyer, P. (2013) 'Where is home?', *TED Global 2013*. Available at: www.ted.com/talks/pico_iyer_where_is_home

King, R., Thomson, M., Fielding, T. and Warnes, T. (2004) *Gender, age and generations*. Sussex: Sussex Centre for Migration and Population Studies, University of Sussex.

Lofgren, O. (1999) *On holiday: A history of vacationing*. Berkeley, CA: University of California Press.

Malmberg, G. (1997) 'Time and space in international migration' in Hammar, T., Brochmann, G., Tamas, K. and Faist, T. (eds.) *International migration, immobility and development*. Oxford: Berg Press, pp. 21–48.

Oppermann, M. (1995) 'Travel life cycle', *Annals of Tourism Research*, 22(3), pp. 535–552.

Orlikowski, W.J. and Yates, J. (2002) 'It's about time: Temporal structuring in organizations', *Organizational Science*, 13(6), pp. 684–700.

Rabinow, P. (1984) *The Foucault reader*. New York: Pantheon.

Robertson, S. (2015) 'The temporalities of international migration: Implications for ethnographic research' in Castles, S., Ozkul, D. and Cubas, M. (eds.) *Social transformation and migration: National and local experiences in South Korea, Turkey, Mexico and Australia*. New York: Palgrave Macmillan, pp. 45–60.

Rytter, M. (2012) 'The semi-legal family life: Pakistani couples in the borderlands of Denmark and Sweden', *Global Networks*, 12(1), pp. 91–108.

Rytter, M. (2019) 'Writing against integration: Danish imaginaries of culture, race and belonging', *Ethnos*, 84(4), pp. 678–697.

Schmidt, G. (2011) 'Migration and marriage: Examples of border artistry and cultures of migration?', *Nordic Journal of Migration Research*, 1(2), pp. 55–59.

Selasi, T. (2014) 'Don't ask where I'm from, ask where I'm a local', *TED Global 2014*. Available at: www.ted.com/talks/taiye_selasi_don_t_ask_where_i_m_from_ask_where_i_m_a_local

Simoni, V. (2014) 'The morality of friendship in touristic Cuba', *Suomen Antropologi: Journal of the Finnish Anthropological Society*, 39(1), pp. 19–36.

Staff (2020) 'Locked out: When and how to let migrants move again', *The Economist*, 436(9205), p. 7.

World Tourism Organization (2020) *International tourism highlights* (2020 edition). Madrid: UNWTO. Available at: www.e-unwto.org/doi/book/10.18111/9789284422456

Yeoh, B. and Lin, W. (2013) 'Chinese migration to Singapore: Discourses and discontents in a globalizing nation-state', *Asian and Pacific Migration Journal*, 22(1), pp. 31–54.

2

MIGRANT, TOURIST, CUBAN

Identification and Belonging in Return Visits to Cuba[1]

Valerio Simoni

Introduction: Ambivalent Belonging and Recognition on Return Visits

In the course of field research among Cuban migrants in Barcelona, I encountered various personal stories and anecdotes about return visits to Cuba.[2] A striking feature in many of these narratives was the value placed on being and behaving like an "ordinary" Cuban when visiting the island. Exemplifying their attunement to the "Cuban lifestyle," Cuban migrants I talked with – who had all left the country in the last thirty years and mostly in the last decade – highlighted their return to simpler routines and behavioral and consumption patterns, in terms of accommodation, food, transportation, dress code, and the rhythm and pace of life more generally. Forget one's mobile phone, forget about checking emails and Facebook daily – via these conversational observations, they presented selves that knew and appreciated what it was to live in Cuba as Cubans. Regularly, such portrayals were contrasted with the attitudes of "other" returning Cuban visitors said to be less sensitive to the Cuban reality and to flaunt their newly acquired foreign tastes and superior socio-economic statuses, a recurrent target being "ostentatious" Cuban Americans coming from the United States. In tension with these narratives, however, were anecdotes by the very same research participants on the differential treatment they regularly received back in Cuba, as "Cubans living abroad" (*los cubanos que viven en el extranjero*). These could be stories of "interested" (*interesados*) kin, friends, and acquaintances that only sought to draw money from the "rich Cuban from abroad," scheming, deceiving, and treating them as they would any other foreign tourist. Such narratives of concrete interactions and events during the migrants' visits spoke of challenges of recognition and belonging.

As convincingly argued by Kathleen M. Adams (2021) and Natalia Bloch and Adams (this volume), much can be gained from exploring the intersecting terrain

DOI: 10.4324/9781003182689-3

of forms of contemporary spatial mobility and from problematizing seemingly fixed boundaries separating tourism, migration, and exile. The drive to categorize and typify, particularly visible in policy discourses and interventions, forecloses the emergence of a range of important questions I wish to address in this chapter. When is one "tourist," "migrant," and "Cuban"? Who is ascribing, endorsing, and assuming such designations? What do these identifications, and the experience of them, evoke, entail, enable, and constrain? Looking at the purposeful emergence of such identifications, I explore the shifting qualities, expectations, and demands associated with them. My broader aim is to contribute to a reflection on when, why, and how these categorizations come to matter, how they bring about or hamper certain modes of being and becoming, as well as the possibility of negotiating, resisting, and overcoming them. My attention is drawn to these issues because they mattered and preoccupied my research participants and came repeatedly to the fore during their visits home and in the ways such visits were experienced and narrated. Accordingly, my attention is as much on the very emergence of belonging and identifications as matters of concern, as it is on unpacking their concrete forms, contents, and effects (these aspects being obviously related).

Belonging has been the object of significant theorization in the social sciences (e.g., Yuval-Davis, 2006; Geschiere, 2009; Candea, 2010; Zigon, 2019). According to Peter Geschiere (2009, drawing on Tania Li, 2000), we may be living in a "global conjuncture of belonging," one characterized by the converging trend, across the world, of "turning *belonging* into a pressing issue" (Geschiere, 2009, p. 6, emphasis in original). Rather than dismissing such concerns with origins, culture, identity, and authenticity as spurious and analytically sterile, it becomes important to understand why and how they emerge, and what they generate. It is time we move beyond interpretations of identity claims as "distress-driven attempts to impose order on an increasingly chaotic world," as Renée Sylvain (2005, p. 355) observes. His critique of reductive and essentialist psychological readings helps de-naturalize the significance of people's concerns with issues pertaining to identity and belonging. Recent studies of indigenous claims and struggles, for instance, draw attention to related politics of recognition, rights, and the securing of resources (see Hodgson, 2002).

Lately, the issue of belonging has been addressed in relation to travel and tourism (see Leite, 2017; Meiu, 2020). Elsewhere (Simoni, 2015) I explored some of its expressions in intimate relations in Cuban tourism and migration, showing how belonging became a matter of concern when intimate relations transgressed established social boundaries (Stoler, 1989), raising doubts about loyalties and the fulfillment of obligations. Scholars addressing the intersections of travel, tourism, and migration have shown how some encounters act as "identity sirens" (Adams, 2019, pp. 163–164), whereby visits to homelands lead migrants to "shift, challenge, or reaffirm sensibilities about their own identities" (p. 152, see also Bidet and Wagner, 2012). In the Cuban visits considered here, it is also clear that the experience and assessment of relations with family, friends, and the country more generally lead returnees to rethink and rearticulate the parameters of their "being Cuban" and what it means to be "Cuban," "migrant," "tourist."

The ethnographic material on which I draw in this chapter comes from 20 months of fieldwork conducted between 2005 and 2020 in Cuba, in Havana, the rural town of Viñales (located 200 km west of the capital), and the beach resort of Santa Maria (30 minutes east of Havana), as well as from four months of research in Barcelona, Spain, since 2012. In all these settings, I engaged mainly with middle-aged Cuban men, who are the main protagonists of the examples in this chapter. Within the ample body of scholarship on Cuban migration and diasporic formations (see, for instance, the contributions in O'Reilly Herrera, 2007), Susan Eckstein (2009), Mette Louise Berg (2011), and Catherine Krull and Jean Stubbs (2018a, 2018b) have pertinently highlighted the heterogeneity of Cuba's diaspora. Eckstein and Berg's (2009) notion of "diasporic generation" thus differentiates the more recent generation of "migrants" from the first wave of Cuban emigrees known as "exiles," who, following the 1959 Revolution led by Fidel Castro, left the country (between the early 1960s until about 1980). Berg and Eckstein also signal a shift from a political to an economically driven migration, starting with the 1990s crisis that struck Cuba after the collapse of the Soviet Union. My research participants fit the "migrant" generation identified by Berg (2011) for Spain, their migration dating from the mid-1990s onward, being relatively diverse in terms of class and racial background, and approximating that of other Latin American "economic migrants," with stronger ties and more frequent visits to family back in Cuba. While the majority of Cuban migrants returning for visits to Cuba come from the United States (Espino, 2013), where the bulk of the Cuban diaspora resides, the ethnographic material presented here refers primarily to return visits by Cubans residing in Europe, notably in Spain.[3]

Awkward Arrivals and the Salience of Belonging

When recounting their latest visit to Cuba, the Cuban migrants I met in Barcelona often featured the initial moments of landing in the country. At the airport, the first awkward encounters with fellow nationals involved the immigration officials screening them and their luggage. These were tense moments for most Cubans I spoke to, as migrants regularly carried gifts for relatives and friends, which could be inspected by airport agents. Legally, no matter how many years they had been living abroad and despite other nationalities acquired, every Cuban citizen is required to present their Cuban passport upon entry, and, during their stay, is officially treated as a Cuban by the authorities, marking a legal difference in status from foreign tourists. On his last visit to Cuba, Nando, a young Cuban man who lived for a decade in Spain, was confronted by a customs officer who discovered he was carrying two mobile phones when he was only allowed to bring in one. The officer intimated he should pay a costly import tax if he wanted to bring in his second phone, and Nando flew off the handle. Unwilling to pay or to leave the phone with the officer, he smashed it on the floor, determined "not to leave them anything." Better destroy it, Nando said, rather than giving "them" the pleasure of keeping his phone.

48 Valerio Simoni

Nando recounted this story with his usual flair and passion, finding complicit ears in the other Cubans listening to him that night, in a Cuban bar in Barcelona. His narrative kick-started a wave of complaints about Cuban officers and, more generally, how the country treated people like them, who simply wanted to visit and help those left behind. These were stories of envious locals, of discrimination and bad treatment that started at the airport and continued in bars, restaurants, and other service locales during the stay. Tragicomic airport stories kept our circle of bar companions busy for much of the evening, with several of Nando's friends complaining of being detained at customs for hours while officers checked their luggage, even as these same officers welcomed foreign tourists with broad smiles ushering them through customs in seconds. People commented on the officers' palpable and almost obscene envy, clearly visible in their spiteful and intense assessing gazes. "And if you complain or make a scandal, they keep you there for hours, or they send you back where you came from," someone commented. Most agreed that it was better to keep a low profile, the advice being not to take issue with any of it (*no coger lucha*). Ramona, a Cuban woman in her 40s who had been living in Europe for over 20 years, went as far as to say that when traveling back to Cuba she "left her brain" in Spain, so as not to get upset by the incongruities one must face.

In discussing the mishaps of arriving back in Cuba, several migrants pondered the differential treatment that awaited Cuban returnees on the one hand and foreign tourists on the other, while both were allegedly there on holidays. "You are less than a tourist, and less than a Cuban," summed up Nando. His reasoning implied that being "a Cuban who lives abroad" back on holidays, generated an amount of envy and frustration that did not apply to foreign tourists visiting the country. The problem seemed to lie in the fact of being so similar, and yet different, slight disjunctures (as opposed to incommensurable disparities) making comparison and moral evaluation all the more obvious and immediate (Trémon, 2018, p. 159). "Here [in Spain] you are a migrant, there the one who lives abroad: you are neither here nor there and are left in the middle of the sea . . . , " concluded one of the Cuban men conversing with Nando. Issues of identity and belonging were clearly brought to the fore and with them the idea that it was hard to find one's place both in the destination and in the country of origin, which misrecognized you not only as an "ordinary" Cuban but also as a "tourist." This sense of misrecognition did not stop at the airport. For many, it continued in even more unsettling ways in relations with friends and family, as the following sections illustrate.

Celebrating Return and Enacting Cuban-Ness

In the summer of 2015, Rolando, a Cuban man in his early 40s whom I first met in 2005 in Viñales, before he migrated to France, was back for a visit with his French wife Amelie and their two children. Before coming to Viñales, they had enjoyed a couple of weeks traveling around the island, staying in all-inclusive resorts, and visiting other areas of Cuba. This was presented as a sort of holiday within the larger visit to Cuba. In the writings of Jennifer Bidet and Lauren Wagner (2012),

Francesca Sirna (2015), Sabine Marschall (2017), and Adams (2019, 2021) we find insightful examples and reflections on the possible combinations, complementarities, simultaneities, and/or compartmentalization of family visits with tourist activities. In the case presented here, what seemed to prevail was a certain separation between foreign-like tourist-modes and Cuban family-visit-modes, with different identifications, subjectivities, and assertions of belonging coming to the fore at different moments. Rolando could get away with being like a foreign tourist in the all-inclusive resorts far from his hometown but felt compelled to align with a more Cuban-non-tourist self – or Cuban-migrant self – when back in the village.

According to Amelie, in the first part of their holiday, Rolando's way of being and relating to her and the children had been more in tune with his behavior back in France, albeit in a tourist mode and context. By way of contrast, she observed that once they got to his hometown and started engaging with their extended family and friends, Rolando's behavior changed in many ways. As she phrased it, he become more of the typical "Cuban macho" character. The tender father who had spent time playing with and caring for the children and "doing family" before getting to Viñales now transformed into the bachelor he had once been, a young man who let his mother and wife tend to the house and children, while he hung out with friends, dwelling in forms of sociability that he celebrated as "typically Cuban," exemplified by easy-going-ness, "hotness" (Simoni, 2013), and a vibrant engagement with music, dancing, drinking, and partying. "When we get here, he becomes like a kid, like when I first met him ten years ago!," said Amelie.[4] But Rolando's wife also expressed her empathy, telling me that she was willing to let him play the "Cuban macho," given how much he must miss his country and his people when in Europe, including his former ways of being and socializing. After all, this was just for the duration of the holiday, and he would soon return to his more "European self" once they were home in France.

Quite revealing of Rolando's duality was that toward the end of their month-long stay on the island, he started complaining that he was tiring of the holiday (which I understood to mean the "family visit" part of it) and that much like the rest of his nuclear family, he too was longing to get back to Europe and his routines there, even if that meant work. What is more, he was not looking forward to returning to Cuba for the next few years. Tired of partying and entertaining people all day, such visits back to Viñales also cost him a fortune. Rolando reasoned that he could help his family better by not returning to Cuba, saving money, and sending it as remittances instead. His absence would thus be more helpful than his presence. This was so also because Rolando accepted his privileged status as a returning migrant and his ensuing obligations toward friends and family. He did not want to disappoint their expectations and wished to be generous with people. On my repeated visits to Viñales after that summer, despite Rolando not having returned for years, people spoke highly of him, as someone loyal to relationships with his loved ones in Cuba.

It is interesting to compare Rolando's case with that of other Cubans who were also back in town from Europe but did not indulge in celebrations and festivities

50 Valerio Simoni

as expected. Their restrained behavior could be judged negatively, interpreted as a sign of lost Cuban-ness, and relinquished allegiance to former ways of being. "He is more French than Cuban" was the criticism leveled at Pedro, a Cuban man who was back on a visit with his French wife and three children and who was rarely seen out at night in local bars and clubs. Pedro and his wife were deemed "boring" for their lack of enthusiasm in partaking in the local festive scene, and this became grounds for questioning his Cuban-ness altogether. As Pedro explained to me in French, he had come back to Cuba after four years of absence and spent most of his days with his mother and visiting a range of relatives, carefully allocating his visits and presents so as not to make anyone jealous. After about three weeks on the island, he was tiring of these routines and found more and more things to complain about – he mentioned the festive excesses, the poor service, people's lack of civility, and disregard for the environment. Pedro was eager to return to France, where he felt more comfortable and attuned to everyday realities and behaviors. His return visit seemed to have reinforced "a sense of belonging to the host country," as observed by Marschall (2017, p. 19) for other returnees, resulting in "further estrangement" and the realization of how much not only one's "old country" but also oneself has changed.

Generosity, Instrumentality, and Opening Up Belonging

Generosity was expected of returnees, particularly during festivities such as those described for Rolando earlier, who in his nights out was always seen inviting people over to his table and offering high-quality rum, beer, soft drinks, snacks, and the like. At stake was the image of someone who had achieved something in life, who had migrated and become wealthier, but who had not forgotten his origins and loyalties, and was willing to redistribute his riches, first among relatives, then among close friends, and finally with lesser friends and acquaintances. The extent of gifts and invitations proffered served to signal social closeness and the degree of intimacy, becoming a powerful index of the strength of the relation at stake (see Zelizer, 2005). The returnees' discernment and sensitivity could help avoid raising feelings of jealousy and discrimination, and included keeping an eye on how relatives, friends, and acquaintances laid claim to, and showed gratitude for, the goods they offered. Occasionally, the Cubans visiting could feel they were being "taken for a ride" and instrumentalized by residents eager to capitalize on their economic resources, much like foreign tourist victims of "*jineterismo*" (Simoni, 2016a), the Cuban notion commonly referring to the "riding" of tourists for instrumental purposes.

This was the scenario evoked in a Barcelona conversation with Gustavo, a Cuban migrant in his 60s who recounted his sexual adventure with two young Cuban women in a Havana hotel, on one of his latest visits to the island. Gustavo had started playing the tourist, addressing the two women in English, banking on the widespread interest in engaging foreign visitors in tourist areas of Havana. Taking on the role of the tourist and hinting that he had hard currency to spend was, for him, a way to seduce the women. After having sex with them, so the story went, Gustavo fell asleep (which he suspected was induced by their having spiked his drink with sleeping pills), and the two women stole all his valuables – money, clothes, shoes, and so on. His narrative, tainted with humor and self-mockery at his tourist-like naïveté, resonated with other stories I had heard of relationships between foreign visitors and *jineteros/-as*, and placed the issue of exploitative forms of intimacy squarely on the table. "Never again!" was the lesson Gustavo drew from this experience: Never again play it like a naïve tourist. In contrast with Gustavo's own prior exploits as a tourist hustler and *jinetero* in the Cuba of the early 1990s, his story highlighted tourism hustling in which he had become the tourist-like victim. This commoditized form of intimacy pushed him to the other side of the Us-Cubans/Them-tourists cleavage so present in Cuba (Simoni, 2015, 2016a).

"People there think they are the smarter ones," Nando told me one evening, referring to the Cubans he had met on his last trip to the island. "They see you as a Euro with legs, as a walking dollar" – another expression I heard repeatedly from tourists in Cuba. The tales of envy, interest, and greed corrupting relationships were entwined with returning to the island as Cubans who lived abroad. They featured unscrupulous friends who, rather than caring for sentiments, showed an interest only in what the migrant could bring economically – the quintessential *amistad interesada* as opposed to true and sincere friendship (Simoni, 2014). What Cuban returnees resented in their engagements with old friends and acquaintances was being "condemned to be a tourist," to borrow on Constance De Gourcy (2010, p. 353), and being exploited as such. More subtly, I would say that people could desire some of the advantages that came with being a tourist (status, privilege) but not its downsides (dupe and gullible). Pushing the reflection further along an existential approach, the impression was that what returnees valued in the "tourist" persona was its promise of "freedom," of opening up unconstrained possibilities for being and becoming, avoiding feeling trapped as "the Cuban who lives abroad," with all the expectations and obligations that came with it.[5]

The more fundamental existential demand, it seems to me, was for the possibility of being, dwelling, and relating not just as one type, member, and representative of a specific group. Uncovering such an existential dimension, I find it useful to draw on Jarrett Zigon's (2018, 2019) recent reflections on "disclosive freedom" (2019, pp. 100–131) as "an openness to possibilities . . . free of the impositions and control of categories and normalization" (2019, p. 105). Criticizing the closed, totalizing, and exclusionary biases intrinsic to "late-liberal politics of identity-focused difference and recognition" (2019, p. 95), Zigon calls for a decentering of approaches to belonging. From identity and the need to identify with one group or another, to possess one quality or another, we move to an emphasis on "*belonging itself*" as the "existential imperative to dwell in openness" (2019, p. 96, emphasis in original), with the notion of "dwelling," and of an "ethics of dwelling," contrasted to the feeling of "being trapped in a world" (Zigon, 2018, p. 119).

This could well be what my research participants aspired to – to dwell in openness and not to feel overly constrained and trapped by one identification. But the expectations weighing on them tended to push belonging-as-identity to the fore, and with it, the need to clarify, assume, and stand by one's positioning, qualities, and loyalties, most notably one's loyalty to those that were receiving them in Cuba. Assuming one's privileged status – as "Cuban from abroad" – meant "handling distributive claims" (Wig, 2020, p. 98, drawing on Ferguson, 2015), fulfilling obligations, and providing the generous kind of care and support that was expected. Revealed here is a tension between different aspects and approaches to belonging: One informed by an ethics of dwelling that eschews the trapping of totalizing identifications – be it "tourist," "migrant," and "Cuban," and their hyphenated combinations – and the other, more identity and loyalty driven, putting emphasis instead on normative expectation and obligation as a privileged member of a certain group.

Downscaling Family, Reshaping Social Life, Redefining Cuban-Ness

In the Cuban cases I explore, the returnees' ties to their families, and the care and responsibilities these ties necessitated, tended to work as a key measure of people's worth, of the fact that they had not forgotten the fundamental duties and obligations that linked them to Cuba (Simoni and Voirol, 2021). Belonging, we may argue following George Paul Meiu (2020), was signified here perhaps less by an "immutable identity," than by "sustaining ties" and "demonstrating one's commitment to local kinship and custom" (2020, p. 10). What such local kinship and custom amounted to, however, was also the subject of debate and dispute, leading my research participants to work over the very contour, meaning, and value of "family" (cf. Olwig, 2012; Adams, 2019). If relationships with one's mother and offspring tended to be left unscathed by such reassessment of who and what counted as family, other kin ties seemed more likely to be weakened, up to the points of estrangement and exclusion.[6] My conversations with Cuban migrants suggested a growing skepticism and scaling down of allegiances and solidarities, in relation not only to one's extended family but also to people in Cuba and the country more broadly.[7] These findings seem to support Geschiere's (2009, p. 27) diagnosis of discourses of belonging as easily lending themselves to fragmentation, purification, and the related unmasking of "fake" members – in the examples I will now consider, the exposing and the exclusion of less deserving, "unproper" kin.

Naomi, a Cuban woman in her 40s I first met in Santa Maria in the summer of 2016, had been living in France for about 20 years but prided herself on coming to Cuba twice a year, each time for at least one month. Having bought a house for her mother several years earlier, she had only recently acquired a new property just for her, as she put it. After so much sacrifice done for her family, she argued, time had come to focus on herself. She had deliberately chosen a secluded place for her new house, as an attempt to escape the poor Havana neighborhood where she had been reared. Naomi did not want people to visit her daily and resented those who visited just to request favors and money. This included her extended family, who had given her ample proof of what they were "really" after: gifts and favors. Jealousy, envy, and "fake smiles" of hypocrisy were all they were able to express, she maintained, and now that she had stopped bringing gifts and visiting, they saw her as "*la mala*," the "bad one" – the wicked relative who had forgotten about her family. But Naomi had by now got over such condemnations, or so she claimed. She was focusing on enjoying and making the most of her time in Cuba, relaxing, partying, and frequenting the "high life" places of tourism and *la farandula* (a local notion evoking "the scene" frequented by celebrities, foreigners, and the "it" people of Cuba).

While evoking a radical reorientation of her social circle and the places she frequented, Naomi also liked to emphasize the fact that, unlike other Cuban migrants, she remained "100% Cuban" in her ways of doing and being in Cuba. The Cubanness she liked to embody was in many ways similar to that enacted by Rolando in Viñales (gendered differences notwithstanding), made of much socializing, partying, drinking, and dancing, and a "typically Cuban" upbeat and euphoric mood. This, it seemed to me, was Naomi's way of dwelling in the aspects of the Cuba she liked while rejecting the more unpleasant encounters with old friends and relatives who only brought her "*problemas*" and never-ending requests. Naomi's predilection was for spending time with people who shared her privileged conditions, namely, foreigners and Cubans who knew what life abroad was like and understood the value of a hard-earned holiday in Cuba.

One night in Barcelona, Nando told us that what was emerging in Cuba was something akin to a new social class: "the Cubans living abroad" (*los cubanos que viven en el extranjero*). When I reported this to Alfredo, another Cuban man who had arrived in Barcelona a couple of years earlier, he very much agreed. When traveling back to Cuba, Cubans like him felt more in tune with others who had experienced that same trajectory. There was a deeply felt commonality, a sense of familiarity and intimacy among those who had traveled, which made it easier to dwell, share, and connect. Another Cuban social formation, which drew together a loose category of transnational subjects – "*los que han viajado*" (those who have traveled) – seemed to be taking shape in Alfredo's reasoning. The experiences and reflections of Nando, Alfredo, and Naomi may offer glimpses of a process of social fragmentation and differentiation. What becomes worth tracing is the shape and content that such differential social formations may take and the way they work toward recalibrating notions of Cuban-ness and belonging.[8]

In reformulating their sense of belonging, returnees like Naomi were at the same time pushing for their own vision of Cuba. We may thus argue that if the migratory experience leads migrants to reimagine the country they left behind, these practices of return contribute to further transforming the homeland and negotiating one's place in it. This was illustrated in the case of Naomi, who refashioned her Cuban-ness and her social milieus and reflected on what aspects of the Cuba she knew deserved to be experienced and cultivated. Future research on returnees' and residents' mutual assessments and the ways in which they confront each other's desires, expectations, and delineations of belonging may help map

54 Valerio Simoni

how different versions and aspects of Cuba and Cuban-ness interact, inform, and respond to one another, enabling us also to ascertain their relative ascendancy or decline. The Cuba favored by Naomi, the social spaces she liked to frequent, and the atmospheres she liked to dwell in seemed to closely approximate what was sought by foreign tourists, with the inflection of her quintessential insider status, that of a "100% Cuban," a non-gullible virtuoso of the *dos* and *don'ts* for enjoying her island. This valued image of herself and her place in Cuba, however, was challenged when meeting other residents, old friends and acquaintances, and her extended family members, who kept reminding her of her difference and privilege, encapsulated by her status as a Cuban living abroad, and the ensuing obligations that fell upon her, including the obligation to share and distribute her resources.

Conclusion: Sticky Identifications and the Demands of Belonging

The research participants whose stories and experiences of return visits to Cuba were presented in this chapter could be seen as aspiring to a sort of holographic persona embodying the best of different worlds and qualities. Rather than a hybrid in-between, we might see this as the ideal of a composite virtuous person who is able to distill and embody valued qualities of the worlds he or she has come to live in. A person who has not forgotten where he or she comes from and is allegedly competent in the best that Cuba and being a Cuban has to offer, but who has also taken stock of what is deemed better elsewhere, and likes to explore the possibilities to be otherwise stemming from it. Analyzing the returns of Filipina domestic workers from Hong Kong, Nicole Constable has reflected on "the ambivalence of not belonging, and the plural vision that might result from diasporic experiences" (1999, p. 208). Such "plural vision," a notion developed by Edward Said (1984), "can be both alienating and inspiring, a source of aware-ness and dissatisfaction, and a source of pleasure and apprehension" (Constable, 1999, p. 224). "In circumstances of change and mobility," continues Constable, "plural vision no longer permits the self the illusion of a unified, bounded, or coherent whole" (1999, p. 224). This was certainly suggested in the complex and oftentimes paradoxical narratives of belonging explored in this chapter.

The demands of belonging, in terms of calls to assume a clear-cut identification and satisfy the expectations and obligations that could ensue, were frequently felt as constraining by my research participants. Whether they took on the role of "tourist," or "migrant" returning home, there could be a reluctance to fully embrace such identifications. Mostly, it seems to me that they were gesturing toward some of the positive aspects that such identifications evoked – such as having been successful abroad or being able to enjoy holidays and celebrate in style back home – while retaining a certain openness and avoiding feeling trapped in them. But this sort of open-ended dwelling, which we could approximate to Zigon's reference to "belonging itself" (2019, p. 96), of lifting weight from issues of identification and categorization to foreground something more akin to a "disclosive freedom"

(Zigon, 2019, pp. 100–131), could easily encounter the resistance of Cuban residents interacting with the returnees. Such resistance, I believe, reveals the manifold and profound emotional, moral, and pragmatic implications that such identifications carry, if not for Cubans returning for a visit, then for those who received them, and for whom being a "tourist," a "migrant," and simultaneously a "Cuban" became a clear marker of status, generative of specific expectations.

We may recall here Hodgson (2002), Sylvain (2005), and Geschiere (2009) reflections on how belonging becomes entangled in politics of recognition and the securing of resources. Given the structural inequalities existing between the retuning migrants and those receiving them (and not unlike those with foreign tourists), Cuban residents could find it legitimate and only normal to call on these temporary visitors to fully assume their privileges, and relate accordingly, beyond any pretenses of being equal. Just as foreign tourists could be prescribed to be generous and share their wealth with disadvantaged Cuban residents (see Simoni, 2016a), so Cubans coming from abroad could be incited to act according to their difference in status. If you wanted to be a successful migrant or a free and leisure-prone tourist, you had to assume the responsibilities that came with it and could not only pick and choose which aspects to retain and which to discard. Such could be the demand at stake, which bolstered the reference to status, identity, and the more totalizing dimensions of belonging, calling for consistency and closure. The "identity-slots" returnees were called to inhabit came with their own expectations, obligations, and indications on how best to fulfill them.[9]

What Cubans on return visits were facing, we may argue, was a call to stay loyal to relationships with and commitments toward, friends, kin, and Cuban people at large. In specifying the terms of what such loyalty implied, and the obligations it included, assumption on what being "tourist," "migrant," and "Cuban" meant featured heavily and were recurrently worked over. This is a testimony of the enduring salience and power of such identifications while also underscoring the importance of anchoring them in the local histories and relational contexts that color their meaning and explain their relevance and value. Rather than dismissing such identifications, predefining their meanings and functions in a priori typologies, or calling for the analytical deconstruction of their distinctiveness, we should remain attentive to their situated and purposeful deployments. We will thus gain further insights into when and how these categorizations come to matter, what kind of relationships, moral obligations, and processes of self- and group-formation they are generative of, and the ways they constrain and/or enable certain modes of being and becoming. We will also gain insights into the possibility, eventually, of escaping and surpassing them. But here again, and beyond supporting the open-endedness and sense of freedom that may result from transcending these categories and identifications, we also ought to ask why are they so resilient, sticky, and tenacious. Part of the answer in the case explored here lies in the highly unequal positions, dependencies, and calls for sharing and solidarity across a North–South divide in which such identifications became entangled and which helped explain their moral weight and force.

56 Valerio Simoni

Notes

1 The chapter revisits and expands on my previous article: Simoni, V. (2019a) «Appartenances et identifications à l'épreuve. Migrants en visite de retour à Cuba, » *ethnographiques.org*, 37, Revenir. Quêtes, enquêtes et retrouvailles, www.ethnographiques. org/2019/Simoni. My thanks go to *Ethnographiques.org* for permissions. Earlier versions of the text benefitted greatly from reviews and feedback of Michaël Busset, Anne-Christine Trémon, Paola Mota Santos, Jean Stubbs, Constance de Gourcy, and Grégoire Mayor. I am extremely grateful to Kathleen M. Adams and Natalia Bloch for their insightful comments and suggestions on the more recent versions of the chapter. The research relied on the generous collaboration of research participants in Spain and Cuba, to whom I extend my deepest gratitude. I thank the Instituto Cubano de Antropología (ICAN) for providing assistance and institutional affiliation during research in Cuba. Funding was received from the Portuguese Foundation for Science and Technology (FCT Post-Doctoral Grant SFRH/BPD/66483/2009), the Swiss National Science Foundation (SNSF *Ambizione* Fellowship, PZ00P1 147946), and the European Research Council (ERC) under the European Union's Horizon 2020 research and innovation program (grant agreement No 759649), which supported my research during the periods 2010–2014 (FCT), 2014–2017 (SNSF), and since 2018 (ERC). Any shortcomings are my own, and sponsoring agencies are not responsible for any use that may be made of the information presented here.

2 All the data and conversation excerpts presented here are based on recollection after the events occurred and were translated into English by the author. Personal names and some details in the examples presented were altered to protect the anonymity of research participants.

3 Albeit accurate numbers for return visits are hard to estimate (Espino, 2013), José Luis Perelló Cabrera (2016) calculates that in 2015, almost 400,000 Cuban migrants returned for a visit, of which about three-quarters were Cuban Americans and one-quarter Cubans residing in other countries. Current studies of Cuban migration also reflect on significant changes in both migratory legislation and Cubans' mobility patterns and how these intersect with further openings of the Cuban government to private enterprise and business endeavors (see Martín Fernandez and Barcenas, 2015; Aja Díaz et al., 2017; Krull and Stubbs, 2018a, 2018b; Bastian, 2018; Simoni, 2019b).

4 For an insightful parallel, see Robert Smith's (2005, pp. 120–146) analysis of return visits by Mexican migrants living in New York and the way such visits entail the negotiation of one's "true mexicanidad" (2005, p. 139), leading to specific co-constructions of ethnicity and gender, and similar suspensions and temporal renegotiation of established family roles.

5 From Nelson Graburn (1983) seminal work on tourism's potential for re-creation and self-creation, to Andrew Causey conceptualization of "utopic space" as the space tourism offers for people to "explore possible ways of being . . . between reality and unrealizable desires" (2003, p. 167), anthropologists have shed light on the utopian dimension in "tourist" ideals, enactments, and forms of relationality (see Simoni, 2016a, 2016b).

6 See Helen Safa (2005) and Heidi Härkonen (2015) for insightful reflections on the enduring importance of matrifocal notions of kinship and family duty in Cuba.

7 Such scaling down is also suggested in Berg's research with Cuban migrants in Spain, who "felt loyal to their families with whom they shared economic hardship and changes, but not to the nation" (2011, p. 153).

8 Krull and Stubbs have drawn on the work of pioneer Cuban anthropologist Fernando Ortiz (1964, cited in Krull and Stubbs, 2018a, p. 189) to reflect on current changes and pluralizations, beyond "the dominant United States-Cuba axis," in notions of "*cubanidad*" – "the quality of that which is Cuban" and "condition of belonging to Cuba" – and "*cubanía*" – "the consciousness of being Cuban and the will to want to be it." This chapter supports such pluralization, highlighting the struggles, negotiations, and competing

views of *cubanidad* and belonging that are born out of encounters between returnee visitors and the people and realities they re-encountered back in Cuba.

9   It is useful to recall here Harri Englund's (2006) critique of approaches placing excessive analytical emphasis on ethical self-formation and self-fulfillment – as exemplified by my research participants' demands to be left in peace, to dwell in the Cuba they liked, the way they liked, with whom they liked, and being who they liked – when such focus leads to insist too much on independence, to assume equal statuses and starting points, and to turn "a deaf ear to demands . . . for a connection or relationship with the affluent world (Ferguson, 2006, p. 22)" (Englund, 2008, p. 36). Englund's call is for a renewed attention to moral obligations and human conditions of dependence, including relations of "deliberate dependencies" and "morally binding pledge[s] to stay loyal to the relationship" (2006, p. 189, cf. Ferguson, 2015, and Wig, 2020). An element that would deserve more attention than I could devote in this chapter is the gendered dimension of such dependencies, as well as their inscription in life stages and generational differences. As hinted by Naomi's story, it was only after she had fulfilled her obligations and secured all the material comforts her mother needed, that she started prioritizing her independence and self-fulfillment.

References

Adams, K.M. (2019) '"Being a tourist in (my own) home": Negotiating identities and belonging in Indonesian heritage tourism' in Leite, N., Casteñeda, Q. and Adams, K.M. (eds.) *The ethnography of tourism: Edward Bruner and beyond*. London: Lexington Books/Rowman and Littlefield, pp. 148–165.

Adams, K.M. (2021) 'What Western tourism concepts obscure: Intersections of migration and tourism in Indonesia', *Tourism Geographies*, 23(4), pp. 678–703.

Aja Díaz, A., Rodríguez Soriano, M.O., Orosa Busutil, R. and Albizu-Campos Espiñeira, J.C. (2017) 'La migración internacional de cubanos. Escenarios actuales', *Novedades en Población*, 26, pp. 40–57.

Bastian, H. (2018) *Everyday adjustments in Havana: Economic reforms, mobility, and emerging inequalities*. Lanham, MD: Lexington Books.

Berg, M.L. (2011) *Diasporic generations: Memory, politics and nation among Cubans in Spain*. New York and Oxford: Berghahn Books.

Bidet, J. and Wagner, L. (2012) 'Vacances au bled et appartenances diasporiques des descendants d'immigrés algériens et marocains en France', *Tracés. Revue de Sciences humaines*, 23, pp. 113–130.

Candea, M. (2010) 'Anonymous introductions: Identity and belonging in Corsica', *Journal of the Royal Anthropological Institute*, 16(1), pp. 119–137.

Causey, A. (2003) *Hard bargaining in Sumatra: Western travellers and Toba Bataks in the marketplace of souvenirs*. Honolulu, HI: University of Hawai'i Press.

Constable, N. (1999) 'At home but not at home: Filipina narratives of ambivalent returns', *Cultural Anthropology*, 14(2), pp. 203–228.

De Gourcy, C. (2010) 'Revenir sur les lieux de l'origine. De la quête de « racines » aux épreuves du retour', *Ethnologie française*, 40(2), pp. 349–356.

Eckstein, S.E. (2009) *The immigrant divide: How Cuban Americans changed the US and their homeland*. New York and London: Routledge.

Eckstein, S.E. and Berg, M.L. (2009) 'Cubans in the United States and Spain: The diaspora generational divide', *Diaspora*, 18(1–2), pp. 159–183.

Englund, H. (2006) *Prisoners of freedom: Human rights and the African poor*. Berkeley, CA: University of California Press.

58 Valerio Simoni

Englund, H. (2008) 'Extreme poverty and existential obligations: Beyond morality in the anthropology of Africa?', *Social Analysis*, 52(3), pp. 33–50.

Espino, M.D. (2013) 'Diaspora tourism: Performance and impact of nonresident nationals on Cuba's tourism sector', *Cuba in Transition*, 23, pp. 416–423.

Ferguson, J. (2006) *Global shadows: Africa in the neoliberal world order*. Durham, NC: Duke University Press.

Ferguson, J. (2015) *Give a man a fish: Reflections on the new politics of distribution*. Durham, NC: Duke University Press.

Geschiere, P. (2009) *The perils of belonging: Autochthony, citizenship, and exclusion*. Chicago, IL: University of Chicago Press.

Graburn, N.H.H. (1983) 'The anthropology of tourism', *Annals of Tourism Research*, 10(1), pp. 9–33.

Härkonen, H. (2015) 'Negotiating wealth and desirability: Changing expectations on men in post-soviet Havana', *Etnografica*, 19(2), pp. 367–388.

Hodgson, D.L. (2002) 'Introduction: Comparative perspectives on the indigenous rights movement in Africa and the Americas', *American Anthropologist*, 104(4), pp. 1037–1049.

Krull, C. and Stubbs, J. (2018a) 'Decentering *cubanidad*: Commodification, cosmopolitanism and diasporic engagement shaping the Cuban migration to post-1989 Western Europe' in Kapcia, A. (ed.) *Rethinking past and present in Cuba: Essays in memory of Alistair Hennessy*. London: Institute of Latin American Studies, pp. 167–210.

Krull, C. and Stubbs, J. (2018b) ' "Not Miami": The Cuban diasporas in Toronto and Montreal' in Fernández, L.R., Wright, C. and Wylie, L. (eds.) *Other diplomacies, other ties, Canada and Cuba in the shadow of the US*. Toronto: University of Toronto Press, pp. 267–303.

Leite, N. (2017) *Unorthodox kin: Portuguese Marranos and the global search for belonging*. Oakland, CA: University of California Press.

Li, T. (2000) 'Articulating indigenous identity in Indonesia: Resource politics and the tribal slot', *Comparative Studies in Society and History*, 42(2), pp. 149–179.

Marschall, S. (2017) 'Tourism and memories of home: Introduction' in Marschall, S. (ed.) *Tourism and memories of home: Migrants, displaced people, exiles and diasporic communities*. Bristol: Channel View Publications, pp. 1–31.

Martín Fernandez, C. and Barcenas, J.A. (2015) 'Reforma migratoria en Cuba e impacto psicosocial en la sociedad cubana', *Novedades en Población*, 21, pp. 26–37.

Meiu, P. (2020) 'Panics over plastics: A matter of belonging in Kenya', *American Anthropologist*, 122(2), pp. 222–235.

Olwig, K.F. (2012) 'The "successful" return: Caribbean narratives of migration, family, and gender', *Journal of the Royal Anthropological Institute*, 18(4), pp. 828–845.

O'Reilly Herrera, A. (ed.) (2007) *Cuba: Idea of a nation displaced*. Albany, NY: State University of New York Press.

Ortiz, F. (1964) 'Cubanidad y cubanía', *Islas*, 6(2), pp. 91–95.

Perelló Cabrera, J.P. (2016) 'Desarrollo del turismo en Cuba: Tendencias, políticas e impactos futuros', *Cuba in Transition*, 26, pp. 229–233.

Safa, H. (2005) 'The matrifocal family and patriarchal ideology in Cuba and the Caribbean', *Journal of Latin American Anthropology*, 10(2), pp. 314–338.

Said, E. (1984) 'Reflections on exile', *Granta*, 13, pp. 157–172.

Simoni, V. (2013) 'Intimate stereotypes: The vicissitudes of being *caliente* in touristic Cuba', *Civilisations. Revue Internationale d'Anthropologie et de Sciences Humaines*, 62(1–2), pp. 181–197.

Simoni, V. (2014) 'The morality of friendship in touristic Cuba', *Suomen Antropologi*, 39(1), pp. 19–36.

Simoni, V. (2015) 'Intimacy and belonging in Cuban tourism and migration', *The Cambridge Journal of Anthropology*, 33(2), pp. 26–41.

Simoni, V. (2016a) *Tourism and informal encounters in Cuba*. Oxford and New York: Berghahn Books.

Simoni, V. (2016b) 'Ethnography, mutuality, and the utopia of love and friendship in touristic Cuba', *Journal of the Anthropological Society of Oxford*, 8(1), pp. 143–167.

Simoni, V. (2019a) 'Appartenances et identifications à l'épreuve. Migrants en visite de retour à Cuba', *ethnographiques.org*, 37. Available at: www.ethnographiques.org/2019/Simoni

Simoni, V. (2019b) 'Tourism, migration, and back in Cuba', *American Anthropologist*, 21(3), pp. 755–760.

Simoni, V. and Voirol, J. (2021) 'Remittances and morality: Family obligations, development, and the ethical demands of migration', *Journal of Ethnic and Migration Studies*, 47(11), pp. 2516–2536.

Sirna, F. (2015) '"Torno a casa in vacanza." L'esperienza del ritorno temporaneo al paese di origine per i piemontesi ed i siciliani emigrati in Francia nel secondo dopoguerra', *Archivio storico dell'emigrazione italiana*, 11, pp. 80–88.

Smith, R.C. (2005) *Mexican New York: Transnational lives of new immigrants*. Berkeley, CA: University of California Press.

Stoler, A.L. (1989) 'Making empire respectable: The politics of race and sexual morality in 20th century colonial cultures', *American Ethnologist*, 16(4), pp. 634–60.

Sylvain, R. (2005) 'Disorderly development: Globalization and the idea of "culture" in the Kalahari', *American Ethnologist*, 32(3), pp. 354–370.

Trémon, A.-C. (2018) 'Sociodicies of (im)mobility: Moral evaluations of stasis, departure and return in an emigrant village (Shenzhen, China)', *Mobilities*, 13(1), pp. 157–170.

Wig, S. (2020) *Into the light. Rifts and relations in Cuba's market transformation*. PhD thesis. Oslo: University of Oslo.

Yuval-Davis, N. (2006) 'Belonging and the politics of belonging', *Patterns of Prejudice*, 40(3), pp. 197–214.

Zelizer, V.A. (2005) *The purchase of intimacy*. Princeton, NJ: Princeton University Press.

Zigon, J. (2018) *Disappointment: Toward a critical hermeneutics of world building*. New York: Fordham University Press.

Zigon, J. (2019) *A war on people: Drug user politics and a new ethics of community*. Berkeley, CA: University of California Press.

3

DIASPORIC IM/MOBILITIES

Migrants, Returnees, Deportees, Expats, Tourists, and Beyond in the Vietnamese Homeland

Long T. Bui

Introduction

"Don't get involved with protests," my mother constantly warned me, "The communists will never let you go back to Vietnam." My mom feared the impact of my budding political involvement on my future ability to travel abroad. With paranoia stemming from the war, she believed that my activities would also affect my family's travel abilities and that she would be put on some no-entry list due to my activities. As a child of postwar refugees, I had little direct connection to the homeland, but my possible exile from it caused much worry for my refugee mother who hoped to retire or visit comfortably in the place she once called home. Meanwhile, there are Vietnamese Americans who are sent back to Vietnam against their will.

Some Vietnamese Americans are voluntarily reconnecting with their homeland, while others are being forcibly deported to it. Given this discrepancy, this chapter explores the forms and dynamics of im/mobility of diasporic Vietnamese. Scholars of return migration and the anthropology of mobility have considered the ways in which "homecoming" is vexed for those who have departed and returned to their homeland (Blitz et al., 2005; Djordjevic, 2013; Wang, 2013). In this chapter, I provide telling instances to enrich our understanding of the dynamics and intersections between exiles, tourists, and migrants, alternating subject positions that implicate moving/stuck Vietnamese Americans. My first example considers exiled Vietnamese who returned to Vietnam as tourists but were detained while there and ultimately expelled from Vietnam. Counterposed to them are "criminal aliens" brought back under duress to Vietnam by the United States, despite not being desired by the Vietnamese government. My second example refers to those Vietnamese Americans who have returned to the Vietnamese homeland to work and/or live and the fluctuating positionalities they occupy as expats/tourists. My analytic focus is on diasporic im/mobilities, a prism that combines the mobility of

DOI: 10.4324/9781003182689-4

members in dispersed postwar communities with the overlapping immobility of others across multi-dimensional spaces.

A growing number of scholars use the concept of return mobilities (rather than simply migration) to describe alternative pathways and transits of repatriated, international students, border-crossers, migrant laborers, holiday vacationers, business-people, and diplomats (Keles, 2022; King and Christou, 2011; Winogrodzka and Grabowska, 2021). Less attention has been paid to immobilities than to mobilities, and how human movement (and its associated meanings) is made difficult or tenuous for those associated with conquered or defunct states (Saraiva and Sardinha, 2016). For members of the South Vietnamese diaspora, I argue that the im/mobilities of migrant workers, tourists, the forcibly repatriated, and retired expats are inextricable from the Vietnam–American War's geopolitical divisions. As refugees from a fallen "ghost nation," their historic status as political exiles and forced migrants adds layered meanings to their "tourist" label (or any label) in present-day Vietnam.

To explain this complex phenomenon, first I provide background on Vietnamese postwar exile and contemporary migration. I situate the reasons why resettled refugees remain unsettled, traversing various landscapes of belonging. After this historical discussion, I discuss the case of criminalized Vietnamese Americans sent back to Vietnam against their will. My online ethnography considers the US tourists of Vietnamese descent imprisoned/exiled by the communist party. Two cases are presented here – those expelled from the United States to Vietnam and those expelled from Vietnam back to the United States. The online ethnography refers only to the second case, while the material for the first case is based on social media and newspaper analysis because I was not in Vietnam when the individuals mentioned were arrested for "subversive" activities. The forcibly repatriated, meanwhile, are part of an ongoing process.

The final section provides ethnographic accounts of expats and tourists, who find it difficult to locate themselves in rapidly changing Ho Chi Minh City/Saigon, the former capital of the South Vietnamese republic. Some expats are still working while others are retired, but many are often confused for tourists. Based on these case studies, I call for increased research about diasporic im/mobilities of subjects finding their way in a world where they do not always fit.

Historical/Political Migrants: Refugees to and From the Homeland

This section highlights the fact that Vietnamese migrants who return to Vietnam are not all the same. Here, we can differentiate between those who opt to move to Vietnam because of the economic opportunities there and those reared in the United States but expelled by the US government for minor infractions under a tough-on-crime stance. Sometimes, those deportees who are forcibly returned often alone without family sit on the same planes with Vietnamese who have been exiled for decades and are now returning to see their families again.

62 Long T. Bui

Today, the communist government welcomes Vietnamese Americans as potential sources of foreign capital while simultaneously casting aspersion on these returnees. Thousands of Vietnamese fled as refugees in 1975 after the fall of South Vietnam to communist forces, and thousands more departed later as economic migrants due to postwar instability. After diplomatic normalizations between Vietnam and the United States in 1995, a growing cohort of overseas Vietnamese made their way back to Vietnam for work, family, nostalgia, or pleasure, while others refused to ever return in protest of the country's authoritarian regime. Yet not all come back voluntarily or feel at ease upon return.

Many refugees headed to the United States did not imagine they would ever step back in the country that they left behind "forever." But their experiences as refugee-turned-returnee yield critical insight into a war-torn diasporic population and its country that no longer formally exists. My analysis is inspired by Natalia Bloch's study of Tibetans in India and her concept of "community embedded in mobility" (2018).[1] South Vietnamese national subjects come from a nation-state viewed as illegitimate, a country that has vanished, which complicates their diasporic returns to the "homeland."

An important factor to consider is how the Vietnamese state polices ethnic Vietnamese-speaking people when they reenter the Vietnamese territory. The interlaced concepts of migration, tourism, and exile inform an investigation into the spatiotemporal disorientations of diasporic return. Since the 1990s, more than 60 Vietnamese Americans have been repatriated against their will with thousands of deportation orders pending. As ethnic studies scholar Ly Thuy Nguyen (2021) writes, "Deportation takes the form of political exile . . . to control borders and regulate entry based on membership" (p. 17–18).

These individuals never volunteered to come back to Vietnam and actively plead and cry out to remain in the United States. Their forced return poses issues, both epistemological and social. How can this double exiled group – once from Vietnam and then from the United States – be characterized? How do we relate forced return-ees from the United States to people exiled from Vietnam? Within a Southeast Asian country governed by "red capitalism" or "market-oriented socialism," divisions between tourist, migrant, and exile are blurred. The criminal line between Cold War friend and enemy persists despite a porous global flow of ideas, capital, and bodies across borders. While all homeland returns involve some emotional ambivalence, the post/socialist context lends additional confusion (Gasviani, 2019; Schwenkel, 2015; Zhang, 2012). In contemporary Vietnam, the ambivalence manifests in the form of "strategies of inclusion towards its diaspora" (Duong, 2016: p. 165). These strategies include perks such as multi-year tourist visas. Vietnamese Americans embody the tensions between two countries formerly at war, but which now operate as trade partners and yet do not fully trust one another. Those visiting the Socialist Republic of Vietnam can be treated simultaneously as insiders and outsiders. Former South Vietnamese veterans once held in communist reeducation camps can later transform into domestic tourists, even though their painful stigma as former prisoners of war and enemies of the communist state continues to haunt them.

Diasporic Im/mobilities **63**

Although they may superficially look the same and follow the same physical paths as other foreign tourists, Vietnamese diasporic returnees are situated differently. A Vietnamese American visiting Vietnam on a tourist/student visa and a criminal "alien" sent back by force both traverse the same kind of geographic space, albeit under very divergent circumstances. Anthropologist Michaela Di Leonardo (2018) addresses ethnic identity and how factors like class play into migrants' situational shifts. As with Italian migrants to the United States who move back to Italy, class and cohort matter for Vietnamese returnees. Those returning to Vietnam are often young adult professionals looking for jobs, tourists, or expats/retirees.

We must constantly challenge identification categories like tourist, migrant, and exile as isolated status markers that exceed the ideological boundaries of the nation (Su, 2017). Juxtaposing those categories, I believe ethnographically grounded examples offer more nuanced understandings of these individuals traversing nationality, legality, and globality. Methodologically, I document online communities and social media networks of deportees. The COVID-19 pandemic limited my ability to return to Vietnam, as I usually do every other summer. I began this project during an unprecedented global lockdown, which arrested migration and shuttered tourism while turning many into temporary exiles. Thus, my ethnography is by necessity virtual and discursive, drawing on news sources and online interviews. The anthropology of mobility is a field that transpires on rapidly shifting grounds. Despite the changing international landscape, the experiences of voluntary returnees with a punitive one-party state resonate with criminalized migrants forcibly brought to Vietnam by the US carceral regime. Thus, I turn to discuss the im/mobilities of criminalized diasporic populations and political exiles.

Political/Legal Exiles: Forced Returns and the Criminally Expelled

To better understand US-born Vietnamese visitors deported to or exiled from Vietnam, we must consider what the United States and Vietnamese criminalizing processes expose, namely, the distinct forms of im/mobilities for diasporic Vietnamese caught in the crosshairs of "national security." The distinction between voluntary and involuntary migrants blurs upon closer examination of the deportee who is sent from the United States to Vietnam. Under a tough-on-crime and anti-immigration stance, President Donald Trump vigorously pursued the deportation of "alien" non-citizens. Many of these people did not obtain citizenship, because they arrived in the United States as children and they and their parents did not understand the naturalization process. Some were even born in the refugee camps, so did not have Vietnamese citizenship either. An agreement signed by Vietnam and the United States in 2008 stipulated that only those Vietnamese who arrived after July 12, 1995 (the date the countries re-established diplomatic relations) could be repatriated. Trump wanted to push that timeline to an even earlier time, though it was understood migrants who came before that date were refugees (Pearson, 2018). A former US ambassador to Vietnam, Ted Osius, viewed deportation as a broken

64 Long T. Bui

promise to refugees: "Their country doesn't exist. South Vietnam isn't a country anymore . . . It's ludicrous to claim they're being sent back to their country . . . which many of them fought for half their lives" (Dunst, 2018). Deporting people who are not wanted in the receiving "enemy" country renders them vulnerable, putting them in a precarious position as double exiles.[2]

Refugees with criminal records encountered deportation orders as adults from old criminal convictions. Many of the Vietnamese being deported had been brought here to the United States as refugees when very young. Some may have been arrested for things like drug possession in their teen years.[3] Arrest records for minors are usually less punitive than for adults, but when harsher laws were imposed (e.g., California's "three strikes" law), those with long-forgotten arrest records were suddenly deported or "repatriated" back to Vietnam, even though some of them had absolutely no memories of life in Vietnam and a few had no relatives at all.[4] The implication is these people are being sent back "home," but they consider the United States their home, as they have lived there for most of their lives. Vietnamese American activists opposed to deportation practices underscore how "the refugee becomes a mode of knowledge production and a critical disruption of hegemonic ideologies, inviting a poetic and political engagement with the forces of power" (Nguyen, 2016: p. 172). Militarized police states endowed with powers of arbitrary detention and with access to personal information shape the unique experiences of exiled deportees, whose micro-narratives and politics do not align with the governments that disavow them.

On Facebook, we find stories like those of Cuong Pham, a mixed-race person who came to the United States at the age of 20 in 1990 on a program for Amerasians, and in the busy-ness of working and becoming a father, never applied for citizenship. In 2000, at the age of 30, he was convicted of indecent assault and battery of children, a sex crime. In 2007, he was convicted of driving under the influence. These are problems linked to the traumas of war and forced migration (Kwan, 2019). Pham was deported on a plane that deposited other deportees in Burma/Myanmar and Cambodia before reaching Vietnam. In Vietnam, he faced difficulty in finding work and received little support from the Vietnamese government which viewed outsiders like him with great suspicion, only receiving them due to diplomatic coercion.

Before introducing findings, my methodology of virtual ethnography requires clarification. Starting in 2018, I monitored various social media sites, including a Facebook group (Southeast Asian Freedom Network) and Twitter for over two years, tracking threats and prominent stories. Some sites were not studied due to privacy issues, such as the Facebook group "Southeast Asian Deportation Public Group" which is for those personally affected or touched by deportation. What I found however from reading the publicly available stories online was that the Vietnamese American deportee remains contested as an identity-in-becoming, one where the sense of betrayal by the United States contributed to their rising political consciousness (Zialcita, 1995). When the Trump presidency transitioned over to Biden, there was still no halt to deportations, especially for a new

Democratic president and congress majority hampered by the legal rules of the previous administration.[5]

Netizens were unflagging in their criticism of ICE deportations. Individuals, reporters, and groups like the Asian Prisoner Support Committee put pressure on Biden not to deport individuals like 29-year-old Ngoc Tran, who was deported by the United States in 2017 for drug convictions incurred as a minor, for which she served time. The Orange County California resident and mother was separated from her children due to her deportation. Tracy La, executive director of the Vietnamese American progressive group VietRISE, consistently spotlights women like Tran, linking their working-class vulnerability and lack of mobility to misogynist violence, as evidenced in the 2021 killing of six Asian spa workers in the city of Atlanta. She tweets, "I believe this violence has been invisibilized . . . I know so many people facing deportation who don't want people to know about it."[6]

To illustrate the diasporic im/mobilities of people affected by the same policies but who were not deported, consider the case of Nam Phong Le, who was not deported due to having US citizenship. Despite going to Vietnam multiple times as a tourist to offer humanitarian aid to orphans, this former social worker found his life upended when he was jailed for stealing retirement benefits from elderly expats in Vietnam. As a 1.5-generation refugee who came to the United States at 11 years old, Le had grown up in poor crime-ridden neighborhoods. Eventually, he got a college education and became a federally employed social worker, returning to Vietnam multiple times as a volunteer tourist to provide humanitarian aid to orphans. Had he not received citizenship as an adult, he would have automatically been sent back to Vietnam. Ironically, Le now wants to return to the homeland permanently, where he hopes to find work which seems elusive for him in the United States due to his status as a felon. Caught in a bind, the 38-year-old feels the need to become an "expat" in Vietnam (in terms of lifestyle), as he remains exiled from the US work system. Growing up in the United States, having arrived in the United States as a child, the Californian speaks English fairly well and was able to obtain a college education. His cultural capital and economic potential as a college-educated Vietnamese American were undercut by his status as a criminalized person. The stories of people like Le demonstrate the ironies of mutually exclusive taxonomies like citizens, tourists, exiles, and migrants.

Vietnamese American returnees enter spaces where they meet locals, immigrants, and non-Vietnamese foreign tourists with whom they share linguistic terrain (English). New norms engendered by these exchanges break presumptions surrounding who people are, what they do, and where they come from (Lee, 2017). Many returnees meet online in support groups, or they meet in cafes, bars, and parks, but generally, they are "off the grid," trying to blend in with the rest of the Vietnamese population (Dunst, 2018). Moving from being "deportable refugees" in the United States to transnational subjects in Vietnam, these "cosmopolitan" exiles residing in Vietnam often find themselves in socially fluid/ambiguous spaces like tourism, where they can find employment as translators, a situation similar to that of Cambodian American deportees (Zelnick, 2018).

This mishmash of labels reveals what sociologist Victoria Reyes (2019) calls a "global borderland" defined by "spatialized configurations of inequalities that are based on differences in nationality and class . . . based on the interaction between the foreign and the local" (p. 3). To illustrate this point, consider the researchers converging on Vietnam every summer, many of them listing themselves as tourists rather than researchers to avoid bureaucratic headaches. One such person I encountered during my research is a refugee who came as a teenager to the United States and later became a scholar of Vietnam. This scholar, Bao, met her partner in Vietnam while conducting research. Due to her partner's political activities, Bao was ultimately placed on a state watchlist.[7] Wherever I spent time with them in Vietnam, we sensed that someone was watching us; we could not enjoy the peace of mind that most tourists take for granted. As a refugee-turned-researcher, Bao, faced trouble as an expungable subject, fearing severed contact with a lover.[8] Their relationship was strained by politics. Bao told me that white Americans, and women in general, are not monitored to the same extent as Vietnamese American men who are always perceived as suspect criminals, much like the re-educated soldiers of South Vietnam. This example speaks volumes about how gendered racialized categories like "tourist" versus returning former "exile" or "refugee" color not only the government's perceptions but also the actions of Vietnamese American men (domestic or foreign), and women and gendered others too, even if to a lesser extent.

Vietnamese American exiles are suspended between countries that have "forgotten" the refugee's plight. The nexus of migrant/tourist/exile affords a non-binary language encapsulating the experiences of Vietnamese who visit the homeland and find themselves fearing arrest during their stay. Insofar as Vietnamese American returnees are vigilantly watched by the government for signs of sedition, former overseas Vietnamese are continually at risk of becoming domestic "enemies." Political scientist Kieu-Linh Valverde (2012) finds that although the Vietnamese government welcomed overseas Vietnamese tourists, "they equally saw the anti-communist overseas population as a direct threat to Vietnam's stability" (p. ix). While Vietnamese people are found everywhere, the Vietnamese from the United States pose the biggest threat, as this is where most South Vietnamese citizens, elites, and political leaders settled. Vietnam's ruling party continues to crack down on US returnees' political activities through vaguely worded penal codes involving categories like "undermining national unity" and "conducting propaganda against the state" (Human Rights Watch, 2016).[9]

Given the Vietnamese government's perception of returnees – be they tourists, researchers, retirees, or expunged refugees – as potential subversives and incendiaries, casual visits can prove risky. This is seen in the case of Michael Nguyen, a working-class 1.5-generation Vietnamese refugee who came to the United States at the age of 10. Nguyen ran an Orange County (California) printing shop and served as the primary caregiver to four daughters. While vacationing in Vietnam in 2019, Nguyen was removed from a tour bus by communist apparatchiks, arrested, and placed in the foreigners' section of a Vietnamese prison. Government officials accused Nguyen of joining a local organization to buy weapons, conduct subversive activities, and incite everyday people to protest – charges that he denied. Nguyen claimed that he was simply a "tourist" visiting aging relatives on his Vietnam vacation. Tried in a Vietnamese court, Nguyen confessed under police interrogation to discussing Vietnam's political affairs on the Internet, something construed as treasonous. In this regard, the policing of tourists involves more than monitoring physical travelers and their online activity, as well. Nguyen served only two years of his 12-year sentence before being expelled from the United States (Randall, 2020). US lawmakers like Representative Katie Porter described Nguyen as a man who "sees injustice in the world and wants to do something about it" (Anderson, 2020). Whatever Nguyen's true intentions, his imprisonment in Vietnam bears relevance for others, as Anh Do, a human rights advocate, underscores: "Look at this person . . . For everyone who returns to Vietnam, this is a warning" (Do, 2019). A month after Michael Nguyen's arrest, Australian retiree Van Kham Chau was also arrested and sentenced to 12 years in prison. Along with two other co-defendants, the 70-year-old former Republic of Vietnam soldier belonged to the New South Wales chapter of Viet Tan, a group branded as terrorists by Vietnam but labeled a peaceful organization by the United Nations. He was accused of recruiting members, although he denies any such activities in Vietnam, despite crossing into Vietnam via Cambodia with false identity documents.

Like many who left as refugees and "made it" in their new countries, Nguyen and Chau returned to Vietnam with economic privilege, but without political potency. They compose part of a "lost generation of exiles who desire political power" but have yet to achieve it (Valverde, 2012: p. 147). This power asymmetry reveals how circuits of tourism enable refugee/returnee politics, and the threat of banishment makes tourism and engaging in politics something returnees think twice about (or obliges returnees to consider their every mundane action while in Vietnam through the lens of potential criminal accusations).

A year before the imprisonment of Michael Nguyen and Van Kham Chau, another exiled tourist made international headlines. In 2018, Will Nguyen (no relation to Michael), a visiting student completing his studies in Singapore, was held by officials in Ho Chi Minh City. The second-generation Vietnamese American was there on a short vacation while pursuing a graduate degree in Singapore when he became swept up in local demonstrations. These protests opposed two controversial draft bills, a measure on cybersecurity and the other on the designation of special economic zones. The protests Will Nguyen joined were part of a nation-wide mobilization against a proposal that would allow Vietnamese land to be rented by foreigners for up to 99 years – a huge boon to Chinese investors hoping to establish not only assembly work factories but also tourist hotels, gambling casinos, and prime resort areas (Tran, 2018a). Tourism directly links to migration here, given the huge boom in Chinese tourism to Southeast Asia and the government's ability to displace local populations in favor of rich outsiders.

68 Long T. Bui

These developments explain why returning tourists might be willing to risk exile to protect their homeland from interlopers. Will Nguyen explains his decision to protest in an interview:

> I was completely awed by this unprecedented display of people power and sought to let the world know what was happening, even tagging international media in some of my Twitter posts. But as the protests grew . . . I began taking a more active role (O' Connell, 2018)[10].

A Vietnamese court convicted Nguyen of disturbing public order and ordered his deportation, sparing him seven years in prison. Nguyen received leniency because he confessed to his crime. He is now a permanent exile from Vietnam, barred from returning.

Nguyen returned to the United States with the US media portraying him as a "defiant" survivor of communist persecution (Foxhall, 2018). Vietnamese state-sponsored media excoriated the outsider/tourist for joining the protests, galvanizing violent action, and plastering protest information online (Chau, 2018). Nguyen's contrasting portrayal in Vietnamese and US media crystallizes a digital "body politics," whereby inchoate public feelings about the nation and diaspora are expressed (Phuong, 2017). What it means to be a part of an imagined community is changing, much like the categories of exile/migrant/tourist, due to shifts in diasporic im/mobilities.

Journalist Michael Tatarski retweeted one of Nguyen's retweets: "Here we see the benefits of a US passport: 10 Vietnamese nationals were jailed for up to 3 years on the same charges filed against Will Nguyen."[11] The journalist notes how the now-exiled Nguyen finds himself in a different predicament from other imprisoned local human rights defenders:

> Nguyen is not a Vietnamese citizen, but an American citizen of Vietnamese descent. This allows him some, albeit limited, "privileges" . . . allowed access to US consular officers, and the authorities have said that his family will be allowed to attend his trial. These are luxuries withheld from many Vietnamese political prisoners, who are often held incommunicado for months – even years – before standing trial (Tran, 2018b).

Nguyen himself invokes his US privilege in a posttrial interview:

> I occupied a nebulous zone; they treated me with gloves on but were at relative ease about what they could say to me. I was "same-same, but different" . . . They knew my actions came from a good place, that they were a natural extension of the nationalism that we, Vietnamese, are taught from birth (O' Connell, 2018)[12].

Diasporic Im/mobilities **69**

With his captors even apologizing for his criminal treatment, Nguyen reflects on being a foreigner, one who would not be treated as a regular "local" criminal. Nguyen deems himself a Vietnam patriot, even though he was technically a tourist, but this category itself can be further parsed out when we expand our lens to include retirees and expats.

Cultural/Emotional Exiles: Retirees and Expats in the Tourist Trap

"What do you mean I can't go?!," my mother bellowed with anger at the Vietnamese airline staff. It turned out that her citizenship status, as it appeared in her passport, meant she could not travel to Thailand on a short holiday while visiting Vietnam. As a US permanent resident, she could not travel as freely as her US-born children with their "fully" American passports. Both US and Vietnamese citizens can travel to Thailand without a visa, but she was somewhere in the middle. With no refund possible for this vacation, my sibling and I were obliged to tour Thailand without her. This trip included our aunt and cousin from Vietnam, who as Vietnamese citizens could freely travel through much of Southeast Asia due to reciprocal travel agreements in the region. Stuck in limbo, as she had been for decades, my mom could only await our return.

For over four decades, my mother held the dubious status of a "permanent resident alien" in the United States. An aging woman with only a third-grade education, she failed the citizenship test multiple times. Yet, she felt so proud to be able to afford this surprise gift for the family. The US dollar's strength in the foreign currency exchange led my mother, a low-wage spa worker, to believe she could be a carefree tourist in her former homeland and other less-expensive countries of the Global South like Thailand. However, her status as an "exile" and her precarity as a non-citizen meant she could not enjoy all the modern-day trappings of a tourist (at least not outside Vietnam).

Tourism has been discussed tangentially in relation to refugee groups (or refugees as tourists), but we need to better understand the returnee's transition from exile to tourist (Inhorn, 2011). Visits to long-lost family members and countries count as tourism, but the gratification of visiting family can be cut short or lost with the prospect of permanent exile or imprisonment (as seen in the examples of Will Nguyen and Michael Nguyen). There is a sociopolitical dimension to the VFR Tourism designation, especially in low-income countries where that is the dominant form of tourism (Pearce and Moscardo, 2005). VFR closely links families in Vietnam and abroad, such that the tourists visiting their family members are not perceived as neutral. Moreover, they can be envisioned as potentially infecting their Vietnamese kin with foreign ideas and thoughts. Media accounts of Vietnamese visitors arrested for suspicious activity invariably cast a shadow over others who merely arrive on holiday or for longer-term stays.

Despite the privileges they enjoy as Americans in Vietnam, diasporic returnees face other issues. Their symbolic association with a former enemy state perceived by communists as a puppet for the United States places an eternal stigma on them as political exiles (Bui, 2018). In my book *Returns of War*, I examined the shift from studying refugee politics to returnee politics, through an ethnography of Vietnamese American youth raised in the United States, who moved back to work or live in Vietnam (to the chagrin of their anticommunist elders).[13] My interviews with returnees revealed that many did not know how to label themselves in a country where it is hard for anyone, Vietnamese or not, to immigrate and settle permanently. According to United Nations data, Vietnam contains the smallest proportion of foreign-born populations after China (Kopf, 2017).[14] Tourism becomes the means for Vietnam to attract foreign income and remains the primary or initial means by which returnees come back, although a burgeoning number of them are economic migrants and retirees. While over four million Vietnamese live abroad, less than an estimated 3,000 overseas Vietnamese have returned permanently to Vietnam.[15] Often yoked to leisure and entertainment, tourism encompasses many activities, but Vietnamese returnee tourism in Vietnam takes on specific forms, including medical tourism (surgery), educational tourism (study abroad), and "voluntourism" (visiting orphanages). Cultural tourism, the biggest category of all, provides a window into distributions of power and value.[16]

The im/mobilities of diaspora refract the multiple privileges of citizenship and forms of cultural exile (Nadurata, 2019: p. 40). Expats with US citizenship may feel emboldened to speak their views, knowing they might be protected by the US government, but they know that they can be arrested, surveilled, and imprisoned, simply for being an outsider.

When I first visited the South Vietnamese historical archives in Ho Chi Minh City to examine war documents for my research, a staff member immediately shooed me away without reason, based on my Americanized appearance, accent, and affiliation with a foreign school. When I returned weeks later, hoping she had forgotten me by then, I pretended to be a clueless tourist who was curious about the library and just wanted to peruse the artifacts. I received immediate admission. This white lie (I was a tourist after all) carried unknown penalties and fear of repercussions. Where does the position of adult tourist begin and where does my status as the child of the diaspora end? Exile/tourism/migration involves more than physical acts of removal/escape; they can be fluid states of mind. As the progeny of Vietnamese refugees including a parent who was a military veteran of the South Vietnamese army, I embodied the enemy, even if I appeared "same-same, but different" to institutional gatekeepers.

Through the diaspora and its varying forms of im/mobility, we can ask: When, where, and how does a refugee (or a child of refugees) who returns to Vietnam – as opposed to Vietnamese economic immigrants of the 1990s onward – feel like a "perpetual foreigner"? Does this person feel like a tourist when traveling with mostly non-Vietnamese tourist caravans from China, South Korea, and Australia? What of aging refugee returnees in Vietnam living on fixed incomes, with modest lifestyles relative to US standards but rich by local standards? In all cases, we must ask if movement and status are forced or willful, permanent, or temporary. Does

Diasporic Im/mobilities **71**

the returnee enter a high or low social position? Does an expat ever cease being an exile? How does a refugee transform into a retiree in the country they left?

Overseas retirees or expats are terms used to describe those people who stay outside their home countries temporarily or permanently. But returning Vietnamese are more than that; they view the United States as their adopted homeland even while linked mentally to their original home. Former refugee Andrew Lam (2018) writes extensively on the personal politics of homeland returns. He worked as a journalist and writer, before retiring permanently in Vietnam. In an online piece entitled "There and Back Again: A Vietnamese Journey," Lam reflects on his blended life in Vietnam as a permanent resident and occasional tourist. At the Cu Chi Tunnel, famous for hiding communist guerillas during the war, he encountered US vets who had done military tours but now circled back to Vietnam as commercial tourists. This tourist site also drew Vietnamese nationals enraptured by the allure of going abroad. Lam observes,

> The middle-aged vets teared up gazing at an old war wound, but [for] the young tour guide . . . She readily confessed that, for her, the tunnel was a relic about which she knew nothing until she got her job . . . 'So you live in California? My dream is to go for a visit.

This young woman hoped to save money for California destinations like Disneyland, Universal Studios, Golden Gate Bridge, and Yosemite Park. If the "tunnel runs toward the bloody past," he concludes, "for this young woman, it leads toward a touristy future." Lam recounts this maxim from a friend that the crossing of borders does not "have to be *outside* of Vietnam," but that these days even "middle-class Vietnamese fly overseas to shop."

Analyzing Lam's narrative of diasporic return, literary scholar Begoña Simal González (2014) believes the writer's "discrepant cosmopolitanism" works across dichotomies as part of a generation that is highly mobile but less politically sensitive compared to their anticommunist elders. González calls attention to the younger generation (now middle-aged or of retirement age) since their patchwork mobile consciousness comprises synchronic moments that do not cohere into any conventional sense of origin and destination. They are part of the diaspora, but their diasporic identifications are unmoored.

Besides being a top Southeast Asian tourist destination, Vietnam is a hotspot for retirees (Quy, 2020). With newly passed laws that enabled foreigners to own real estate (but not land outright), Vietnam opened its doors to investors to supplement remittances. With preferential treatment and faster approval for business permits, well-to-do diasporans are settling in Vietnam amid familiar comforts like the American-style suburbs "to which they grew accustomed during their exile" (Ly, 2003).[17] My research participant Lam constitutes part of the 1.5 generation. With a child's memory of the war, Lam had returned to Vietnam to find his "roots," before settling there permanently. His father was a high-ranking South Vietnamese military officer, so his family was obliged to flee. Well-connected people who did not escape as refugees were exiled from communist civic life and the mainstream economy. Yet, his wealthy family held onto some financial assets that allowed Lam to return/retire comfortably in senior-friendly Vietnam.

Yet, the haunting memory of war persists as a collective wound for all in the South Vietnamese diaspora, and this trauma is where the psychic life of the tourist/expat resonates with that of the migrant/deportee and exile/prisoner – despite wildly disparate experiences. I interviewed finance worker and television producer Anh-Thu Nguyen who grew up as a Vietnamese American born in the United States. She now resides in the Little Tokyo enclave of District One, the most touristy part of Saigon. While bouncing around nice restaurants with Nguyen, I asked her how she identifies. She was clearly at pains to label herself, alternating between "Vietnamese" and "foreigner," despite having lived in Vietnam for over a decade.[18] She hesitated to embrace the term "immigrant" as, for her, it connotes economic struggle, which she did not quite know compared to her refugee parents. Equally problematic was the term "expat," which for Nguyen connoted the retired "Aussies" hanging out in bars or the Korean foreign workers shacked up in their suburban condos. She did not know where she would retire, debating whether to go back to the US or stay in Vietnam forever.

The homeland orientations of Nguyen's own family are polarizing. Her mother enjoys coming back every year to visit family, but her father has only returned twice since 1975. She attributed his reluctance to the trauma he experienced as a persecuted former soldier in reeducation camps run by the communist victors. The parents' competing senses of homeland as well as tourism (aversion versus attraction) frame Nguyen's mental vacillation and liminality of "being always here and there."

Like Lam and Le, Nguyen is open about her queer identity and participated in Vietnam's first LGBT+ public pride events in Vietnam. Their stories tell me that the intersection of exile, migration, and tourism operates via the intersectionality of ethnicity, gender, and sexuality (Piña, 2022). Attention to queer exiles (estranged from the nation/family), sexual migrants (denied same-sex marriage visas), and LGBT tourists (surveilled for "morality" and appearance) shape the subcultures not visible to the heteronormative eye, as anthropologist Natalie Newton (2012) found in her study of "les" women in Saigon, which bound together in a subculture of foreign and local lesbians. Diasporic im/mobilities hinge on the condition of queer diasporas. That is, we need to consider how to "queer" the given binary of Vietnamese national outsider and insider, given that queer people are frequently relegated to the outside of the biological and national family. In doing so, we recognize that non-binary subjects are already profiled as "subversive" to heteronormative cultures and societies.

During the earlier phases of the COVID-19 pandemic, Nguyen feared returning to the United States, since Vietnam was safely handling the crisis while the United States was an epicenter of infection at the time. If she left Vietnam and attempted to return, she would be barred or put in the foreigner/tourist category, obliged to pay for lodging and quarantine accommodations in a hotel, even though she has a home in Vietnam. In a time of global lockdown, the question of exile/migrant/tourism entails new geographic alignments and border closures, turning tourists into temporary exiles and isolated captives. Nguyen, like other expats, debated going back to the United States to receive her COVID-19 shots, given Vietnam's shortage. This would require an indefinite stay until Vietnam reopens and being barred from the adoptive/ancestral homeland. Nguyen and others' intent to return to the United States for vaccinations differs from the "medical tourism" of non-citizen travelers coming to the United States to do the same thing. The diasporic im/mobilities of return exceed any singular frame in a world that is changing as fast as the people moving (or not) within it.

Conclusions

This study highlighted the ambiguous status of Vietnamese Americans exiled to and from Vietnam. It considers the tenuous standing of precarious subjects from overseas migrant communities in their diasporic im/mobilities, whether as former refugees or children of refugees. By tracking the transits and trappings of the repatriated deportee and (deportable) tourist, I offer an avenue for expanding upon studies of exile, tourism, and migration. In juxtaposing discussions of the plight of the deportee with that of Vietnamese American expats, I invite us to ponder other avenues for studying im/mobile people in a more politicized fashion. This contrasting discourse resists the tendency to apply "politics" only to people who are arrested and deported by the Vietnam or US government. Someone working or retired in Vietnam can be repatriated based on a range of social activities. In highlighting the politics of im/mobility alongside the stories of Vietnamese American refugees, their offspring, and loved ones in the homeland, we can gleam empathy (or the limits of it) for these groups and others, and an appreciation of the complexities shaping their translocal lives. Implicit in the cases presented here is that we ask not only where people belong, but whether we care enough to attend to their specific needs. There is an ethics to exile.[19]

When members of the postwar South Vietnamese diaspora return to their homeland, it is never clear what they are returning to, given the circuitous detours taken by migratory subjects, from activism to entertainment. Their diasporic im/mobilities illustrate how the simple meanings attached to terms such as tourist, refugee, and migrant appear at odds with what is happening on the ground. My examples speak to the incommensurability of multi-sited living. In these instances, we find critical voices that can address the multiple worlds which we traverse and are, sometimes, held in place.

Notes

1 Bloch's (2018) study of Tibetan refugees in India tracks a range of mobile subjects that include newcomers, second-generation refugees, seasonal migrants, tourists, and expats. She found that no one single term captures the community's diversity and levels of dispersion.

2 On an international level, Trump's deportation policy forced poorer nations to take America's "criminals." It imposed international pressure with threats of visa sanctions on any "recalcitrant" country. Such hardline policies retraumatize refugee communities and tear families apart by sending refugees into countries from which they are estranged, indifferent, or adverse to them.
3 Postwar resettlement programs for Vietnamese refugees lacked full institutional support, resulting in high rates of gang activity and "deportability" (Chow, 2005).
4 In this state, a punitive "three strikes" law punishes individuals for life due to small crimes, and felony charges that dissolve their legal permanent status and prevent them from ever applying to citizenship (Lum, 2018).
5 This coincided with the dozens of Vietnamese deported to Vietnam from Cambodia and banned from entering the country for years.
6 See https://twitter.com/_TracyLa/status/1377049103545212930 (Accessed: May 31, 2021). Given the sensitive legal issues faced by individuals posting on these sites, I revealed my research objectives but did not contact or chat with any of the people who were active in these groups. Instead, I conducted a deep active online presence to understand different sorts of experiences shared by the members of these groups.
7 This is a pseudonym used to protect my colleague's identity.
8 She would also be facing disenfranchisement from the country on which her credentials as a scholar are based. That would mean a lot of retooling as a scholar, probably not something she would take lightly.
9 This relates to the Cuban case, where Cuban Americans are treated as corrosive agents by Cuba's communist government (Gosin, 2017; Bradford, 2016).
10 A YouTube video posted by an anonymous source showed Nguyen bleeding from his head, beaten, and dragged through the street by plain-clothed police.
11 Twitter @miketataraski (July 23, 2018).
12 "Same same but different" is a common expression throughout parts of Asia and speaks to contradiction and cultural connection.
13 I did ethnographic fieldwork in Vietnam between 2008 and 2016, a time of great anxiety a confusion over the future of the diaspora. I found that while ordinary people in Vietnam welcomed old friends and opportunities for cultural exchange, they are critical of overseas Vietnamese and their display of arrogance, ignorance, and wealth.
14 Vietnamese nationals' passports only allow them to visit 40 countries. Vietnam is one of the countries with the least powerful passport rankings, according to the World Economic Forum's Passport Index. In contrast, the passports of Vietnamese from the United States placed third overall on passport power rankings, enabling US citizens to freely roam the planet with abandon and protection (VnExpress, 2016).
15 This figure does not include those who repeatedly renew their three-month visas (Viet-NamNet Bridge, 2011).
16 In their study of Vietnamese Australian returnees in Vietnam, Thu Nguyen and Brian King (1998) examine ethnic tourism and Visiting Friends and Relatives (VFR) tourism, focusing on acts performed by migrants and long-term exiles to reestablish heritage links. Whereas the Vietnamese American tourists they interviewed showed positive optimism for Vietnam's future and society, longtime Vietnamese expats living in Vietnam voiced concerns about the country's political situation, unsatisfactory sanitary conditions, and personal safety.
17 This news article follows the life of Linda Vo who owns a spacious California-styled mansion in a "Viet Kieu Village" near Ho Chi Minh City's riverfront and drives an SUV with American flag pillows. Unlike the European or Korean foreign expats, this ethnic expat remembers a prior era: "Here, we remember America . . . There, we remember Vietnam. We have two countries. Maybe someday, we will lose our memory and it won't matter."
18 While VK used to be derogatory, according to An-Thu Nguyen, it was reclaimed or neutralized, but the feeling of being a cultural outsider remained. This was mostly due to her heavy American accent while speaking Vietnamese.

19 All my research participants told me that upon returning to Vietnam, they felt more authentically Vietnamese, even if they encountered social barriers to acceptance. Despite policing by a "corrupt, failed socialist government," as well as experiences of "racism and isolation," international travel enables these globetrotters to be more routed than rooted, concomitantly "coming home" and "going away" (Small, 2013, p. 73).

References

Anderson, P. (2020) 'Orange County man returns home, shares details of imprisonment in Vietnam', *NBC Los Angeles*, 28 October. Available at: www.nbclosangeles.com/news/local/orange-county-returns-home-shares-details-of-imprisonment-in-vietnam/2451326/

Blitz, B., Sales, R. and Marzano, L. (2005) 'Non-voluntary return? The politics of return to Afghanistan', *Political Studies*, 53(1), pp. 182–200.

Bloch, N. (2018) 'Making a community embedded in mobility: Refugees, migrants, and tourists in Dharamshala (India)', *Transfers*, 8(3), pp. 36–54.

Bradford, A. (2016) 'Remembering Pedro Pan: Childhood and collective memory making in Havana and Miami, 1960–2000', *Cuban Studies*, 44(1), pp. 283–308.

Bui, L. (2018) *Returns of war: South Vietnam and the price of refugee memory*. New York: New York University Press.

Chau, H. (2018) 'Xet xu ong William Nguyen', *Tuoi Tre Online*, 13 July. Available at: https://tuoitre.vn/20-7-xet-xu-ong-william-nguyen-20180713093631229.htm

Chow, G. (2005) 'Exiled once again: Consequences of the congressional expansion of deportable offenses on the Southeast Asian refugee community', *Asian Law Journal*, 12(1), pp. 103–136.

Di Leonardo, M. (2018) *The varieties of ethnic experience*. Ithaca, NY: Cornell University Press.

Djordjevic, B. (2013) Politics of return, inequality and citizenship in the post-Yugoslav space. *CITSEE Working Paper Series*, 29.

Do, A. (2019) 'Last year he went on vacation to Vietnam. Now he faces 12 years in prison', *Los Angeles Times*, 25 June. Available at: www.latimes.com/la-me-vietnamese-prison-nguyen-20190625-story.html

Dunst, C. (2018) 'The Deportees Caught in Trump's Immigration War', *Southeast Asia Globe*, 12 December. Available at: https://southeastasiaglobe.com/the-vietnamese-deportees-caught-in-trumps-immigration-war/

Duong, L. (2016) 'Diasporic returns and the making of Vietnamese American ghost films in Vietnam', *MELUS: Multi-Ethnic Literature of the United States*, 41(3), pp. 153–170.

Foxhall, E. (2018) 'Houstonian will Nguyen returns to Twitter with defiance after arrest, detention in Vietnam', *The Houston Chronicle*, 27 July. Available at: https://m.chron.com/news/houston-texas/article/Will-Nguyen-who-was-detained-in-Vietnam-returns-13111091.php?utm_campaign=twitter-mobile&utm_source= CMS%20Sharing%20Button&utm_medium=social

Gasviani, G. (2019) 'The role of the Soviet past in contemporary Georgia', *Caucasus International*, 9(1–2), pp. 37–50.

Gosin, M. (2017) ' "Bitter diversion": Afro-Cuban immigrants, race, and everyday-life resistance', *Latino Studies*, 15(1), pp. 4–28.

Human Rights Watch (2016) *Vietnam: Events of 2016*. Available at: www.hrw.org/world-report/2017/country-chapters/vietnam

Inhorn, M. (2011) 'Diasporic dreaming: Return reproductive tourism to the Middle East', *Reproductive Biomedicine Online*, 23(5), pp. 582–591.

Keles, J. (2022) 'Return mobilities of highly skilled young people to a post-conflict region: The case of Kurdish-British to Kurdistan – Iraq', *Journal of Ethnic and Migration Studies*, 48(3), pp. 790–810.

King, R. and Christou, A. (2011) 'Of counter-diaspora and reverse transnationalism: Return mobilities to and from the ancestral homeland', *Mobilities*, 6(4), pp. 451–466.

Kopf, D. (2017) 'In one metric of diversity, China comes in dead last', *Quartz*, 27 December. Available at: https://qz.com/1163632/china-still-has-the-smallest-share-of-incoming-migrants-in-the-world/

Kwan, Y. (2019) 'Providing asset-based support for Asian American refugees: Interrogating transgenerational trauma, resistance, and affective capital', *New Directions for Higher Education*, 186, pp. 37–47.

Lam, A. (2018) 'There and back again: A Vietnamese journey,' *Boom California*, 21 March. Available at: https://boomcalifornia.com/2018/03/21/there-and-back-again/

Lee, J. (2017) *The politics of translingualism: After Englishes*. London: Routledge.

Lum, L. (2018) 'Group addresses incarceration among Asian Americans, Pacific Islanders', *Diverse Issues in Higher Education*, 1 May. Available at: https://diverseeducation.com/article/115575/

Ly, P. (2003) 'In Vietnam, finding the comforts of home', *Washington Post*, 12 October. Available at: www.washingtonpost.com/archive/politics/2003/10/12/in-vietnam-finding-the-comforts-of-home/39fc9244-2182-4ae4-b1eb-bc970fe188b0/

Nadurata, E. (2019) *Crip'in Migration: Examining the elderly migrant experience in Filipino American literature*. MA thesis. Los Angeles, CA: University of California.

Newton, N. (2012) *A queer political economy of "community": Gender, space, and the transnational politics of community for Vietnamese lesbians (les) in Saigon*. PhD thesis. Irvine, CA: University of California.

Nguyen, L.T. (2021) *Revolutionary others: Migratory subjects and Vietnamese radicalism in the US during and after the Vietnam War*. PhD thesis. San Diego, CA: University of California.

Nguyen, T. and King, B. (1998) 'Migrant homecomings: Viet Kieu attitudes towards traveling back to Vietnam', *Pacific Tourism Review*, 1(4), pp. 349–361.

Nguyen, V. (2016) 'Refugeography in "post-racial" America: Bao Phi's activist poetry', *MELUS: Multi-Ethnic Literature of the United States*, 41(3), pp. 171–193.

O' Connell, T. (2018) ' "I argue to this day that I have done nothing wrong", says arrested US citizen', *Southeast Asia Global*, 17 August. Available at: https://southeastasiaglobe.com/will-nguyen-interview/

Pearson, J. (2018) 'US seeks to deport thousands of Vietnamese protected by treaty: Former Ambassador', *Reuters*, 12 April. Available at: www.reuters.com/article/us-usa-vietnam-deportees/u-s-seeks-to-deport-thousands-of-vietnamese-protected-by-treaty-former-ambassador-idUSKBN1HJ0OU

Pearce, P. and Moscardo, G. (2005) 'Domestic and visiting friends and relatives tourism' in Buhalis, D. and Costa, C. (eds.) *Tourism business frontiers*. London: Routledge, pp. 70–77.

Phuong, T. (2017) 'Saint, celebrity, and the self(ie): Body politics in late socialist Vietnam', *Positions: East Asia Cultures Critique*, 25(4), pp. 821–842.

Piña, D.A. (2022 'White supremacy in rainbow: Global pride and black lives matter in the era of COVID', *New Sociology: Journal of Critical Praxis*, 3, pp. 1-10.

Quy, N. (2020) 'Vietnam among top 10 countries for retirement', *VN Express International*, 6 January. Available at: https://e.vnexpress.net/news/news/vietnam-among-top-10-countries-for-retirement-report-4037643.html

Randall (2020) 'Vietnamese Am held prisoner in Vietnam for 2 years freed', *AsAmNews*, 27 October. Available at: https://asamnews.com/2020/10/27/michael-nguyen-is-resting-with-family-in-orange-county-after-his-surprise-release-from-a-vietnamese-prison

Reyes, V. (2019) *Global borderlands: Fantasy, violence, and empire in Subic Bay, Philippines*. Palo Alto, CA: Stanford University Press.

Saraiva, A. and Sardinha, J. (2016) '"My country, my pain; my child, my love": Aging Azoreans in San Jose, California and ancestral homeland return (Im) mobilities', *Inter-DISCIPLINARY Journal of Portuguese Diaspora Studies*, 5, pp. 7–23.

Schwenkel, C. (2015) 'Socialist mobilities: Crossing new terrains in Vietnamese migration histories', *Central and Eastern European Migration Review*, 4(1), pp. 13–25.

Simal-González, B. (2014) 'Andrew Lam's narratives of return: From Viet Kieu nostalgia to discrepant cosmopolitanisms' in Oliver-Rotger, M. (ed.) *Identity, diaspora and return in American literature*. New York: Routledge, pp. 93–114.

Small, I. (2013) 'The Vietnamese transnational(s)' in Barker, J., Harms, E. and Lindquist, J. (eds.) *Figures of modernity in Southeast Asia*. Honolulu: University of Hawaii Press, pp. 72–75.

Su, P. (2017) '"There's no solidarity": Nationalism and belonging among Vietnamese refugees and immigrants in Berlin', *Journal of Vietnamese Studies*, 12(1), pp. 73–100.

Tran, A. (2018a) 'Vietnam: Workers protest proposed lease of economic zones to China', *The News Lens*, 24 July. Available at: https://international.thenewslens.com/article/10049

Tran, V. (2018b) 'Freedom of assembly on trial in Vietnam', *New Naratif*, 19 July. Available at: https://newnaratif.com/journalism/freedom-assembly-trial-vietnam/

Valverde, K. (2012) *Transnationalizing Viet Nam: Community, culture, and politics in the diaspora*. Philadelphia, PA: Temple University Press.

VietNamNet Bridge (2011) 'Viet Kieu bring money, but also knowledge and technology', *VietNamNet Bridge*, 24 January. Available at: http://english.vietnamnet.vn/fms/special-reports/4011/viet-kieu-bring-money – but-also-knowledge-and-technology.html

VnExpress (2016) 'Vietnam has one of the least powerful passports in Southeast Asia', *VnExpress International*, 18 September. Available at: https://e.vnexpress.net/news/news/viet-nam-has-one-of-the-least-powerful-passports-in-southeast-asia-3470103.html

Wang, C. (2013) 'Politics of return: Homecoming stories of the Vietnamese diaspora', *Positions: East Asia Cultures Critique*, 21(1), pp. 161–187.

Winogrodzka, D. and Grabowska, I. (2021) '(Dis)ordered social sequences of mobile young adults: Spatial, social and return mobilities', *Journal of Youth Studies*, 24, pp. 1–17.

Zelnick, J. (2018) 'Cambodian American deportable refugees and transnationalism' in Howell, J., Altamirano, D., Totah, F. and Keles, F. (eds.) *Porous borders, invisible boundaries? Ethnographic perspectives on the vicissitudes of contemporary migration*. Arlington, VA: American Anthropological Association, pp. 91–98.

Zhang, L. (2012) 'Afterword: Flexible postsocialist assemblages from the margin', *Positions: East Asia Cultures Critique*, 20(2), pp. 659–667.

Zialcita, F. (1995) 'State formation, colonialism and national identity in Vietnam and the Philippines', *Philippine Quarterly of Culture and Society*, 23(2), pp. 77–117.

4

STUDENT MIGRATION AS AN ESCAPE FROM PROTRACTED EXILE

The Case of Young Sahrawi Refugees

Rita Reis

Introduction

This chapter concerns people who were once nomads searching for water and pastures who suddenly found themselves imprisoned in refugee camps, victims of a failed decolonization process. Their territorial homeland, Western Sahara, was a Spanish colony (1884–1976) and is today a non-self-governing territory (San Martín, 2010). The failed decolonization process in tandem with the 1975 Mauritanian–Moroccan invasion of Western Sahara spurred the flight of about half the population (San Martín, 2010). Today, the refugee camps of Tindouf, Algeria, are more than a place of exile: They have served as the Sahrawi Arab Democratic Republic (SADR) headquarters since its proclamation in 1976. SADR and its national political project of independence for the Sahrawi people were spearheaded by the Liberation Front of Saguia al-Hamra and Wadi Dhahab (POLISARIO Front), established in 1973 to combat Spanish occupation. Contrary to refugee camps' stereotypic association with stagnation, the Sahrawi refugee camps are considered "central margins" (Fiddian-Qasmiyeh, 2015), where inhabitants are involved in multiple transnational processes. One such transnational process that stands out is that of educational mobility.

***

"I prepared this for an activity with a boy with autism, who reacts very well to textures," Amal told me as she got into my car and showed me what she had made: A rectangle with several glued objects of different sizes and textures. Amal, a 26-year-old Sahrawi refugee, and I were on our way to pick up one of her colleagues, as we headed to the farm near Badajoz, Spain, where they worked. They were employed by an association that facilitated occupational therapy with horses. Amal started a session, helping a boy mount a horse, and we went for a ride. In her sweet way, she sang to him, "you know, he gets very relaxed when I sing to him in Hassanyia."[1]

DOI: 10.4324/9781003182689-5

When we first met, Amal was in her 20s and had been living in Extremadura for over a decade. As a child, she spent several summers there, through the Holidays in Peace program (*Programa Vacaciones en Paz*) that offers summer vacations for Sahrawi refugee children. When she turned 13 – marking the end of her eligibility for the Holidays in Peace program – Amal's Spanish host family decided to foster her so that she could continue her education in Spain. Upon graduation in 2018, Amal opted to stay in Spain and started working as an occupational therapist, thus moving from being a refugee student to a migrant. Like many of my research participants, she obtained formal status as a stateless person,[2] and despite the distressing geographical distance from her family, she did not consider making a permanent return to the camps.

Recent media images represent the so-called "refugee crisis" as comprised entirely of newcomers requiring immediate aid in temporary camps. However, most of the world's refugees live in protracted exile (Milner, 2016), experiencing a chronic "permanent temporariness" (Bailey et al., 2002). Nevertheless, many traverse camp borders, integrating different types of mobilities, including those for economic purposes. By considering such mobilities and assuming that there are "'overlapping' and 'multiple' refugeehoods" (Fiddian-Qasmiyeh, 2012, p. 293), we can more accurately address how refugees "actively respond . . . to displacement" (Fiddian-Qasmiyeh, 2020, p. 3). Moreover, a more nuanced understanding of the voluntary movements of forcibly displaced persons enables us to better acknowledge that – even when living in protracted refugee contexts – people seek improved conditions and meaningful lives (Schielke, 2009) and are driven by "imaginative geographies, emotional valences, social relations and obligations" (Carling and Collins, 2018, p. 911).

The case of the Sahrawi people is pertinent as it illustrates the intersection of exile and different forms of mobility. However, Sahrawis' contemporary movements should not be considered simply legacies of their nomadic heritage (Wilson, 2017). In this sense, Sahrawi student mobility must be analyzed within a framework that considers the intersection of multiple mobility processes, including transnational movements, migrations, displacements for medical reasons, nomadism, vacations, and education. We must also consider the educational programs offered to refugee populations and their relation to the construction of imagined communities (Anderson, 2006).

This chapter analyzes the intersections between exile, educational mobilities, and migration by spotlighting the perspectives of young Sahrawis living in Extremadura, Spain, and by focusing on transgenerationality. I examine how, after 40 years in exile, the paths and expectations of young people who left camps to study contrast with those of their parents and siblings who remained in the camps. The findings presented here draw from 24 months of ethnographic fieldwork conducted between April 2018 and March 2020.[3] I spent 16 months in Spain's province of Extremadura and eight months in the city of Algiers (Algeria), observing the daily lives and future aspirations of Sahrawi youth living in these locales. The names and some personal details concerning my research participants have been changed to

80 Rita Reis

protect their privacy. Due to length constraints, this chapter focuses exclusively on the data collected in Spain. However, the long-term duration of my fieldwork including participant observation in Algiers and the development of sustained relationships with several research participants enabled me to access alternate universes and to gain insights into the viewpoints of parents and siblings who remained in refugee camps.

During my research in Extremadura, I conducted interviews with students and members of the Sahrawi community, Spanish host families, representatives of the POLISARIO Front, and leaders who oversee programs for Sahrawi refugees (e.g., Holidays in Peace). I partook in the daily lives of Sahrawi youngsters, their Spanish host families, and members of Extremadura's broader Sahrawi community. I also lived with and accompanied my research participants in their routine activities, hanging out with them as well as their host families in formal and informal contexts, ranging from work settings to relaxed chats over tea. Besides studying Arabic together and sharing a house with one of my closest female Sahrawi research participants, we participated in political and cultural events related to the Sahrawi cause.

This chapter is divided into three sections, each of which reflects the mobility trajectories of most of my research participants. I begin by discussing the summer program Holidays in Peace as a cornerstone for transnational mobility routes in childhood and adolescence. I also explore how this summer program contributes to strengthening relations of solidarity and cooperation with the refugee camps. Next, I examine student mobility as an avenue for establishing oneself in Spain, situating the analysis of the SADR's transnational education model (Chatty, Fiddian-Qasmiyeh and Crivello, 2010) within debates on educational policies. This section not only highlights mobility trajectories among protracted refugee populations (Fiddian-Qasmiyeh, 2015, 2020) but also underscores the importance given to education as a life-changing factor (Crivello, 2009; Holland and Yousofi, 2014; Bartlett et al., 2015). Finally, I examine Sahrawi refugee-students' experiences as they transitioned into economic migrants during their stays in Spain, highlighting the dynamics of this period which is marked by migratory desire. In this final section, I also compare current-day trajectories with those undertaken by my research participants' parents and siblings who returned to the camps.

Holidays in Peace Program: Holidays and Transnational Trajectories Among Children

> The first day you don't forget. I was one of the few children who were coming [for] the first summer. . . . Most of my friends [were returning for another] summer . . . [and already] had their [host] family . . . .. I didn't know what was in front of me. . . . Then [the person in charge] calls me [and] says . . . "this is your new family" and the first thing I remember [is that] I turned my back on them and started to cry. . . . On top of that, . . . you don't know how to speak Spanish, you are super lost! But my [host] family helped me a lot because they

understood the situation, I remember they put me in the car and the first thing we did was to shop for clothes and have an ice cream [laughs].

(Bashir, 28 years)

I heard many stories like Bashir's. When talking about Holidays in Peace, all my research participants remembered their "first summer." For most of them, it was the first time they left the refugee camps and their mothers. Stories about their surprise at discovering light switches or learning how to swim in a pool were often recounted with a mix of nostalgia and amusement – for Sahrawis and host families alike. Eventually, I was able to observe the arrival of one group of Sahrawi Holidays in Peace participants in Extremadura. Watching the children arrive, holding hands, some suspicious, others frightened or seeking familiar faces, made me remember Bashir's words. Except for a few cases where my research participants left the camps for health reasons or partook in the Italian Holidays in Peace program, almost all participated in several sessions of the Spanish program. Many of them forged enduring bonds with their host families, having subsequently been fostered by them to continue their studies in Spain after aging out of participation in the program.

***

The program that became known as Holidays in Peace at the beginning of the 21st century has existed since 1976. The program sent Sahrawi children to Algiers during the summer months when temperatures in the Sahara Desert usually exceed 50°C. Since then, Holidays in Peace has operated continuously in different countries (i.e., Denmark, Switzerland, Greece, United States, France, Germany, and Italy), but Spain has remained the main destination. The Spanish Holidays in Peace program is overseen by the Sahrawi Ministry of Youth and Sports, in the refugee camps, and by the Friends of Sahrawi People Associations (*Amigos del Pueblo Saharaui*), in Spain. It is a solidarity program for Sahrawi children between the ages of 8 and 12. Initially, participants were selected based on school grades and family history (e.g., having parents killed in war); however, in recent years, the only condition for participation in the program is age (Bonilla Pérez, 2021). Each year, the number of available slots is determined by how many Spanish families enroll as hosts. The program's main objectives are to enhance children's health conditions by facilitating access to specialized medical care and a more varied diet and to offer a temporary escape from the extreme summer heat in the camps. The program also serves to raise international political awareness about the Sahrawi cause. Additionally, Holidays in Peace has a touristic, recreational dimension, since children go on vacations and participate in leisure activities – something overlooked when discussing exile. According to Sahrawi Holidays in Peace leaders overseeing the program and members of various Spanish associations involved in the process, more than 10,000 children participated in the program annually between 1990 and 2000. From 2007 on, these numbers dropped dramatically, especially during the economic crisis. The year 2018 registered an increase, with approximately 4,000 participants, roughly the same as in 2019. The program has been on hiatus since the advent of the COVID-19 pandemic.

82 Rita Reis

Several anthropologists have hailed the Holidays in Peace as "a unique transnational network of care" (Crivello et al., 2006, p. 30). The protracted exile experienced by Sahrawi refugees has given rise to dynamics that span multiple generations, as illustrated in this program. First, several generations of the same Spanish family have been hosting Sahrawi youth and/or participating in associated activities, including fundraising and political campaigns (Reis, 2020a). Second, several generations of the same Sahrawi family participate in the program at any given time (e.g., siblings and nephews/nieces of my research participants), often staying with the same host families. Such was the case with Mali, a 27-year-old Sahrawi woman who has been living in Spain since her adolescence and, in 2019, facilitated the fostering of her 7-year-old niece by her long-standing host family, just as her older brother had done for her when she was younger. Mali was thrilled by her niece's arrival, but she was not the only one: Mali's older brother traveled from another city to greet the little girl at the airport. I remember observing the two of them, noting how the little girl remained close to her uncle, while the other children hovered near the buses that were to take them to "their" locations.

***

"You'll have one more child in your house, . . . we were told, and it is true," Bea told me when we met. In her 60s, she is an experienced host mum, in charge of a local solidarity association that organizes Holidays in Peace in a small town in Extremadura. Through her, I came to know most of the host families, learning more about their experiences with "their" children. Many families referred to their Sahrawi children as "another son" or "another daughter," establishing family relations and deep emotional bonds (Crivello et al., 2006; Bonilla Pérez, 2021).

These family relationships established through the program nurture a certain kind of solidary tourism to the refugee camps. Especially during Holy Week, many host families travel to the camps to visit "their" child's family. Although the host parents highlight this as the primary reason, many also mentioned the importance of witnessing first-hand the harsh conditions in which Sahrawi refugees live (see Hudgins, 2010), something they would not have done had it not been for this connection with "their" child. Pilar, a Holidays in Peace host mum in her forties, is a good example of this. When we first met, she had never traveled to the camps due to the challenging living conditions: "I don't want to be ungrateful, but I don't know if I can [handle it]." Eventually, she did, telling me upon return how everything had gone very well and that the following year she planned to revisit the camps, and she did. For Pilar, like others, going to the camps allowed her to strengthen her relationship with "her" Sahrawi child through the reciprocity of the visit (Mauss, 2001). Pilar also considered her visits to the camp crucial for raising her awareness of the home situations of the young participants. As she told me, "If it wasn't for the girl, I would never have gone there."

Solidarity is, undoubtedly, an important dimension of host families' flows toward the refugee camps that become tourist destinations (Bloch, 2018; Popović, 2018). Most of the host families that participated in my research were not aware of Western Sahara's conflict before hosting a child. Some of them traveled to the refugee

Sahrawi Student Migration and Exile   **83**

camps after hosting and were received in their child's family's house, giving rise to what Holt (2017) calls "intimate aid." Holt uses this expression to refer to the direct humanitarian relation between Spanish and Sahrawi families. In short, one could argue that beyond comprising a national project for child and youth transnational mobility, Holidays in Peace promotes a close relationship between exile and solidarity tourism, in both children and their host families.

In addition to sparking solidarity tourism, the relationships young Sahrawi participants establish with their host families while participating in the summer program set the stage for longer stays in Spain. As Amal, age 26, recounts:

> My family from here [Spain] had spoken with my family from there [refugee camps], [to] ask them how they would feel if they did the papers [Spanish legal documents] for me so that I could come here [Spain] to study [year-round after aging out of the summer program]. [In Spain, I'd] be able to graduate, since I [would] not have opportunities there . . . at the beginning, they [the biological parents] didn't accept [the proposal] . . . but in the end, they [did].

And as 28-year-old Bashir told me:

> In the third summer, the [host] family invited me to stay, and I did not [want to] . . . I mean, imagine! You don't have the maturity to analyze what they were offering you or to be aware of what that meant, so I told them "No! No way! How am I going to stay here?!" I wanted to be in my camp, with my friends, with my mother, you know? . . . Later, . . . [due to] the insistence of the [host] family and my [biological] mother's persuasion: "it's going to be a good opportunity, you have to take it . . ." . . . [I discovered] she was absolutely right! Right now, I think I've adapted, I am even integrated, and . . . everything is wonderful!

From Summertime to Study Abroad: Transnational Student Mobilities

Leaving the refugee camps to pursue education in Spain is not always easy for Sahrawi youth. Amal's recollections of her arrival illustrate some of these challenges:

> I came with a little fear, sorrow too . . . I had a worse time when I got here [Spain], they took me to a school . . . I didn't speak [Spanish] or understand it well. The truth is that the school helped me a lot, I had great teachers and my classmates were also good and supported me all the time. I remember that at recess I would sit in a chair, away from everyone [laughs], but that was only for a few months.

Due to cooperation between Spanish civil society and the refugee camps, after Amal's years with Holidays in Peace ended, she was fostered by her host family.

84 Rita Reis

This process was essential for her continued studies in Extremadura. Her story illustrates experiences shared by many of my research participants in Spain: Adapting to a new country, school, and a new family's daily routines, all of which are very different from summer routines and conditions back home. Like most families in the camps, Amal's family sent four of their five daughters to Algeria for secondary education, and later to attend universities. Her oldest brother studied in Libya, while the youngest one attended school in the camps. Amal was the only one to go to Spain for secondary education, due to a direct agreement between her biological and host family. From that point in time until she began working in 2018, Amal visited her family every summer.

***

As with Bea (who permanently hosted several Sahrawi children) notes, and as Amal's and Bashir's experiences attest, these "family" bonds created during the summers have the potential to help integrate Sahrawi exiles into the host society through education (Chatty et al., 2010; Gómez Martín, 2016; Reis, 2019). The stories of Amal and Bashir show that often such possibilities are initiated by the host families. Hosting Sahrawi children and adolescents to enable them to pursue their studies during the academic year is a well-established form of cooperation in Spain, currently carried out under the Madrasa Project.[4] Transnational education has become a characteristic of SADR which, since its creation, has been sending its young generations abroad.

For Sahrawi people engaged in nation-making in exile, there is a close relationship between education and war. This is reflected in Bashir's observation that "they say that there is no Sahrawi who does not have a family member killed in the war or a relative who has studied in Cuba." Although very different, both education and war were – and still are – central to the process of nation-building and daily life in the refugee camps. On the one hand, the war mobilized men, leaving the construction of the camps in the hands of women (Caratini, 2006), and allowing their children to travel abroad to fulfill the "duty of a good Sahrawi citizen" (Chatty et al., 2010, p. 38). Children's education rapidly became an important parental goal (Bartlett et al., 2015, p. 1165), personified in mothers. This challenges the popular imagery of refugee camps as stagnation zones (Malkki, 1995; Agier, 2008). In this sense, one could argue that war and education are two "processes by which the nation came to be imagined, and, once imagined, modelled, adapted and transformed" (Anderson, 2006, p. 141) in the context of exile. Additionally, this educational model so prevalent among Sahrawi exiles contrasts with other refugee contexts, where the impossibility of studying outside of refugee camps has "created a 'deadlock situation,'" eliminating or greatly limiting "opportunities to learn through interaction with the outside world" (Oh and van der Strouwe, 2008, p. 595).

War and education formed the cornerstones of Sahrawi society in exile. Beyond building an independent state, the POLISARIO Front led a social revolution (Gimeno Martín, 2007), aimed at weakening the tribal social order (Caro Baroja, 2008). Education was seen as central to this social revolution; it guaranteed a

Sahrawi Student Migration and Exile **85**

population that "could better serve the causes of liberation and nation-building" (Farah, 2010, p. 30): In short, education was seen as essential for developing the (future) independent Western Sahara. For this reason, schools were among the first structures to be built in the camps. National adult literacy campaigns were quickly established to address profound illiteracy (Farah, 2010). Velloso Santisteban and Vinagrero Ávila argue that the Sahrawis were able to "raise an educational system in the desert" (2016, p. 159), with its own curriculum (Farah, 2010) and mandatory attendance (Corbet, 2018). Presently, the education system in the refugee camps comprises kindergarten, primary school, and secondary education (Velloso Santisteban and Vinagrero Ávila, 2016). Despite the existence of two high schools, most students are sent to third countries for high school.[5] By ensuring equal access to education for both boys and girls, SADR broke with the trend of universities as "enclaves of privilege," recognizing "the critical role of higher education in nation-building and peacemaking" (Wright and Plasterer, 2010, p. 43).

Establishing a comprehensive national educational system in the refugee camps posed challenges that ultimately led prompted the SADR to embrace a transnational education model (Chatty et al., 2010) by establishing different protocols. Drawing on bilateral agreements based on the "principles of the Non-Aligned Movement and South-South cooperation"[6] (Fiddian-Qasmiyeh, 2015, p. 60), the SADR secured educational opportunities for its younger population in countries such as Algeria, Libya, Syria, and Cuba.[7] Solidarity partnerships and cooperative protocols with organizations in several European countries (Farah, 2010) enabled additional educational opportunities for Sahrawis. Often this process is deeply connected to Holidays in Peace, as the cases of Amal and Bashir illustrate. Besides its educational component, these cooperative protocols have a political dimension, as they promote support for and strengthening of the Sahrawi cause abroad, as noted earlier.

One characteristic of the Sahrawi camps related to their embryonic state structure is that, despite being entirely dependent on humanitarian aid (Betts et al., 2011), they are not managed by international organizations. Rather, SADR bodies are closely involved in all camp-related activities. Sahrawi refugee camps have frequently been hailed as "ideal" refugee camps, offering examples of good humanitarian practice (Chatty et al., 2010) and "female-friendly" environments (Fiddian-Qasmiyeh, 2014). This has attracted Western funding which, in turn, enables their educational institutions to function more adequately – albeit with difficulties.

Education is similarly entwined with the political projects of other populations living in prolonged exile, such as in the case of Tibetan refugees in India (see Bloch, 2017). Like SADR, the Tibetan Government in Exile has established its own free and universal primary and secondary-level educational system, as well as other types of schools aimed at ensuring the continuity of a Tibetan "displaced culture" in a context where culture "has become a tool of political struggle" (Bloch, 2017, p. 80). In both cases, education is considered a key element in the formation of future generations, given that it is in schools "where the process of nation-building in exile takes place" (Bloch, 2017, p. 81).

86 Rita Reis

The political context that initially motivated these student mobilities is today permeated by other factors. In particular, students' personal desires now play a role in their movements. This is especially visible in the post-graduation aspirations of my research participants and their families. In this sense, even when they are neither moved by the logic of the "global educational hierarchy" (Hansen and Thøgersen, 2015, p. 3) nor explicitly seeking to "take advantage of social and economic opportunities in Western societies" (Olwig et al., 2010, p. 4), the long decades of exile have fostered changes in motivations for study abroad. Whereas in the past student mobilities were embraced on behalf of the nation, with a scheduled return date and the objective of applying the knowledge acquired *in situ*, today these travels are infused with individual perspectives that transcend the educational protocol goals and do not necessarily include permanent returns. Nonetheless, many of my research participants contribute to the development of the camps by implementing projects related to their areas of expertise, especially in the realms of health, education, and women's empowerment.

As I observed during fieldwork, my research participants viewed a permanent return as regressing to the "refugee condition(s)" (Corbet, 2018, p. 342), i.e., life with neither professional opportunities nor economic stability. In a way, one could argue that while education can break cycles of poverty (Crivello, 2009; Bartlett et al., 2015), it simultaneously gives rise to another exile, as Beidid told me: "It breaks my heart being away but I can't come back because I don't have anything to do there . . . no job, nothing!" Holland and Yousofi observed how young Afghans, especially females, pursuing "a better future through higher education" (2014, p. 241), are faced with strong family reactions. This is very different from the Sahrawi context. As Nayat told me: "From a very young age I have had the support of my father to study. He always wanted me to study . . . [and] instilled in us [me and my sisters] that we had to study and be independent women." In sum, Sahrawi student mobilities must be considered as "lived processes of (im)mobility, departure, arrival, emplacement and displacement" (Fiddian-Qasmiyeh, 2015, p. 3), permeated by individual desires, in a period strongly marked by hopes for economic migration (Gómez Martín, 2016; Reis, 2020b).

Coming Back? Student Mobilities Gone Permanent

After drinking a hot beverage on a winter evening, Amal, Beidid, and I walked through Badajoz's downtown. We huddled together as we walked, hoping to protect ourselves from the freezing cold. Amal had just returned to Spain from the refugee camps, after spending one month with her family. "You know, I drove [while I was] there! My father kept asking why I didn't drive here!," she laughed, "it is not like here – I told him!" We started discussing whether we would walk alone after dark in the camps, given how easy it was to get lost. I reminisced: "I used to take the cars' path, otherwise I would get lost." Amal agreed with me: "So did I! And plus, close to my house, there are some dogs . . . that bite!" Beidid also shared with us a frightening experience she had while wandering alone at night, "trust me when I say I fainted!" This small talk reveals how their lives and experiences in the refugee camps were described with a blend of nostalgia.

Although sharing desires to return to the camps, for Amal and Beidid, this was not a valid option at the time, given the lack of employment opportunities and the need to send remittances: As Mali used to tell me frequently, "I have to help them, there are no jobs in the camps." From the biological family's perspective, this was an acceptable reason for not returning. Nevertheless, negotiating the social transition from student to economic migrant on return to the refugee camps is not a linear process. Students' "non-return" upon completion of their studies confounds the objectives of the educational programs, contributes to the emptying of camps, and further exacerbates the lack of highly qualified professionals in the camps, particularly in the health and educational sectors. Their "non-return" differentiates these youth both from members of the prior generation who ultimately returned and from those of their peers who returned (such as their siblings). Their non-return also differentiates them from the elders who remain in the camps. There are other differences, as well. Sabih, a man in his 30s who I interviewed in one of the camps, offered an illustrative story of his siblings:

> We have a problem not found elsewhere in the world, . . . we have an experience, . . . [every] year we have sent our generations out. . . . For example, in my family: we are four, . . . [I studied] in Syria, . . . my brother [spent] fourteen years in Cuba! . . . My sister, seven years in Libya. And the other sister stayed in the camps. I have a [different] culture [life experience], my brother too, my sister [who studied in Libya has a culture of her own] that is different [again]. . . . And we live in the same family. . . . It is the same . . . flower, but it is not the same petal.

Whereas in the past, the differences created by educational experiences were observed upon return to the camps, today some return permanently (mostly those who studied in Algeria) and others do not. Moreover, there are also differences between those who stayed in Spain upon completing their studies and other Sahrawis who arrived there as economic migrants in adulthood. Salma, aged 26, never studied in Spain. After reaching Holidays in Peace's age limit for participation, she returned to the camps, remaining there to care for her grandparents. After their deaths, she moved to Spain as an economic migrant. Salma was the only Sahrawi woman I knew who wore a veil daily. As for the others, they only veiled themselves for specific events related to the Sahrawi cause.

If, in the past, economic migration was difficult to pursue and socially frowned upon, today among the biggest challenges my research participants face is the social pressure of living and working in Spain while maintaining a reputation for adhering to proper gendered norms and behaviors in Spain's Sahrawi community or when visiting the camps. This is particularly true for females. Several authors (Chatty et al., 2010; Fiddian-Qasmiyeh, 2014, 2015) note that returning to the camps after a long period of absence prompts criticism and some degree of rejection, especially for females. My Sahrawi friends were very aware of and concerned about this, especially given the negative connotations associated with living in Spain, which is perceived as (negatively) "Westernized" (Bloch, 2014, p. 150). "I don't know about you, but I'm not the same person here and there!," Beidid told Bashir. Although Bashir admitted paying attention to his behavior and interactional style while back in the camps, he concluded that he put less effort into altering his behavior than Beidid.

Additionally, remaining in Spain is accompanied by feelings of guilt (Jackson, 2008). This guilt centers around being away, failing to return, and having the chance for a better life while one's family remains unable to escape poor living conditions in the camps. Hamdi, who has lived in Spain since he was thirteen years old, was 26 when we met. Speaking about his adaptation, he recounted how he thought about his family constantly:

> We were having a meal and, suddenly, I thought "I'm fine, I'm going to eat but my family can't eat this, I don't know what they're eating now" I was constantly thinking about [my family in the camps] . . . it was as if I was self-ish being very well and knowing that [my] family [was] not.

Mali, who followed a similar mobility trajectory, moved to Spain after several summers of Holidays in Peace, due to a health condition. She finished secondary education there and became an economic migrant. During my research, she was working in a nursing home, something she did not like, but the need to send remittances back home made it necessary. Mali called it "the fucking remorse." She continued by stating that this feeling was always present: When she accomplished something and immediately remembered that "they are there" and did not have access to the same opportunities, as when she turned on the air conditioning in the summer and remembered the extreme heat her family endured in the camps.

Sahrawi youth living in Spain and making annual return visits to the camps reveal important generational gaps when compared to elders. More specifically, these differences can be observed through the changes in the education programs' outcomes and how these young people focus their life projects more on individual rather than collective perspectives. However, as I witnessed during my research, worries concerning how their behaviors were observed, perceived, and questioned – especially, but not only, by the elders – were ever present.

Although refugee student mobility and, later, migration are experiences shared by different generations, the experiences of my Sahrawi friends are quite different from that of their parents and grandparents. Also, their personal expectations regarding their futures are radically different from those of their parents' generation (Koselleck, 2004). Whereas until the 1990s, most Sahrawis who studied abroad returned to the camps and participated *in situ* in nation-building and the struggle for independence, today the return is conceptualized differently and does not necessarily entail permanence. For instance, Nayat, a 29-year-old Sahrawi woman, living in Spain shared her conversation with her husband about the possibility of moving back to the camps. "He told me: 'imagine we go back, we have our *khayma* [tent] and then what?'"

Nayat left the refugee camps at an early age and went to Italy and later to Spain where she acquired most of her education. She married Hassan, who was also Sahrawi and had resided in Spain since a young age. Both are highly skilled and very active in the Sahrawi cause. As Hassan told me after stating that he did not intend to return to the camps, "I contribute more to the cause from Spain." As a prominent lawyer, Hassan helps the Sahrawi community with legal issues and participates (as an international observer) in trials of Sahrawi activists tried in Moroccan courts. Nayat and Hassan represent the new generation of Sahrawis trained in Spain: They met in Spain, married in the refugee camps, established their careers in Spain, and they actively contribute to the cause, without anticipating a definitive return. As Gómez Martín (2016) argues, by developing "inventive strategies," Sahrawi young people can maintain their fight for independence and, at the same time, improve their lives.

The aforementioned lack of viable employment in the camps has led to increased migratory movements especially among males, constituting a new "cycle of movement" (Chatty et al., 2010, p. 77). This was particularly visible in Amal's and Mali's families since the older brothers of both Amal and Mali had moved to Spain as economic migrants (Amal's brother left his wife and children behind in the camps). In cases where men move alone, they economize by sharing households with one another to focus on sending remittances. Up until recently,[8] it was a time of neither war nor peace for the Sahrawi, and this "ambivalent temporality of the 'meanwhile'" (Solana, 2016, p. 84) rendered economic migration a seemingly viable life solution. This also changed the educational programs' outcomes and created additional generational gaps.

Conclusion

> "Don't forget that you're Sahrawi, you're not Spanish," my brother used to tell me every time I came to Spain.
>
> (Amal)

Amal's comment expresses a common theme among my research participants, especially the female ones: Keeping up with the family expectations and behaving "properly" in Spain. Leaving the refugee camps to study and becoming an economic migrant is a negotiated process (Holland and Yousofi, 2014). This process entails balancing between helping family members in the camps, participating in the cause, and maintaining one's Sahrawiness.

Although transnational student mobility programs originated as and remain a "political project of the government in exile" (Bloch, 2017, p. 135), the passing of over four decades has changed those agendas, as well as families' and young people's

90 Rita Reis

expectations. Whereas before, the parental generation that studied abroad returned to the camps and the political cause, today's younger generation participates in the cause differently, from abroad. Through the trajectories of my research participants – representing shared paths for Sahrawi youth – I have shown how these young people's lives are permeated by transnational movements, shaping their life prospects. Beginning with participating in Holidays in Peace, then being fostered by one's host family to study abroad, and ultimately becoming an economic migrant is currently the typical trajectory for Sahrawi exiled youth. Thus, the Sahrawi case enables us to observe the intersection of exile, holidays, educational mobility, and economic migration. Studying abroad and migrating appear as strategies for escaping protracted exile and pursuing a better future (Fiddian-Qasmiyeh, 2015; Hansen and Thøgersen, 2015). However, to understand youths' trajectories from refugee camps to Spain, we must also consider the flows in the opposite direction – the travels of host families to the camps, and the centrality of solidarity tourism in this process. Even though it was not a central theme of this chapter, solidarity tourism has been an important dimension of my research (especially the relation between political commitment and solidarity) and has informed this analysis (Reis, 2020a). Embodied in a nation-building process, the outcomes of Sahrawi student mobilities have become an avenue for personal change (Holland and Yousofi, 2014) and an escape from protracted exile.

Notes

1   A dialect of Arabic spoken in northwest Sahara.
2   A stateless person is not considered as a national by any state. Presently, it is easier to obtain this status than citizenship, and it has become a frequent legal solution for Sahrawis in Spain.
3   This research was financed by the Portuguese Foundation for Science and Technology (SFRH/BD/128517/2017).
4   This collaborative program between SADR and Spanish associations enables teenagers aged 13 years and older to be hosted by families to enable education in Spain. Students stay in Spain during the academic year and return to the refugee camps in the summers. It offers a legal framework for these mobilities, avoiding (future) "custody" problems between host and biological families, as occurred in the past.
5   Additionally, the Sahrawi national education system is supported by a network of vocational education and special training institutes for children with disabilities. Finally, it is worth mentioning the existence of the University of Tifariti's unique project that, in collaboration with several institutions, aims to promote university education in camps, strengthen relationships, and send Sahrawi students to associated universities.
6   South–South cooperation is understood by Fiddian-Qasmiyeh as "encompassing a wide range of initiatives developed by Southern state and non-states [sic] actors in support of individuals, communities, and peoples across the Global South" (2015, p. 11). Moving beyond the dichotomy of North as donor and South as receiver, the South–South cooperation is based on "mutual benefit, solidarity, reciprocity and non-interference in the national sovereignty of other states" (2015, p. 18).
7   Due to political turmoil, protocols with Libya and Syria were suspended.
8   In November 2020, after the Moroccan military's repression of a civilian pacific demonstration in Guerguerat Strip was met with UN silence, the POLISARIO Front broke the 1991-cease-fire agreement and returned to armed struggle.

References

Agier, M. (2008) *On the margins of the world – The refugee experience today*. Cambridge: Polity Press.

Anderson, B. (2006) *Imagined communities: Reflections on the origin and spread of nationalism*. London: Verso.

Bailey, A.J., Wright, R.A., Mountz, A. and Miyares, I.M. (2002) '(Re)producing Salvadoran Transnational Geographies', *Annals of the Association of American Geographers*, 92(1), pp. 125–144.

Bartlett, L., Rodríguez, D. and Oliveira, G. (2015) 'Migration and education: Sociocultural perspectives', *Educação e Pesquisa*, 41, pp. 1153–1170.

Betts, A., Loescher, G. and Milner, J. (2011) *The United Nations High Commissioner for Refugees (UNHCR): The politics and practice of refugee protection*. London and New York: Routledge.

Bloch, N. (2014) 'Constructing borders within Diaspora "born refugees", newcomers and bargaining Tibetan identity', in Posern-Zieliński, A. and Mróz, L. (eds) *Middle grounds, ambiguous frontiers and intercultural spaces*. Poznań: Instytut im. Oskara Kolberga, pp. 135–154.

Bloch, N. (2017) 'Beyond integration. Tibetan Diaspora's separation strategy in multicultural India', in Posern-Zieliński, A. (ed.) *The world of encounters. The role of migration and ethnicity in the contemporary world*. Poznań: Instytut im. Oskara Kolberga, pp. 75–95.

Bloch, N. (2018) 'Making a community embedded in mobility – Refugees, migrants, and tourists in Dharamshala (India)', *Transfers*, 8(3), pp. 36–54.

Bonilla Pérez, N. (2021) 'Children's rights promotion in Sahrawi refugee camps: A study on the vacaciones en paz programme from a child rights-based approach', *Schriftenreihe Junges Afrikazentrum (JAZ)*, 11, pp. 1–53.

Caratini, S. (2006) 'La prisión del tiempo: los cambios sociales en los campamentos de refugiados saharauís', *Cuadernos Bakeaz*, 77, pp. 1–16.

Carling, J. and Collins, F. (2018) 'Aspiration, desire and drivers of migration', *Journal of Ethnic and Migration Studies*, 44(6), pp. 909–926.

Caro Baroja, J. (2008) *Estudios saharianos*. Madrid: Catarata.

Chatty, D., Fiddian-Qasmiyeh, E. and Crivello, G. (2010) 'Identity with/out territory: Sahrawi refugee in transnational space', in Chatty, D. (ed.) *Deterritorialized Youth – Sahrawi and afghan refugees at the margins of the Middle East*. New York: Berghahn Books (Studies in Forced Migration, 29), pp. 37–84.

Corbet, A. (2018) 'Au-delà de l'exil: mobilités des étudiants sahraouis et impacts de leur retour dans les camps', in Boulay, S. and Correale, F. (eds) *Sahara occidental – conflit oublié, population en mouvement*. Tours: Presses universitaires François-Rebelais, pp. 337–352.

Crivello, G. (2009) '"Becoming somebody": Youth transitions through education and migrations – evidence from Young Lives, Peru', *Young Lives – An International Study of Childhood Poverty, Working Paper*, 43, pp. 1–27.

Crivello, G., Fiddian, E. and Chatty, D. (2006) 'Mobility and the care of Sahrawi refugee youth', *Anthropology News*, 47(5), pp. 29–30.

Farah, R. (2010) '"Knowledge in the service of the cause": Education and the Sahrawi struggle for self-determination', *Refuge: Canada's Journal on Refugees*, 27(2), pp. 30–41.

Fiddian-Qasmiyeh, E. (2012) 'Invisible refugees and/or overlapping refugee Dom? Protecting Sahrawis and Palestinians displaced by the 2011 Libyan uprising', *International Journal of Refugee Law*, 24(2), pp. 263–293.

Fiddian-Qasmiyeh, E. (2014) *The ideal refugees: Gender, Islam, and the Sahrawi politics of survival*. Syracuse, NY: Syracuse University Press.

Fiddian-Qasmiyeh, E. (2015) *South-South educational migration, humanitarianism and development – views from the Caribbean, North Africa and the Middle East*. London: Routledge.

Fiddian-Qasmiyeh, E. (2020) 'Introduction – Refugee in a moving world: Refugee and migrant journeys across disciplines', in Fiddian-Qasmiyeh, E. (ed.) *Refuge in a moving world – Tracing refugee and migrant journeys across disciplines*. London: UCL Press, pp. 1–19.

Gimeno Martín, J.C. (2007) *Transformaciones socioculturales de un proyecto revolucionario: la lucha del pueblo saharaui por la liberación*. Caracas: Caracas, Programa Cultura, Comunicación y Transformaciones Sociales, CIPOST, FaCES, Universidad Central de Venezuela.

Gómez Martín, C. (2016) 'De exilios a migraciones económicas. La movilidad espacial de los saharauis como parte del "ingenio aguzado de la supervivencia"', in Barreñada, I. and Ojeda, R. (eds) *Sahara Occidental 40 años después*. Madrid: Catarata, pp. 105–116.

Hansen, A.S. and Thogersen, S. (2015) 'The anthropology of Chinese transnational educational migration', *Journal of Current Chinese Affairs*, 44(3), pp. 3–14. doi:10.1177/186810261504400301.

Holland, D.G. and Yousofi, M.H. (2014) 'The only solution: Education, youth, and social change in Afghanistan', *Anthropology & Education Quarterly*, 45(3), pp. 241–259.

Holt, B. (2017) *Western Sahara, Sahrawi Arab democratic republic: Protracted Sahrawi displacement and camping*. Abidjan: CreateSpace Independent Publishing Platform.

Hudgins, K. (2010) 'Student development tourism: A growing trend to what end?', *Anthropology News*, 51(8), pp. 29–29.

Jackson, M. (2008) 'The shock of the new: On migrant imaginaries and critical transitions', *Ethnos: Journal of Anthropology*, 73(1), pp. 57–72.

Koselleck, R. (2004) *Futures past – On the semantics of historical time*. New York: Columbia University Press.

Malkki, L.H. (1995) *Purity and exile: Violence, memory, and national cosmology among Hutu refugees in Tanzania*. Chicago, IL: Chicago University Press.

Mauss, M. (2001) *Ensaio sobre a Dádiva* (Edições 70). Lisbon: Edições 70 (Perspectivas do Homem).

Milner, J. (2016) 'Protracted refugee situations', in Fiddian-Qasmiyeh, E. et al. (eds) *The Oxford handbook of refugee & forced migration studies*. Oxford: Oxford University Press, pp. 151–162.

Oh, S.A. and van der Strouwe, M. (2008) 'Education, diversity and inclusion refugee camps in Thailand', *Comparative Education Review*, 52(4), pp. 589–617.

Olwig, K.F., Valentin, K. and Dalgas, K.M. (2010) *Research project education, mobility and citizenship*. Århus: Danish School of Education – Århus University and Department of Anthropology – University of Copenhagen, pp. 1–14.

Popović, M. (2018) *Tourism in contested regions: A typology of tourists visiting the refugee camps of Western Sahara*. MSc Dissertation. Ljubljana: University of Ljubljana.

Reis, R. (2019) 'Mobilities from the Exile: the Sahrawi student migrations', in Rafik Khalil, R.M. and Malit, F.T. (eds) *Recent migrations and refugees in the MENA region*. London: Transnational Press London, pp. 65–80.

Reis, R. (2020a) 'Vacaciones en Paz: los refugiados saharauis entre el activismo político y la solidariedad española', in Schuster, P.K. and Valenzuela-Moreno, K.A. (eds) *Trayectorias y Jornadas: Transnacionalismo en Acción*. London: Transnational Press London.

Reis, R. (2020b) 'Sahrawi student mobilities: exile routes among young refugees', *Cahiers de L'Ouest saharien*, 12, pp. 55–74.

San Martín, P. (2010) *Western Sahara – The refugee nation*. Cardiff: University of Wales Press.

Schielke, S. (2009) 'Ambivalent commitments: Troubles of morality, religiosity and aspiration among young Egyptians', *Journal of Religion in Africa*, 39(2), pp. 158–185.

Solana, V. (2016) '"No somos costosas, somos valiosas." La lucha de las Mujeres Saharauis Cuarenta Años Después', in Barreñada, I. and Ojeda, R. (eds) *Sahara Occidental 40 Años Después*. 1a. Madrid: Catarata, pp. 81–91.

Velloso Santisteban, A. and Vinagrero Ávila, J.A. (2016) *Educación en Palestina, Sáhara Occidental, Iraq, Guinea Ecuatorial y para refugiados.* Madrid: UNED – Universidad Nacional de Educación a Distancia.

Wilson, A. (2017) 'Ambivalences of mobility: Rival state authorities and mobile strategies in a Saharan conflict', *American Ethnologist*, 44(1), pp. 77–90.

Wright, L.A. and Plasterer, R. (2010) 'Beyond basic education: Exploring opportunities for higher learning in Kenyan refugee camps', *Refuge*, 27(2), pp. 42–56.

5

THE INTERSECTIONS BETWEEN TOURISM AND EXILE

Justice Tourism in Bethlehem, Palestine

Rami K. Isaac

Introduction

> International tourists are genuinely conceived [of] as an opportunity for residents and refugees to tell their stories and have their stories known outside of Palestine. Tourists were expected to go back home and communicate, on their terms. These tourists were not only regarded as witnesses but also as participants in the realization of a new, hopeful, and bright future.
>
> (Rami Kassis, Director of Alternative Tourism Group, interview, January 15, 2020, Beitsahour)

In this chapter, I offer a case study of justice tourism in Bethlehem, Palestine, to illustrate how this form of travel embodies intersecting forms of mobility. I argue that Palestinian refugeehood has become a "tourist attraction" and examine how tourism to refugee-related sites in Bethlehem aims at building empathy and solidarities between two mobile subjects – international tourists and Palestinian refugees. Bethlehem is an international religious destination and tourism is the main source of income for locals, especially in the form of pilgrimages (Çakmak and Isaac, 2012; Isaac, 2021). However, due to the ongoing conflict between Israel and Palestine, new forms of tourism are gaining ground in Palestine. Increasingly, tourists are drawn to Palestinian refugees: They arrive hoping to tour the refugee camps, visit Bethlehem's Segregation Wall, and view Banksy's Walled Off Hotel. Bethlehem thus showcases the intersection between tourism (as well as a pilgrimage) and exile, as it encompasses various overlapping forms of travel, all colored by politics.

As Natalia Bloch and Kathleen M. Adams noted in the introduction to this volume, "while scholars have traditionally researched and theorized tourism, migration, and exile separately, social reality blurs these seemingly fixed categorical boundaries." Accordingly, this chapter explores the dynamics that transpire when

DOI: 10.4324/9781003182689-6

refugees are the "tourist attraction" and maps out the motivations and experiences of tourists visiting the aforementioned Bethlehem sites. I also discuss justice tourism's potential for creating empathy and solidarities between international tourists and Palestinian refugees.

Recent tourism research has seen growing interest in the connection between tourism and justice (Higgins-Desbiolles, 2008; Isaac and Hodge, 2011; Guia, 2021). Some of this consideration has focused on mainstream tourism outcomes and how justice can be augmented (Jamal and Higham, 2021). Other research has centered on alternative tourism outcomes, where increased commodification has greatly limited justice benefits (Guia, 2021). Less explored, however, is how justice tourism intersects with other forms of mobility (Bloch, 2021). Justice tourism is broadly conceptualized as a type of deliberate travel oriented toward supporting social, political, and environmental sustainability. Justice tourism aims to address contemporary tourism inequities by mapping a footpath to a more equitable world order. As Regina Scheyvens (2002) observes, justice tourism is a type of tourism that develops solidarity, mutual recognition, and equity between "guests" and "hosts" while also providing local communities with economic, social, and cultural benefits and supporting self-determination. Scheyvens (2002, pp. 105–119) delineates five forms of justice tourism. These include the "hosts" recounting their stories of past (or current) oppression, tourists learning about poverty issues, visitors engaging in voluntary conservation work, vacationers doing voluntary development work, and revolutionary tourism. In contrast to Scheyvens, Freya Higgins-Desbiolles (2009), as well as Rami K. Isaac and Darlene Hodge (2011), shares a narrower conceptualization of justice tourism as involving visiting places where people are currently experiencing injustice and human rights violations. For these authors, justice tourism should contribute to fundamental transformations of the contemporary global order, as suggested in this chapter concerning Palestine.

In this case, justice tours take visitors through Bethlehem neighborhoods and adjacent Jewish settlements as well as Palestinian refugee camps (such as Deheisha refugee camp) to illustrate Israel's alleged injustices toward Palestinians (Isaac, 2010, p. 31). These tours also visit Palestinian political and religious institutions, some of which Israeli authorities have shut down over the years. In both Bethlehem and the Deheisha refugee camp, Palestinian families host the tourists and recount their suffering under Israeli occupation. These visiting tourists want to witness political history, oppression, and hardships with "their own eyes" (see Adams, 2001). Tourists' motivations and experiences in refugee sites are important to examine, as tourists' perspectives in conflict-ridden destinations such as Palestine have been relatively neglected by researchers.[1] Furthermore, this study highlights the importance of qualitative research for empathy-building. As Adams states, such approaches have "tremendous potential . . . for engendering empathy, an important but sometimes under-emphasized aspect of critical tourism studies" (Adams, 2021, p. 698).

96 Rami K. Isaac

Context of the Study

Bethlehem is a city located in Palestine's central West Bank, approximately 10 km south of the city of Jerusalem. As the capital of the Bethlehem Governate, which covers 660 km[2], Bethlehem includes 10 municipalities and three refugee camps[2] (UN OCHA, 2010). Since the early 20th century, Palestine's political circumstances have changed dramatically, most notably with the 1948 creation of Israel and the 1967 war, when Israel occupied the West Bank and the Gaza Strip (Morris, 2004; Weizman, 2007; Halper, 2008). These events have had lasting repercussions for Palestinians, most of whom became refugees (Morris, 2004).

Today, many Palestinians live in camps in Jordan, Lebanon, and Syria and within the West Bank and the Gaza Strip (Morris, 2004). The refugee camps are the result of the 1948 uprooting of Palestinian villages during the first Arab–Israeli war and the subsequent Six-Day War in 1967 (Carter, 2006). In Bethlehem, there are three refugee camps: Aida Camp, with an estimated refugee population of 3,150; Al-Deheisha Camp, with a population of 15,000; and Al'Aza Camp (or Beit Jibrin), the smallest camp on the West Bank with approximately 1,800 residents. The Palestinians residing in these camps cannot return to their homes, because Israel has denied Palestinians rights of return (Hazboun, 1992; Masalha, 2003).

In November 2000, the Israeli prime minister approved a plan to build a Segregation Wall between the northern and central regions of the West Bank, which was later extended to the southern region (Applied Research Institute, 2005, p. 20). Construction started in June 2002. In most areas, the wall consists of an electric fence aligned with dirt paths, barbed wire, and trenches, with a general width of 60 m. In some sections, the wall is 68 m high. Once completed, it will be 771 km long and approximately 6–8 m high (Applied Research Institute, 2005, p. 20). The entire wall is built on Palestinian territory, resulting in further confiscation of land. The United Nations International Court of Justice voted in 2004 that the wall breaches international law and ordered its dismantling (Gelbman and Keinan, 2007). Not surprisingly, both the wall and the refugee camps have become destinations for justice tourism.

Methodology

This research entailed both qualitative and quantitative methods, including word frequency count and content analysis of online reviews posted by tourists who joined alternative tours in Bethlehem. Holsti (1969, p. 14) gives us "a broad definition of content analysis as, 'any technique for making inferences by objectively and systematically identifying specified characteristics of messages'" (Thurlow, 2007, p. 67). A word frequency count complements the content analysis. Combining those methods provides a good overview of the primary emphases of the reviews.

The most popular Google site for Bethlehem tourism reviews is Tripadvisor, the world's biggest travel platform that largely comprises travelers' destination, accommodation, and attraction reviews. There are plenty of alternative tours offered in

Bethlehem, including those whose itineraries include visits to the Segregation Wall and the refugee camps, so I opted to focus on reviews of those alternative tours. These were identified via google searches within the alternative tour reviews for "alternative Bethlehem," "refugee camp," "Segregation Wall," or "Separation Wall."

I selected only those reviews containing at least one full sentence for analysis, ruling out single-word reviews (such as "great," etc.) as they were too brief to provide research insights. I analyzed reviews in all languages since Tripadvisor automatically translates reviews into English. Yet, although automatic translation technologies have immensely improved, they remain imprecise. Therefore, I scrutinized translated reviews and disqualified incomprehensible reviews. There were no reviews available before 2005 because the tourism industry was hard hit by the second Intifada (Çakmak and Isaac, 2012); therefore, only reviews posted after that time were considered. More specifically, I looked at the reviews posted between 2005 and 2014, as this research study was conducted in 2014. In total, 513 reviews were selected for analysis. The program NVivo was used for the word frequency count, while Taguette was used for the content analysis. I was able to trace the traveler's national origin for 325 out of the 513 reviews (63.4%). The vast majority (28.9%) of reviews analyzed were authored by individuals from the United States, followed by England (10.8%), Germany (7.7%), Canada (4%), and the Netherlands (4%). The frequencies of the other countries were too small to be taken into consideration.

I also took several (justice/political) tours in and around Bethlehem. I joined six guided tours organized by the Alternative Tourism Group (ATG), engaging in participant observation as we walked to sites such as military roadblocks and checkpoints at the entrance to Bethlehem, during visits to the Aida Refugee Camp, and while being hosted by Palestinian families in Bethlehem. Recently, in February 2020, I accompanied a group of 18 German tourists who visited the Segregation Wall to understand their reactions to and experiences during the tour. I focused my participant observation and my conversations with tourists on how the guide leveraged his/her narrative and how the alternative tour company presented the culture, history, and politics of Palestine and its complex relationship with Israel.

What Transpires on a Justice Tour of Bethlehem?

Our 2020 tour of the wall, led by a tour guide from ATG in Bethlehem, lasted for 4 hours. The tour started at the entrance to Bethlehem, where we looked at the massive Segregation Wall and adjacent checkpoint Gilo 300. There, the guide shared the history of Bethlehem. He focused on the Rachel's Tomb area (Kubit Rahil in Arabic) that was once a lively, economic hub of Bethlehem. Rachel's Tomb had been one of Bethlehem's heritage sites for centuries, due to its historical significance. For this particular justice tour, this site was significant because of its location in a contested zone of occupied Palestine, dominated by the Segregation Wall (see Isaac and Platenkamp, 2016; Selwyn, 2010). There, the guide continued his storytelling about the wall's construction and its socioeconomic impacts on the inhabitants of Bethlehem. From the Rachel's Tomb area, the tour group walked along the wall where we stopped at several shuttered souvenir shops and restaurants that had completely closed down due to the building of the wall and the departure of the majority of the areas' inhabitants. As one of the German tourists in his mid-30s stated, "I appreciated the thorough explanation of the history surrounding Rachel's Tomb area and the current political situation, it helped to provide an important perspective of the lives of those living in proximity to the Wall."

Later we stopped at Claire Anastas's family home. The home was slated to be surrounded by the wall on three sides. The annexation forced most families to leave the neighborhood, but some of them, such as the Anastas family, could not afford to leave and thus remained. Claire's extended family moved into their three-story home in 2000 before the Segregation Wall was constructed in this area. Claire opened a home goods shop and her husband John, a mechanic, operated a workshop on the ground floor. They made a comfortable living in this once-busy and affluent tourism neighborhood of Bethlehem. But with the wall's construction, Claire Anastas's family was forced to close their businesses and is now struggling with huge debts. The tourists were overwhelmed by the physical experience as every window of the house faced the wall. Tourists had an opportunity for extended discussions with Claire Anastas, regarding her family situation.[3] They also talked to the owners of local restaurants and other residents in the area to understand the wall's impacts on their businesses. When a tourist asked one of the restaurant owners how businesses was before the wall, he replied:

> We used to receive groups of tourists almost every day for lunchtime, but now we barely receive any tourists as a result of the wall. All tourists go through the checkpoint and immediately move to visit the Nativity Church and do not stop here. No tourists like to have lunch facing the Segregation Wall.

Here is how one of the German tourists I accompanied, a political science student in her mid-20s, described her experience:

> I wanted to convince myself about [sic] the inhuman way of separating people who have been friends. I was interested to see the wall and refugee camps, I heard about it on TV and read about it in the newspapers. We discuss this issue with our friends, it is one of the themes that interest me. Moreover, once you see the wall, you can understand more about what is happening here.

This visitor's comments parallel motivations expressed by another German tourist I interviewed:

> [I joined the tour] to witness the disaster of the apartheid wall in Palestine and Israel's violations of human rights and humiliation, in order to feel and

Intersections Between Tourism and Exile **99**

understand the physical situation of the Palestinians' suffering. Furthermore, over the years I had plenty of discussions, disputes, and debates about the wall with friends in Palestine, so logically I visited the wall.

On one of my visits to the wall and the refugee camps in Bethlehem, a guide working for ATG shared his reflections with me concerning his feelings about the tour. As he stated, "Silence feels for many tourists [sic] the only apposite response when the scale of the experience exceeds narration of the desperate situation of Palestinians living near to [sic] the wall." He further explained that ATG chose to create tailor-made, unconventional tourist packages, including classical religious tours as well as interpretive tours and homestays. These were to serve the basic requirements of "normal" tourists visiting Palestine. What makes them unique and critical for counter-discourse, however, is the narrative. It is the narrative that enables these tours to potentially serve as powerful tools for re-articulating places, identities, and people in Palestine. Visitors are introduced to Palestinian people's daily struggles and various structures of occupation, including the wall, the refugee camps, and the checkpoints restricting Palestinians' movements.

Many tourists appeared to respond emotionally to these narratives and images. As one of the German tourists on our tour, a woman in her mid-50s, admitted,

> I felt sad and frustrated, [sic] the feeling of being nothing and not being able to do anything against this terrible system. I developed a lot of empathy towards [sic] the Palestinian people because of my experience of living in Berlin before 1989 when the city was divided by the Berlin Wall.

Another German retired tourist from the same group commented, "I was impressed how the people who are not allowed to pass the border do [sic] cope with it." As these comments and others suggest, in the context of Palestine, justice tourism is a form of tourism that allows travelers to encounter the "truth" of Israeli oppression and Palestinian suffering (Isaac and Hodge, 2011). In other words, justice tourism in Bethlehem aims at building empathy and solidarities between two mobile subjects – tourists and Palestinian refugees.

Tourists' Encounters With Refugees

The following section discusses the tours offered to tourists, as well as the role of the guides, both of which played a significant part in the online reviews.

Table 5.1 illustrates the most frequent words used by tourists in their online reviews, most of which were positive and were generally linked to the commentary about the tour itself and specific tour guides. The words "tours," "Bethlehem," "great/good/amazing," and "Palestine" were mentioned most often. Visitors were very enthusiastic about the tour and the sites they visited, including the stories they heard about their guide's life and the people they spoke to during the tour, such as refugee camp residents. These included refugees' stories of flight from home and

TABLE 5.1 Most frequently used words

Words	Frequency	Words	Frequency
Tours	956	Life	131
Bethlehem	621	Local	127
Great/good/amazing	410	Friends	122
Palestine	406	Refugee	114
Guiding	318	Politics	113
Recommend	244	Jerusalem	108
History	244	Learn	102
Knowledgeable	199	Thank	98
Experiences	191	Understanding	89
Wall	189	Banksy	87
Interesting	176	Personal	78
Israel	166	Perspective	76
Camp	144	Story	75
People	142	Conflict	72

hopes to return someday. These visitor accounts are evocative of the life stories I heard from my guide when I took one such tour in 2020. Most guides tell their own life story and share details about their upbringing and educational background. On the 2020 tour, I took, our guide told us how he had worked in Israel as a tiler until 1991 when the checkpoints and closures began. The closures emerged from a "pass system" which required that every Palestinian obtain a permit to enter Israel for work, effectively curtailing Palestinians' right to free movement. Our guide also revealed that he was a political activist and had spent six years in an Israeli prison due to his political activities. Ultimately, he told us he felt he had wasted most of his life under occupation and explained that he was searching for alternative work. Among the most promising jobs in Bethlehem are those in tourism. Therefore, he enrolled in a training program offered by the Ministry of Tourism and Antiquities for tour guides and ultimately passed the exam. Accordingly, he ended up in the tourism industry as a guide.

As revealed in the online reviews, tourists recommended such tours to others because of the personal encounters with locals and the unconventional sites visited – their reviews emphasized that these tours were different from the general tours offered to tourists. The authors of the reviews found their experiences "interesting," noting that they learned about the situation in Bethlehem, the complex political conflict, the history behind it, and how people were living under occupation within the walls that excluded them from the rest of the world.

Reviewers' online comments conveyed that they appreciated that they could see local daily life and could talk to people about their perspectives, everyday struggles, and political conflict. Many tourists left feeling like they had made new friends during the tour – with tour guides or residents of the refugee camps. As one of the reviewers stated, "I started out as a stranger, and I left as a friend." Another reviewer wrote, "After the tour, I made friends with a local tour guide living at the refugee

Intersections Between Tourism and Exile **101**

camp. Not only do I want to recommend tours to others, but also, I want to specifically recommend the tour guide Abood."

Beyond the sites visited during the tours, the guides played a significant part in tourists' online feedback. Tourists comment not only on the guides' personal stories of their refugee experiences but also on the stories of the people living in the refugee camps and tourists' feelings while there. For instance, one male American reviewer described the Bethlehem refugee camp tour as "deeply moving and sad." The most frequently mentioned negative emotions were sadness and somberness. Participants found it sad to see how people lived in the refugee camps and how they were forced to live under occupation. Although none of the reviews mentioned specific stories recounted during the tours, many comments suggested that hearing stories of refugee life made the tour an "emotional experience." One reviewer, a 38-year-old German, commented:

> He [the tour guide] gave us a comprehensive history of the camp, as well as the Palestinian plight, [and], described what it is like to live in the camp under such outrageous conditions. [He] explained the state of current affairs of the camp, and then shared with us his personal and tragic family's [sic] story.

Another reviewer, a Dutch male, commented on his tour guide's story: "As the story unfolded, we were drawn in . . . we listened to Salah's story with bated breath." While the tourist did not share Salah's story in his review, one of the guides I knew working at the ATG in Bethlehem told me how Salah organizes his tours:

> He [Salah] takes visitors to the "disturbing places" such as the Segregation Wall at the entrance to Bethlehem. He first tells them the story of the wall's erection and the consequences of the wall to the residents' livelihoods. Then he explains that at [sic] twelve years earlier, people were living at that exact spot, with shops and restaurants, and [that it] used to be one of the commercial hubs in Bethlehem, but now it is a complete ghost area. Tourists . . . usually remain silent to [sic] reflect on the incredible force of this wall.

One of the concepts appearing in the frequency table pertains to the "experience" of the tours. As one reviewer wrote, "It is sad how a land and people are separated in this way." Another reviewer noted, "Walking in the refugee camps in Bethlehem deeply shocked me, and embarrassed me, it made me sad about the Israeli crime against humanity, imprisoning the people of Palestine systematically, and the Segregation Wall is one climax of the [sic] Israeli politics." Yet another reviewer commented, "I didn't feel good because it is not [a] good situation and not good for the people who live there, I felt sad and depressed afterward for such [sic] situation. I felt sadness filling my heart and helplessness that I am not able to really [sic] help."

Guiding and recommendations of specific guides were frequent themes in the reviews. As one 40-year-old American reviewer stated, "Salah gives you a good

102 Rami K. Isaac

insight into what daily life in Bethlehem looks like and is experienced for [sic] the city's inhabitants, from the refugee camps, the consequences of the wall, and the settlements." Another reviewer, a 47-year-old German man, noted, "Our tour was conducted by a resident of the camp, who provided an in-depth look and explanation about the history of the camp through the present day."

Tourists' Responses to Banksy's Solidarity Art in Bethlehem

Most of the online reviews I analyzed expressed admiration for the graffiti on the wall, particularly the artwork created by Banksy, the popular English street artist. His identity remains unknown. Banksy is perhaps the most famous contemporary street artist alive today. His work often depicts controversial political images. Banksy visited Palestine several times, especially Bethlehem, where he produced various artworks on the West Bank Segregation Wall and other places. His thought-provoking art – addressing political and social issues – was his way of showing his solidarity with the Palestinian people. In 2006, he wrote, "Palestine is now the world's largest open-air prison and the ultimate activity holiday destination for graffiti artists" (Banksy, 2006, p. 136). In 2007, the artist organized an exhibition in Bethlehem to draw attention to Palestinian poverty and the impacts of the Segregation Wall. Additionally, Banksy financed the construction of the Walled Off Hotel in Bethlehem, which is a hotel, museum, and art gallery exhibiting his work (Davis, 2018). This endeavor contributed significantly to drawing visitors and boosting the Palestinian economy (Khader, 2019, p. 140). The hotel entrance is widely identifiable thanks to Banksy's artistic depiction of a chimpanzee dressed as a hotel porter. The museum is filled with political artworks by Banksy and other artists. For instance, one piece by Banksy represents Lord Balfour, sitting behind his wooden desk preparing to sign the declaration that resulted in the establishment of a Jewish homeland in Palestine and the expulsion of Palestinians from their homes, resulting in a global Palestinian diaspora.

The Walled Off Hotel has eight rooms and hosts tourists whose stays average one or two nights. Every room is decorated with works that simultaneously depict oppression and hope. In addition, every window in the hotel faces the Segregation Wall. The hotel also features an interactive tour. For example, visitors can pick up a phone in the entrance hall and hear a voice saying, "This is the Israeli officer giving [sic] you five minutes to evacuate your house; the Israeli forces will bomb your home." The museum aims to do more than simply display art: A video offers historical facts about the conflict. Most of the German tourists I accompanied were impressed by the Banksy Museum in the Walled Off Hotel. As one tourist told me, "It provides a great [sic] help to understand the situation from a Palestinian perspective." Tourists also commented on the graffiti on the wall facing the hotel, viewing them as artworks that told real stories about daily lives and the suffering of Palestinians. As one Dutch male reviewer noted, "I consider these graffiti as pieces of art that told real stories about the daily lives and suffering of Palestinians, but

Intersections Between Tourism and Exile **103**

also about the conflict between Palestine and Israel." Moreover, the tourists liked that some graffiti portrayed the situation humorously and admired that it shifted from simply depicting the ugly reality to enabling new ways of expressing the sad feelings surrounding the wall.

Many reviewers considered their overall experience at the Banksy Walled-Off Hotel as "interesting." They saw their time there as an opportunity to educate themselves on the cultural, historical, and political context of Palestinian lives in Bethlehem. As one female German reviewer stated, "I learned the messier and painful sides of the story." Although the German group, which I interviewed, came to see Banksy's art, they also encountered the stories behind it. The reviews posted by tourists suggested that they gained a deeper understanding of the Palestinian struggle, the Israeli settlements, and how they affect the lives of Palestinians under occupation. This was also reflected in my interview with a retired female German tourist who visited the Banksy Walled-Off Hotel. As she told me, "The art of Banksy in the hotel is mostly based around [sic] political and societal issues, making it thought-provoking. It provides clear stories of the daily struggle of the Palestinian people under this brutal occupation." Another female German tourist stated:

> It is a must-see place in Palestine, you can't only visit the Nativity and other religious places, and not visiting [sic] the wall, and the Walled-Off Hotel. It is as if you didn't visit Palestine. And when you visit Israel, you have to go to Yad Vashem, which is the museum and memorial to the victims of the Holocaust. One needs to always see and remember what people can do to other people, and I always recommend visiting both these places to my friends.

Tourists' Responses to the Segregation Wall and Refugee Camp

This section focuses on the responses and experiences of tourists who visited the Segregation Wall in Bethlehem and the refugee camps. Most respondents had negative responses to the wall and the Palestinian suffering caused by it. A female German tourist in her mid-50s stated,

> I visited the wall to see the injustice in the world in general, to feel it. As Germans we are related to Israel, we want to protect Israel but we don't want Palestinians to suffer either. So, one can't build a wall and let the others suffer, one should learn from the [sic] history.

This respondent conveys feelings of guilt due to the persecution of Jews during World War II and arguably before. She supports the state of Israel, but not at the cost of Palestinians' suffering. Another tourist referred to the history of the Berlin Wall:

We, as Germans, had a wall, and being in Palestine one must definitely visit the wall and see it and must know about the situation in Palestine. I was born in Berlin and there was the Berlin Wall. And as a child, I always saw it as we used to live not far from it. Therefore, I was confronted with the wall during my childhood, so once I visited Palestine, I said, "I must see the wall." I hope that this wall will be destroyed in the end, one should not lose hope.

Another popular political tour organized by the ATG in collaboration with the Israeli tour operator Olive Trees is the "One Day Tour." The tour includes a visit to the Segregation Wall and one of the refugee camps. In the camp, the local guide invites refugees to talk about their life and the history of their exile. Most of these stories refer to the 1948 war. As one of the refugees in the camp recalled,

Zionist militias attacked us in Western Jerusalem and killed many people without any reason. Many Palestinian cities and villages were destroyed. More than 750,000 were expelled from their homes, and we have become refugees waiting to go back home.

He also added that the 1948 events should not be erased from collective memory: "Israel does its best to silence us, banning us from talking about the *Nakba*[4] in schools so the younger generations will not know what happened."

During the tour, the tourists were also tutored in the symbolism of a giant "Key of Return" at the entrance to the Aida Camp. The 9-m-long key symbolizes Palestinian refugees' right of return, as guaranteed by UN Resolution 194. One of the reviewers, a male from the Netherlands, commented,

I didn't know about the refugee camps or how many of them are in Bethlehem. I visited my Palestinian friends, and they took me to Aida camp . . . it was a very thought-provoking experience. Especially the key at the entrance of [sic] the camp and [the] explanations we had there. This is a reality that no one can ignore. People have to go back home, and this key symbolizes their right of return.

And, as another reviewer stated, "These Palestinians used to live in what is now called Israel and are not allowed to go back to their homes. All refugees have the right to go back home." As these quotes illustrate, the tours evoked political and emotional responses from tourists.

Tourists' Motivation and Experiences at the Refugee Camps

My analysis of 513 reviews of alternative tours in Bethlehem posted on Trip Advisor has enabled me to identify tourists' motivations and experiences. Listed in the following are themes that emerged in these reviews.

Tree 1: motivations

Nodes:

- Learning/education (211)
- Different perspectives (168)
- See everyday life with their own eyes (142)
- Understanding (85)

Tree 2: experiences

Nodes

- Positive experience (amazing/excellent/great, etc.) (198)
- Authentic/real experience (53)
- Unforgettable/memorable experience (46)
- Eye-opening (41)
- A highlight of the trip (35)
- Mixed feelings (23)

Tree 1: Motivations

Tourists' varied motivations are often interconnected. Content analysis revealed that tour participants' main motivation was "learning/education." However, what the tourists learned differed, and this is why some other nodes from the tree "motivation" are connected to "seeing everyday life."[5]

Politically oriented tourists[6] visit Jerusalem to show their support for one or the other of the two primary groups in conflict in the city, while other tourists "are more politically neutral . . . [they] are just curious to learn more . . . [about] the conflict and how it manifests itself in Jerusalem" (Brin, 2006, p. 215). ATG offers tourists an opportunity to stay a couple of nights at one of the refugee camps, which helps refugees economically. As a refugee who hosted tourists at his home in the camp noted, "tourism connects Palestine and Palestinian refugees to the outside world, giving voice to the Palestinians who otherwise are silenced by the state of Israel." Bloch (2021) made similar observations regarding Tibetan refugees in India and their attempts to employ tourists as allies in the diaspora's political struggle for international recognition and self-determination.

As noted earlier, an important tourist motivation is to learn about and witness Bethlehem's history. However, participants on the alternative tours are not only hoping to learn about Bethlehem's religious sites but also aspiring to better understand the political conflict that caused Palestinians' refugeehood. The alternative tours bring these stories to light.[7] As a 30-year-old American reviewer stated,

> We saw the refugee camps and talked about the tenuous relationship between Israel and Palestine. I HIGHLY encourage any traveler in Israel to visit

Bethlehem and meet Abood to learn another part of the story in this complicated "relationship," seeing the settlements, Separation wall, refugee camp, and art as a form of protest will surely open your mind and world view.

Another female British student's review noted, "Salah's political tour through Bethlehem is one you will never forget, as it will educate you about the entire historical, cultural, and political context of the Israeli-Palestinian conflict and the consequent situation Palestinians find themselves in."

The second most frequently noted motivation that propelled tourists to visit these Bethlehem sites was to learn or educate themselves about different perspectives. Many European and North American tourists believe that the mainstream news offers them access to only one side of the story, which favors the Israelis. As one female Jewish-American tourist commented, "Being raised in a Zionist family and hearing the Israeli narrative most of my life, it was important to me to hear the Palestinian narrative." Another middle-aged American female tourist from Washington DC wrote:

> Salah's tour was exceptionally informative and provided a different point of view than the U.S. media often gives us. He took his time during the tour, we never felt rushed, and his English is superb. We were a small group so the tour felt very intimate and personal, and I can honestly say I left Palestine/ Israel with a completely different perspective.

Likewise, a 42-year-old tourist from Great Britain made a similar comment:

> If you want to know the facts about the Palestinian-Israeli conflict first-hand, see the refugee camps and a different side to Bethlehem, hear the personal stories, and also facts about the city's ancient history, you should definitely go on this tour and meet him [Abood, the guide]. I had a really great time and I understand things so much better now.

And a 47-year-old Canadian male commented:

> He [the recommended guide] does not glorify Palestinian conduct, or Israel's. In 6–8 hours, you will see a part of Israel that was not designed for you to see. But you cannot possibly understand this place without a visit to the West Bank. This is the best way to make that visit. Do not hesitate.

Tree 2: Experience

The second tree focuses on the tour participants' experiences and reveals how tourists felt after the tour. Most striking is that most of the tourists who visited refugee camps and the Segregation Wall found it a positive experience. As one reviewer summed up, "this tour provided us with great experiences, interesting places to visit, and a very good guide, Abood." Similarly, another reviewer, a female from Germany wrote: "It was an amazing and insightful experience about a country that is struggling for its identity and land."

Moreover, the participants felt that they gained insights into the "real" and "authentic" Bethlehem (13.34% out of 513 reviews). As a male reviewer from the United States stated:

> This tour is unique as it shows you the real Palestine – it is very different from what is shown in western media. You will see the real neighbourhoods and Michael explains the history of how they came to be. He showed me a side of Palestine and the attractions it has to offer that are not provided by other tour companies or in any guidebook. His explanations are thorough and unbiased.

Likewise, tourists considered their experience as "eye-opening." Fairday, a male from the Netherlands, observed, "Seeing the refugee camps and having the chance to speak to the locals through Rami really opened my eyes and my heart to the Israeli-Palestinian conflict." Similarly, Anne, a 52-year-old from Canada noted, "At the end of a very interesting and eye-opening day, we left him [their guide] at the border crossing with a better grasp of the challenges lying ahead for his people."

These first-hand experiences made their visits unforgettable, something that will stay with them forever. As Noor observed, "Salah's political tour through Bethlehem is one you will never forget, as it will educate you on the entire historical, cultural and political context of the Israeli Palestinian conflict and the consequent situation Palestinians find themselves in." Likewise, another female reviewer from the Netherlands, Rose J., stated "In addition to driving and guiding us, Michael provided historical context and insight along the way. I not only enjoyed the tour but also learned a lot from Michael that day, taking home memories that will stay with me forever."

Often the tours were booked at the last minute or even accidentally. The participants happened to encounter the guide by chance and were invited to join the tour. For many, visiting the refugee camp turned out to be "the highlight" of their trip. As Marcel, a 49-year-old tourist from the Netherlands, summed up, "Visiting a refugee camp at the Separation Wall was definitely the highlight of the tour." And a female American tourist stated, "We met Abood [the guide] by accident and had one of our best days in Israel."

Finally, many tourists mentioned experiencing a range of emotions, both positive and negative. Krisnelvik, a 48-year-old male from the Netherlands wrote, "I recommend Alternative Tourism Group to everybody interested in cultural, political, and human issues, it was fun, interesting, and heartbreaking at the same time." And Jessica, a 32-year-old from the Netherlands reflected, "To end our day, Abood took us to Aida Refugee camp and the different locations of Banksy Art including the Separation Wall across the Walled Off Hotel. I must admit I felt both sad and hopeful about the Palestinian plight." These findings are in line with

108 Rami K. Isaac

Gila Oren et al.'s (2021) study, which demonstrates that negative emotions can contribute to an overall positive tourist experience since the main motivation of the tourists they studies was not fun and recreation but rather to gain knowledge about the situation in situ. Similarly, the tourists' primary motivation for the selection of these Bethlehem tours was to educate themselves about the situation there, especially the political conflict.[8]

Conclusion

Justice tourism is important for Palestine since it shows tourists the injustice and human rights violations occurring there. Justice tourism can be defined not by tourists' experience, but by their responses to the experience (Isaac and Hodge, 2011). It might well be that these self-selecting tourists were naturally inclined to be persuaded toward supporting the Palestinian cause or were already sympathetic, but even so, changed attitudes were observed in a prior study (Isaac and Hodge, 2011, p. 107). Moreover, these alternative tour operators hope that tourists will return home and communicate the refugees' stories of Israel's alleged injustice so that these stories become known outside Palestine. These refugee aspirations vis-à-vis tourists call to mind Bloch's case study which demonstrated that Tibetan refugees in Dharamshala "achieve their collective goals through the skillful use of tourist attraction status" (Bloch, 2021, p. 23). Here tours expose tourists to injustice as framed and perceived by oppressed groups – among them, refugees – in the hope that tourists will become "advocates of justice causes" (Kassis, 2006). ATG, therefore, creates space for encounters with the refugees living in refugee camps. As Kassis et al. (2016, p. 49) observe of tourism in Palestine, "the conviction is that only then will tourism realize its potential for both travelers and visited."

This chapter explored the intersection of two forms of mobility in Bethlehem, namely, tourism and exile, by analyzing tourists' experiences visiting the Segregation Wall and Palestinian refugee camps. Justice tourism in Bethlehem thus brings together tourists and refugees, enabling refugee voices to be heard. For local alternative tourism agencies such as ATG, tourism is a means for those living in exile to connect to the outside world and build solidarity networks. Tourists visiting Bethlehem are tutored so that they can "become holders of the knowledge that will one day lead to equity, democracy and human rights for all" (Kassis, 2006). Richard Clarke's observations about political tours carried out in the West Bank town of Hebron are apt here:

> These tours differ from classical models of propaganda and ideology in that they are based on practice. Groups of people are led around the city, to be exposed to "the reality" of the situation. They are encouraged to imagine what it must be like to live there, to appreciate the proximity of the other side, and to take these experiences home with them to tell others.
>
> *(Clark, 2000, p. 18)*

Palestinians are finding it hard to have their voices heard, and intensive efforts are needed to ensure that Palestinian voices are heard in tourism. Palestinian refugeehood has become a tourist attraction and this form of tourism aims at building empathy and solidarities between two mobile subjects – international tourists and Palestinian refugees. The relationship between Palestine, Israel, and tourism is inherently political. Ultimately, this chapter has demonstrated how justice tourism and tours provided at refugee camps – places of encounter between tourists and exiles – can make fundamental contributions toward empathy building.

Notes

1 Some exceptions include Adams (2001), Buda (2012), Lisle (2016), and Isaac and Platenkamp (2016).
2 These Palestinian refugees are dependent on the United Nations Relief and Works Agency for Palestine Refugees in the Near East (UNRWA). This relief and human development organization, established in 1948, operates in all three refugee camps.
3 This case was previously discussed in Isaac and Platenkamp (2016).
4 Nakba, otherwise known as the Palestinian Catastrophe, refers to the destruction of Palestinian society and the Palestinian homeland in 1948 and the permanent displacement of most Palestinian Arabs.
5 The motivation of "seeing everyday life" aligns with research conducted by Boyd (2000), Brin (2006), and Isaac and Eid (2019). It includes both private and organized group excursions to sites related to the Israeli–Palestinian conflict.
6 Eric Brin (2006) uses the expression "politically-oriented tourists" in his work on politics and tourism in Jerusalem.
7 Most tourists visit Palestine despite the conflict since their main motivation is pilgrimage or visiting religious sites in Bethlehem (Çakmak and Isaac, 2012; Isaac, 2010; Shepherd et al., 2020).
8 For similar findings, see Farmaki (2013), and Isaac and Çakmak (2016).

References

Adams, K. (2001) 'Danger zone tourism: Potentials and problematics for tourism in tumultuous times' in Teo, P. Chong, H.K and Chang, T.C. (eds.) *Interconnected worlds: Southeast Asia tourism in the 21st Century*. Cambridge: Pergamon Press, pp. 267–281.
Adams, K. (2021) 'What western tourism concepts obscure: Intersections of migration and tourism in Indonesia', *Tourism Geographies*, 23(4), pp. 678–703.
Applied Research Institute (2005) *The Israeli assault on Bethlehem triangle*. Jerusalem: Applied Research Institute.
Banksy (2006) *Wall and piece*. London: Century.
Bloch, N. (2021) *Encounters across difference. Tourism and overcoming subalternity in India*. Boulder, New York and London: Lexington.
Boyd, S.W. (2000) 'Heritage tourism in Northern Ireland: Opportunity under peace', *Current Issues in Tourism*, 3(2), pp. 150–174.
Brin, E. (2006) 'Politically-oriented tourism in Jerusalem', *Tourist Studies*, 6(3), pp. 215–243.
Buda, M.D. (2012) 'Hospitality, peace and conflict: "Doing fieldwork" in Palestine', *The Journal of Tourism and Peace Research*, 2(2), pp. 50–61.
Çakmak, E. and Isaac, R.K. (2012) 'What destination marketers can learn from their visitors' blogs: An image analysis of Bethlehem, Palestine', *Journal of Destination Marketing and Management*, 1, pp. 124–133.

Carter, J. (2006) *Palestine: Peace not apartheid*. London: Simon & Schuster.

Clarke, R. (2000) 'Self-presentation in a contested city: Palestinian and Israeli political tourism in Hebron', *Anthropology Today*, 16(5), pp. 61–85.

Davis, T. (2018) Welcome to the walled off: A visit to Banksy's hotel in Bethlehem. *The Jerusalem Post*. Available at: www.jpost.com/jerusalem-report/welcome-to-the-Walled-off-a-visit-to-banksys-hotel-in-bethlehem-544463.

Farmaki, A. (2013) 'Dark tourism revisited: A supply/demand conceptualization', *International Journal of Culture, Tourism and Hospitality Research*, 7(3) pp. 281–292.

Gelbman, A. and Keinan, O. (2007) 'National and transnational borderlanders' attitude towards the security fence between Israel and the Palestinian Authority', *Geo Journal*, 86(4), pp. 279–291.

Guia, J. (2021) 'Conceptualizing justice tourism and the promise of posthumanism', *Journal of Sustainable Tourism*, 29 (2–3), pp. 503–520.

Halper, J. (2008) *An Israeli in Palestine: Resisting dispossession, redeeming Israel*. London: Pluto Press.

Hazboun, S. (1992) 'A socioeconomic study of the Beit-Jibrin refugee camp, Bethlehem', *Journal of Arab Affairs*, 11(1), pp. 54–66.

Higgins-Desbiolles, F. (2008) 'Justice tourism and alternative globalization', *Journal of Sustainable Tourism*, 16(3), pp. 345–364.

Higgins-Desbiolles, F. (2009) 'International solidarity movement: A case study in volunteer tourism for justice', *Annals of Leisure Research*, 12(3–4), pp. 333–339.

Holsti, O.R. (1969) *Content analysis for the social sciences and humanities*. Reading, WI: Addison-Wesley.

Isaac, R.K. (2010) 'Alternative tourism: New forms of tourism in Bethlehem for the Palestinian tourism industry', *Current Issues in Tourism*, 13(1), pp. 21–36.

Isaac, R.K. (2021) 'Pilgrimage tourism to Palestine: The 'come and see' initiative in Palestine' in Darius, L. (ed) *Pilgrims: Values and identities*. Wallingford: CABI Publishing, pp. 188–201.

Isaac, R.K. and Abu Eid, T. (2019) 'Tourists' destination image: An exploratory study of alternative tourism in Palestine', *Current Issues in Tourism*, 22(12), pp. 1499–1522.

Isaac, R.K. and Çakmak, E. (2016) 'Understanding the motivations and emotions of visitors at Tuol Sleng genocide prison museum (S-21) in Phnom Penh, Cambodia', *International Journal of Tourism Cities*, 2(3), pp. 232–247.

Isaac, R.K. and Hodge, D. (2011) 'An exploratory study: Justice tourism in controversial areas. The case of Palestine', *Tourism Planning & Development*, 8(1), pp. 101–108.

Isaac, R.K. and Platenkamp, V. (2016) 'Concrete u(dys)topia in Bethlehem: A city of two tales', *Journal of Tourism and Cultural Change*, 14(2), pp. 150–166.

Jamal, T. and Higham, J. (2021) 'Justice and ethics: Towards a new platform for tourism and sustainability', *Journal of Sustainable Tourism*, 29(2–3), pp. 143–157.

Kassis, R. (2006) *'The Palestinians and justice tourism: Another tourism is possible'*. Available at: http://atg.ps/study-center/articles.

Kassis, R., Solomon, R. and Higgins-Desbiolles, F. (2016) 'Solidarity tourism in Palestine: The alternative tourism group of Palestine as a catalysing instrument of resistance' in Isaac, R.K., Hall, C.M. and Higgins-Desbiolles, F. (eds) *The politics and power of tourism in Palestine*. London: Routledge, pp. 37–52.

Khader, J. (2019) 'Dystopian dark tourism, fan subculture and the ongoing *Nakba* in Banksy's Walled-Off heterotopia' in Isaac, R.K., Çakmak, E. and Butler, R. (eds.) *Tourism and hospitality in conflict-ridden destinations*. New York: Routledge, pp. 137–152.

Lisle, D. (2016) *Holidays in the danger zone: Entanglements of war and tourism*. Minneapolis, MN: University of Minnesota Press.

Masalha, N. (2003) *The politics of denial: Israel and the Palestinian refugee problem.* London: Pluto Press.

Morris, B. (2004) *The birth of the Palestinian refugee problem revisited.* Cambridge: Cambridge University Press.

Oren, G., Shani, A. and Poria, Y. (2021) 'Dialectical emotions in a dark heritage site: A study at the Auschwitz death camp', *Tourism Management*, 82. https://doi.org/10.1016/j.tourman.2020.104239.

Scheyvens, R. (2002) *Tourism for development: Empowering communities.* London: Pearson.

Selwyn, T. (2010) 'Ghettoizing matriarch and a city: An everyday story from the Palestinian/Israeli borderlands', *Journal of Borderlands Studies*, 24(1), pp. 39–55.

Shepherd, J., Laven, D. and Shamma, L. (2020) 'Autoethnographic journeys through contested spaces', *Annals of Tourism Research*, 84. https://doi.org/10.1016/j.annals.2020.103004.

Thurlow, JDB (2007) *Why are some learners more successful than others in the completion of an ABET course? – A case study at a publishing company. Research report submitted as part of the requirements of a master's degree in education.* School of Education Faculty of Humanities University of the Witwatersrand. Available at: https://wiredspace.wits.ac.za/bitstream/handle/10539/4771/JThurlow-8704642G-MEd-ResearchReport.pdf?cv=1&isAllowed=y&sequence=1

United Nations Office for the Coordination of Humanitarian Affairs (UNOCHA) (2010) 'Shrinking space: Urban contraction and rural fragmentation in the Bethlehem Governorate', *UNOCHA Survey Report.* Available at: www.un.org/unispal/document/auto-insert-203128/.

Weizman, E. (2007) *Hollow land: Israel's architecture of occupation.* London: Verso.

6

CRAFTING ACTIVISTS FROM TOURISTS

Volunteer Engagement During the "Refugee Crisis" in Serbia

Robert Rydzewski

Introduction

In 2015 and 2016, Serbia witnessed not only an unprecedented number of asylum seekers but also an unprecedented influx of pro-refugee volunteers from the Global North. In their itinerant volunteerism or activism, as some term it (Cantat, 2020, p. 107), they resembled tourists; they moved freely across the Balkan state borders, enjoying the advantages of their privileged passports and a surplus of time and mobility, and became active at asylum seekers' stopover and immobilization spots. These mostly (but not exclusively) young people spontaneously formed self-organized groups to support asylum seekers from the Global South whose movement toward Western Europe was often perceived as undesirable and thus restricted (Bloch, 2020, p. 223). In this exceptional period, described as "the long summer of migration" (Kasparek and Speer, 2015), reception or transit centers (or simply refugee camps) in the Balkan Peninsula became the axes of two highly mobile groups. These intersecting mobilities produced not only structural and hierarchical stratifications (Tesfahuney, 1998, p. 501) but also new forms of political action and solidarity.

Researchers have studied volunteers' involvement in various humanitarian and natural crises (e.g., Dass-Brailsford et al., 2011; Helsloot and Ruitenberg, 2004; Whittaker et al., 2015), and European scholars have become increasingly interested in civil society's response to the so-called "refugee crisis[1]" along the Balkan route. Many have analyzed it from the perspective of grassroots activist groups supporting asylum seekers (Koca, 2016; Sandri, 2017). Although not novel (see Cantat, 2016; Sandri, 2017), volunteer involvement in recent refugee crises constitutes a significant evolution in scale and quality when compared to that of former times. Researchers on the Greek island of Lesbos, for example, noticed that the first to help asylum seekers arriving on the shores were the residents of the coastal villages

DOI: 10.4324/9781003182689-7

(Afouxenidis et al., 2017; see also Papataxiarchis, 2016). Further research has suggested that volunteer groups in Greece, by supporting people on the move, established new social spaces for asylum-seeker protection that filled institutional gaps (Chtouris and Miller, 2017).

Volunteers' motivations – self-fulfillment and an impulse to do good (Chtouris and Miller, 2017, p. 70) – resemble volunteer tourism, which is often described in terms of "making a difference" in the lives of those from the Global South (e.g., Vrasti, 2013). But it is also a practice that enables the acquisition of professional skills and experience and contributes to self-growth – a subject broadly discussed in studies of voluntourism (e.g., Sin, 2009). Thus, it is primarily beneficial to the volunteers themselves. Scholars such as Erik Cohen (1979, p. 182) define tourism as traveling beyond the boundaries of one's everyday life space during time off from professional duties and suggest "there is some experience available 'out there', which cannot be found within the life space, and which makes travel worthwhile" (1979, p. 182). Furthermore, volunteer tourism, which addresses those travelers partaking in development and humanitarian projects, is part of the "moralization of tourism" (Butcher, 2003). According to Butcher, disillusionment with contemporary societies motivates travelers to infuse leisure practices with deeper meaning by joining projects that replenish the natural environment or "traditional" cultures and simultaneously foster a sense of personal accomplishment (2003, p. 16–22). Such an approach to the activities of "episodical volunteers" (Handy et al., 2006) enables us to put in dialogue literature on migration, activism, and tourism. It is also promising for investigating the interrelations between leisure time, work, and new forms of social and political activism that emphasize the volunteer's self-actualization.

However, scholars of volunteerism/activism and tourism/voluntourism differ in their emphases, perhaps reflecting their geographical orientations. While volunteer tourism researchers mostly analyze young privileged middle-class white subjects in the Global South (e.g., Adams, 2001; Bloch, 2011; Vrasti, 2013), the scholars addressing activists supporting asylum seekers (Theodossopoulos, 2016; Kallius et al., 2016; Simsa, 2017) primarily focus on European Union (EU) countries. Serbia, a country that lies within the geographical boundaries of continental Europe but not within the EU is the bottleneck for entry into the EU and often escapes scholarly attention.

In this chapter, I highlight the blurred boundaries between tourism, activism, and asylum seeking and illuminate the points of entanglement between white privileged subjects from the Global North supporting asylum seekers from the Global South. In particular, I examine volunteers' and asylum seekers' intersecting mobilities along the Balkan route to spotlight how these encounters foster novel avenues for solidarity and political activism. I address the following key questions: (1) What are the points of intersection between the volunteers and asylum seekers and how did they change in the course of the refugee crisis and its aftermath? (2) What are the social and personal conditions for the geographically mobile volunteer? (3) What are the similarities and differences between the movement of volunteers,

114 Robert Rydzewski

tourists, and refugees? (4) How do volunteers interact with the refugees and how does this interaction influence the solidarity movement?

Generally, scholars approach the phenomenon of new volunteer groups helping asylum seekers (which emerged in 2015 in Europe) from the perspective of volunteer humanitarianism or horizontal solidarity movements. These are generally self-organized groups without previous experience in refugee protection that are motivated by humanitarian reasoning (Sandri, 2017, p. 2). These groups do not have permanent structures, collectively determined goals, or mechanisms of political influence (Cantat, 2016; Koca, 2016; Chtouris and Miller, 2017). On the other hand, scholars of tourism and voluntourism in the Global South highlight egocentric and individualistic orientations, which can be driven by the need for adrenaline (Adams, 2001), authenticity (Bruner, 2005), or the neoliberal rationalization that drives young people to seek aid programs credentials and experience necessary for employment (Vrasti, 2013, p. 22). My approach to volunteerism in Serbia aligns with research on volunteerism. I characterize volunteering as an unpaid activity that (1) reflects individual moral choice, one's biography, and global circumstances (like privatization and 'NGOization' of aid and development programs), while (2) offering possibilities for self-realization, personal and professional fulfillment (Choudry and Kapoor, 2013). Volunteers operating along the Balkan route have an affinity with volunteer tourism which also provides reciprocally beneficial relations with receiver aid. But, as opposed to volunteers, volunteer tourists usually pay tourist operators to participate in formalized NGO projects (Mostafanezhad, 2014, p. 11; Mostafanezhad, 2016, p. 15).

I suggest that self-development was a key factor in volunteers' decision-making processes about whether or not to engage during the "refugee crisis" in Serbia. Sensibilities about self-development impacted the volunteers' personal motivations, how they organized themselves, as well as their geographical mobility which intersected with the mobility of asylum seekers. Consequently, volunteers became involved in asylum seeker protection only when they saw it as an opportunity for self-realization. Thus, volunteering combines leisure, tourism, and professional aspirations. Over time, however, the primary motivations for volunteering often changed, and volunteers became activists on behalf of asylum seekers in their own countries, thereby simultaneously pursuing self-actualization and social justice. Volunteering became a bridge between individual needs and collective responsibility.

Field Sites and Methodology

My analysis is based on data collected between October 2015 and October 2016[2] while working in two grassroots organizations supporting asylum seekers in two border zones. Both organizations were primarily composed of short-term volunteers from the Global North. I started my research with Border Free Association, which operated in the reception center in Preševo, a town in southern Serbia on the border with North Macedonia and Kosovo. My second research location was Subotica and its surroundings, on the Serbian–Hungarian border, where a grassroots group called Fresh Response operated from June 2015 until the last months of 2016. In contrast to Border Free Association, this group deployed mobile activists along the border as well as in asylum seekers' unofficial settlements and transit centers. Occasionally, I also visited different transit centers elsewhere in Serbia and North Macedonia. My ethnographic fieldwork was grounded in activist research, which entails acquiring theoretical knowledge through action (Hale, 2006; Goldstein, 2014; Sandri, 2017). As Charles Hale (2006, p. 87) explains, this method advocates positioning oneself within the political alignment of the organized group, which in this case entailed assisting asylum seekers. My research data were derived from participant observation and consisted of living and working with volunteers, taking fieldnotes on my observations, and conducting unstructured interviews with both asylum seekers and activists. Additionally, I interviewed local community members and representatives of transnational NGOs to contextualize volunteers' work.

Since I was involved in volunteer operations, I should explain my motivations. I came to North Macedonia to do fieldwork for my PhD project on the transitions of post-Yugoslav cities. After three months in the field, plagued by troubles related to legalizing my stay, I chose to move to Preševo due to that city's complex ethnic relations and interesting political transition. From June 2015 to March 2016, Preševo was a transit zone, with asylum seeker arrivals fluctuating between 100 and 1,200 per day. Observing these exhausted people, sleeping on the street with little or no assistance (at the time) while awaiting travel permits, I became inspired to join one of the grassroots movements assisting[3] asylum seekers and to eventually carry out research in the reception center.

From Summer 2015 until late winter 2016, the clandestine Balkan route was temporarily opened, becoming a quasi-legal corridor into the EU. For those with money and resources, it was a viable entryway into the EU. Asylum seekers were obliged to stop at one of the reception centers in Serbia to secure a 72-hour permit to cross the country (Beznec et al., 2016; Cantat, 2020; Rydzewski, 2020a). These Balkan Peninsula camps were, in fact, EU extra-territorial confinement spaces created during its asymmetrical negotiations with candidate countries (Mitrović, 2014). The Preševo reception center soon became Serbia's largest, most developed government facility, with a capacity of over 600 people and a total staff of 150–200.[4] It was also home to dozens of local and international NGOs, as well as grassroots groups that supported asylum seekers. There were several other refugee camps scattered around the country, which created points of entanglement between asylum seekers from the Global South arriving *en masse* and volunteers from the Global North who engaged (in a very flexible manner) in the former's protection.

Volunteer Response on the Balkan Route

Lesley Hustinx and Frans Lammertyn (2003) describe the classic "modern" volunteer organization structure as entailing hierarchical divisions of labor and strong, clearly defined figures of authority. Such organizations distinguish between members

116 Robert Rydzewski

and non-members, are highly structured, and provide rewards for long-term membership and dedication to the organization's values and goals. In contrast, volunteer organizations in post-industrial societies are characterized by informality, decentralized initiatives, and autonomy from external oversight. Their members have project-oriented objectives and are attracted by personal interests and preferences rather than organizational targets. Volunteers' self-oriented courses of action override subordination to the organization's collective goals, resulting in loose, temporary involvement in the organization's structure and activities (Hustinx and Lammertyn, 2003, p. 175). As my ethnography illustrates, new flexible forms of social engagement satisfy volunteers' travel desires and offer face-to-face intercultural encounters, as well as the joy and fulfillment associated with doing meaningful work that benefits others.

The grassroots groups operating on the Western Balkan route were diverse in nationality and work style. Initially, their presence and actions were spontaneous. Members of the self-organized groups arrived in their own cars, packed with food, clothes, tents, and raincoats, and distributed these supplies at different sites, following asylum seekers and adjusting to the constantly changing situation. Their operations were coordinated by weak and ephemeral groups or *ad hoc* established associations that communicated with each other via online platforms.

As the number of arriving volunteers grew over time, volunteers began to coordinate their actions with other aid organizations, enhancing their effectiveness and enabling them legalized stays in Serbia. For example, once foreign volunteers operating adjacent to Border Free Association became more formalized, they were allowed to erect tents in front of the official camp and attend meetings hosted by the camp authorities.[5] In this messy "grey space" (Yiftachel, 2009, p. 243) – between the institutionalized camp space and that of the host territory – at the edge of formality and informality, the volunteers benefited from their proximity to the institutionalized camp.

The formalized Balkan corridor created during the long summer of migration enabled approximately one million asylum seekers to cross the Balkan states and reach the EU with relative safety. However, by the end of 2015, the gates to the EU began closing and by early 2016, only asylum seekers from war-torn countries such as Syria, Afghanistan, Iraq, and Eritrea were permitted to travel through the Balkan corridor. The established reception and transit centers along the corridor began to serve not only as places of sanctuary and care for those seeking protection but also as places of confinement and as instruments for racial and ethnic segregation (Beznec et al., 2016, p. 16; Martin et al., 2020, p. 749; Mitrović and Vilenica, 2019, p. 11). In November 2015, following Austrian recommendations, the Preševo center authorities introduced segregation of "genuine refugees" and "economic migrants."[6] Only the former were allowed into the center. "Economic migrants," in contrast, stayed in the volunteer-operated tents or avoided Preševo altogether. Particularly in early 2016, Serbia's selective and imprecise transit center admission policy left many people on the move without assistance. This gap was filled by local and foreign volunteers operating in the informal spaces beyond the central authorities' jurisdiction.

Points of Intersection

Volunteers and asylum seekers followed each other and responded to each other's needs. Volunteers moved across the Balkan Peninsula, speedily adjusting to local environments, and cooperating with different organizations to provide support to asylum seekers wherever their paths crossed, be it in bus and train stations, unofficial settlements, or official refugee camps. Asylum seekers' high mobility within the Balkan Peninsula and volunteers' independence from formal organizations, financial autonomy, and operational flexibility created various points of intersection where these two groups met and interacted.

In the summer of 2015, in the northern part of the country, various independent volunteers operated on both sides of the Serbian–Hungarian border and in the area around Subotica. Their work was temporary, chaotic, and highly unstructured. When Hungary sealed its southern border in September 2015 with a 175-km border barrier, the flow of asylum seekers turned toward Šid on the Serbian–Croatian border, and the volunteers piled into their cars and pursued them. Several weeks later, some volunteers moved to Preševo, where the new reception center was just opening. In the spring of 2016, when unofficial refugee settlements started reappearing around Subotica in northern Serbia, the grassroots groups returned there, but this time they were better organized. A 19-year-old German volunteer Olga, whom I met in Preševo, explained how and why she changed her location:

> I was here another time, five weeks ago. Then my motivation was that I had free time before my university started. Back then, a friend of mine worked in Opatovac[7] on the Croatian-Serbian border. There were enough volunteers, and we heard about Preševo. We heard that the situation there was tense. So, six of us came down in two cars. Yeah, we had a look around and we started trying to help.

To improve the effectiveness of their work and to adjust to asylum seekers' constantly changing locations, the volunteers moved to different parts of the country and cooperated with various local humanitarian actors. For example, members of Subotica's *ad hoc* Fresh Response initiative previously worked in various refugee camps, unofficial settlements, or transit and reception centers in Idomeni (Greece), Preševo (Serbia), Opatovac and Slavonski Brod (Croatia), or even in Libya and collaborated with formal and informal groups. To do so, they often had to overcome various ideological differences. For instance, the secular group Fresh Response decided to work with the Christian organization Eastern European Outreach, a group experienced in supporting socially disadvantaged people in northern Serbia.

Volunteers' lack of institutional affiliation and non-compliance with national laws and local social norms allowed them to reach asylum seekers in unofficial settlements, bus and train stations, and on the routes. A good example was a group of volunteers from Stuttgart (Germany) that wanted to set up a field kitchen

118 Robert Rydzewski

immediately adjacent to the North Macedonian–Serbian border posts. One of the volunteers, a male in his twenties, told me about how the group came to Preševo:

> There was a guy who called up people and bought the cooking machine [field kitchen]. We collected clothes and other things and we just came here, and we wanted to cook for refugees, share food and tea . . . But we face problems; they [the police] don't want to permit us to cook, we need to register as volunteers. It all depends on people here and what they think of us, and what they want. If they are open-minded or want only money. If we do not cook here, we will go somewhere else.

Central to this group of volunteers' challenges were the sanitary requirements they had to fulfill in order to operate as food distributors at the border. No one could explain why the officials sought to fulfill the sanitary conditions right at the border and ignored them 15 km away from the reception camp. But most important was the volunteers' readiness to relocate to another place in Serbia or beyond if they felt their work in the current location was senseless. Significantly, the volunteers could react to shifting situations more rapidly than international NGOs and transnational agencies. This was the case with the onset of heavy rainfalls in the autumn of 2015, when volunteers handed out raincoats bought in local shops, while the UNHCR could only offer water-absorbing blankets.

In the summer and autumn of 2015, when the Balkan corridor borders were still open, the Preševo camp and its surroundings were in utter chaos. People lined up on the main street, sometimes for as long as two days, to register themselves as asylum seekers. Exhausted by the journey, they slept on the street with little to no assistance. Garbage was scattered everywhere, the two portable toilets were overloaded, and the street was becoming a sewage drain. Used clothes, emergency reflective blankets, and other waste covered the entire neighborhood, contributing to the suffocating smell of decomposing garbage and excrement. In this period, volunteers and asylum seeker interactions mostly transpired during short meetings and addressed basic needs such as providing medical attention, baby care, food, and other materials. But, as German volunteer Olga explained, when there was time and space, they also tried to provide emotional support:

> If there is nothing important to do, we will just talk to people in the line, because I have a feeling that a lot of refugees must carry so much emotional stuff. So, we ask them how they feel, where they are from, and it seems that telling us their stories helps them.

Olga's comments illustrate that for volunteers, it was important to connect and share stories. Céline Cantat, who researched local solidarity movements supporting asylum seekers in Belgrade (Serbia), argues that this sort of volunteers' approach represents "opposition to the Serbian government and to a top-down mode of relating to people on the move" and builds alternative modes of asylum seeker support (Cantat, 2020, p. 108). Furthermore, the visibility of human pain and struggles also motivated volunteers to stay and try to offer relief. Providing hot tea and blankets to asylum seekers queuing outdoors, distributing clothes to those camping, and protesting at the Greek–North Macedonian or the Serbian–Hungarian border gave them a feeling that they were doing something meaningful.

However, when asylum seekers' suffering became less visible, cloaked behind gray UNHCR tents when the Balkan corridor was closed in March 2016, young volunteers concluded that their stay in Preševo had become senseless. They soon decided to travel to Idomeni in Greece, where a new unofficial refugee camp was emerging. As two Swiss tourists in their late 20s explained, they'd been traveling in Southeast Asia and upon learning of the asylum seekers' situation in the Balkans, they decided to detour to Preševo in Serbia. However, when they saw that the situation there was not as grave as they had imagined, they assumed their help was not needed and decided to travel to Idomeni. The compulsion to do something meaningful can produce restless activists, i.e., volunteers who quickly detach themselves from a particular location or organization and move onward to new destinations.

The closure of the Balkan corridor with the Turkish–EU agreement of March 2016 altered asylum seekers' movements: Their journey northward was forcefully stopped, but their movement within Balkan states intensified. Asylum seekers traveled from south to north and again to the south or in any other direction. This chaotic movement was punctuated by stopovers in refugee camps, unofficial refugee settlements, and bus and train stations, but it enabled asylum seekers to regain some agency and rekindled hopes that they could eventually reach the EU (Rydzewski, 2020a). Official and unofficial camps transformed from transit hubs to places obliged to accommodate hundreds of people for lengthy, yet undefined periods. The living conditions in unofficial settlements and most state-run camps were unbearable. Asylum seekers experienced extreme poverty, frigid temperatures, and health care negligence.

The closure of the Balkan corridor and the hyper-mobility of asylum seekers also impacted the interactions between volunteers and refugees. In the era of closed borders, these two groups spent weeks and even months, closely collaborating on repetitive attempts to cross the border, which were usually unsuccessful. These close collaborations fostered stronger bonds between the two parties. A 25-year-old Moroccan man described his close relationship with one Greek volunteer:

> She came from the sky like an angel, but volunteers come and go. I saw her in Idomeni, and after that I didn't see her for a long time, and then I saw her again there. She asked me if I wanted to help them [the volunteers] with clothing distribution. I agreed to come . . . She helped me a lot. She gave me some clothes because I didn't have any. She gave me socks, food, we listened to music together. Thanks to her I forgot about bad things. I had hard times and she helped me . . . These volunteers were like family to me.

120 Robert Rydzewski

Volunteers also moved along the Balkan route in search of sites congested with asylum seekers, because only in those places could they satisfy their desires to feel useful and accomplished. The length of their stays and the type of work they did in each new location depended on their personal desires and the asylum seekers' situations: The "graver" the site and the direr the asylum seekers' situations, the greater the draw. Authenticity was also a factor: As Natalia Bloch writes (2011, p. 259), in the eyes of volunteers, no place guarantees more authenticity than refugee camps, because no one chooses to live in exile in precarious conditions, one can only be forced into it. Thus, these sites often appear as the utmost "real" places.

Overlapping Terrain: Volunteer Tourism and Activism

Most of the volunteers I met were single males and females in their 20s or 30s who were generally well-educated middle-class citizens of the Global North.[8] The classic literature generally describes those volunteering their time in support of refugees as "activists," defined as autonomous groups "moved into action by a variety of motives ranging from humanitarian compassion to more critical stances toward national and European border policies" (Cantat, 2020, p. 105). However, in actuality, they resemble volunteer tourists. Those who were still students used their university vacation periods to get involved, while others volunteered during their work vacations. A significant number of volunteers came to Serbia as part of a gap year. Generally, their stays in the camp lasted from a couple of days up to two weeks. Those volunteering for longer periods often relocated, following asylum seekers in tandem with the changing situation, as noted earlier.

Sotiris Chtouris and DeMond Miller claim that one of the major reasons their interviewees were drawn to volunteer was because they lacked clearly defined professional and educational aims. They believed that volunteering might lend structure and meaning to their lives (Chtouris and Miller, 2017, p. 70; see also Hustinx and Lammertyn, 2003, p. 177). The wish to fulfill one's own interests while supporting asylum seekers in their journeys was also evident among the foreign volunteers I worked with in Serbia. This observation is shared by voluntourism researchers who claim that beneficiaries of volunteering are more often aid givers than aid receivers (Sin et al., 2015). Some of my interviewees' comments reveal that their own needs for social and cultural capital as well as their desires to experience "real" life played a crucial role in their decisions to travel to Serbia. My co-workers' common motivation was a need to see the situation on the ground, and thereby be better equipped to assess the contradictory media reports on the "refugee crisis." Not only does this reflect a distrust of media and national institutions, which fail to provide reliable information, but it also echoes themes found in certain kinds of tourism. A Polish student in her 20s, Sabina, explained her desire to engage in Preševo:

> I had to come here to see it with my own eyes because the media coverage is . . . , it is all so grotesquely presented and the vocabulary used is just terrifying. A week of anti-migrant and anti-refugee demonstrations [in her home

country] motivated me to come down here to see it for real, I wanted to meet those people to be able to understand why they had decided to migrate.

As these comments illustrate, pro-asylum seekers volunteers in Serbia share objectives with danger zone tourists whose itineraries are inspired by the imagery of nightly news reports from the world's tumultuous zones (Adams, 2001, p. 269). But volunteers arrived in the Balkans not only to observe and verify world events but also to act in response to news images. A 27-year-old traveler from Spain, who abandoned his journey around Europe to come volunteer in Serbia, explained:

> There are plenty of reasons why I have come here. I wanted to travel, move around, I didn't want to stay in Spain. I have been traveling for last [sic] two years and now I want to do something different, something more meaningful, so I realized that this would be a great combination of traveling, visiting different places and being useful. A chance to enjoy doing something meaningful.

Similar to the danger-zone travelers studied by Kathleen M. Adams (Adams, 2001, p. 273), volunteers in Serbia tended to stress satisfaction in doing something meaningful and maintaining their identities as activists and humanitarians. This allowed them to locate themselves higher than tourists in the imaginary hierarchy of travelers because they acted not for themselves, but for others. This represents one extreme practice of social differentiation, "a practice which separates these 'adventurers' from the masses of package tourists, as well as from ethnic tourists" (Adams, 2001, p. 269).

School holidays brought rises in the numbers of volunteers in Serbia and more traveler-like attitudes. The precarious nature of post-industrial labor, or "risk society" (Beck, 1992) wherein employment based on short, flexible contracts, producing a lack of social security and long periods without work (not to be confused with holidays) is also noteworthy here. These emergent new labor standards invite us to rethink the relationship between work and leisure. Some claim that in periods when people lack a guaranteed income, free time is not leisure but a vacuum that requires filling (Rojek, 2001, p. 121). Wanda Vrasti (2013) emphasizes the importance of understanding volunteering as yet another means to secure social and cultural capital, arguing that neoliberal rationalization and emotional dictums turned volunteering into a good "for an economy where credentials and expertise are no longer enough to secure employment" (2013, p. 22). In other words, Vrasti explains that neoliberal capitalism forces individuals to treat all their actions, including leisure time, like work or an investment in one's future ability to work (2013, p. 86). Katarzyna's story illustrates these calculations. A well-educated Polish woman in her mid-30s had left a prior job and was hoping to shift to a humanitarian field. Like many other activists, Katarzyna learned about the situation on the Western Balkan route from the media. Lacking professional humanitarian experience, she saw volunteering as a good opportunity to gather new experiences that

122   Robert Rydzewski

would be required for future work in the relief sector. Likewise, Filipe, a Swiss left-wing politician in the early stage of his career, revealed similar motives. For him it was not the experiences gained in Preševo that mattered most: It was the public image of himself that he built via his social media posts and photos from the camp.

Finally, in my case, biographical and mundane circumstances influenced my decision to engage in voluntary work in Serbia: my visa-free stay in North Macedonia had expired and my work visa was delayed. I wanted to fill the gaps between my research stays in North Macedonia and had the luxury of free time amidst my normal professional duties. Having been expelled from North Macedonia, I wanted to await readmission to a nearby country. Thus, had I not conducted research in North Macedonia, I would probably not have engaged in refugee protection in Serbia. My decision arose not only from my professional aspirations but also from a sense of moral calling. I appeared in Preševo as a privileged white male from the Global North, hoping to help address the material effects of global injustice. I chose Preševo because of its similarities in history and ethnic composition to Tetovo, a city in western North Macedonia that had been my primary field research site. But I also wanted to see what was happening in the places spotlighted in the media. As a young anthropologist, I believed my research should be socially and politically engaged. Thus, I decided to shift my research focus from the transformations of post-Yugoslav cities to the "refugee crisis" in the Serbian section of the Western Balkan route (Rydzewski, 2020b). Self-actualization is often intertwined with humanitarianism or compassion. To put it another way, a socially responsible self is evidenced by the need to respond to human tragedy and reduce suffering (see Fassin, 2012). Such actions also contribute to one's personal development. Foreign volunteer engagement shows that individual life projects, including professional, political, and moral choices, comingle with the motivation to fight global injustice.

Moving Beyond Volunteer Tourism

Not unlike backpacker tourists who set off on trips with a particular route in mind, only to shift course as the journey unfolds, the foreign volunteers encountered situations upon arrival in Serbia that differed markedly from their expectations. Many came with the idea of providing basic humanitarian aid. Sabina explained to me how she understood her work in the first days of her stay in Preševo:

> The whole work of a volunteer is that you must decide whether the situation is so tragic that you must help, or this person can wait because our resources are so small that we are not able to help everyone, so it is quite difficult. We work in this line to the camp . . . and we help these people get on the buses, we make tea, we also organize family gathering points for those separated during the registration process, where family members or friends can find each other after they leave the camp. Additionally, in this line, we distribute information, water, and food, we try to calm people down because this is a tense situation.

Newly arrived foreign volunteers were emotionally affected by meeting dislocated families traveling with children, encountering wounded asylum seekers, and hearing their gut-wrenching stories. It was not only the Serbian state (and the EU) that exercised selective assistance to asylum seekers arriving from war-torn countries but also the volunteers themselves. They were, particularly at the beginning of their voluntary service, eager to provide individualized help to Syrians and other "exemplary victims" (Malkki, 1996, p. 384). During their stay in the camps, volunteers often established strong relationships with one or a few asylum seekers to whom they provided more individualized help. For instance, the aforementioned Polish woman, Katarzyna, was moved by the story of a large family traveling with an infant and decided to bring a bag of baby food, teddy bears, and clothes under the cover of night.

Some volunteers' impulsiveness and "unprofessional" behavior reduced the impersonality of encounters between refugees and volunteers[9] while simultaneously paving the way for selectivity and reinforcing the inequality between the help giver and the help receiver. Such dynamics situate volunteers not far from volunteer tourism, where inequality is embedded in the asymmetrical relations and volunteer tourists' imposition of conscious-salving aid does not entail reflection on the actual needs of the people they seek to help and the consequences of their actions (Birrell, 2010). These dynamics are illustrated by the case of an American woman who traveled from New York to volunteer in Preševo for two weeks. Given the distance she traveled, it would have been more beneficial for asylum seekers and the local community if she had sent the money spent on the transcontinental flight to a local organization supporting refugees than flying to Europe. But as volunteer tourism critiques suggest "volunteer trips aim to alleviate their guilty conscience at the expense of locals, whose needs remain unaddressed, whose jobs are replaced by unskilled volunteers and who are condemned to perform low-wage service work for the enjoyment of Western tourists" (Vrasti, 2013, p. 9).

The volunteers' short but intensive meetings with people on the move – face-to-face interactions, conversations, sharing food, playing with children, and providing individual support – often resulted in long-term relations loaded with mutual expectations which did not match the stereotypical image each had of the other. The volunteers' humanitarian intentions to alleviate asylum seekers' suffering were predicated on the assumption that the recipients of their help were weak, unable to proceed with their journeys, and in need of immediate help. Volunteers were frustrated wherever this picture was disrupted by the asylum seekers' entrepreneurship, strategic network building, or simply their desires to regain a measure of control over their lives by modifying aid in their own way. The volunteers' perception of asylum seekers as passive receivers of aid reproduces colonial and paternalistic approaches characteristic of humanitarian help (see Malkki, 1996; Minn, 2007). The case of Patrick, a 45-year-old single man from Germany, illustrates volunteers' paternalism and denial of asylum seekers' agency. During his volunteer work in Greece, Patrick established a strong relationship with a Kurdish refugee family. Following the closure of the refugee camp in Idomeni, Patrick maintained contact

124 Robert Rydzewski

with them and offered financial support, so they could rent a flat in Thessaloniki. However, the family did not wish to stay in Greece and wanted to use the money to pay a smuggler to take them to Germany or at least to Serbia, where Patrick was volunteering at the time. Patrick, in turn, was not keen to pay for a smuggler and refused. His Kurdish friends then suggested he secure documents to enable them to relocate to Germany. Patrick did not feel he could manage the process of relocating them to his country. The family assured him that he could provide this assistance because a Spanish activist had already done so for them – but they were uninterested in moving to Spain. Learning that "his" family had another volunteer assisting them also triggered ambivalent emotions for Patrick. On the one hand, he was angry that they had not informed him, because he and the Spanish man could have cooperated and combined funds to improve the family's situation in Greece. On the other hand, he felt betrayed and cheated – he thought that they were "his" family and that he had been their only "friend" for all these months. This type of relationship between volunteers and asylum seekers often involves a sense of possessiveness on the part of the volunteers, leading to the aid giver's attempts to control the aid taker's journey. The strong ties create mutual expectations, as Patrick's case illustrates. However, the ties also produce certain attitudinal shifts: Volunteers who might be described as "volunteer tourists" or "diversionary tourists" – those who try to "escape from boredom and the meaninglessness of a routine" (Cohen, 1979, p. 186) – became transnational political activists who support "their" asylum seekers on different stages of the journey. Occasionally, volunteers' social media advocacy for asylum seekers informs the public about the situation on the Balkan route. Likewise, their presence at official meetings enabled people on the move to gain vital information about migration law and human rights and, in some cases, even facilitated their border crossings. Such actions implicitly and explicitly delegitimized border securitization and contested border regimes, lending volunteers a degree of political force.

Over time, volunteers' sensibilities about their roles shifted, moving from defining themselves as humanitarian actors meeting basic physiological needs to transnational activists lobbying for asylum seekers' rights and supporting them financially or/and emotionally through the different stages of their journeys. Witnessing the harsh EU border regime and human suffering prompted volunteers to take more critical, active stances both in Serbia and in their home countries. Sometimes, they returned to the same camp after several weeks for another short stay. Sometimes, they traveled throughout the country to meet a refugee they had gotten to know elsewhere on the Balkan route. Other times, they would cable money or simply ask another volunteer working in a particular refugee camp to take care of refugees they had come to know. This was the case for Julia, a university student from Switzerland, who ran a temporary refugee kitchen in Idomeni (Greece). She contacted me via another volunteer I had met in Preševo, to ask about the situation on the Serbian–Hungarian border, and suggested taking special care of one Syrian family whose trip from Greece to Serbia she was partially financing. Such networks of volunteers built transnational solidarity groups supporting asylum seekers throughout the Balkan route.

Crafting Activists from Tourists 125

The relation between volunteers and asylum seekers often resembled the sponsorship offered by tourists to their hosts in the Global South (see Adams, 1992, p. 547). The "special assistance" provided secretly to a particular asylum seeker with whom the volunteers established a friendship ranged from extra food packages or additional clothes to large sums of money that enabled the receivers to survive a longer period of being stranded on the Balkan route or financed a further clandestine journey to the EU. In critical situations, such as when refugees were brutally beaten by border guards or cheated by smugglers, it was the volunteers, not the state officials or employees of international NGOs or agencies, who were the first to be contacted. This relationship was based on reciprocity. On the one hand, the volunteers gained a sense of performing meaningful actions, experience in the humanitarian sector, and firsthand asylum seekers' stories that they could capitalize on in the future course of their professional and social lives. For instance, upon her return to Switzerland, Julia worked with a local university to establish a language school for refugees which complemented the insufficient language courses provided by the state. Another example is that of Katarzyna who developed her activities during "the refugee crisis" in Serbia and upon returning to her home country created one of the largest civil society groups supporting newcomers there. On the other hand, the asylum seekers gained the long-term financial and emotional support necessary to face an extremely dangerous journey to the EU, as was noted earlier.

Conclusions

Drawing on ethnographic fieldwork along the Balkan route and theories from migration, activism, and tourism studies, I examined the intersecting spatial mobilities of the volunteers and asylum seekers in Serbia, at the doorstep of the EU. This chapter shows different mobilities of the people who are at contrasting hierarchical positions of the EU border regime: The European volunteers freely crossed the border while the refugees' movement was denied and suppressed by criminal and state actors. The Balkan corridor's closure caused refugees to become entrapped in the viciously hypermobile circle of the Balkan circuit (Stojić Mitrović and Vilenica, 2019: 540) which was followed by volunteers. These two mobilities – that of refugees and volunteers – in the opposite directions highlight the global inequality surrounding the right to move created by migration regimes.

However, these privileged mobilities and vulnerable immobilities established at the fringes of the EU are the new points of intersection of two highly mobile groups. What emerged at the junctions where these groups intersected – refugee camps, bus and train stations, or unofficial asylum seekers' settlements – were new forms of solidarity based on reciprocal benefits (though sometimes marked by uneven power relations that fostered patronizing environments). The volunteers engaged in the asylum seekers' protection in Serbia, not unlike volunteer tourists. Both volunteers and volunteer tourists often sought self-realization, personal and professional fulfillment, and were motivated to travel by highly mediatized

126 Robert Rydzewski

important social and political events, making it difficult to draw a line between the two groups. Yet, the volunteers involved in the operation along the Balkan route went beyond self-development. Witnessing global injustice, inequality created by the EU border regime, or denial of human rights, they turned into activists operating in transnational spaces. These volunteers' movements are based on both self-actualization and altruism. They supported people on their way to the EU both materially and emotionally and built transnational groups and networks. Furthermore, some of them set up or engaged in pro-refugee organizations upon return to their home countries. Consequently, as my research suggests, volunteers' tourist-like encounters with refugees can be transgressive experiences that lay the foundation for solidarity movements.

Notes

1 Although there is not one definition of the "refugee crisis," it is usually characterized as period of time in 2015 and 2016, during which European institutions failed to control, manage, and govern migration toward the EU (Kasparek, 2016, p. 2). Therefore, the question of whose crisis the "refugee crisis" was is a legitimate one. De Genova suggests that it is "a crisis of state sovereignty that is repeatedly instigated, first and foremost, by diverse manifestations of the autonomous subjectivity of human mobility itself" (2017). Thus, the term "refugee crisis" I use in quotation marks because it was not a crisis of refugees but of the EU border control that by multiplication of the Frontex agency budget (Guiraudon, 2018, p. 151), violence, exceptional or "emergency" governmental measures tried to restore the control over its borders.
2 This research was funded by the National Science Centre, Poland (Grant No. 2015/17/N/HS6/00694). I thank Kathleen M. Adams and Natalia Bloch for their numerous and constructive comments on this chapter.
3 During my new fieldwork in Serbia, I was deeply engaged in the volunteers' operations. Among my obligations were distribution of food to asylum seekers, maintaining contact with other NGOs, welcoming and supervising new volunteers, and representing volunteers at official camp meetings.
4 For more on the Preševo reception center, see Mandić (2018).
5 Due to the fact that all foreigners arriving to Serbia were required to register with the police within 48 hours of arrival, foreign volunteers closely cooperated with a local nongovernmental organization called the Youth Office. The Youth Office provided volunteers with legal representation for administrative matters and allowed the volunteers to use its offices and storage rooms. The local NGO staff actively cooperated with camp authorities, and on occasion, they were incorporated into transnational organizations. Such collaboration was helpful when it came to lobbying state officials and relief agencies for grassroots initiatives.
6 "Refugees," "asylum seekers," or "economic migrants" in my research settings were very vague and politicized terms. First of all, because the status of people traversing the Balkan Peninsula changed during the so-called refugee crisis several times. Furthermore, these categories are highly politicized and created on the basis of international law, which labels its holders, and according to these labels, the right to protection is guaranteed.
7 Opatovac is a town on the Croatian–Serbian border where the reception center functioned in the summer of 2015.
8 During my fieldwork, I met volunteers from Australia, the United States, Austria, the Czech Republic, Germany, Poland, Spain, Switzerland, and other EU and EFTA countries.
9 This is a critique of volunteer aid projects noted by Erica Bornstein (2003, p. 73).

References

Adams, K. (2001) 'Danger zone tourism: Potentials and problematics for tourism in tumultuous times' in Teo, P., Chang T.C. and Ho K.C. (eds.) *Interconnected worlds: Southeast Asia tourism in the 21st century*. Cambridge: Pergamon Press, pp. 267–281.

Adams V. (1992) 'Tourism and Sherpas, Nepal: Reconstruction of reciprocity', *Annals of Tourism Research*, 19(3), p. 534–554.

Afouxenidis, A., Petrou, M., Kandylis, G., Tramountanis A. and Giannaki, D. (2017) 'Dealing with a humanitarian crisis: Asylum seekers on the eastern EU border of the Island of Lesvos', *Journal of Applied Security Research*, 12(1), pp. 7–39.

Beck, U. (1992) *Risk society: Towards a new modernity*. London and New York: Sage.

Beznec, B., Speer, M. and Stojić Mitrović, M. (2016) 'Governing the Balkan Route: Macedonia, Serbia and the European Border Regime', *Research Paper Series of Rosa Luxemburg Stiftung Southeast Europe*, 5. Available at: www.rosalux.de/en/publication/id/14554/governing-the-balkan-route.

Birrell, J. (2010) 'Before you pay to volunteer abroad, think of the harm you might do', *The Guardian*, 14 November. Available at: www.theguardian.com/commentisfree/2010/nov/14/orphans-cambodia-aids-holidays-madonna.

Bloch, N. (2011) Urodzeni uchodźcy. Tożsamość Pokolenia młodych Tybetańczyków w Indiach. Wrocław: Fundacja na rzecz Nauki Polskiej.

Bloch, N. (2020) 'Beyond a sedentary other and a mobile tourist: Transgressing mobility categories in the informal tourism sector in India', *Critique of Anthropology*, 40(2), pp. 218–237.

Bornstein, E. (2003) *The spirit of development: Protestant NGOs, morality, and economics in Zimbabwe*. Stanford: Stanford University Press.

Bruner, E.M. (2005) *Culture on tour: Ethnographies of travel*. Chicago, IL: University of Chicago Press.

Butcher, J. (2003) *The moralisation of tourism. Sun, sand . . . and saving the world?* London and New York: Routledge.

Cantat, C. (2016) 'Rethinking mobilities: Solidarity and migrant struggles', *Intersections. EEJSP*, 2(4), pp. 11–32.

Cantat, C. (2020) 'The rise and fall of migration solidarity in Belgrade', *Movements. Journal for Critical Migration and Border Regime Studies*, 5(1), pp. 96–124.

Choudry, A. and Kapoor, D. (2013) *NGOization: Complicity, contradictions and prospects*. London and New York: Zed Books.

Chtouris, S. and Miller, D.S. (2017) 'Refugee flows and volunteers in the current humanitarian crisis in Greece', *Journal of Applied Security Research*, 12(1), pp. 61–77.

Cohen, E. (1979) 'A phenomenology of tourist experience', *Sociology*, 13, pp. 179–201.

Dass-Brailsford, P., Thomley, R. and Hurtado de Mendoza, A. (2011) 'Paying it forward: The transformative aspects of volunteering after Hurricane Katrina', *Traumatology*, 17(1), pp. 29–40.

De Genova, N. (2017) *The borders of "Europe": Autonomy of migration, tactics of bordering*. Durham, NC: Duke University Press.

Fassin, D. (2012) *Humanitarian reason: A moral history of the present*. Berkeley, CA, Los Angeles, CA and London: University of California Press.

Goldstein, D.M. (2014) 'Lay the body on the line: Activist anthropology and the deportation of the undocumented', *American Anthropologist*, 116(4), pp. 839–849.

Guiraudon, V. (2018) 'The 2015 refugee crisis was not a turning point: Explaining policy inertia in EU border control', *European Political Science*, 17, pp. 151–160.

128 Robert Rydzewski

Hale, C.R. (2006) 'Activist research vs. Cultural critique: Indigenous land rights and the contradictions of politically engaged anthropology', *Cultural Anthropology*, 21(1), pp. 96–120.

Handy, F., Brodeur, N. and Cnaan, R.A. (2006) 'Summer on the island: Episodic volunteering', *Volunteering Action*, 7, pp. 31–42.

Helsloot, I. and Ruitenberg, A. (2004) 'Citizen response to disasters: A survey of literature and some practical implications', *Journal of Contingencies and Crisis Management*, 12, pp. 98–111.

Hustinx, L. and Lammertyn, F. (2003) 'Collective and reflexive styles of volunteering: A sociological modernization perspective', *Voluntas: International Journal of Voluntary and Nonprofit Organizations*, 14(2), pp. 167–187.

Kallius, A., Monterescu, D. and Rajaram, P.K., (2016) 'Immobilizing mobility: Border ethnography, illiberal democracy, and the politics of the "refugee crisis" in Hungary', *American Ethnologist*, 3(1), pp. 25–37.

Kasparek, B. (2016) 'Routes, corridors, and spaces of exception: governing migration and Europe', *Near Futures Online 1, Europe at a Crossroads*. Available at: http://nearfuturesonline.org/routes-corridors-and-spaces-of-exception-govern-ing-migration-and-europe/.

Kasparek, B. and Speer, M. (2015) 'Of hope. Hungary and the long summer of migration', 9 September 2015. Available at: https://bordermonitoring.eu/ungarn/2015/09/of-hope-en.

Koca, B.T. (2016) 'New social movements: "Asylum seekers welcome UK"', *European Scientific Journal*, 12(2), pp. 96–108.

Malkki, L. (1996) 'Speechless emissaries: Asylum seekers, humanitarianism, and dehistoricization', *Cultural Anthropology*, 11(3), pp. 377–404.

Mandić, D. (2018) 'A migrant "hot potato" system: The transit camp and urban integration in a bridge society', *Journal of Urban Affairs*, 43(6), pp. 799–815.

Martin, D., Minca, C. and Katz, I. (2020) 'Rethinking the camp: On spatial technologies of power and resistance', *Progress in Human Geography*, 44(4), pp. 743–768.

Minn, P. (2007) 'Toward an anthropology of humanitarianism', *The Journal of Humanitarian Assistance*. Available at: https://sites.tufts.edu/jha/archives/51.

Mitrović, S.M. (2014) 'Presenting as a problem, acting as an opportunity: Four cases of socio-political conflicts taking the presence of migrants as a focal object in Serbia', *Glasnik Etnografskog Instituta SANU*, 62(1), pp. 67–81.

Mitrović, S.M. and Vilenica, A. (2019) 'Enforcing and disrupting circular movement in an EU Borderscape: housingscaping in Serbia', *Citizenship Studies*, 23(6), pp. 540–558.

Mostafanezhad, M. (2014) 'Volunteer tourism and the popular humanitarian gaze', *Geoforum*, 54, pp. 111–118.

Mostafanezhad, M. (2016) *Volunteer tourism popular humanitarianism in neoliberal times*. London and New York: Routledge.

Papataxiarchis, E. (2016) 'Being "there": At the front line of the "European refugee crisis" - part 1', *Anthropology Today*, 32, pp. 5–9.

Rojek, C. (2001) 'Leisure and life politics', *An Interdisciplinary Journal*, 23(2), pp. 115–125.

Rydzewski, R. (2020a) 'Hope, waiting, and mobility. Migrant movement in Serbia after the EU-Turkey Deal', movements. *Journal for Critical Migration and Border Regime Studies*, 5(1), pp. 75–96.

Rydzewski, R. (2020b) *"Refugee crisis" – An anthropological case study of the Serbian part of the western Balkan route*. PhD dissertation. Poznań: Adam Mickiewicz University.

Sandri, E. (2017) '"Volunteer humanitarianism": Volunteers and humanitarian aid in the Jungle refugee camp Calais', *Journal of Ethnic and Migration Studies*, 44(1), pp. 65–80.

Simsa, R. (2017) 'Leaving emergency management in the refugee crisis to civil society? The case of Austria', *Journal of Applied Security Research*, 12(1), pp. 78–95.

Sin, H.L. (2009) 'Volunteer tourism – 'Involve me and I will learn'?', *Annals of Tourism Research*, 36(3), pp. 480–501.

Sin, H.L., Oakes T. and Mostafanezhad, M. (2015) 'Traveling for a cause: Critical examinations of volunteer tourism and social justice', *Tourist Studies*, 15(2), pp. 119–131.

Tesfahuney, M. (1998) 'Mobility, racism and geopolitics', *Political Geography*, 17(5), pp. 499–515.

Theodossopoulos, D. (2016) 'Philanthropy or solidarity? Ethical dilemmas about humanitarianism in crisis-afflicted Greece', *Social Anthropology*, 24(2), pp. 167–184.

Vrasti, W. (2013) *Volunteer tourism in the global south: Giving back in neoliberal times.* New York: Routledge.

Whittaker, J., McLennan, B. and Handmer, J. (2015) 'A review of informal volunteerism in emergencies and disasters: Definition, opportunities and challenges', *International Journal of Disaster Risk Reduction*, 13, pp. 358–368.

Yiftachel, O. (2009) ' "Critical theory and gray space", Mobilisation of the colonized', *City*, 3(2–3), pp. 247–263.

7
PANAMA'S TEMPORARY MIGRANTS IN THE TOURISM ERA

Carla Guerrón Montero

> Ships go between these islands as if they were streets,
> the cords of the ships touching the branches of the trees.
>
> (Fernando Colón, 1892, p. 164)

> The sea is history.
>
> (Derek Walcott, 1986, 364)

Introduction

When Samuel Robinson sailed aboard the steamship RMS Dom from Kingston, Jamaica, to the city of Colón, Panama, in 1881, he did not imagine he was to build a life in that country. The journey from Jamaica to Panama was designated Route No. 10 by the Royal Mail Steam Packet Company (RMSPC), owned by the British government. As a deck passenger on the steamship – for Samuel could not afford the cost of an elegant cabin reserved for wealthier passengers – he merely dreamed of succeeding in a land that promised to become "the Constantinople of the Pacific . . . one of the great places of the earth" (Fraser, 1913, p. 93).

Samuel, an Afro-Antillean, was one of the thousands of laborers who migrated from the Antilles during the 19th and 20th centuries to work on various construction projects, beginning with the construction of the Panamanian railroad (1850–1855), followed by the failed French efforts to build a canal across the isthmus (1880–1890), the successful US-led construction of the Panama Canal (1904–1914), and the construction of the Canal's third set of locks (1940–1942). He was among the first group of workers to arrive in Panama to initiate the construction of the Panama Canal for the *Compagnie Universelle du Canal Interocéanique* (Worldwide Company of the Interoceanic Canal) in the 1880s. Samuel left Jamaica because he

DOI: 10.4324/9781003182689-8

Tourism and Panama's Temporary Migrants **131**

did not think it possible to attain economic security and upward social mobility on an island where slavery was abolished only on paper. He knew that the disastrous post-emancipation economic, social, and environmental conditions in Jamaica and around the Caribbean limited his opportunities. Hence, like men before and after him, he traveled to Panama. Many of his relatives, especially those with specific skills (craftsmen, teachers, preachers, lawyers, and doctors) had previously made similar journeys to New York City, so for Samuel migration was a viable option.

In Panama City, Samuel found modest accommodations in a neighborhood of migrant Jamaicans, Barbadians, Saint Lucians, and Martinicans. He planned to take advantage of the high wages promised by the French *Compagnie*, work for a few years as a manual excavation laborer, save enough to return to Jamaica, and buy a plot of rural land. But his life took a different course when in 1884, he met Marion Nightingale, a beautiful Barbadian Black woman. She was working as a washer-woman for Canal workers, hoping to return to her island at the first opportunity. Samuel and Marion formed a family and settled in Panama City. When the French efforts to build the Canal failed and the *Compagnie* went bankrupt, Samuel found a job with the railroad company and Marion continued to wash clothes, only now for railroad workers.

Samuel is representative of the people who altered the "experience of mobility" (Cresswell, 2006, 2010) on the steamship routes of the RMSPC in the 19th century. The company – which was meant to transport mail, packets, and eventually luxury passengers on a predominantly transatlantic trade route between the Antilles and England – was transformed by the demand for migrant worker transportations within the Antilles and from the Antilles to Central America, especially to Panama (Figure 7.1). The luxury passengers who sailed this route to reach various tourist and work-related destinations were far outnumbered by laborers flocking to a promised working paradise.[1] An estimated 200,000 people sailed to Panama from not only the Caribbean islands of Jamaica, Barbados, St. Lucia, St. Vincent, and Grenada but also Martinique, Guadeloupe, Haiti, and Cuba during the period between 1850 and 1950, affecting the routes, the ships, and the overall experience of mobility throughout the company's networks. These workers, in fact, "transformed [the ships] socio-culturally by their presence" (Anim-Addo, 2013, p. 33).

Samuel and his fellow workers changed not only the routes they traveled but also the societies where they settled, temporarily or permanently. The story of Samuel, emblematic of the lives of Caribbean Afro-Antilleans, demonstrates the importance of engaging with the histories of places and peoples by looking at how multiple travel routes and personal experiences intersect. For example, Samuel's voyage to Panama, regarded as a place of transit due to its geopolitical situation, came about due to two historical circumstances beyond his control. First, his ancestors had been forcibly transported from West, Central, and South Africa to Jamaica by the Spaniards and the English starting in the 17th century. Second, after the abolition of slavery in England's colonies in 1834 (and in Jamaica in 1838), Afro-Antilleans were regarded as ideal mobile manual laborers and regularly navigated along routes in the Caribbean, Central America, and Europe.

FIGURE 7.1 Afro-Antillean migrants on Colon Island, 19th century

Source: Author unknown; courtesy of Tito Thomas

Indeed, movement and connectedness characterize the historical experiences of Afro-Antilleans in Central America and the Caribbean. During the past 24 years, I have been immersed in these intricate histories, particularly in Panama and Grenada (Guerrón Montero, 2006, 2009, 2011, 2015, 2020). In this chapter, I draw on the insights gained from this engagement to call into question the dichotomous ideas about travel widely used in mobilities research. In doing so, I accept the invitation put forth by the editors of this volume, Kathleen Adams (2021) and Natalia Bloch (2020), to challenge certain neatly established categories in tourism and migration studies by analyzing the politics of mobility in Panama. For Panama, the tourism industry has become a transnational device that allows for the reinterpretation of the nation's complex trajectory; thus, I explore ways in which the labels tourist, migrant, local, guest, host, voluntary migration, forced migration, home, and away from home can be unpacked in this context. Furthermore, I propose that studying the process of nation-building can contribute to a more nuanced understanding of tourism and migration. The chapter is based on my long-term research in Panama City and the Archipelago of Bocas del Toro. This research, initiated in 1996, combines qualitative and quantitative methods, including archival research,

Tourism and Panama's Temporary Migrants 133

long-term ethnographic fieldwork, and in-depth interviewing, in addition to census surveys and surveys of tourists and hotel owners.

Mobilities and Autonomies in Neoliberal Capitalism

Over the last 15 years, the new mobilities paradigm has emerged in the social sciences. This paradigm considers the physical movement of peoples and objects, along with their connections to the virtual movement of ideas, images, and information. By engaging with movements and connectedness, it raises awareness of the mobility or lack thereof among peoples, capital, technologies, commodities, and images (Burns and Novelli, 2008; Cresswell, 2006; Hannam et al., 2006; Sheller and Urry, 2004).

Since tourism is a quintessential vehicle for the circulation of peoples, ideas, objects, and commodities, it is not surprising that this paradigm has been applied to its analysis (Dürr and Jaffe, 2012; Salazar, 2010; Sheller and Urry, 2004). Studies have compared the mobilities of cosmopolitan tourists versus the presumed immobilities of the tourism workers (Cresswell, 2001; Bloch, 2020), addressed the phenomenon of lifestyle migration (McIntyre, 2013; Cohen et al., 2013), and examined extreme mobilities such as the experiences of "global nomads" (Kannisto, 2015). By highlighting the intersections of travel, tourism, and migration, these studies challenge such deeply held dichotomous concepts in tourism research as home and away from home, tourist and local, or host and guest (Chambers, 2009; Adams, 2019; Guerrón Montero, 2019). Given that the experiences and realities of tourism are rarely so binary, such reconsiderations are not merely intellectual exercises; they are necessary.

Because the new mobilities paradigm ultimately addresses the history and contemporary reality of neoliberal capitalism, I propose that it can interact fruitfully with the conceptual framework known as the autonomy of migrations. The autonomy of migrations seeks to study migratory mobilities as both subjective and objective. It positions the subjective practices, demands, and experiences that are expressed in migratory movements in relation to the "objective causes" that determine them (Mezzadra, 2005, p. 144). It also focuses on the moments in which migrants "act as citizens," exercising their right to citizenship through practices that exemplify the essential economic and social role they play in the societies where they live. Rather than treating migrants as objects responding solely to "push" and "pull" forces or viewing refugees as helpless victims, this theory recognizes a significant measure of independence on their part in its analysis of migratory movements (De Genova et al., 2018, p. 241). It insists that individuals labeled "migrants" and "refugees" play a large role in directing their own mobility and stresses the "claims to space" they make as part of this process (Papastergiadis, 2018; Mezzadra, 2005; De Genova et al., 2018).

The autonomy of migrations approach counters the normative binary concept of mobility by allowing us to consider the subjective reasons why a person moves from one place to another, yet without ignoring the very real objective conditions

134 Carla Guerrón Montero

(economic, environmental, social, and political) that also propel migratory movements. It proposes that the struggles of migrant groups and the networks they develop, which extend far beyond territorial boundaries, are key (Mezzadra, 2005, p. 146), without glorifying either timid or extreme forms of global nomadism. By studying migrations and tourism through this lens, we can address the role of mobilities in the history and contemporary reality of capitalism and understand its transformation through the subjective experiences of workers, the people who really move the system – people such as Samuel Robinson, who was introduced earlier and whose story will resume later. We can see how these movements represent "historically specific social formations of human mobility that manifest themselves as a constitutive (subjective, creative, and productive) power within the more general capital-labor relation" (De Genova et al., 2018, p. 241). As Sandro Mezzadra (2012) states,[2]

> The struggles around mobility cut through the history of capitalism, since the first enclosure in England mobilized the local rural population and since the first slave ship crossed the Atlantic. It could even be said that the friction between a "politics of migration" and a "politics of control" constitutes the nucleus of the history of capitalism (p. 163–164).

It is worth stressing once again that the "autonomy of migrations" framework invites us to center on the personal, culturally grounded reasons people move, travel, and stay. It does not deny that external structural forces in the global environment can make people move. Its major contribution is to counter the notion that people are merely pawns in a game whom outside forces can move at will. If we put this framework in dialogue with the mobilities paradigm, we can challenge such presumably fixed dichotomies as "mobile tourists" and "immobile locals."

Panama's Narratives of Nation-Building

The Isthmian country of Panama embodies the politics of mobility. After becoming independent from Spain in 1821, it was annexed to Colombia as a province for 81 years. Upon independence from Colombia in 1903, it became dependent economically and politically on the United States (Figure 7.2). There are two competing – somewhat mutually exclusive – narratives as to how Panama as a nation-state was built. The first one emphasizes what I call the "fluidity of mobilities," while the counternarrative stresses a sedentary origin. According to the first narrative, Panama was built on a foundation of deterritorialized connections resulting from its geopolitical condition as a place of transit. As a result, it attracted people from almost every continent in the world, making Panama one of the most ethnically diverse territories in the Americas. Afro-Antilleans, Chinese, Greeks, Italians, Indians, French, Spanish, Chileans, Colombians, and US citizens (to name a few) have settled in the Isthmus at one point or another, fostering remarkable ethnic

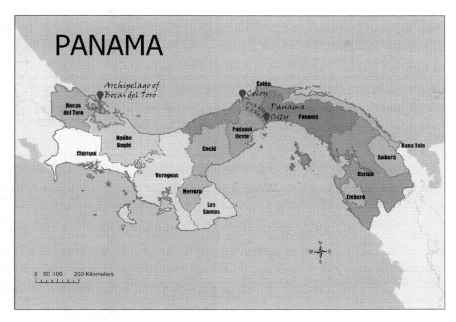

FIGURE 7.2   Map of Panama
Source: Map by Carol Lyell

diversity. Its population of 4,396,000 (2021) encompasses eight indigenous groups and at least two distinct Afro-Panamanian groups. There are also Asian Panamanians, rural and urban mestizo groups, and – more recently – lifestyle migrants, in particular from the United States. The counter-narrative proposes that the nation grew by affirming claims to fixed historic and cultural origins. This foundational myth anchors Panama in the Spanish conquest, making the nation fundamentally Hispanic. It is supported by the fact that Panama's history is marred by several periods of ethnic cleansing.

The two narratives coexist today, in Panama's tourism era. Starting in the 1990s, Panama underwent dramatic political, social, and economic transformations. Following 21 years of dictatorial rule, the first democratic regime invested in tourism as the most viable alternative for Panama's future. In the 21st century, Panama has become a tourism and lifestyle migration mecca, with the tourism industry a major force through which local, national, and global representations of identities intersect. In this context, I propose that a third narrative has emerged: Panama is, and has always been, a "multicultural nation." This narrative does not address what multiculturalism entails or whether it is a problematic concept. It simply embraces and celebrates ethnic groups whose cultural practices have remained distinct and distinguishable. That embrace, however, does not translate into public policies that provide equal opportunities to historically marginalized ethnic groups. Here the struggles of marginalized groups cast as "temporary migrants" are occluded by the

136 Carla Guerrón Montero

rhetoric of multiculturalism, now eagerly espoused by the Panamanian government. Conversely, tourists and lifestyle migrants are welcomed in this rereading of Panama's nation-building narrative.

The Archipelago of Bocas del Toro in the northwestern corner of Panama, part of Bocas del Toro province, represents a microcosm of the multicultural elements found in Panama, including Afro-Antilleans, Chinese, indigenous groups (particularly Ngöbe), Panamanian Latinos (the term used in Panama to refer to mestizos), and lifestyle migrants, mostly from Europe and North America. Afro-Antilleans represent the largest and most dominant group in the Archipelago. The Archipelago has approximately 17,000 inhabitants distributed across nine inhabited islands.

My ethnographic research there centered on exploring the histories of Afro-Antillean populations, to which Samuel Robinson belonged. Afro Antilleans in Bocas del Toro are descendants of peoples enslaved by Irish, English, and Scottish families in Jamaica and Barbados. They arrived in the Archipelago in the early 1800s. They are also descendants of Antillean workers who migrated involuntarily or voluntarily to Panama in the 19th century to participate in the infrastructural projects mentioned earlier, as well as to work on small banana plantations and for the United Fruit Company (UFC) (Carles, 1952; Heckadon Moreno, 1980; Waisome et al., 1981).

The 19th century was a period of prosperity for the region, due in part to the presence of the UFC. Bocas Town boasted five consulates, several bilingual newspapers, and thriving businesses owned by merchants from Germany, Italy, Spain, Lebanon, the United States, Jamaica, China, and England (Stephens, 1987, p. 14). This period ended in the early 1900s when the UFC moved its headquarters from Bocas Town in the Archipelago to Almirante on the mainland due to an outbreak of the "Panama Disease," a soil-borne fungus which, according to Steve Marquardt, "was less a natural disaster than a product of industrial-scale, globalized agriculture" (2002, p. 7).

This meant Bocas del Toro Town was no longer the center of the province's commercial activities: "the government thought, 'Bocas is not worthwhile [*Bocas no está en nada*]' and lost interest in the place" (interview S. C., May 2, 2002). From the 1960s until the early 1990s, Archipelago life was characterized by a stagnant economy, organized around UFC's limited production, small-scale agriculture and fishing, and service-oriented jobs (bureaucratic, medical, and educational). Bocas del Toro became known as a "punishment zone" for ill-behaved bureaucrats or government workers. It took the development of a strong tourism industry in the mid-1990s to turn things around. Tourism produced important changes in the configuration of the Archipelago (Guerrón Montero, 2004, 2006) and ultimately became the foundation of the reconstruction of the Panamanian nation, but along very different lines.

The Stories of Samuel and Marta

Putting the mobilities paradigm in conversation with the autonomy of migrations approach is especially apt for analyzing the African Diaspora as a process and a condition (Patterson and Kelley, 2000). Samuel Robinson's path of mobilities goes beyond the specific period I describe in the beginning of this chapter, and far beyond that of his ancestors. His ancestors were enslaved peoples, the victims of incessant comings and goings, "from one shore to the other of the same ocean, from the slave ports of West and Central Africa to those in the Americas and Europe" (Mbembe, 2016, p, 43). As Achille Mbembe (2016) deftly notes, peoples of African descent are the only human beings "whose flesh was transformed into a thing and their spirit, the living crypt of capital, in merchandise" (p. 30). The circulation of peoples of African descent was needed in an economy that required "colossal capital" to function (p. 26); this circulation was accompanied by their transformation into menacing objects that needed to be protected, broken, or destroyed, in order to dominate them.

Samuel was classified as a temporary economic immigrant; he assumed (as was expected of him) that he would return to Jamaica after a period of working in Panama. Yet he chose to put down roots, build a family, and adjust to being treated as an outsider, not only by Panamanians of different ethnic origins but also by the "Creoles," fellow Afro-Antilleans who had settled there before him. They called Samuel "jumeco," "negro," or "drifting coconut."[3] He did not expect that his children and grandchildren would have to repeatedly prove and reprove their allegiance to the nation where they were born or that this nation would deny them the right to belong. And he certainly never expected that, in the 21st century, he and his descendants would become tourism attractions, or that the cultural practices that had been perceived as alien by non-Antillean Panamanians would become markers of official multiculturalism in the tourism era.

But that is what happened. Because of the isolation they endured – both inside and outside the Canal Zone and in the Archipelago of Bocas del Toro – Afro-Antilleans maintained many distinguishing features such as language, religious traditions, and architecture. They developed institutions to sustain themselves, including schools, lodges, benevolent societies, and churches (GWC, SCRBC, 72/2; Westerman, n.d., p. 22). Samuel would have never dreamed that today, "Afro-Antilleans typify the primary symbols of Panama as a constructed nation: cosmopolitan, [with] transnational ties, and [as] the bridge of the world" (Guerrón Montero, 2020, p. 150).

Mezzadra (2004) stresses that, to enrich our understanding of migration's complexities, we must place the subjectivity of the migrant at the center of our explorations (p. 269). The histories of Afro-Antilleans in Panama, where they oscillated between temporary and permanent status and embraced a cosmopolitan identity resulting from their long history of mobility, provide an excellent illustration of these complexities. I have previously noted (Guerrón Montero, 2006, 2020) that – while geographically bounded and assumed to be isolated – Panamanian Afro-Antilleans now assert their identities as a group with enough transnational connections to understand worlds that elude the country's other ethnic groups. They have repositioned themselves through participation in transnational circuits. Specifically, their long-held connection with the diaspora extends to the Caribbean, Central America, the United States, and the United Kingdom. As Gregory Higginbotham

138 Carla Guerrón Montero

(2012) states, if we understand the Afro-Antillean diaspora as a population scattered across different nation-states that identify with a single origin, we will see how this concept "gives identities the opportunity to cross borders and boundaries . . . and form racial, ethnic and cultural commonalities and solidarities at the transnational level" (p. 196).

For instance, it is common for Afro-Antillean women to travel throughout Panama for teaching and nursing job posts. Many Afro-Antillean men choose to work as crew members on cruise ships for months at a time, returning home for a few weeks only twice a year. This migration pattern is also common in other parts of the Atlantic coast of Central America, particularly among Afro-Antillean populations with a command of the English language. These experiences allow Afro-Antilleans to see themselves as more worldly than other ethnic groups in Panama and, in some cases, than the tourists and lifestyle migrants with whom they often engage in the tourism era.[4]

For our purposes, it is important to understand the significance of lifestyle migrants. These are relatively affluent individuals who move, either permanently or temporarily, to places where they can maintain or improve their quality of life (Benson and O'Reilly 2009, p. 621). The term encompasses residential migrants who are retired and who move permanently or semi-permanently; seasonal lifestyle migrants or "snowbirds"; and migrants who are not of retirement age. In general, lifestyle migration (Korpela, 2009; Torkington, 2012) or lifestyle mobilities (Benson and O'Reilly, 2018; Hayes, 2015) refers to "the transnational domiciliary relocation of people" from the Global North to the Global South (Hayes, 2015). Recognizing the inequalities and asymmetries of contemporary migration regimes, scholars of mobilities define lifestyle migration as a kind of mobility that is practiced mostly by the upper and middle classes of the Global North (Banks, 2004; Benson and O'Reilly, 2009; Hoey, 2005). In Bocas del Toro, most lifestyle migrants are from the United States (Spalding, 2013). The steady flow of lifestyle migrants into Panama has resulted in great measure from a series of policies carried out by successive Panamanian administrations since the 1990s.[5] Their presence has had a significant impact on tourism and its participants.

To illustrate this point, let us consider the experience of a consummate "tourate,"[6] Marta Simpson,[7] whose life has been entangled with that of lifestyle migrants for more than 20 years. Marta has engaged with tourism on many fronts since the industry developed in Bocas del Toro. An Afro-Antillean, she was born on the island of Providencia, Colombia, where she lived until 1976 when she moved to the Archipelago of Bocas del Toro at the age of 16. When she was 13, her mother found work on the nearby island of San Andrés, so she stayed with her sisters and her aunt in Providencia. For Marta, her mother's departure to San Andrés marked the beginning of her role as a homemaker. Three years later, Marta's mother met a Bocatorenean and moved with him to Bocas. Marta left Providencia when her mother returned to take her to Bocas del Toro.

In 1976, this voyage required taking a ship from San Andrés to the Panamanian city of Colón and another ship from Colón to Bocas del Toro. Marta did not expect

Tourism and Panama's Temporary Migrants   **139**

to stay in Bocas del Toro beyond the three months granted in her tourist visa. Yet she did stay; she married, had five children, divorced, worked, went to church, and met tourists, lifestyle migrants, and anthropologists (Guerrón Montero, 2020). Though she built a life in Panama, Marta, like many others, became a person in exile. She remained in a state of uncertain displacement for 31 years as an undocumented person – a temporary migrant in the 20th and 21st centuries in a country where she had lived for most of her life, very much like Samuel in the 19th and 20th centuries.

Through her interactions with tourists, lifestyle migrants, and anthropologists, Marta accumulated great cultural capital while also gaining some economic capital. Her work as a cook, hostess, and administrator on different properties owned by lifestyle migrants did not allow her to accumulate much wealth, but she accessed economic capital tangentially through material support and sponsorships offered by these lifestyle migrants. Her affiliation with foreigners also brought her a degree of prestige. Ultimately, Marta's interactions with tourists, lifestyle migrants, and anthropologists earned her a good deal of cultural, symbolic, and social capital. Her skilled cultural brokerage on behalf of lifestyle migrants and tourists allowed her to fulfill her dream of becoming a permanent resident in Panama and, soon after, to return to her beloved Providencia. Once her legal status was resolved, Marta visited her island, thanks to the economic support of a good friend of hers from California who is a "snow-bird" lifestyle migrant. Returning to Providencia for the first time after 31 years was a very emotional experience for Marta: "When I landed in Providencia, I wanted to kiss the floor. I cried and cried; I could not believe I was able to return after 31 years" (July 16, 2020)[8] (Figure 7.3).

Marta has been back six more times since her first trip in 2004. She has returned to visit her dying father, see friends, and explore other parts of Colombia such as Cartagena. Because she did undocumented work for most of her life, she did not receive a pension when she retired. Thus, she chose to use what she had saved from her employment to return to Providencia and stay for a month because it is there where she feels the happiest. During our online conversations in June 2020, she told me:

> Right now, talking to you, I want to be there. When I see a picture of my beaches, I want to be there. Sometimes I sit here on my balcony overlooking my neighbor's home and my mind runs to Providencia and I imagine I am there looking at the dawn. What I want to say is that knowing that you are in the place where you were born is enough to give you the greatest happiness in life. It does not matter how many beaches you visit or what you eat.

To further explain her point of view to me, Marta asked me: "How do *you* feel when you return to Ecuador?" I could certainly understand Marta's sentiments, as – despite being able to return to my home country often, and despite feeling like a tourist there sometimes – I feel renewed excitement and joy every time I travel to

FIGURE 7.3 Marta in Providencia

Source: Photo by Vivian Archibold Dawkins

Ecuador. In fact, after more than 24 years of living in the United States, I also still see myself as a migrant just as Marta does.

As a tourist in her native country, Marta had sampled new dishes, enjoyed beaches that catered to tourists, and explored tourist sites, while also visiting old family members and friends (known as VFR tourism), cooking and going on trips

Tourism and Panama's Temporary Migrants **141**

with them, visiting the places on the island she loved as a child, and being surprised by new bridges and buildings that were not there before. She even recalled with excitement how, on her way back to Panama in 2018, she was unexpectedly upgraded to the first class:

> To travel in first class, oh my God! It was my happiest trip ever. I felt as if I were in a five-star hotel, or restaurant, with the little towel to clean your hands and the champagne. I had no idea what the little towel was for, or where to find the food tray in my seat, but I just watched what the person sitting next to me did and followed her lead.
>
> *(July 16, 2020)*

Marta's thirst for experiences, knowledge, and interactions is uncommon. Her fearless drive to experiment with behaviors or activities (and certainly with flavors) that are not usually part of Afro-Antillean life is equally uncommon (Guerrón Montero, 2020). But her experience of mobility and displacement is not unusual. Marta left Providencia to settle in Bocas and has a family network in not only Providencia, San Andrés, and Cartagena in Colombia, but also Colón and Panama City in Panamá, Limón in Costa Rica, and New York City in the United States. These circuits that are ever present in her life trajectory are characteristic of the experiences of Afro-Antilleans. I found it ironic that Marta is now partially immobilized because of a medical problem with her sciatica and because of the current global COVID-19 pandemic. Yet even amidst these challenges, Marta is certain she will recuperate and will be ready to hop on her next trip back to Providencia. She only wonders whether and how she will be able to ride a motorcycle there, as moto-taxis are the only means of transportation available.

Marta's story brings to the forefront the subtle complexities that are missed if we ignore the subjectivities of those who migrate. Marta considers Bocas del Toro her home; there she has children, grandchildren, and friends. At the same time, her other home, the place where she is "always happy," is the island of Providencia. If we apply binary categories such as "mobile guest" and "immobile host" to people like Marta, we miss the opportunity to understand how the lives of Bocatoreneans and permanent or temporary visitors are entangled. Marta, for example, was able to become a permanent resident thanks to the support of lifestyle migrants who facilitated money and contacts so she could hire a lawyer and legalize her status. Later, they also made her dream of returning to Providencia a reality in 2004 and beyond. In 2005, when she received the news that her father was terminally ill, a group of friends – all lifestyle migrants and tourists – gathered enough money to send her on a plane to Providencia within days. Most of these lifestyle migrants arrived in Bocas as tourists, became enamored with the Archipelago, and decided to move there part- or full-time. Real estate agent Chris, for example, loved what he perceived as the quaint atmosphere of the Archipelago, in glaring contrast with the endless busyness of his native New York. Once he made local friends in Bocas, particularly Marta, the Archipelago became his second home. He purchased a house on Colon

142 Carla Guerrón Montero

Island and invited Marta to live there rent-free with the understanding that she would upkeep the property. Chris can be assured that his house is well-cared for and that when he arrives in Bocas, Marta will take care of him like a son. Marta's honed hospitality skills make her the perfect hostess for Chris, while Chris offers Marta the opportunity to have a pleasant living arrangement.

In one way or another, the tourism-related activities by Afro-Antilleans in the Archipelago are a great example of James Clifford's (1992) concept of traveling in dwelling. While Chris can visit Bocas yearly and maintain a second home in the Archipelago, most Bocatoreneans never leave Bocas del Toro, yet their lives are also intertwined with the lives of temporary or permanent lifestyle migrants or passing tourists. For instance, Linda – an Afro-Antillean cook – has developed good relationships with some lifestyle migrants in town. She even has two international "daughters-in-law." Her oldest son, Edgar, is the boyfriend of an Italian woman whose family owns a restaurant in town; while she is in Italy, he spends time with two additional Bocatorenean girlfriends. Juan, Linda's second son, is also interested in meeting women from abroad; he has a girlfriend from the United States who stays in regular contact with him. Linda believes that her sons should not have more than one girlfriend but thinks that they are simply being "young men." Because of Edgar's relationship with the family from Italy, Linda has become acquainted with other Italians in town. Her husband takes her to one of the Italian restaurants in Bocas once a year as a special treat. Linda longs for her annual visit to the restaurant, where she orders a different dish every time she visits. David Livingston, the son of an Afro-Antillean man and an indigenous woman, owns a small hostel in Bocas. For him, as long as the people who stay at his hostel (from countries as diverse as Japan, Sweden, and Israel) have a good time, become friends with him, and send him postcards and stamps from their travels to add to the "stamp board" prominently featured in the hostel, he is happy charging them low rates.

Afro-Antilleans from the larger diaspora regularly visit Panama as tourists and engage in what has been termed "roots tourism" (Dillette, 2021). This is true of any diasporic group and, as Adams (2021) has noted, that fact remains elusive until we add nuance to the categories we use to understand mobilities. Just like Marta when she traveled to Providencia, these diasporic tourists spend time both with their families and in tourism activities in Bocas and Panama City, such as the annual Grand Afro-Antillean Fair organized by the Society of Friends of the Afro-Caribbean Museum of Panama (SAMAAP). SAMAAP is an organization founded in 1981 by Afro-Antilleans in Panama and abroad to keep the Afro-Antillean Museum alive. The fair is a two-day event that, for the last 33 years, has occurred during carnival time, around February (a time established for the convenience of Afro-Antilleans in Panama, the United States, and the Antilles). Most of its audience is composed of Afro-Antilleans from the diaspora, but it is open to the public. The fair used to take place on the patio of the museum, but in 2014 it was moved to the ATLAPA Conventions Center, located in the prosperous San Francisco neighborhood, to accommodate larger crowds. At the fair, Afro-Antilleans dressed in tunics and wearing *kofias*[9] walk alongside children parading with banners that read "We are proud of our Black race." Performances of the quadrille, the May Pole dance, and sokah music[10] are highlights of the event, which culminate with the election of the African Queen. Here the Afro-Caribbean, the African, the pan-African, the Afro-Antillean, and the Afro-Panamanian all mix, thus signaling that Afro-Antilleans belonging to the African diaspora are a group that is integral not only to the construction of the Panamanian nation-state but to the modern world as we experience it (cf. Patterson and Kelley, 2000).

Conclusions: Who Are the Temporary Migrants?

Antonio Hardt and Sandro Mezzadra (2017) note that, regardless of structural inequalities and asymmetric power relations, the mobility of migrants vindicates the right of people to freedom of movement as an essential human liberty. Lifestyle migrants and "global nomads" (primarily from the Global North) have the resources and cultural capital to take advantage of this right in a steady manner, but people in the Global South also engage in mobilities. The Martinican writer and philosopher Édouard Glissant (2006) called it "circular nomadism," the right to invoke more than one set of roots and more than one culture as legitimate.

The autonomy of migrations paradigm challenges the distinctions between migrant and refugee, or voluntary and forced migration, by recognizing the subjectivity of those who move. Samuel, for instance, voluntarily moved to Panama to work on the construction of the Panama Canal, along with thousands of Afro-Antilleans, but in a system that some scholars have called neo-slavery or semi-slavery (Diez Castillo, 1981, pp. 67–68; cf. Westerman, 1980, p. 27). The massive migration of Black bodies to Panama, Latin America's "blackening period" (Andrews, 2004, p. 10), produced anxiety among the Panamanian elites. I stated earlier that Samuel would have been surprised to learn that his descendants would have been denied their right to citizenship in the country where they were born. But this is exactly what happened when several laws against Afro-Antilleans were passed in 1926, and more so in the 1941 constitution, which not only prohibited further migration of English-speaking Black peoples but also denied citizenship to Afro-Antilleans born in Panamanian soil. Afro-Antilleans were labeled alien competitors and usurpers.

By integrating the mobilities paradigm with the autonomy of migration concept, we can also incorporate the experiences of lifestyle migrants in a much more complex way. As we have seen, Samuel moved because conditions were difficult in Jamaica at the time, and the opportunities for upward social mobility promised by Panama were compelling. Marta traveled to Panama to follow her mother, who had moved there in search of upward mobility and opportunities not available to her in Colombia. But Chris, the lifestyle migrant whose story I shared earlier, also traveled to Bocas del Toro in search of upward mobility and overall better quality of life. In more than one way, Marta facilitated both for Chris, by helping him navigate the Panamanian legal system, taking meticulous care of his investment while he works in the United States, and introducing him to life in a quintessential Caribbean paradise.

144 Carla Guerrón Montero

A framework that considers the multiple reasons that motivate people to move rather than fixating on one cause is necessary if we are to discern the intricate contexts of mobility. While Afro-Antilleans were temporary migrants in Panama for a long period, their "permanence" in Panama has solidified partly because of tourism. Tourism has given Afro-Antilleans the opportunity to present and represent identities that would otherwise have been suppressed within the national context. Men and women in Bocas acquired a "space" for cultural-political autonomy. In the meantime, new "temporary migrants" have arrived, also enticed by local authorities but for very different reasons. These are the lifestyle migrants, for whom the categories "migrant" and "tourist" are intertwined (Adams, 2021).

Samuel's and Marta's stories are examples of the real and tangible limitations of movement. And yet, their stories are also excellent examples of the autonomy of migrations and the resourcefulness of migrants. What is important to highlight here is that, amidst these circumstances, there is ambivalence. The advent of the tourism industry provides Afro-Antilleans with an opportunity to challenge the national meta-narrative, which has kept them in the category of "temporary migrants" since their arrival to Panama in the mid-19th century. By looking at mobilities from the perspective of nation-building and by looking at the subjectivity of the migrant stories, we gain a fuller understanding of the categories of tourist, migrant, local, guest, host, voluntary migration, forced migration, home, and away from home. Afro-Antilleans' position as diasporic individuals who are as savvy and worldly (or even more so) as the tourists and lifestyle migrants they encounter can only be understood when we reflect upon their position in the history of the construction of the Panamanian nation-state. Only when we see that there are at least two competing narratives in existence (the fluidity of mobilities and the sedentary origin narrative), can we recognize that Afro-Antilleans were never the sedentary "others" they were assumed to be. They are unrecognized cosmopolitans in the construction of the nation-state in Panama.

Notes

1 At the time, Panama was viewed as a "working paradise" for those in great need of economic support. For most others, however, the Panama Canal Zone was perceived as a dangerous place because of the historic experiences of Americans, French, and British in the Caribbean and the Panama Canal Zone, which were marked by malaria, yellow fever, and death (Baldwin, 2005, p. 224).
2 This and other translations from Spanish to English are my responsibility.
3 The term "jumeco" is used pejoratively in Panama to refer to a person of Jamaican origin.
4 In contrast, Anna Spalding (2013) states that the lifestyle migrants perceive Afro-Antilleans as unsophisticated and carrying an air of superiority.
5 These policies included tax exemptions for properties destined for tourism activities, discounts for health insurance and other benefits (Law 8 of 1994), and the elimination of visa requirements for targeted populations (Executive Decree 248 of 2001).
6 Andrew Causey (2003) defines a tourate as a local person in a tourist destination who interacts directly and frequently with tourists, in contrast with those living in tourism destinations who rarely engage with visitors.

7 I have used pseudonyms to refer to the men and women with whom I interacted in the Archipelago.
8 The Archipelago of San Andrés, Providencia, and Santa Catalina is a department of Colombia consisting of two island groups and eight outlying banks and reefs in the Caribbean Sea.
9 The *kofia* is a brimless cylindrical cap with a flat crown, worn by men in East Africa.
10 Sokah or soca originated in Trinidad and Tobago in the early 1970s and developed into a range of styles during the 1980s. It combines calypso with East Indian rhythms.

References

Adams, K.M. (2019) '"Being a tourist in my (own) home": Negotiating identity between tourism and migration in Indonesia' in Leite, N., Castañeda, Q, and Adams, K.M. (eds.) *The ethnography of tourism: Edward Bruner and beyond*. Lanham, MD, Boulder, CO, New York and London: Lexington Books, pp. 148–165.

Adams, K.M. (2021) 'What western tourism concepts obscure: Intersections of migration and tourism in Indonesia', *Tourism Geographies*, 23(4), pp. 678–703.

Andrews, G.R. (2004) *Afro-Latin America, 1800–2000*. New York: Oxford University Press.

Anim-Addo, A. (2013) 'Steaming between the Islands: Nineteenth century maritime networks and Caribbean archipelago', *Island Studies Journal*, 8(1), pp. 25–38.

Baldwin, J. (2005) 'The contested beach: Resistance and resort development in Antigua, West Indies' in Cartier, C. and Lew, A.A. (eds.) *Seductions of place: Geographical perspectives on globalization and touristed landscapes*. London and New York: Routledge, pp. 222–241.

Banks, S.P. (2004) 'Identity narratives by American and Canadian retirees in Mexico', *Journal of Cross-Cultural Gerontology*, 19(4), pp. 361–381.

Benson, M. and O'Reilly, K. (2009) 'Migration and the search for a better way of life: A critical exploration of lifestyle migration', *Sociological Review*, 57(4), pp. 608–625.

Benson, M. and O'Reilly, K. (2018) *Lifestyle migration and colonial traces in Malaysia and Panama*. London: Palgrave Macmillan.

Bloch, N. (2020) 'Beyond a sedentary other and a mobile tourist: Transgressing mobility categories in the informal tourism sector in India', *Critique of Anthropology*, 40(2), pp. 218–237.

Burns, P. and Novelli, M. (2008) 'Introduction' in Burns, P. and Novelli, M. (eds.) *Tourism and mobilities: Local-global connections*. Wallingford: CABI, pp. 1–14.

Carles, R.D. (1952) *La Ciudad de Colón y la Costa de Oro*. Panamá: El Independiente.

Causey, A. (2003) *Hard Bargaining in Sumatra: Western travelers and Toba Bataks in the marketplace of souvenirs*. Honolulu, HI: University of Hawai'i Press.

Chambers, E. (2009) *Native tours: The anthropology of travel and tourism*. Long Grove, IL: Waveland Press.

Clifford, J. (1992) 'Travelling cultures' in Grossberg, L., Nelson, C. and Treichler, P. (eds.) *Cultural studies*. New York: Routledge, pp. 96–116.

Cohen, S.A., Duncan, T. and Thulemark, M. (2013) 'Introducing lifestyle mobilities' in Cohen, S.A., Duncan, T. and Thulemark, M. (eds.) *Lifestyle mobilities: Intersections of travel, leisure and migration*. Farnham: Ashgate, pp. 1–18.

Colón, F. (1892) *Historia del Almirante Don Cristóbal Colón en la cual se da particular y verdadera relación de su vida y de sus hechos, y del descubrimiento de las Indias Occidentales, llamadas nuevo-mundo*. Madrid: Imprenta de Tomas Minuesa.

Cresswell, T. (2001) 'The production of mobilities', *New Formations*, 43, pp. 11–25.

Cresswell, T. (2006) *On the move: Mobility in the modern western world*. London and New York: Routledge.

146 Carla Guerrón Montero

Cresswell, T. (2010) 'Towards a politics of mobility', *Environment and Planning D: Society and Space*, 28(1), pp. 17–31.

De Genova, N., Garelli, G. and Tazzioli, M. (2018) 'Autonomy of asylum? The autonomy of migration-undoing the refugee crisis script', *The South Atlantic Quarterly*, 117(2), pp. 239–265.

Dillette, A. (2021) 'Roots tourism: A second wave of double consciousness for African Americans', *Journal of Sustainable Tourism*, 29(2–3), pp. 412–427.

Diez Castillo, L.A. (1981) *Los cimarrones y los negros antillanos en panamá*. Panamá: Impresora R. Mercado Rudas.

Dürr, E. and Jaffe, R. (2012) 'Theorizing slum tourism: Performing, negotiating and transforming inequality', *European Review of Latin American and Caribbean Studies*, 93, pp. 113–123.

Fraser, J.F. (1913) *Panama and what it means*. London, New York, Toronto and Melbourne: Cassell and Company.

Glissant, É. (2006) *Tratado del todo-mundo*. Barcelona: Editorial El Cobre.

Guerrón Montero, C. (2004) 'Afro-Antillean cuisine and global tourism', *Food, Culture, and Society*, 7(2), pp. 29–47.

Guerrón Montero, C. (2006) 'Tourism and Afro-Antillean identity in Panama', *Journal of Tourism and Cultural Change*, 4(2), pp. 65–84.

Guerrón Montero, C. (2009) 'The "three roots" of Panama's cultural heritage: The construction of racial and national identities in simulated tourism' in Baud, M. and Ypeij, A. (eds.) *Cultural tourism in Latin America: The politics of space and imagery*. Leiden and Boston, MA: Brill Academic Publishers, pp. 45–68.

Guerrón Montero, C. (2011) 'On tourism and the constructions of 'Paradise Islands' in central America and the Caribbean', *Bulletin of Latin American Research*, 30(1), pp. 21–34.

Guerrón Montero, C. (2015) 'Tourism, cultural heritage and regional identities in the isle of spice', *Journal of Tourism and Cultural Change*, 13(1), pp. 1–21.

Guerrón Montero, C. (2019) 'Tourism' in *Oxford bibliographies in "anthropology."* Available at: https://www.oxfordbibliographies.com/view/document/obo-9780199766567/obo-9780199766567-0025.xml

Guerrón Montero, C. (2020) *From temporary migrants to permanent attractions: Tourism, cultural heritage, and Afro-Antillean identities in Panama*. Tuscaloosa: University of Alabama Press.

Hannam, K., Sheller, M. and Urry, J. (2006) 'Mobilities, immobilities and moorings', *Mobilities*, 1(1), pp. 1–22.

Hardt, M. and Mezzadra, S. (2017) 'October! To commemorate the future', *The South Atlantic Quarterly*, 116(4), pp. 649–668.

Hayes, M. (2015) 'Moving South: The economic motives and structural context of North America's emigrants in Cuenca, Ecuador', *Mobilities*, 10(2), pp. 267–284.

Heckadon Moreno, S. (1980) 'Nota al Lector' in Reid, C. (ed.) *Memorias de un criollo bocatoreño*. Panamá: Litho-Impresora Panamá, pp. 7–14.

Higginbotham, G. (2012) Seeking roots and tracing lineages: Constructing a framework of reference for roots and genealogical tourism', *Journal of Heritage Tourism*, 7(3), pp. 189–203.

Hoey, B. (2005) 'From Pi to Pie: Moral narratives of noneconomic migration and starting over in the postindustrial Midwest', *Journal of Contemporary Ethnography*, 34(5), pp. 586–624.

Kannisto, P. (2015) *Global nomads and extreme mobilities*. Farnham: Ashgate.

Korpela, M. (2009) 'When a trip to adulthood becomes a lifestyle: Western lifestyle migrants in Varanasi, India' in Benson, M. and O'Reilly, K. (eds.) *Lifestyle migrations: Expectations, aspirations and experiences*. Aldershot: Ashgate, pp. 15–30.

Marquardt, S. (2002) Pesticides, parakeets, and unions in the Costa Rican banana industry, 1938–1962', *Latin American Research Review*, 37(2), pp. 3–36.

Mbembe, A. (2016) *Crítica de la razón negra: Ensayo sobre el racismo contemporáneo*. Barcelona: Futuro Anterior Ediciones.

McIntyre, N. (2013) 'Mobilities, lifestyles and imagined worlds: Exploring the terrain of lifestyle migration' in Cohen, S.A., Duncan, T. and Thulemark, M. (eds.) *Lifestyle mobilities: Intersections of travel, leisure and migration*. Farnham: Ashgate, pp. 193–207.

Mezzadra, S. (2004) 'The right to escape', *Ephemera*, 4(3), pp. 267–275.

Mezzadra, S. (2005) *derecho de fugal: Migraciones, caudatan y globalización*. Madrid: Traficantes de Sueños.

Mezzadra, S. (2012) 'Capitalismo, migraciones y luchas sociales: La mirada de la Autonomía', *Nueva Sociedad*, 237, pp. 159–178.

Papastergiadis, N. (2018) *The turbulence of migration: Globalization, deterritorialization and hybridity*. Hoboken, NJ: John Wiley & Sons.

Patterson, T.R. and Kelley, R.D.G. (2000) 'Unfinished migrations: Reflections on the African diaspora and the making of the modern world', *African Studies Review*, 43(1), pp. 11–45.

Salazar, N. (2010) *Envisioning Eden: Mobilizing imaginaries in tourism and beyond*. New York and Oxford: Berghahn Books.

Sheller, M. and Urry, J. (2004) 'Introduction: Places to play, places in play' in Sheller, M. and Urry, J. (eds.) *Tourism mobilities: Places to play, places in play*. London: Routledge, pp. 1–10.

Spalding, A.K. (2013) 'Lifestyle migration to Bocas del Toro, Panama', *International Review of Social Research*, 3(1), pp. 67–86.

Stephens, C. (1987) 'Bosquejo histórico del cultivo del banano en la provincia de bocas del toro (1880–1980)' in Moreno, S.H. (ed.) *Publicaciones especiales revista panameña de Antropología*. Panamá: Asociación Panameña de Antropología, pp. 1–50.

Torkington, K. (2012) 'Place and lifestyle migration: The discursive construction of "glocal" place-identity', *Mobilities*, 7(1), pp. 71–92.

Waisome, F.A., Priestley, G. and Maloney, G. (1981) 'Documento Central del Primer Congreso del Negro Panameño' in Maloney, G. (ed.) *Memorias del Primer Congreso del Negro Panameño*. Panamá: Impresora de la Nación, pp. 62–103.

Walcott, D. (1986) *Collected Poems: 1948–1984*. New York: Farrar, Straus, & Giroux.

Westerman, G. (1980) *Los Inmigrantes Antillanos en Panamá*. Panamá: Impresora de la Nación.

Westerman, G. (n.d.) *Papers, 1886–1988*. Schomburg Center for Research in Black Culture, Manuscripts, Archives and Rare Books Division, Sc MG 505 [GWC, SCRBC].

8

INTERSECTIONS OF TOURISM, CROSS-BORDER MARRIAGE, AND RETIREMENT MIGRATION IN THAILAND

Kosita Butratana, Alexander Trupp and Karl Husa

Introduction

This chapter examines the intersections of tourism and migration in the context of retirement and marriage migration in Thailand. In recent decades, the volume of spatial mobility processes has continuously increased. Not only has the complexity of spatial patterns advanced dramatically, but also the types of population groups involved. Thailand has become one of the most popular tourist destinations worldwide and is a prominent hotspot for international retirement migration. This increase in senior migration attests to desires to spend "sunset years" abroad, where one can enjoy a better, more affordable lifestyle in a more pleasant environment, often with a local partner. In the Thai context, retirement migration patterns predominantly consist of male senior citizens from Europe, North America, Australia, and some East Asian countries settling in Thailand. Male retirement migration to Thailand also has a counter-mobility, with converse selectivity. Many younger Thai women, and to a much lesser extent gay men, enter relationships with foreign men, followed by a cross-border migration to the partner's country of residence. Thai women who migrated through marriage or other intimate relationship with foreigners have become a significant component of the Thai diaspora. This diaspora is distinctive in many European countries and, in turn, generates dynamics for visiting friends and relatives (VFR) tourism.

Our analysis draws on semi-structured interviews, surveys, and participant observation to better understand so-called Western retirement migrants in Thailand and Thai marriage migrants in Europe. We argue that the development of short-term mobilities entailing various types of leisure and business tourism influences and co-creates long-term stays and vice versa. Both mobility patterns (marriage migration and retirement migration) often originate from a tourist experience and a "host–guest" relationship which can then lead to a longer-term stay. Such a long-term stay

DOI: 10.4324/9781003182689-9

Tourism, Marriage, and Retirement Migration **149**

may be as a retirement migrant in Thailand or movement as a cross-border migrant out of Thailand. The difference between "tourists" and "long-term stayers" (such as retirement migrants) has become increasingly blurry, and both "types" are often attracted by similar motivational factors. Intersections between tourism and migration also exist in marriage-related migration. Thai–Western couples often initially meet in Thailand's tourist areas and decisions about more permanent moves can be preceded by mutual short-term visits.

Allan M. Williams and C. Michael Hall's (2002) discussion of the tourism and migration nexus outlined various types of tourism-informed mobility. They argued that tourism can lead to migration and entails dynamics of both consumption (e.g., long-term tourism, second homes, and retirement migration) and production (e.g., entrepreneurial, labor, and return migration). Tourism-induced migration often arises following mass tourism (Gustafson, 2002; Stallmann and Espinoza, 1996). A tourist's deepening relationship with a destination following repeat visits can sometimes trigger new forms of mobility, with tourism potentially leading from temporary visits to a more permanent migration. Moreover, migration must be understood as a prerequisite for VFR tourism (Williams and Hall, 2002, p. 38). Here, migration leads to a form of tourism where friends and relatives visit each other. According to the UN World Tourism Organization (UNWTO, 2019, p. 7), VFR tourism[1] accounts for 27% of all international travel movements. There are manifold ways in which tourism and migration re-enforce each other, and it is often "impossible to draw neat boundaries around the two because they constantly intersect, sometimes within one and the same individual" (Salazar, 2022, p. 141). While the interconnections between tourism and migration are incontestable, state mobility regimes grounded in (tourist) visas, work permits, and different types of residence and immigration statuses differ significantly and reflect the problematic presumption that these two forms of mobility are mutually exclusive (Glick Schiller and Salazar, 2013; Koslowski, 2011; Bui and Trupp, 2020).

The empirical evidence on retirement migration to Thailand presented in this chapter draws primarily from a broader project[2] aimed at critically examining international retirement in Thailand. Our focus was on the nexus of long-stay tourism and the (semi-permanent) immigration of foreigners: We sought to address the extent, structure, causes, and consequences of rapidly growing senior migration to Thailand, using the Hua Hin/Cha-am region,[3] a tourism hotspot, as an example. Empirical data were collected between 2010–11 and 2016 via three surveys. The first study entailed 44 semi-structured interviews and addressed a narrow range of topics, including the relationship between tourism, availability of attractive partners in the area under study, and male-dominated retirement migration. The second survey was more extensive and consisted of questionnaires and semi-structured interviews of 112 "Western" migrants. The participants of the surveys were migrants from Europe, North America, Australia, and New Zealand who had lived in the study area for at least three months at the time of the research. In contrast to other studies on similar subjects, no age limit was set for research participation. However, persons engaged in gainful employment in Thailand were excluded. Since more than four-fifths of the respondents lived on acquired pensions and only slightly less than 20% earned their

150 K. Butratana, A. Trupp, and K. Husa

living from savings or similar sources, the term "retirement migrant" is used here in a somewhat broader sense. Among other issues, this survey addressed the living conditions of migrants, their needs and desires, and integration problems. A third questionnaire-based survey was conducted in 2016 among 203 "Western" migrants and focused on the development and characteristics of long-stay tourism in the Hua Hin/Cha-am region. In addition, the third author of this chapter (Karl Husa) has been researching the Hua Hin/Ch-am region since 2005, visiting retirees' second homes and conducting informal conversations about their lives as foreigners in Thailand.

The empirical data on marriage migration stem from an ongoing PhD research project by Kosita Butratana on Thai marriage migration to Austria. Kosita designed and conducted semi-structured interviews, supported by a quantitative survey, among Thai migrants in Austria, and carried out participant observations both in Austria and Thailand. Initial contact with research participants was made through personal networks and social media which enabled meetings with Thai women outside our pre-existing networks. The first author of this chapter – Kosita – has established trust and rapport with the research participants over seven years. These relationships led to invitations into migrants' private homes and workplaces and allowed participation in everyday activities. In addition, participant observation took place in Thai Buddhist temples, Thai restaurants, bars, and Thai festivals in Austria as well as in migrants' family homes in Thailand. Moreover, Kosita was also living as a Thai migrant in a cross-cultural relationship in Austria herself. A questionnaire was used to interview 85 Thai women between the ages of 23 and 77, who reside in Austria and are married to (or have intimate relationships with) Westerners/Austrians. The questionnaire covered topics such as the women's socio-economic background before and after migration, reasons for migration, previous travel experience, the role of social and transnational relations (including home visits), and the overall marriage migration experience. Out of these 85 survey respondents, 30 women participated in semi-structured interviews. For the semi-structured interviews, purposeful qualitative sampling was applied to identify individuals who have different characteristics and traits to showcase the complexity and diversity of marriage migrants. In keeping with standard research practices, we use pseudonyms for all the research participants discussed here.

In this chapter, we outline the distinct characteristics of retirement and marriage migration, noting some of the overlapping terrains with tourism. This is followed by a contextualization of Thai mobilities in relation to the development of inbound and outbound movements. Next, we offer empirical evidence to illustrate how tourism and migration in the context of retirement and marriage intertwine, overlap, and influence each other.

Retirement, Tourism, and Migration

While conventional forms of mobility are often associated with labor migration and economic push and pull factors (Williams and Hall, 2002), in contrast, retirement migration and amenity migration constitute "new" forms of mobility that arise less from economic necessity and more from personal leisure and lifestyle preferences. Although these forms of migration have been around for some time, their increased frequency and expanded geographical range in recent decades render them "novel" (Rainer, 2019). Senior citizen migration is therefore a particular form of consumption-led migration as opposed to production-led types of spatial mobility (Bell and Ward, 2000). Consumption-related mobilities have also been categorized under the broader heading of amenity or lifestyle migration, with amenity migration defined as the movement of people for pleasure enhanced by the allure of experiencing different lifestyles rather than for economic reasons (Chipeniuk, 2008; Benson and O'Reilly, 2016). Désirée Bender et al. (2018), however, argue that retirement migrants are often motivated by social or financial challenges in their home countries, rather than simply searching for a better lifestyle. On the other hand, since retirees depend neither on employment nor on other local economic structures and are in most cases already freed from family responsibilities such as childcare, they have fewer decision-making constraints (McHugh et al., 1995).

International retirement migration has been defined as a "highly selective migration process which redistributes (retired) individuals – and their concomitant incomes, expenditures, health, and care needs – across international boundaries" (Williams et al., 1997, p. 220). It is a type of movement that blurs the distinction between tourism and migration. Retirement migrants move, "migrate, oscillate, circulate or tour between their home and host countries" and any effort "to categorize their moves fails as the individuals themselves periodically alter their migration patterns and thus their legal status" (O'Reilly, 2007, p. 281). Indeed, the characteristics of retirement migration suggest a strong convergence with touristic mobility. Especially when considering "lifestyle migrants" or "amenity-seeking migrants" drawn by the destination country's services and attractions, the overlapping terrain between "tourist" and "migrant" becomes clear, since both types of travel are driven by the same motivational factors. Moreover, the overlap becomes more palpable when one considers that the target areas of mass tourism and international senior citizen migration coincide to a great degree. Furthermore, the fact that opportunities for consumer-oriented, "amenity-seeking" migrants were initially generated by the tourism industry (Hall and Williams, 2002) indicates that mass tourism is often a precursor to subsequent migration processes. Considering this, the relationship between prior voyages as a tourist and subsequent migration plays an important role and influences the decision to migrate (Husa et al., 2014). These dynamics suggest the importance of considering these two phenomena in conjunction. In short, due to these strong overlaps, we concur with many authors who consider clear delineations between different mobility types ranging from tourism to migration to be problematic (Williams and Hall, 2002).[4]

Within Southeast Asia, Thailand, Malaysia, the Philippines, and – more recently – Vietnam and Cambodia have become attractive destinations for long-stay tourists and retirees from affluent countries of the Global North. The economic importance of this flow is demonstrated by the fact that during the last two decades several governments and entrepreneurs in the region have been increasingly promoting

152 K. Butratana, A. Trupp, and K. Husa

their countries as ideal retirement destinations (Husa et al., 2014, p. 139). As the first country in Southeast Asia to court affluent retirees from "Western countries," Malaysia initiated a retiree program called "Silver Hair" in 2002 and introduced the so-called "Malaysia My Second Home (MM2H)" initiative in 2006 (Wong et al., 2017).[5] In the Philippines, a Special Resident Retiree Visa Program is available to any foreigner older than 35 years (Gorvett, 2010). Moreover, the Philippine Retirement Authority has launched a global retiree recruitment initiative called "Plan METJACK," an acronym for the main source countries or regions, i.e., Middle East, Europe, Taiwan, Japan, America, China, and Korea (Toyota and Xiang, 2012, p. 710). More recently, Vietnamese and Cambodian developers have begun to promote popular tourist destinations in their countries as retirement options. Thailand has also established a foreign retiree program enabling participants to obtain a one-year renewable visa. This is not, however, an entirely new phenomenon for this country: The settlement of large numbers of foreign nationals goes back to the Vietnam War. Many American soldiers who were stationed in Thailand during the Vietnam War remained there after the conflict ended, ultimately wedding local women.

The influx of long-term tourists and retirement migrants has a significantly biased gender ratio in favor of men.[6] Almost everyone knows the stereotypical image of a somewhat overweight, mostly gray-haired man with a sunburnt face accompanied by a beautiful Thai woman, half his size and age (Veress, 2011, p. 203). In Thailand, one of the new focal points of international retirement migration is the region around the town of Hua Hin. The area is touted as Thailand's new "retirement haven," together with the tourist center Cha-am. The region has a rapidly growing expatriate population, and a considerable percentage of so-called *farang* (the Thai term for Western foreigners[7]) have settled here after retirement. This phenomenon is obviously not limited to Hua Hin. Other important tourist centers in Thailand, such as Bangkok, Pattaya, Phuket, Chiang Mai, and some parts of northeastern Thailand, show significant numbers of Western immigrants. The main reason we selected Hua Hin for our study is that this area is considered Thailand's growing new touristic center, especially since the 2004 tsunami. This growth extends beyond the tourism sector: The region is increasingly becoming a hotspot for *farang* immigration and the epicenter of a booming real estate market.

Marriage Migration and Tourism

Marriage-related migration has been conceptualized as a broad category of marriage mobilities encompassing three distinct sub-forms (Charsley et al., 2012). The first sub-form is known as family formation or marriage migration, in which a permanent resident of a country marries a person from overseas and the foreign spouse migrates to join their partner. A second sub-form discussed in the literature is migration to reunite with a married partner (family/spousal reunification), wherein a migrant later brings a spouse back home. The third sub-form encompasses other contexts where marriage plays an important factor in migration. For example, this sub-category includes dependent or tied migration, where both partners are migrants but one is the primary migrant and the partner accompanies the initial migrant. Katharine Charsley (2012, p. 29) argues that many of these sub-forms of international partnerships

> are accepted as unproblematic, . . . [whereas] marriage between, say Europeans or other groups considered culturally compatible are rarely subjected to the same sort of scrutiny that marriages between racial groups or between groups identified as "different" face.

Marriage migrants have complex migration trajectories which may include return, circular, or transnational migration (Ishii, 2016; Charsley, 2012). The directions of marriage migratory patterns are diverse, including North–North, South–South, and North–South trajectories, and marriage-related migrants may include men, children, and the elderly (Ishii, 2016). Yet, globally, most international marriage migrants are female and follow a Global South to Global North migration pattern mirroring female labor migration (Constable, 2011; Fresnoza-Flot, 2021).

The existing literature identifies various drivers of global cross-border marriage migration. Some authors highlight the affluence gap between economically more and less advanced countries as one potential driver (Jones and Shen, 2008; Constable, 2005). Others examine how media representations and migrant narratives foster imaginings of a better life, which in turn can stimulate marriage migration (Lapanun, 2012). Many partners from Thailand's villages in transnational marriages have gained material wealth (e.g., new houses, cars, jewelry, or mobile phones) and adopted new roles as family providers through these unions (Angeles and Sunanta, 2009). Such examples and "global imaginations" (Appadurai, 1996, p. 55), constructed through media reports and friends' or relatives' narratives, can be compared with the notion of the tourist gaze (Urry, 2002) and how popular images propel tourists' mobilities (Adams, 1984). The expectations of an upcoming journey for potential tourists and migrants alike are pre-constructed through information and images transmitted via social media, TV programs, movies, newspapers, and stories of other tourists or migrants.

A few authors, such as Williams (2012), have suggested that increased mobility has enhanced the relationship between international tourism and cross-border marriage migration, creating more chances for intimate relationships to develop across international borders. Before COVID-19, the UNWTO recorded 1.5 billion international tourist arrivals in 2018, with Thailand ranking among the top ten destinations, counting 39.8 million arrivals (UNWTO, 2020). Mass tourism attractions and a well-developed service sector in many countries offer multiple opportunities for social interaction between domestic visitors, international tourists, and local residents. Previous studies highlight linkages between the (red-light)-entertainment industry, sex trade, and international marriage and migration (Brennan, 2004). As scholars note, women in some parts of the world opt to migrate to another country to toil in menial jobs rather than work in the local sex tourism trade (Mix and Piper, 2003).

Another area where marriage migration and tourism are closely intertwined is the context of VFR tourism. Each round and type of migration creates a new network and new spatial settings of friends and kin (Williams and Hall, 2002). Bo-Young Moon et al. (2019) state that VFR tourism is mainly travel to one's original or previous home, to a place where left behind family members and friends reside. In addition to visiting friends and relatives, VFR tourists may also visit nearby attractions, restaurants, and other leisure facilities. Importantly, however, VFR tourism can flow in both directions following the friends and family network (Dwyer et al., 2014; Williams and Hall, 2002).

Within the Thai context, intimate cross-cultural relations between Thais and Westerners date back to the late Ayutthaya period in the 17th and 18th centuries when an increasing number of international and European merchants came to the country. However, the first major push factors for larger-scale cross-border relationships and marriages occurred in the second half of the 20th century during and after the Vietnamese–American War (Cohen, 2003). At that time, American soldiers were stationed in Bangkok and other provinces, and tens of thousands of Vietnam-based GIs went to Thailand on "Rest and Recreation" (R&R) leaves. Most military bases in Thailand as well as the R&R zones were "surrounded by a 'pleasure belt' of restaurants, bars, massage parlors, hotels, nightclubs and brothels" (Meyer, 1988, p. 70). Thai women increasingly entered relationships with American military men. The sex work origins of most Thai women who married American soldiers created an association between sex work, sex tourism, and marriage to foreigners in the Thai collective memory (Bishop and Robinson, 1998).

Since that time, despite manifold political, economic, and ecological crises, Thailand has developed into a mass tourism destination and is positioned in the top four for tourism earnings globally (UNWTO, 2020). This immense volume of international tourists is supported by a strong network of transport facilities and cross-border connections as well as by a highly developed service and hospitality sector geared toward international tourists and the expatriate population of various budgets. In many Thai–Western marriages, men met their Thai partners while visiting Thailand. Such meetings may happen by chance, be planned by one of the partners or by a friend, or be arranged by matchmaking and marriage agencies (Cohen, 2003; Zimmermann, 2014).

From Tourist to Retirement Migrant

It is often assumed that potential retirement migrants' destination choices are mainly influenced by former touristic activities. Only the second step, the "fine-tuning" – where one selects the exact location or kind of the desired environment – is supposed to be more heavily influenced by state-run or private marketing initiatives (Williams and Hall, 2002; Jaisuekun and Sunanta, 2016). Our research addressed the growing importance of retirement migration to Thailand, highlighted the tourism–retirement link, and confirmed the great influence of touristic activities on subsequent migration (Husa et al., 2014).

In the case of Hua Hin/Cha-am, most immigrants had considerable experience with Thailand from earlier travels, long before settling in the country. In the 2010–11 survey, only one in 11 respondents reported "jumping into cold water," i.e., not having been to Thailand a single time before moving there. One-third of the respondents had even traveled to the country ten or more times, and many had been regular visitors (on annual trips, for example), thus already felt sufficiently acquainted with Thailand, its culture, and its people well before they decided to move there (Husa et al., 2014; Vielhaber et al., 2014). The 2016–17 survey, which focused mainly on long-stay tourists, produced similar results: Almost one-third of the respondents had a long history of travel to Thailand which was either leisure- or business-related, and almost 40% had already been to the Hua Hin/Cha-am more than once. Extensive travel to Thailand for business reasons was mentioned by a few migrants. These included tour guides and tour operators who supervised or organized group tours, employees of international corporations who were sent to Thailand as expats, a former diplomat, and a military advisor. Furthermore, approximately 19% of the respondents said that they would seriously consider moving to Thailand after retiring. The destinations visited during previous trips to Thailand are not surprising – these long-stay tourists usually focused on mass tourism hotspots. Hence, most immigrants to Thailand had already traveled extensively and accumulated abundant experience in the country – whether for touristic or business reasons – before they decided to settle there.

Personal relationships with local residents in the study area, however, were a negligible factor in the choice of Hua Hin or Cha-am as a retirement destination. In contrast to some studies of international retirement migration to relatively non-touristic, up-country destinations in Thailand (e.g., Koch-Schulte, 2008) where the retirement destination choice was influenced primarily by wives and girlfriends from the region, such factors seemed to play only minor roles in migration to touristic areas.

The proximity to the ocean, favorable climatic, and calm, safe atmosphere make Cha-am and Hua Hin highly popular among "Western" retirees. Cha-am is also less touristy which scores an additional bonus for some of the respondents. The lower cost of living in Thailand and retirement migrants' affection for Thai culture and people also play important roles. Many foreign residents consider Cha-am – a smaller and lesser-known site – "quieter" and "more Thai," with significantly "fewer *farang*" than in Hua Hin, which all enhance its appeal:

> It's a quiet beach area with a lot of Thai people coming from Bangkok every weekend. . . . So you have low prices and you still have the Thai culture. And that's very important.
>
> *(Arvid, Norway, 46 years, Cha-am)*

> There is less stress, fewer tourists, it's quiet and a lot less expensive.
>
> *(Pierre, Switzerland, 51 years, Cha-am)*

It is noteworthy that these ex-tourists try to avoid other tourists by choosing what they perceive to be less touristic locations. This can also be seen as a strategy to dissociate themselves from mass tourism (Week, 2012).

156 K. Butratana, A. Trupp, and K. Husa

TABLE 8.1 Reasons for migration to Thailand

	Nr.	%	% of respondents (112)
Health problems, better climate	28	17.3	25.0
Lower costs of living	23	14.2	20.5
Customs and culture	16	9.9	14.3
Occupational possibilities	17	10.5	15.2
Because of Thai spouse/partner	17	10.5	15.2
Problems in country of origin	6	3.7	5.4
To enjoy one's retirement	15	9.3	13.4
Searching for "adventure"	7	4.3	6.3
Recommendation by friends	8	4.9	7.1
Other	25	15.4	22.3
Total	**162**	**100.0**	

Source: Husa et al., 2014, p. 161

In Hua Hin, the royal family's summer palace imbues the town with a sense of safety and "quality" – expressed in the elegant townscape and upscale audience. Another advantage of Hua Hin noted by retirement migrants is the extremely expat-friendly infrastructure: Many shopping and entertainment venues cater to Western desires and are particularly appreciated by expats. Also, sex tourism is rather underdeveloped there compared to other destinations such as Pattaya, making Hua Hin more family-friendly in the eyes of many research participants. Finally, respondents noted that Hua Hin has a higher-class clientele. Additional reasons immigrants offered for the selection of Hua Hin, as opposed to other regions of Thailand, were favorable climatic conditions (less heat and a milder rainy season), proximity to Bangkok, cleanliness, and the attractive countryside surrounding the city:

> It seems cleaner, it's fairly modern. You have most of the amenities that people are looking for. And it's fairly quiet.
>
> *(John, United Kingdom, 53 years, Hua Hin)*

> I like it because of the weather, it's cool, it's close to the beach, it's only two and a half hours from Bangkok, and when the king was healthy, he lived here. And what's good enough for the king, that's good enough for me.
>
> *(Paul, United Kingdom, 68 years, Hua Hin)*

Respondents' reasons for leaving their home country for an extended period were generally associated with retirement, a factor allowing many of them to fulfill a long-cherished dream. However, in fact, there were also other reasons that led to this decision, including warm climate that promised to alleviate health problems and the relatively low cost of living enabling a higher standard of living (see Table 8.1). Other destinations with equally favorable climate and low costs of living scored significantly lower than Thailand as preferred migration destinations. Several interviewees who had already lived in Mediterranean countries before moving to Thailand (mostly in Spain) complained about the significant cost of living increases there and about the cold, damp winter months – not so in Thailand. Other alternative warm and inexpensive destinations considered by the respondents were ultimately deemed too politically unsafe or dangerous due to high crime rates (Kenya, Central America, Cambodia, and Vietnam), too conservative (Malaysia, Indonesia), or lacking sufficient levels of medical care (Laos and Cambodia).

Contact with the local population clearly played a subordinate role in interviewees' decisions to relocate to Cha-am/Hua Hin, since approximately half of the respondents were not personally acquainted with any Thais before moving. Only 15% had met their Thai partners before choosing to move. In contrast to other surveys (Howard, 2008; Koch-Schulte, 2008), the availability of attractive Thai partners was seldom mentioned explicitly as an important reason for migrating to Thailand. However, because around 91% of the respondents were men and only a very small portion relocated with a Western partner, it seems pertinent to take a closer look at the role of women in this migration process. When research participants were queried about the importance of relationships with Thai women as a motive, desires for a lasting and stable relationship were given great importance. Most respondents saw the factor of the "availability of women" in conjunction with a permanent life partner and the desire to share a life with someone. For example, in response to our question about the extent to which the sexual availability of Thai women figured into his calculus, Wesley, a 62-year-old American migrant in Hua Hin stated:

> No, no, actually it's not. I know it sounds like a lie but it's not. I'd like just to meet one nice person. One nice person would be wonderful and the lady I am with right now is very nice and we get along well together.

Interview data indicate that expats who had already lived in Thailand for long periods of time and who reached retirement age no longer prioritize sexual encounters with Thai women. However, the possibility of easily obtaining a young, attractive partner as an older single man was highlighted in several conversations. As Mike, a 62-year-old British retiree in Hua Hin explained:

> I suppose having a young woman around you is a good boost for your ego. In the West if I try to talk to someone your age, in England, she would run and get the policemen. . . . I'd rather look at something pretty than look at something that's all wrinkled and horrible.

As Mike's comments convey, the imagery of both men and women, including the social role of Thai women compared to that of Western women, is quite stereotypical. Thai women's "submissiveness" and male superiority were often perceived as

158 K. Butratana, A. Trupp, and K. Husa

desirable (also see Brennan, 2004). For instance, Paul, a 68-year-old British migrant in Hua Hin, commented:

> They [Thai women] give you respect which you don't get back in the UK or in Europe. You have respect, you give them security, they give you appreciation. It is as simple as that.

Although Thai women's traditional role is not mentioned as a primary reason for relocating, the Western male gaze and stereotypical perceptions about Thai women are important dimensions of the retirement migration experience. In general, most respondents appear to consider their lives in Thailand quite satisfying. However, as Klaus, a 55-year-old German living in Hua Hin, observed, when asked whether he had found the paradise he was seeking:

> more or less, but after some time even living in paradise becomes boring. After a few years you find out that the same problems you had at home emerge, sometimes even worse – if you weren't capable of getting along alone at home, you will also have problems managing things in your life here.

Female immigrants to Thailand remain a minority, but their numbers have increased steadily in recent years as Christina Vogler's (2015) study on retirement migration to Northern Thailand demonstrates. One of Vogler's (2015, p. 49) Swiss participants, Christine, who lives with two other Swiss women in a Swiss settlement north of Chiang Mai, explains her decision to move to Thailand as follows:

> Before, I was here on vacation a lot. My daughter was on an exchange year in Thailand, even here in Chiang Mai! That was the reason why I came to Thailand in the first place. Then I took in an exchange student from Thailand myself. I always call her "daughter of my heart." I was still a lot in contact with her and her family years after. In the end, she even became the owner of my land here. Because she is Thai she could buy the land. As a European, I can't buy land.

While Western retirement migration is dominated by single men, increasingly single women and couples are also relocating to Thailand, as studies indicate (Horn et al., 2016; Vogler, 2015).

Tourism and Marriage Migration

Tourist hotspots in Thailand represent social spaces for forming intimate relationships and generating subsequent travel and marriage migration. In Austria, the number of Thai migrants has significantly increased in recent decades since Thailand became one of Austria's most important long-distance tourism destinations. The Thai population in Austria currently constitutes the second largest Southeast Asian group, growing from 40 Thai citizens in 1971 to 4,000 in 2012 and 5,006[8] in 2020 (Statistik Austria, 2020). More than 80% of Austria's Thai population is female, and over 60% of them are married to Austrian men (Butratana and Trupp, 2014). Simultaneously, Austrian tourist arrivals in Thailand increased from 46,717 in 2003 to 86,987 in 2011 (Alpha Research, 2012, p. 508) and 1,116,656 in 2018 (Ministry of Tourism and Sports, 2020). Smaller numbers of Thai migrants are students as well as both high- and low-skilled labor migrants (Butratana and Trupp, 2011).

Some tourist zones, including areas in Bangkok, Pattaya, Phuket, Hua Hin, and Koh Samui, feature various tourist attractions, restaurants, bars, clubs, and massage parlors where tourists and local people meet and interact (Statham et al., 2020). Indeed, 42 (49.4%) out of 85 survey respondents met their Austrian male partner in a tourist place in Thailand. Most of the women we interviewed were also employed in service- and/or tourism-related occupations in Thailand at the time they met their partners, working as waitresses, receptionists, bar workers, masseuses, hairdressers, or small business owners. The majority of Thai marriage migrants interviewed (50.6%) met by coincidence (or "destiny," as many highlighted in our conversations) or through introductions by friends and relatives (38.8%). Only a small percentage initially met through other channels such as matchmaking agencies or online forums.

Many of these intimate relationships originating in such tourist places entailed an initial joint domestic trip within Thailand (mainly sponsored by the male Western partner), followed by mutual cross-border visits before decisions for more permanent marriage migration were made. For example, one of the interview partners, Nee, was born and raised in a village in the northeastern region of Thailand, 450 km from Bangkok. Born into a large family with eight siblings, she comes from a socioeconomically poor background. Nee dropped out of school after the fourth grade, at the age of 11, to support her family and to fulfill the expected role of a good daughter by working in a grocery shop. At the age of 16, she met her Thai boyfriend and they decided to move to Bangkok to find better-paid jobs. In Bangkok, both worked in garment factories. She became pregnant and after the birth of the child, they decided to return to their home province. While Nee started a small business as a mobile seller at a bus station, her boyfriend began to gamble, routinely getting drunk, and behaving irresponsibly toward the family, which eventually led to the breakup of their relationship. Nee then decided to move back to Bangkok on her own to find a new job and escape the reminders of these negative personal experiences. She initially worked in a factory and then as a salesperson at a popular clothing market, where she met many foreign clients with whom she could also practice English. At the age of 25, she entered another relationship with a Thai boyfriend. For Nee, that was worse than the first one. As she explained, she "jumped out of a frying pan into the fire," suffering from her partner's behavior which included gambling, drinking, and domestic violence. She separated from her Thai boyfriend and after being single for a while, she met her future Austrian husband, Karl, while he was visiting Thailand as a tourist. They first met by coincidence in Bangkok's Silom area which features a popular night market as well as many restaurants and bars. Nee highlighted in our conversations that meeting her foreign partner was "destiny." Karl was five years older than her, was also single at the time, and often visited Southeast Asia for business-related trips. Nee showed him some of the famous tourist attractions in Bangkok, and Karl subsequently invited her for a holiday to Thailand's islands. After this trip, Nee asked him to visit her family in northeastern Thailand. Nee was impressed that Karl was happy to become acquainted with another part of Thailand and that he appreciated meeting her family. After spending time together in Thailand, Karl returned to his home country and applied for a tourist visa for Nee so that she could visit him in Austria. During this visit, the relationship further evolved, and after one year, she decided to marry him and move permanently to Austria. Nee's son grew up with his grandparents in Thailand. He received regular support and remittances from his mother and eventually became a parent himself. Nee's story demonstrates how internal migration can lead to international migration and how shorter tourism and leisure-related stays can culminate in cross-border marriage.

As Mary Beth Mills (1997) illustrates, at least two forces come into play in shaping migration decisions in the Thai context: One refers to the obligations of a good and dutiful daughter propelled by traditional family values (*bun khun*), and the other is the desire to be a "modern" (*than samay*) woman who wants to experience a new and different lifestyle. Further drivers for cross-border marriage migration include the affluence gap between more and less developed countries, imagined better lives, the role of migrant networks, and – as outlined earlier – the increased interactions between "hosts" and "guests" in globalized tourism and entertainment zones (Lapanun, 2012; Butratana and Trupp, 2021).

As noted earlier, the tourism-led migration hypothesis suggests that previous tourism experience can play an important role in the migration decision-making process, a statement that has received little attention in the study of international marriage migration. However, our research data offer new nuances to our understanding of how these processes of tourism and migration comingle. Our data show that 24 (18.2%) of all Thai female respondents had previously worked or lived abroad and that 52 (61.2%) had international tourist experience before moving to Austria. However, the majority (34) of these international tourism experiences took place within Asia, particularly Southeast Asia, while 16 women indicated previous travel experience to the EU. For example, Peet graduated from the University of Fine Arts in Thailand and studied English at a private school. After completing her education, she worked for an international chain hotel in Thailand, but she wanted to travel and explore places beyond Asia. Via a Thai friend's network, she got a job as a housekeeper in Greece for ten months. Peet was able to save some money which she used for domestic trips in Greece and for further travel to Austria where she stayed with a friend from Thailand. During her stay, she took a job as a part-time housekeeper in a hotel in Austria and decided to extend her visa and stay longer (which due to different immigration laws would not be possible nowadays). During her stay in Austria, she met her partner Tom at a party which

Tourism, Marriage, and Retirement Migration **161**

ultimately led to her decision to stay in Austria permanently and study German. Peet eventually found a new job as a graphic designer for a company, enabling her to further develop the skills she acquired back in Thailand at the University of Fine Arts. Peet is proud that she – as a Thai woman – could impress her Austrian co-workers and achieve success in her chosen career. The initially planned short-term visit to Austria turned into a long-term commitment, both privately and professionally. Since she lived in Austria, she could pursue her passion for travel and she visited many European countries. Her experience reverses the common theme of the Western male traveler meeting his partner abroad, thereby challenging dominant assumptions and stereotypes of male-directed processes in marriage migration. While her story differs from the dominant narratives in our data, it represents important diversities along geographical and gendered mobilities.

In contrast to Peet, other interviewees had no prior travel experience in Austria. Often following bad experiences in Thailand, these women reached a point in life where they were ready for radical change. As Nut, a 48-year-old Thai woman from eastern Thailand, explained: "[Approximately 25 years ago] I decided to cross the Rubicon, even though at that time I did not even know where Austria was located. I had no idea what this country looked like. And what awaited me." Earlier, Nut, who was a single mother needing to support her children, moved from her hometown in eastern Thailand to Bangkok to work in a bar. On her fourth day at work, she met Christian who was on holiday in Thailand. He visited her every day and, after several meetings, Christian asked Nut to quit her job at the bar and offered to support her financially to which she agreed. In that period, Christian visited Thailand every three to four months on business trips. During his visits, she invited him to her hometown while he invited her to travel to Thailand and Southeast Asia. They had a long-distance relationship between Austria and Thailand for two years. Christian then asked her to visit his home country, Austria, and she accepted the invitation. She applied for a tourist visa, which enabled her to spend six months in Austria. They then returned to Thailand together, decided to marry, and prepared for a more permanent move to Austria. Nut was very excited about her first visit to Austria which was her first trip beyond Southeast Asia. In Austria, Christian and his family were great sources of support for her. She recalls In introduced her to Thai restaurants and Thai markets in Austria. In the beginning, she faced two big challenges. First, she had to leave her children behind in Thailand. They were eventually allowed to join her in Austria. The other big challenge was language. Initially, she did not speak German. The first years were thus difficult, and she often felt lonely. However, she has been calling home regularly and usually visits Thailand at least once a year. While Nut still misses the left-behind family in Thailand, she appreciates the formalized social security system in Austria.

Few of the women interviewed were well-traveled internationally before their migration for a cross-border marriage, showing that independent travel to Europe or Austria before marriage generally played a minor role in the marriage migration decision-making process.

162 K. Butratana, A. Trupp, and K. Husa

Visiting Friends and Relatives Tourism

In a globalized world of increasing interconnectivity and mobility, it is not surprising that migrants travel between their current and original homes and that they receive visits from their left-behind relatives and friends. While some migrants decide to cut off relationships with their country of origin after arrival in the new destination, the majority maintain contact with family members (Dwyer et al., 2014). Empirical evidence from our research suggests that all 85 marriage migrants we interviewed maintain contact with their family or relatives in Thailand. The majority do so frequently, through phone calls or social media communication (Table 8.2). Over the last six years, 82 out of 85 (97.6%) respondents made a trip back home to Thailand, with most trips lasting between two and eight weeks. Our data indicate that marriage migrants spend more time and more money during their trips to Thailand than the average European tourist visiting Thailand (Ministry of Tourism and Sports, 2020).

All except one of the respondents travel to Thailand to spend time with family and relatives. Thai women we interviewed stay in their parents' or relatives' homes,

TABLE 8.2 Aspects of visiting family and relatives in Thailand

		Nr	%
Frequency of contact	Twice a week or more	77	90.6
	Once a week	5	5.9
	Once a month	3	3.5
Mode of contact*	Phone	84	98.8
	Social media	83	97.6
Frequency of trip to Thailand	Every year	50	58.8
	Every two years	24	28.2
	Every three years	7	8.2
	Every five to six years	2	2.4
	Never	2	2.4
Reasons for trip to Thailand*	Visiting family and relatives	81	95.3
	Holiday	64	75.3
Typical travel companions from Austria*	None (solo travel)	33	38.8
			63.5
			32.9
	Husband	53	9.4
	Children	27	
	Friends	7	
Travel spending per Thailand trip in EUR	0	2	2.4
	<1,000	2	2.4
	1,001–2,000	9	10.6
	2,001–5,000	27	31.8
	5,001–10,000	30	35.8
	>10,000	15	17.6

Source: Own survey; n = 85; *multiple answers possible

with only a few opting to book hotels instead. While there, they spend a great deal of money taking family members out to restaurants, renovating their parents or their own homes, and meeting other familial material needs (such as buying new mobile phones for relatives and purchasing everyday household and food items, such as rice or milk products). For example, on her recent trip to Thailand, Ploy visited her hometown in the northern highland region and then invited her elder sister for a trip to the eastern gulf coast resort region of Pattaya. Ploy stated: "I am really happy and so proud to have a trip with my sister. Because she never ever left our village." Most respondents state that the decision to marry an Austrian man is also tied to family interests or obligations. Supporting parents and family members plays a major role for most marriage migrants in Thai society, especially for daughters, in keeping with *Bun khun*. *Bun khun* is an expression of gratitude and reciprocity to parents and others from whom one previously received essential support. Reciprocity is also considered a way to improve stores of merit in popular Buddhism (Tosakul, 2010, p. 191).

However, when Thai marriage migrants visit their home country, they often need to mediate the competing demands of their (Thai) families and their Western partner, children, or friends accompanying them on the return to the homeland. Many of the Thai women we interviewed do so by making use of the additional leisure and shopping opportunities in Thailand. Before or after visiting their left-behind family, they continue to visit other tourist areas within Thailand or other Asian countries. As also shown by Kathleen M. Adams (2021) who examined tourism patterns of the Toraja,[9] homebound travel involves interwoven activities combining family and cultural events with visits to local tourism sites. VFR tourism also flows in the other direction, when family members, relatives, or friends from Thailand visit Austria, though in smaller numbers and with lower frequency.

Generally, VFR tourism is strongly focused on visiting and staying with family members rather than friends, reflecting the crucial role of family values and obligations in Thai society. However, at the same time, Thai women and especially their Austrian partners hope to experience other destinations and leisure activities in Thailand, necessitating travel itineraries that satisfy both left-behind family members and Austrian partners and family.

Conclusion

The continuous and growing influx of Western tourists to Thailand has influenced more permanent forms of movement in the context of retirement and marriage migration. Our data show that most Western retirement migrants residing in Thailand had already traveled extensively for leisure and recreation or business purposes before they decided to settle in the country. Many thus transformed their favorite holiday destination into a second or even first home, often after retiring. Features enjoyed during their travels and holidays, such as the warmer, more appealing climate and lower costs of living, are also the main reasons for these more permanent moves. In contrast to other studies of international retirement migration to Thailand (Koch-Schulte, 2008), where the target destination choice was strongly influenced by wives and girlfriends from that region, such factors played a relatively minor role in our research. However, interview data shed light on some Western men's stereotypical images of Thai women and how their perceptions of local women (as available and subservient) played an important role in migration decisions. The low costs of living, wide range of services, and, in most cases, a positive image of the destination area formed during previous stays as tourists are still the most important drivers for this increasingly heterogeneous group of not only senior, mostly single migrants but also single women and couples, to select Thailand for the rest of their "golden years" (Horn et al., 2016; Vogler, 2015).

In the context of marriage migration, tourism and migration mainly intersect through two dynamics. First, Thailand's tourism hotspots are social spaces where international tourists meet Thai women (and men) who are frequently internal migrants themselves working in the hospitality and service sector. This is where intimate relationships often originate, leading to domestic holidays within Thailand, mutual cross-border visits, and eventually marriage and the Thai partner's migration to a new country. Only a minority of the marriage migrants in Austria had prior travel experience in Austria or other European countries. While studies show that Thai and Southeast Asian outbound tourism to Europe has increased in recent years (Bui and Trupp, 2020), these travel experiences do not seem to lead to desires to make the holiday destination a second home.[10] Second, the Thai marriage migrants abroad not only helped establish transnational networks and flows for remittances, ideas, values, and lifestyles, motivating still more women to marry and move abroad (Statham et al., 2021) but also produced an increase in VFR tourism. Thai migrants in Austria regularly visit their home countries for both leisure and family purposes. Home visits and financial support for relatives also reflect Thai women's socio-culturally specific gendered expectations surrounding obligations to parents and family members (Angeles and Sunanta, 2009). Future research on Thai marriage migration might consider non-heterosexual relationships as well as the migration experiences of Thai men.

Our chapter examined the intersecting terrain between tourism and migration in the Thai context. We have shown how tourism intertwines and overlaps with retirement migration and marriage migration and how these varied forms of contemporary spatial mobility influence each other. The chapter thus contributes to recent discussions aimed at overcoming the "binary between tourism and migration that has plagued classic Western models of travel" (Adams, 2021, p. 683; Bloch, 2020). The COVID-19 pandemic has strongly impeded mobility between Austria and Thailand, as elsewhere in the world. In April 2020, in the early stage of the pandemic, this chapter's first author, a Thai citizen (Kosita) was barred from entering Austria by emigration officials at the Lost Angeles airport, despite her marriage to an Austrian citizen and possession of a Schengen visa for the EU. Since

Tourism, Marriage, and Retirement Migration **165**

then, countries have been regularly updating their COVID-19 entry regulations and VFR travel between Austria and Thailand is possible under certain conditions. Thailand even pioneered the so-called "Phuket Sandbox" in July 2021, allowing fully vaccinated and tested foreign tourists to enter Phuket Island, and subsequently other parts of Thailand. However, the evolution of virus variants, rising COVID-19 infection rates, and continuously changing travel restrictions and quarantine regulations, made many Thai marriage migrants and Austrian tourists stay home. The pandemic has also led to the shutdown of most international tourist destinations in Thailand, prompting the return migration of many newly unemployed domestic hospitality and service industry employees in Thailand. Future research on the tourism and migration nexus in Thailand may further examine these pandemic-induced reverse migration dynamics.

Notes

1 UNWTO statistics lists VFR together with "health, religion, other" into one purpose of visit category.
2 This is a joint research project of the Department of Geography and Regional Research, University of Vienna, and Suan Dusit University, Thailand, entitled "Searching for Paradise? International Retirement Migration to Thailand" (Husa et al., 2014).
3 The study area consisted of the town of Hua Hin, situated approximately 200 km south of Bangkok on the western Gulf of Thailand, and the beach town of Cha-am (located 20 km north of Hua Hin), which is primarily known for its coastal strip, Cha-am Beach.
4 For example, a special type of retirement mobility which strongly blurs the boundaries of tourism and migration is the Japanese *rongusutei* (long-stay tourism), i.e., officially organized, long-term trips for Japanese retirees. This type of mobility, organized by the Japanese Long-Stay Foundation for Japanese pensioners on behalf of the Japanese government since 1992, is defined as "a style of staying abroad for a relatively long time in order to experience the life and culture in a . . . destination and contribute to the local society while leaving the [sic] economic resources in Japan" (Ono, 2008, p. 151).
5 In 2021, the Malaysian government introduced a number of new rules such as significantly increasing the expected minimum monthly income from offshore sources.
6 The results of the 2010 population census showed an increase in the number of foreigners from 192,000 Westerners (Europeans, North Americans, Australians, and New Zealanders) in 2000 to approximately 260,000, tellingly three-quarters of them male.
7 The term *farang* originally derives from *Frank,* a Germanic people that became powerful in Central and Western Europe during the Middle Ages. The term was then used in the Mediterranean areas to refer to Western Europeans in general and spread further to many parts of Asia and the Pacific. In Thailand, the term was taken over from Muslim traders during the Ayutthaya period who used *farang* to refer to the Portuguese in Southeast Asia. More recently, *farang* is used to name "all Caucasians and the West in general" (Kitiarsa, 2010, p. 61).
8 Deploying the criterium of country of birth (rather than nationality), Statistik Austria counts 6,420 Thai people in Austria, whereas 5,471 of them are female.
9 The Toraja are an indigenous group in Sulawesi, Indonesia.
10 Most Thai tourists visiting Europe spend less than a week there and characteristically engage in a rather rushed consumption of tangible and classical cultural tourist attractions, pursuing experiences that seem exotic, and shopping (Trupp and Bui, 2015; Bui and Trupp, 2020).

166 K. Butratana, A. Trupp, and K. Husa

References

Adams, K.M. (1984) 'Come to Tana Toraja, "Land of the heavenly kings"': Travel agents as brokers in ethnicity', *Annals of Tourism Research*, 11(3), pp. 469–485.

Adams, K.M. (2021) 'What Western tourism concepts obscure: Intersections of migration and tourism in Indonesia', *Tourism Geographies*, 23(4), pp. 678–703.

Alpha Research (2012) *Thailand in figures 2010–2011*. Bangkok: Alpha Research.

Angeles, L.C. and Sunanta, S. (2009) 'Demanding daughter duty: Gender, community, village transformation, and transnational marriages in Northeast Thailand', *Critical Asian Studies*, 41(4), pp. 549–574.

Appadurai, A. (1996) *Modernity al large: Cultural dimensions of globalization*. Minneapolis, MN and London: University of Minnesota Press.

Bell, M. and Ward, G. (2000) 'Comparing temporary mobility with permanent migration', *Tourism Geographies*, 2(1), pp. 97–107.

Bender, D., Hollstein, T. and Schweppe, C. (2018) 'International retirement migration revisited: From amenity seeking to precarity migration?', *Transnational Social Review*, 8(10), pp. 98–102

Benson, M. and O'Reilly, K. (2016) *Lifestyle migration: Expectations, aspirations and experiences*. Abingdon: Routledge.

Bishop, R. and Robinson, L.S. (1998) *Night market: Sexual cultures and the Thai economic miracle*. New York and London: Routledge.

Bloch, N. (2020) 'Beyond a sedentary other and a mobile tourist: Transgressing mobility categories in the informal tourism sector in India', *Critique of Anthropology*, 40(2), pp. 218–237.

Brennan, D. (2004) *What's love got to do with it? Transnational desires and sex tourism in the Dominican Republic*. Durham, NC and London: Duke University Press.

Bui, H.T. and Trupp, A. (2020) 'Asian tourism in Europe: Consumption, distinction, mobility, and diversity', *Tourism Recreation Research*, 45, pp. 4–18.

Butratana, K. and Trupp, A. (2011) 'Thai communities in Vienna', *Austrian Journal of South-East Asian Studies*, 4(1), pp. 183–190.

Butratana, K. and Trupp, A. (2014) 'Thai female migration to Austria' in Husa, K., Trupp, A. and Wohlschlägl, H. (eds.) *Southeast Asian mobility transitions: Issues and trends in migration and tourism*. Vienna: Department of Geography and Regional Research, University of Vienna, pp. 220–236.

Butratana, K. and Trupp, A. (2021) 'Gender, class, and paradoxical mobilities of Thai marriage migrants in Austria', *Singapore Journal of Tropical Geography*, 42(1), pp. 85–106.

Charsley, K. (2012) 'Transnational marriage' in Charsley, K. (ed.) *Transnational marriage. New perspectives from Europe and beyond*. New York and London: Routledge, pp. 3–22.

Charsley, K., Storer-Church, B., Benson, M. and Van Hear, N. (2012) 'Marriage-related migration to the UK', *International Migration Review*, 46, pp. 861–890.

Chipeniuk, R. (2008) *Defining amenity migration: Results from a survey of experts*. Smithers: University of British Columbia.

Cohen, E. (2003) 'Transnational marriage in Thailand: The dynamics of extreme heterogamy' in Bauer, T. (ed.) *Sex and tourism: Journeys of romance, love, and lust*. New York: The Haworth Hospitality Press, pp. 57–82.

Constable, N. (2005) 'Introduction: Cross-border marriages, gendered mobility, and global hypergamy' in Constable, N. (ed.) *Cross-border marriages. Gender and mobility in transnational Asia*. Philadelphia, PA: University of Pennsylvania Press, pp. 1–16.

Constable, N. (2011) *Cross-border marriages: Gender and mobility in transnational Asia*. Philadelphia, PA: University of Pennsylvania Press.

Dwyer, L., Seetaram, N., Forsyth, P. and King, B. (2014) 'Is the migration-tourism relationship only about VFR?', *Annals of Tourism Research*, 46, pp. 130–143.

Fresnoza-Flot, A. (2021) '"Men are butterflies, women are hindlimbs of an elephant": Thai women's gendered being in transnational spaces', *Gender, Place & Culture*, 28(5), pp. 680–701.

Glick Schiller, N. and Salazar, N.B. (2013) 'Regimes of mobility across the globe', *Journal of Ethnic and Migration Studies*, 39, pp. 183–200.

Gorvett, J. (2010) 'Southeast Asia lures retirees with affordable luxury', *The International Herald Tribune*, 22, p. 12.

Gustafson, P. (2002) 'Tourism and seasonal retirement migration', *Annals of Tourism Research*, 29(4), pp. 899–918.

Hall, C.M. and Williams, A.M. (2002) 'Conclusions. Tourism-migration relationships' in Hall, C.M. and Williams, A.M. (eds.) *Tourism and migration. New relationships between production and consumption*. Dordrecht: Springer, pp. 277–289.

Horn, V., Bender, D., Hollstein, T. and Schweppe, C. (2016) ' "Moving (for) elder care abroad": The fragile promises of old-age care facilities for elderly Germans in Thailand' in Horn, V. and Schweppe, C. (eds.) *Transnational aging: Current insights and future challenges*. New York and London: Routledge, pp. 163–177.

Howard, R.W. (2008) 'Western retirees in Thailand: Motives, experiences, wellbeing, assimilation and future needs', *Ageing & Society*, 28, pp. 145–163.

Husa, K., Vielhaber, C., Jöstl, J., Veress, K. and Wieser, B. (2014) 'Searching for paradise? international retirement migration to Thailand – A case study of Hua Hin and Cha-am' in Husa, K., Trupp, A. and Wohlschlägl, H. (eds.) *Southeast Asian mobility transitions: Issues and trends in migration and tourism*. Vienna: Department of Geography and Regional Research, University of Vienna, pp. 137–167.

Ishii, S.K. (2016) 'Marriage migrants as multi-marginalized transnational diaspora' in Ishii, S.K. (ed.) *Marriage migration in Asia. Emerging minorities at the frontier of nation-states*. Singapore: NUS Press and Kyoto University Press, pp. 1–23.

Jaisuekun, K. and Sunanta, S. (2016) 'Lifestyle migration in Thailand: A case study of German migrants in Pattaya', *Thammasat Review*, 19(2), pp. 89–103.

Jones, G. and Shen, H. (2008) 'International marriage in East and Southeast Asia: Trends and research emphases', *Citizenship Studies*, 12, pp. 9–25.

Kitiarsa, P. (2010) 'An ambiguous intimacy: Farang as Siamese occidentalism' in Harrison, R.V. and Jackson, P.A. (eds.) *The ambiguous allure of the west. Traces of the colonial in Thailand*. New York: Cornell University Press, pp. 57–74.

Koch-Schulte, J. (2008) *Planning for international retirement migration and expats: A case study of Udon Thani*. Thailand: University of Manitoba.

Koslowski, R. (ed.) (2011) *Global mobility regimes: A conceptual reframing*. New York: Palgrave Macmillan.

Lapanun, P. (2012) 'Social relations and tensions in transnational marriage for rural women in Isan, Thailand' in Hayami, Y., Koizumi, J., Songsamphan, C. and Tosakul, R. (eds.) *The family in flux in Southeast Asia. Institution, ideology, practice*. Chiang Mai: Silkworm Books, pp. 483–503.

McHugh, K.E., Hogan, T.D. and Happel, S.K. (1995) 'Multiple residence and cyclical migration: A life course perspective' *The Professional Geographer*, 47(3), pp. 251–267.

Meyer, W. (1988) *Beyond the mask*. Saarbrücken: Verlag Breitenbach.

Ministry of Tourism and Sports (2020) *Tourism Statistics*. Bangkok: Ministry of Tourism and Sports. Available at: www.mots.go.th/more_news_new.php?cid=411.

Mills, M.B. (1997) 'Contesting the margins of Thai modernity', *American Ethnologist*, 24(1), pp. 37–61.

Mix, P.R. and Piper, N. (2003) 'Does marriage 'liberate' women from sex work? Thai women in Germany' in Piper, N. and Roces, M. (eds.) *Wife or worker? Asian women and migration*. Lanham, MD: Rowman & Littlefield, pp. 53–72.

Moon, B.-Y., Yang, S.-H. and Lee, T.J. (2019) 'Married immigrant women's VFR tourism as the way to ethnic minority group acculturation', *Journal of Tourism and Cultural Change*, 17, pp. 544–561.

Ono, M. (2008) 'Long-stay tourism and international retirement migration: Japanese retirees in Malaysia' in Haines, D.W., Minami, M. and Yamashita, S. (eds.) *Transnational migration in East Asia: Japan in a comparative focus*. Osaka: National Museum of Ethnology, pp. 151–162.

O'Reilly, K. (2007) 'The rural Idyll, residential tourism, and the spirit of lifestyle migration' in *Conference proceedings of thinking through tourism* (Association of Social Anthropologists). London: London Metropolitan University.

Rainer, G. (2019) 'Amenity/lifestyle migration to the Global South: Driving forces and socio-spatial implications in Latin America', *Third World Quarterly*, 40(7), pp. 1359–1377.

Salazar, N.B. (2022) 'Labour migration and tourism mobilities: Time to bring sustainability into the debate', *Tourism Geographies*, 24(1), pp. 141–151.

Stallmann, J.I. and Espinoza, M.C. (1996) *Tourism and retirement migration* (Faculty Paper Series 97/3). College Station: A&M University, Department of Agricultural Economics.

Statham, P., Scuzzarello, S., Sunanta, S. and Trupp, A. (2020) 'Globalising Thailand through gendered 'both-ways' migration pathways with 'the West': Cross-border connections between people, states, and places', *Journal of Ethnic and Migration Studies*, 46(8), pp. 1513–1542.

Statham, P., Scuzzarello, S., Sunanta, S. and Trupp, A. (eds.) (2021) *Thai-western mobilities and migration: Intimacy within cross-border connections*. New York and London: Routledge.

Statistik Austria (2020) *STATcube Statistische Datenbank*. Vienna: Statistik Austria.

Tosakul, R. (2010) 'Cross-border marriages: Experiences of village women from Northeastern Thailand with Western men' in Yang, W.-S. and Lu, M.C.-W. (eds.) *Asian cross-border marriage migration: Demographic patterns and social issues*. Amsterdam: Amsterdam University Press, pp. 179–199.

Toyota, M. and Xiang, B. (2012) 'The emerging transnational "retirement industry" in Southeast Asia', *International Journal of Sociology and Social Policy*, 32(11/12), pp. 708–719.

Trupp, A. and Bui, H.T. (2015) 'Thai outbound tourism to Austria: Trends and issues', *SDU Research Journal Humanities and Social Sciences*, 12(1), pp. 1–14.

UNWTO (2019) *UNWTO tourism highlights*. Madrid: UNWTO.

UNWTO (2020) *UNWTO tourism highlights*. Madrid: UNWTO.

Urry, J. (2002) *The tourist gaze*. Thousand Oaks, CA: Sage.

Veress, K. (2011) 'Vom Sextouristen zum Strandpensionisten?' in Husa, K., Nissel, H. and Wohlschlägl, H. (eds.) *Südost- und Südasien. Demographische, soziale und regionale Transformationen*. Vienna: Department of Geography and Regional Research, University of Vienna, pp. 203–248.

Vielhaber, C., Husa, K., Jöstl, J., Veress, K. and Wieser, B. (2014) 'Paradise found? Experiences of Farang retirement migrants in Hua Hin and Cha-am, Thailand' in Husa, K., Trupp, A and Wohlschlägl, H. (eds.) *Southeast Asian mobility transitions: Issues and trends in migration and tourism*. Vienna: Department of Geography and Regional Research, University of Vienna, pp. 168–195.

Vogler, C.M. (2015) *Receiving and providing care abroad. Interactions between international retirement migration and the elderly care sector in Chiang Mai, Thailand*. MA thesis. Vienna: University of Vienna.

Week, L. (2012) 'I am not a tourist: Aims and implications of "traveling"', *Tourist Studies*, 12(2), pp. 186–203.

Williams, A.M. and Hall, C.M. (2002) 'Tourism, migration, circulation and mobility. The contingencies of time and place' in Hall, C.M. and Williams, A.M. (eds.) *Tourism and migration. new relationships between production and consumption*. Dordrecht: Springer, pp. 1–52.

Williams, A.M., King, R. and Warnes, A.M. (1997) 'A place in the sun. International retirement migration from northern to Southern Europe', *European Urban and Regional Studies*, 4(2), pp. 115–134.

Williams, L. (2012) 'Transnational marriage migration and marriage migration. An overview' in Charsley, K. (ed.) *Transnational marriage. New perspectives from Europe and beyond*. New York: Routledge, pp. 23–40.

Wong, B.K.M., Musa, G. and Taha, A.Z. (2017) 'Malaysia my second home: The influence of push and pull motivations on satisfaction', *Tourism Management*, 61, pp. 394–410.

Zimmermann, C. (2014) "Love me, love me forever" – Thai women's pre-migrational hopes, dreams, and images of love and marriages with western men, in Husa, K., Trupp, A. and Wohlschlägl, H. (eds.) *Southeast Asian mobility transitions: Issues and trends in migration and tourism*. Vienna: Department of Geography and Regional Research, University of Vienna, pp. 196–219.

9

THE TOURIST, THE MIGRANT, AND THE ANTHROPOLOGIST

A Problematic Encounter Within European Cities

Francesco Vietti

Prologue: Turin, June 20, 2019

> When I saw the Gran Madre church for the first time, here in Turin, I felt like I had been electrocuted. The church is in fact very similar to the Pantheon in Rome, whose architect is the famous Apollodorus of Damascus. Damascus is my beloved city, where I was born and raised, and so seeing this church in Turin I suddenly felt at home, I realized that somehow I could restart my life, which had been interrupted by the war.

Farid tells the group of tourists how Turin's architectural heritage, in an interplay of harmonies and memories, helped him feel "at home" when he arrived in the city at the end of his escape from Syria. This is June 20, World Refugee Day, and Farid is leading a walk through the streets of Turin's district of Porta Palazzo, Italy. This is not an impromptu job – Farid has taken part in a long training course to become an intercultural guide with the *Migrantour* project. Through this initiative, he also puts to use the professional skills he gained before leaving Syria. In Damascus, before the outbreak of the conflict, Farid was, in fact, the director of a tour company and worked mainly with Italian tourists visiting his country.

At the next stage of the walk, we are to meet with the *imam* of the nearby Peace Mosque. The group crosses the market square and enters the courtyard of a tenement house. Several generations of immigrants live in the building: Sicilians, Calabrians, and Apulians who arrived in Turin from southern Italy between the 1950s and the 1970s, attracted by work opportunities in the automotive industry; as well as Moroccans, Chinese, Nigerians, and Romanians who have come to the city in the last 30 years, mostly joining the construction and trade sectors.

"Have any of you ever entered a mosque in Italy?," Farid asks as the group approaches. Everyone shakes their heads. "I actually thought it was forbidden,"

DOI: 10.4324/9781003182689-10

comments a woman in her fifties. "No, no, you can enter freely, but you have to follow some rules," Farid explains, describing how they should prepare for the meeting. In a few minutes, the group is ready to enter: I am at the end of the line next to Chiara, a young anthropologist who serves as the local coordinator of the project. Chiara has attended every stage of the training course as a tutor and continues to support the work of intercultural guides by organizing daily walks.

Once inside, *imam* Hassan invites the group to sit in a circle and offers mint tea and dates as a sign of welcome. "As you can see, this is not a real mosque, but a simple prayer room in an old warehouse," he explains. "However, we have tried to make it pleasant, thanks to the work of our best craftsmen. People come here to pray, but also to relax, to study, to meet their friends and fellow villagers. The mosque is a point of reference for the entire community."

Introduction

The aforementioned ethnographic sketch presents the protagonists and the context of the "problematic encounter" that I will discuss in this chapter on the intersections of tourism, migration, and exile in European cities. In the foreground, is a Syrian refugee who works as a guide on urban tourism itineraries. Next to him is a group of tourists, primarily composed of people who reside in the city where the tour takes place. Chiara, the practicing anthropologist who pursues her profession outside the university, joins them inside. Finally, in the background, there is the city of Turin, with its Porta Palazzo district, the landing place of several generations of internal and international immigrants, a district dotted with small mosques hidden in the buildings' courtyards, almost invisible and seemingly inaccessible to those who do not belong to the community of the faithful.

Considering the various individuals in this scene, who can be called "local" and who "foreign"? What is the otherness that each of them seeks? How do their views of the city and its cultural heritage vary? In the following pages, I address these questions with the aim of developing a critical analysis of *Migrantour*, a European project for which I was the scientific coordinator from 2009 to 2019. My research is based on a body of 50 in-depth interviews conducted with migrants, tourists, students, and members of the project staff, as well as on prolonged observations of the decision-making processes that developed the initiative, and of the vast number of publications produced by the partners in the project (internal and external evaluation reports, promotional materials, a visual archive, press releases, etc.).[1] *Migrantour* is a network of groups in 20 cities where first- and second-generation migrants have created intercultural urban itineraries and accompanied walks aimed at tourists, residents, and students. Their objective is to showcase the contributions that migration has made over time to the transformation of these cities and their cultural heritage. This initiative involved numerous anthropologists (in addition to myself), who envisioned *Migrantour* as an opportunity for applying their knowledge and contributing to public interest anthropology, an emphasis in the discipline (Adams, 2005).

172 Francesco Vietti

This contribution is part of a wider reflection on the connections between various forms of mobility in the contemporary world. Although tourism, migration, and exile have long been the subjects of different studies and separate theories, a quarter of a century has passed since Arjun Appadurai indicated that "tourists, immigrants, refugees, exiles, guest workers" collectively constitute "an essential feature of the world" capable of influencing "the politics of (and between) nations to a hitherto unprecedented degree" (Appadurai, 1996, p. 33). This, in his terms, was a complex "ethnoscape" worthy of scholarly attention. Likewise, in the same period James Clifford (1997) indicated a need to study ethnographically the "travelling cultures," observable in those "transit sites" passed through by different types of travelers, as well as by powerful global forces such as media images and commodities.

Since the early 2000s, large metropolises (hubs of globalization thanks to the networks of transnational ties woven "from above" and "from below") have become a key context in which scholars have applied the new mobility paradigm (Urry, 2000) and explored different varieties of the migration-tourism nexus. As noted by C. Michael Hall and Allan Williams (2002), the stark contrast between production and consumption – connoting migration and tourism, respectively, in terms of labor and leisure – has thus gradually been disrupted. The erosion of this artificial division highlights that migrants and tourists are subjected to similar processes involving imagination of the "elsewhere" (with reference to both the places they come from and the places they aspire to reach) and symbolic representation of "otherness" (in respect of local people they meet). However, exploring this hybridity, with its connections and overlaps, does not mean neglecting or underestimating the profound differences between mobility regimes (Shamir, 2005; Koslowski, 2011; Glick Schiller and Salazar, 2013), which are often reinforced in the neoliberal world by systems of control, surveillance, and governance over freedom of movement. It is, therefore, necessary that we not de-politicize the issue. Rather, we must focus our attention on the status hierarchies and conditions of inequality and exclusion produced by the opportunities and constraints embodied in these intersecting forms of (im)mobility.

From this theoretical perspective, the scenario described in this chapter's prologue can be defined for all intents and purposes as a border encounter. Not the kind that occurs on the external borders of Europe (Lauth Bacas and Kavanagh, 2013), but rather the type that occurs along the internal borders within European cities. Urban borders mark (un)equal access to public spaces as well as conflicts over interpretations of local heritage between the majority of citizens and the different immigrant minority residents (Pastore and Ponzo, 2016). Just as the Mediterranean beaches of Lesbos and Lampedusa constitute borders, borders also exist in the districts of Milan, Paris, Brussels, and Lisbon,

> that distinguish natives from foreigners, locals from strangers, "legals" from "illegals," Europeans from Others. However, the fluidity of the borders of (in)visibility, as they are variously traversed, transgressed, and reconfigured

Tourist, Migrant, and Anthropologist **173**

> provides insight into how borders, with their many dichotomies, map onto long histories of – and new possibilities for – sociocultural exchange and transformation. The migrations currently taking place . . . amid the contexts of tourism attest to ongoing, transformational encounters across the shifting borders of (in)visibility, (il)legality, and difference.
>
> *(Cabot and Lenz, 2012, p. 178)*

It is precisely these "transformative encounters" that I focus on here, using the case study of the *Migrantour* project to examine the conditions that make them possible in the urban environment. Via this case study, I also explore the potential and limits of these encounters for realizing the aspiration to live together "in difference," which constitutes one of the possible outcomes of the relations produced by mobility (Nowicka and Vertovec, 2014).

In the following two sections, I begin by offering historical context for my analysis, discussing the prior forms of tourist engagement with cultural diversity in European expositions and immigration districts. Then, I discuss the *Migrantour* project, reflecting on strategies and challenges for configuring encounters between tourists and migrants as transformative experiences, capable of generating actions to achieve greater "mobility justice" (Sheller, 2018).

From Slumming to Mobility Justice

The intersections of tourism, migration, and exile date back to the final decades of the 19th century, i.e., to the very origins of tourism as a specific social phenomenon of modernity. In those years, two forms of encounter with ethnic and cultural otherness emerged in European cities: The Universal Expositions with pavilions that often included colonial-style displays of indigenous peoples from European imperial realms (Blanchard et al., 2011) and tours of the neighborhoods where, in those same years, growing numbers of immigrant workers were settling, attracted by the rapid industrialization of the metropolises. In Victorian London, the practice of slumming, i.e., going for a walk in the slums of East London, such as Whitechapel and Shoreditch, was established among the wealthy classes who wanted to see how the poor lived (Koven, 2004). This "fashionable mania," as the newspapers' headlines described the practice of slumming in the late 19th century (The New York Times, 1884), spread rapidly to the United States as well, where the phenomenon was consolidated in all its complexity and ambiguity. If, on the one hand, "going to the slums" for many wealthy bourgeois was nothing more than a voyeuristic pastime, an entertainment for which the spectacle of poverty was the object of an itchy curiosity for brutality, promiscuity, and exoticism (Heap, 2009), for others, this experience took on a different value. The tours in the New York neighborhoods where "the other half" lived inspired philanthropists, intellectuals, and politicians and gave rise to the birth of charitable associations and important reforms in the social welfare field (including public housing). Immigrants' miserable living conditions in Chinatown, Harlem, and the overcrowded tenements of

174 Francesco Vietti

Manhattan's Lower East Side (where people went to see "Jews and Italians") were thus brought to the center of public opinion and political debate (Riis, 1971).

Among those fascinated by the Babel of languages, cultures, and customs by which immigration had transformed European and North American metropolises in the early 20th century, were not just artists and tourists but also anthropologists. A mixture of attraction and repulsion, of wonder and dismay, seized, for example, Claude Lévi-Strauss upon his arrival in New York in 1941. Landing in America as an exile, without citizenship, fleeing Vichy France via a daring voyage by ship from Marseille to Martinique, the great French anthropologist, while walking the city streets, observed how New York foreshadowed its future cultural landscapes:

> New York (and this is the source of its charm and its peculiar fascination) was then a city where anything seemed possible. Like the urban fabric, the social and cultural fabric was riddled with holes. All you had to do was pick one and slip through it if, like Alice, you wanted to get to the other side of the looking glass and find worlds so enchanting that they seemed unreal.
>
> *(Lévi-Strauss, 1977, p. 261)*

Indeed, after World War II, with the growth of mass tourism, an increasing number of cities began to compete for international tourists by promoting their attractiveness in terms of cultural diversity. The Chinatowns, in particular, with their high degree of aesthetic elaboration and architectural stylization, became a global symbol of the affirmation of "ethnic neighborhoods" as places of entertainment and consumption (Wong and Chee-Beng, 2013). A recognizable feature of these areas became the commercial offerings of shops and restaurants where visitors could buy exotic products, consume unusual foods and drinks, and participate in events and shows related to different cultural traditions, as in the case of the Chinese New Year. In addition to tourists passing through, these attractions offered citizens residing in other districts of the city opportunities for "traveling-in-dwelling" (Clifford, 1997), creating the illusion of being able to travel to the East without having to take an intercontinental flight (Lin, 1998).

The proliferation of migration in the "age of migration" (Castles et al., 2014) has transformed many emigration countries in Mediterranean Europe into new immigration destinations. Over the past three decades, many of the neighborhoods currently involved in the *Migrantour* project, from Marseille's Panier to Rome's Esquiline, have become sites of "daily multiculturalism" (Wise and Velayutham, 2009). As anthropologists Volkan Aytar and Jan Rath (2012) noted in a well-known study on the subject:

> The growing tourism and leisure industries in these neighbourhoods offer opportunities to natives and immigrants, skilled and unskilled, and males and females alike. They participate as organizers of cultural events, as web designers, as owners of cafes, coffee shops, restaurants, travel bureaus, hotels,

souvenir shops, telephone and Internet shops, but also as waiters, cooks, dishwashers, and janitors. . . . Together, they engender "globalization from below" and create mainstream but unique products in terms of innovation, production, and consumption. . . . In our globalizing world – where local difference and place identity are increasingly important – heritage and cultural diversity have become crucial components of the cultural capital of post-industrial societies.

(p. 2)

It is indeed an ambivalent process. On the one hand, immigrant entrepreneurs' agency is highlighted and strategically managed tourism narratives stress representations of the neighborhoods where they live and work as places where tourists can "visit the whole world in a city." Such accounts challenge the dominant discourses that describe those districts as dangerous and degraded (Rath, 2007). In this sense, despite the narratives, depiction of immigrants as those forever on the social margins of the city, passively awaiting policies that somehow integrate them, tourism constitutes an arena in which immigrants demonstrate that they are active and central to the practice of "city-making": that they are people capable of negotiating with political and institutional actors and can develop their own vision of the future of society (Çağlar and Glick Schiller, 2018). On the other hand, numerous studies show how public administrations and investors with significant financial capital have the power to implement policies "from above" and channel resources to initiate gentrification processes, which in many cases result in excluding resident immigrants from the benefits brought by the visitor flows. Ultimately, this can lead to immigrants' progressive marginalization, if not expulsion, from the areas redeveloped for tourism (Shaw et al., 2004). From this perspective, as well as from an economic point of view, the subordination of migrants is reaffirmed and consolidated at the cultural level by the processes of folklorization and trivialization of their otherness. As Wendy Brown (2009) astutely observes, the superficial consumption of "the Other" leads to tolerance, a liberal democratic discursive depoliticization of both the sources of political problems and solutions to them. The uncomplicated celebration of "diversity" and "difference" effectively silences contestation and conflict, and therefore any further calling for justice and equality.

Faced with this risk, an ethically and politically critical approach to issues entailed in the intersections of migration, tourism, and exile in the city should strive to promote what Mimi Sheller called "mobility justice." In her *Manifesto*, Sheller (2018) proposes a multi-scalar approach, moving from the level of individual bodies to the level of the street, the city, the nation, and the globe. Transversal to these five layers is the invitation to "take action" to put in place social practices, infrastructures, and narratives that can support migrants in their "struggles for the right to the city and the public sphere . . . with a politics of occupation and presence in public space that disrupts normalized mobility spaces and offers epistemic alternatives" (Sheller, 2018, p. 30).

176 Francesco Vietti

A Crooked, Open, Modest City

Migrantour is an initiative launched in 2009 in Turin, which blossomed over the following decade in Italy and Europe, aided by financing from the European Commission during two biennial planning periods (2014–15 and 2018–19). Currently, the network is consolidating through the Erasmus+ exchange program and includes the cities of Turin, Milan, Genoa, Florence, Rome, Bologna, Cagliari, Catania, Parma, Bergamo, and Pavia in Italy; Marseille and Paris in France; Lisbon in Portugal; Valencia and Barcelona in Spain; Brussels in Belgium; Copenhagen in Denmark; Utrecht in the Netherlands; and Ljubljana in Slovenia. It is, therefore, an entity that over time has assumed significant dimensions (especially in Italy): The organization trained over 600 intercultural guides and created about 40 intercultural urban itineraries; over 30,000 people took part in the walking tours carried out in the various cities and over 5 million European citizens were reached by communication campaigns promoted by the network partners. These numbers, therefore, invite a serious critical analysis of the initiative highlighting the outcomes, while acknowledging the weaknesses and risks involved.

In the following three subsections, I organize my reflections drawing on the three ethical dimensions of building and dwelling outlined by American sociologist Richard Sennett (2018): crookedness, openness, and modesty.

Claim #1: We Are Crooked

> In an essay on cosmopolitan life, Immanuel Kant observed in 1784 that "out of the crooked timber of humanity, no straight thing was ever made." A city is crooked because it is diverse, full of migrants speaking dozens of languages; because its inequalities are so glaring.
>
> (Sennett, 2018, p. 2)

The starting point of *Migrantour* is the recognition that our societies are marked by differences and inequalities. Global cities are "crooked" because the living conditions, opportunities, and resources of the people who live in them are unequal. Likewise, the neighborhoods targeted by *Migrantour* for its itineraries are "crooked" because they experience internal rifts, conflicts, and borders. In an attempt to explore such complexity and convey it by way of guided visits, the project opted for co-construction of itineraries, so that, through participatory methodology, intercultural guides represent their own issues and visions of the city. The training course each of the network's cities provides starts with mapping, or rather counter-mapping (Campos-Delgado, 2019), a process whereby migrants involved in the initiative can highlight their neighborhoods, routes, and places of significance in the urban fabric. Starting with map-making, each intercultural guide proceeds to describe their own map to the other members of the training group, thus sharing certain aspects of their life story. Mutual learning established in this way constitutes the basis for consolidating a real "community of practice," wherein intercultural guides become part of a group producing new knowledge and skills from mutual and prolonged interactions (Wenger, 1998).

The second phase of the walks' co-planning process includes a fieldwork phase, during which the intercultural guides conduct ethnographic research involving participant observation, in-depth interviews, and collection of visual documentation. This research aims to move the intercultural guides from the first level of autobiographical narration to that of grappling with the life stories of others, be they other migrants or other citizens who live and work in the neighborhoods included in the project. In this phase, the role of the anthropologists involved in *Migrantour* is particularly important, as they intervene as trainers as well as tutors in research methodologies. In some cases, the collaborations initiated by the project involved entire departments or degree courses in anthropology, as in the case of Paris, where since 2014 *Migrantour* has been collaborating with an MA course in Anthropology and Ethnology at the University of Paris-Descartes. As Houlaïmatu, an intercultural guide originally from Guinea Conakry, says:

> In my country, I was a journalist. But when I arrived in France, I realized that people only see me as a refugee. Going into the field with the students, when I speak, they listen to me attentively. Nobody looks at me with pity, they see me as I would like everyone to see me: as a person who is there because she has something to offer.

And as Pia, an ethnology student, observes her experience with *Migrantour*:

> Participating in the design is an enriching experience on a personal and professional level. In fact, each stage of the construction of the itinerary has allowed us to refine and put into practice knowledge acquired at the University. Furthermore, the doubts, changes, and difficulties we have encountered on the ground have prompted us to reflect and redefine our specific way of acting. For me, it was the first contact with the world of work as an anthropologist.

A particularly delicate representational issue arises from the connection between the personal experiences of the guides and the variety of life stories they collect from the field. The crucial question here is how to represent this complexity through a narrative that does not oversimplify social reality, normalizing the existence of allegedly homogeneous immigrant communities from a cultural point of view. In the early years of the project's development, in my capacity as a scientific coordinator, I felt that *Migrantour* should necessarily practice what the postcolonial theorist Gayatri Ch. Spivak (1990) defined it as "strategic essentialism," i.e., to consciously proceed to produce a reification of cultural differences in order to achieve the political goal of giving voice to people traditionally marginalized in the public and media arena. During the creation of the itineraries, the intercultural guides, therefore, chose a series of objects (food and handicraft products), photographs, music, and so on, to be used during walks as symbols to evoke stories and

178 Francesco Vietti

experiences. However, this strategy revealed its pitfalls over the years and generated criticism from some participants in the walks, as well as project partners, and members of the scientific community evaluating the impact of the initiative. As they observed, this approach of "strategic essentialism" effectively produced new stereotypes through the commodification of cultural differences.

Therefore, *Migrantour*'s efforts have progressively focused on avoiding producing normalized, pacified, and univocal narratives, leaving room for the emergence of contradictions, conflicts, and resistances that span the cities involved in the project. For example, to create the itinerary in Matongé, a neighborhood known for its many Congolese migrant-run shops and restaurants, *Migrantour* Brussels took the approach of the *Collectif Mémoire Coloniale et Lutte contre les Discriminations* (Colonial Memory and Fight against Discrimination Collective). This group of activists and researchers arranged conferences, public events, and communication campaigns to broaden awareness of the history of Belgian colonialism in Africa; a history still somewhat removed or silenced, but which consequences – in terms of current discrimination and racism – remain embedded in the urban fabric, including in Brussels. The "decolonial walking tour" in Matongé starts from Lumumba square, a site of conflicting memory where one can clearly see the controversial way Belgian society represents its recent past: In 2018, the place was re-named by the municipality of Brussels in honor of Patrice Lumumba, the key figure in the history of Congolese independence murdered in 1961; however, the center of the square remains home to the statue of King Léopold II, the imperial ruler of Congo from 1885 to 1908, whose administration was characterized by systematic atrocities. Not surprisingly, in 2020, Lumumba square was the site of Belgium's major *Black Lives Matter* demonstrations. The itinerary also includes a focus on (de)colonization and gender: A stop in front of an anonymous building that today hosts a clothing store reveals the forgotten story of the *Union des femmes coloniales* [Union of Colonial Women]. Going back to the 1950s, the building housed a kind of "training center" to prepare Belgian women to fulfill the role of "good colonial wives" and properly oversee indigenous servants.

From this perspective, *Migrantour*'s projects can today be compared to other similar initiatives that aspire to "radicalize" tourism by making it a tool for spreading anti-hegemonic narratives to a wider audience, to denounce the power structures underlying the inequalities linked to class, race, gender, and sexual orientation (Cheng et al., 2010).

Claim #2: Open the City

> An open city would of course tolerate differences and promote equality . . . but would more specifically free people from the straitjacket of the fixed and the familiar, creating a terrain in which they could experiment and expand their experience.
>
> (Sennett, 2018, p. 9)

Sennett's thesis is that the main political challenge of our time is the clash that pits the proponents of a "closed society" – that is a segregated, segmented city with an anti-democratic regime of control – against those who instead support the possibility of an open society and an "open city," which presupposes a different way of thinking and living in the urban space. Along these lines, the *Migrantour* project proposes an initiative aimed at "opening up the city," making it accessible, and trying to deconstruct some of the internal borders.

The third phase of the training course for intercultural guides targets precisely this goal. A deeper intercultural reading of the tangible and intangible heritage characterizing the neighborhoods where the walks occur therefore embraces two strategies: (a) a search for new, unprecedented meanings that can suggest different readings of already consolidated elements of the urban heritage and (b) the valorization of sites that are not usually perceived as culturally significant or that are represented in the public discourse as "no-go zones." In the ethnographic sketch that opened this chapter, both categories are discernable.

The tangible and intangible heritage presented during the walks is interpreted as the outcome of social action (Harrison, 2010) that involves interactions between the intercultural companions' subjective point of view, the experiences of those who live and work in the neighborhoods, and the elements of the urban landscape. In this way, *Migrantour* aspires to contribute to effectively implementing the Convention on the Value of Cultural Heritage for Society, signed by the Council of Europe in 2005 in Faro, Portugal. This convention foresaw the recognition and strengthening of "heritage communities" composed of people "who value specific aspects of cultural heritage which they wish, within the framework of public action, to sustain and transmit to future generations" (Council of Europe, 2005, p. 2). *Migrantour* promotes imagery of first- and second-generation immigrants as a group with a "plural identity" and a "right to [benefit from] cultural heritage" and "take part in the selection of new cultural expressions aimed at belonging to the notion of cultural heritage" (Zagato, 2015, p. 147).

The issues related to heritage-making are inherently political, since deciding what should be remembered within a society is closely linked to issues of power and identity. This explains why in most cases the stories, memories, and representations of migration maintain a peripheral position, a marginal role in the historical, cultural, and social narrative of nations (Hintermann and Johansson, 2010). Nevertheless, as noted by Laurence Gouriévidis (2014), migration is no longer a "non-place of memory" in European cities. Building on Gérard Noiriel and Marc Augé, Gouriévidis notes that migrants, after having long been excluded from public discourse on cultural heritage, have gradually gained visibility in sites central to the construction of national identity (see also Basso Peressut and Pozzi, 2012). For many cities in it's network, *Migrantour* has become an integral part of this process, establishing a synergy with museums interested in involving immigrant communities in reinterpreting their collections. In Genoa, for example, *Migrantour* collaborates with *MEM – Memoria e Migrazione* (MEM – Memory and Migration), a museum dedicated to the history of Italian emigration. This museum has identified the *Migrantour* walks as a tool for connecting the stories of Italian emigrants who left the port of Genoa between the 19th and 20th centuries with those of immigrants who now live in the city.

180   Francesco Vietti

In cases such as this, *Migrantour* proves to be useful for integrating institutional and authorized representations of migration. In other situations, however, the walks include elements of what we could define as "dissonant heritage," to borrow the category proposed by G.J. Ashworth and J.E. Tunbridge (1996). These sites are characterized by an "aesthetic of subversion" capable of "disrupting and challenging any representational system that aims at reducing migrant subjectivities to mere bodies without words," restoring to migrants a subjectivity denied by political and media representations (Mazzara, 2015, p 460). As Mercedes, a Peruvian intercultural guide at *Migrantour* in Milan attests:

> The stop I love most during the walk along Padova street is that of the mural of Santa Sarita. Sarita Colonia is a saint not recognized by the church, a very popular figure in Peru who is invoked as a protector by the poorest and most marginalized people in society. The mural was created by a Peruvian artist who portrayed Sarita as a very determined girl, staring at you defiantly. It is a very beautiful image, it is as if she had become the protector of all of us, Latin American immigrants, who live in the area. Sarita tells us to have courage, not to be ashamed of who we are.

Migrantour's commitment to the "open city" is not without contradictions and counterproductive effects. In the very act of including neighborhoods and spaces usually neglected by tourism in the walks, the project triggers or contributes to gentrification dynamics. The more successful the initiative is, the greater the chances that institutions and investors will see in *Migrantour* an ally to support "redevelopment" interventions aimed to increase the attractiveness and prestige of certain zones considered "degraded." To limit the risks associated with this perspective, the network has increasingly sought to entrust the project's development to people who manage the walks not as a stand-alone activity, but as part of a broader commitment to social cohesion in the area. This is the case, for example, in Lisbon, where *Migrantour* is organized by the *Associação Renovar a Mouraria* (Renovate the Mouraria Association), a company that has, for many years, managed the *Casa Comunitária da Mouraria* (Mouraria Community Center), a meeting space offering services for the neighborhood's citizens, or in Catania, where the walks are organized by the *Trame di Quartiere* (Neighborhood Stories/Networks)[2] as part of a series of initiatives aimed at regenerating the San Berillo neighborhood "from below." In this way, intercultural itineraries can become a tool for the residents themselves "to understand the everyday places where they live, work, shop, and socialize. . . . [It] also provides them with a basis for fighting proposed changes that often destroy the centres of social life, erase cultural meanings, and restrict local participatory practices" (Low, 2011, p. 391).

Claim #3: Practice Modesty

> The ethical connection between urbanist and urbanite lies in practicing a certain kind of modesty: living one among many, engaged in a world that does not

mirror oneself. Living one among many enables . . . richness of meaning rather than clarity of meaning. That is the ethics of an open city.

(Sennett, 2018, p. 302)

Building and inhabiting the open city is possible, Sennett argues, only if we commit ourselves to "practicing a certain kind of modesty" (Sennett, 2018, p. 302). This is a modesty project which in *Migrantour*'s vision should also characterize the attitude of those involved in tourist interactions, both that of the guides and that of the visitors. Living harmoniously with others, moving in a world that can never fully represent us (otherwise it could not represent others at the same time), accepting the feeling of only being partially "at home" (so that others can also feel a little "at home") emerges from learning. It is therefore not surprising that *Migrantour*, initially conceived as a tourist experience, has increasingly become a form of public pedagogy (Biesta, 2012). In many cities in the network, the main audience for the walks consists of primary and secondary school pupils, as well as groups of university students and adults engaged in training courses. For all of these groups, the walks are configured as an activity included in the Global Citizenship Education programs. These programs, promoted at the international level by UNESCO and implemented at the local level by a wide range of educational institutions, NGOs, and grassroots organizations, focus "on expanding the consciousness and the competencies of students to prepare them for [the] opportunities and problems of globalization" and encourage students "to develop understanding and awareness of cultural differences that are part of their everyday experience" (Dill, 2013, p. 2).

Faced with growing demand from schools, the intercultural guides have therefore trained themselves to work more effectively with children and young people and have partially adjusted the itineraries and language used during the walks to make them suitable for groups of different ages and educational levels. Finally, *Migrantour* has developed classroom educational materials for teachers to use before and after the city walks in order to expand upon the topics addressed during the tours. In the words of Laura, an Italian teacher at a secondary school in Rome:

> With each passing year, I bring more and more classes to experience Migrantour, because compared to a few years ago the opportunities to really work on intercultural themes have decreased as if we had reversed course. Migration is spoken of only with regard to the illegal immigrant landings, no one thinks of the hundreds of thousands of second-generation children who attend school every day. It is also important for the children of Italians to be aware that not only does Italy have a long history of migration behind it, but that also perhaps their own future will lead them to emigrate to live and work in another country.

Designing a tour for children and students often requires developing different, more innovative tools to translate the itinerary's content into a symbolic representation

182 Francesco Vietti

that is compelling for young people. For example, Rashid, an intercultural guide who relocated with his Roma family from former Yugoslavia, offered *Migrantour Turin* his experience in creating wooden marionettes and puppets: He delivers some of the main themes of the walking tours he leads in Turin through a series of street art performances. In contrast, in Bologna, an intercultural tour tackles the challenges related to conveying the experiences of second-generation immigrants to young people in a different fashion. The Bologna itinerary was designed by the members of *Next Generation Italy*, a local association of youngsters born in immigrant families, and aims to prompt students and teenagers to reflect on the situation of their peers who, despite being born and living in the same city, do not have Italian citizenship. The walk is therefore combined with group discussions concerning civil and political rights and equal opportunities. Students are invited to contribute also after the tour, uploading video and audio content to the association's blog and social media sites

Educationally oriented companies based in the same cities as the projects are the primary developers of these types of activities, as they have the possibility of offering schools these walks as part of their cultural mediation services. A typical case is *Migrantour* Naples, undertaken by Casba, a social cooperative created by and composed solely of intercultural mediators. In other cities in the network, where the project is linked to people operating in the tourism sector, the public pedagogy function of *Migrantour* falls under the framework of responsible tourism. This label, formalized in 2002 by the Cape Town Declaration issued at the World Summit on Sustainable Development, identifies certain forms of tourism that embrace guiding principles pertaining to economic, social, and environmental responsibility. These principles include a commitment to guarantee "the well-being of host communities," to involve "local people in decisions that affect their lives and life chances," to contribute positively "to the conservation of natural and cultural heritage," and to propose experiences to tourists "through more meaningful connections with local people, and a greater understanding of local cultural, social and environmental issues" (International Conference on Responsible Tourism in Destinations, 2002, p. 3). *Viaggi Solidali* (Solidarity Travel), the Italian tour operator that organizes *Migrantour* in Turin, Florence, and Rome, and *Baština Voyages* (Heritage Travel) which coordinates *Migrantour* Paris, are members of national and international associations that foster this kind of ethical approach to tourism and hospitality.

Responsible tourism initiatives, as well as Global Citizenship Education programs, are "embedded in a certain understanding of global creative capitalism" and rooted in "highly particular Western liberal individualism" (Dill, 2013, p. 4). To avoid the pitfalls of "multicultural tolerance" (Brown, 2009), intercultural walking tours must therefore prompt experiential learning based on a critical pedagogy conceived in terms of a "pedagogy of hope" (hooks, 2003). Building on Paulo Freire's insights, bell hooks envisions education as the practice of freedom that enables us to restore our sense of connection and create community. By imagining the city as "a classroom without boundaries," we can make inroads in our pursuit of a more socially engaged understanding of how human groups and spaces are shaped by institutionalized systems of domination (race, sex, and nationalist imperialism).

The everyday learning generated by the intercultural walks can produce changes that are all the more profound when people are stimulated to critically contemplate their own underlying assumptions. This is best accomplished by "situating those assumptions in broader theoretical and conceptual contexts as well as political-economic structures" (Cunningham, 2010, p. 25, cited in Cheng et al., 2010–2011, p. 118). It is under these conditions that the problematic urban encounters between migrants, tourists, and anthropologists can effectively become transformative.

Conclusions

In February 2020, 10 years after its birth, *Migrantour* stopped its activities for the first time. The COVID-19 pandemic and the consequent lockdown that hit all of Europe caused a prolonged closure of schools and the collapse of domestic and international tourism. For a few months, the project continued to live online only, then, when cities gradually reopened in late spring, the walks began to be offered again following the necessary health precautions. Farid, wearing his mask, returned to accompany the Porta Palazzo walk in Turin.

The world to which migrants and tourists have returned, with great difficulty moving and gathering, has been profoundly transformed by the pandemic and its cultural, social, economic, and political consequences. There is no doubt that the neighborhoods characterized by the highest rates of immigrant residents were among the zones most penalized by the lockdown, because of overcrowding and the concentration of marginalized residents working in part-time or informal jobs, where they could not benefit from the protections guaranteed to other groups. New and serious inequalities have emerged in the urban fabric of European cities.

The summer of 2020 offered unprecedented uncertainty for tour operators who had to quickly reconfigure their activities. Travel abroad has been restricted or strongly discouraged almost everywhere, and European governments have directed citizens toward domestic tourism, to be carried out within the borders of individual countries, aimed at rediscovering local territories and local cultural heritage. National and regional restrictions on tourist mobility risk producing a superficial (and in some respects dangerous) celebration of the unique and specific identities of nearby places, "our places," invariably described as safer, and therefore more beautiful and preferable to a distant elsewhere imagined as insecure and therefore "to be avoided." However, tourism's intersection with migrations may indicate a different approach that involves demonstrating how the local is inevitably entangled with the global and illustrating how identity is inextricably linked to otherness. This approach deconstructs the presumed purity and authenticity of traditions and products in order to foster a cosmopolitan and intercultural vision of heritage. In this new context, initiatives similar to *Migrantour*, which exists primarily in large cities, could also be tested in small and medium-size centers, as well as in rural

184 Francesco Vietti

areas, where the tangible and intangible heritage linked to migration is less visible and more physically dispersed.

In facing these challenges, anthropology can play an important role both at the analytical level and in applied terms. The study of migration and tourism from the perspective that Sherry B. Ortner (2016) termed "dark anthropology" has yielded a large body of ethnographic research documentation denouncing the dimensions and practices of domination, exploitation, suffering, and oppression produced along the external and internal borders of "Fortress Europe." To complement this approach, it seems useful to also turn our attention to the dimensions of coexistence, sharing, and conviviality to explore possible spaces for dialogue, intimacy, cooperation, care, friendship, and reciprocity (Hemer et al., 2020). It is in this interpretative framework that we can place the case study of the *Migrantour* network, and it is from this perspective that together with other colleagues, we will continue to apply anthropological insights to the development and constant critical review of the initiative. As Erve Chambers lucidly wrote:

> Even the most "value free" stance finds its appeal ultimately in a belief that it is better for our world to have the knowledge of anthropology than not, and even the most empirically minded among us generally imply that a world enlightened by anthropology will somehow be a better world. This is not necessarily true; it is at least possible to imagine that it is not at all true. But our assumptions of value are necessary. Without them, we cannot sustain a discipline acceptable to us.
>
> *(Chambers, 1987, p. 329)*

Notes

1 All the names in the chapter have been replaced with pseudonyms. I take this opportunity to thank all of the intercultural guides and colleagues who have collaborated with *Migrantour* in recent years. I also thank Meghann Ormond, cultural geographer at Wageningen University, whose critical reflections on the project have significantly contributed to the analysis I present here (for a critical reflection on our shared experience of being in pivotal roles in *Migrantour* and *Roots Guide* projects, see Ormond and Vietti, 2022)

2 The Italian name of this association is difficult to translate into English because it is highly metaphoric. "Trame" in Italian is "weft" and refers to weaving, but in a symbolic way, it also stands for "plot," the plot of a story. The idea is that the association is interested not only in the stories of the San Berillo neighborhood but also in the economic, political, and social structures, connections, and networks that characterize this part of the city.

References

Adams, K.M. (2005) 'Public interest anthropology in heritage sites: Writing culture and righting wrongs', *International Journal of Heritage Studies*, 11(5), pp. 433–439.

Appadurai, A. (1996) *Modernity at large. Cultural dimensions of globalization*. Minneapolis, MN: University of Minnesota Press.

Ashworth, G. and Tunbridge, J. (1996) *Dissonant heritage: The management of the past as a resource in conflict*. Chichester: Wiley

Aytar, V. and Rath, J. (eds.) (2012) *Selling ethnic neighborhoods: The rise of neighborhoods as places of leisure and consumption*. New York and London: Routledge.

Basso Peressut, L. and Pozzi, C. (eds.) (2012) *Museums in an age of migrations*. Milan: Politecnico di Milano.

Biesta, G. (2012) 'Becoming public: public pedagogy, citizenship and the public sphere,' *Social & Cultural Geography*, 13(7), pp. 683–697.

Blanchard, P., Boëtsch, G. and Jacomijn Snoep, N. (eds.) (2011) *Exhibitions. L'invention du sauvage*. Paris: Actes Sud.

Brown, W. (2009) *Regulating aversion: Tolerance in the age of identity and empire*. Princeton, NJ: Princeton University Press.

Çağlar, A. and Glick Schiller, N. (2018) *Migrants and city-making: Multiscalar perspectives on dispossession and urban regeneration*. Durham, NC: Duke University Press.

Cabot, H. and Lenz, R. (2012) 'Borders of (in)visibility in the Greek Aegean' in Nogués-Pedregal, A.M. (ed.) *Culture and society in tourism contexts*. Bingley: Emerald Group Publishing Limited, pp. 159–179.

Campos-Delgado, A. (2019) Counter-mapping migration: Irregular migrants' stories through cognitive mapping', *Mobilities*, 4, pp. 488–504.

Castles, S., de Haas, H. and Miller, M.J. (2014) *The age of migration: International population movements in the modern world*. Basingstoke: Palgrave Macmillan.

Chambers, E. (1987) 'Applied anthropology in the post-Vietnam era: Anticipations and ironies', *Annual Review of Anthropology*, 16, pp. 309–337.

Cheng, W., Barraclough, L. and Pulido, L. (2010) 'Radicalising teaching and tourism: A people's guide as active and activist history', *Left History*, 15(1), pp. 109–125.

Clifford, J. (1997) *Routes: Travel and translation in the late twentieth century*. Cambridge, MA and London: Harvard University Press.

Council of Europe (2005) *Council of Europe framework convention on the value of cultural heritage for society*. Available at: https://rm.coe.int/1680083746.

Cunningham, K. (2010) 'Putting the anthropological toolkit to use in international and intercultural learning', *Practicing Anthropology*, 32(3), pp. 23–26.

Dill, J.S. (2013) *The longings and limits of global citizenship education: The moral pedagogy of schooling in a cosmopolitan age*. New York and London: Routledge.

Glick Schiller, N. and Salazar, N.B. (2013) 'Regimes of mobility across the globe', *Journal of Ethnic and Migration Studies*, 39, pp. 183–200.

Gouriévidis, L. (ed.) (2014) *Museum and migration. History, memory and politics*. London and New York: Routledge.

Hall, C.M. and Williams, A.M. (eds.) (2002) *Tourism and migration. New relationships between production and consumption*. Dordrecht: Springer.

Harrison, R. (2010) 'Heritage as social action' in West, S. (ed.) *Understanding heritage in practice*. Manchester: Manchester University Press, pp. 240–276.

Heap, C. (2009) *Slumming. Sexual and racial encounters in American nightlife, 1885–1940*. Chicago, IL: University of Chicago Press.

Hemer, O., Povrzanović Frykman, M. and Ristilammi, P.M. (eds.) (2020) *Conviviality at the crossroads. The poetics and politics of everyday encounters*. Basingstoke: Palgrave Macmillan.

Hintermann, C. and Johansson, C. (eds.) (2010) *Migration and memory: Representations of migration in Europe since 1960*. Innsbruck, Wien and Bozen: StudienVerlag.

hooks, b. (2003) *Teaching community: A pedagogy of hope*. New York and London: Routledge.

International Conference on Responsible Tourism in Destinations (2002) *The Cape Town declaration*. Available at: https://responsibletourismpartnership.org/cape-town-declaration-on-responsible-tourism/.

Koslowski, R. (ed.) (2011) *Global mobility regimes: A conceptual reframing*. New York: Palgrave Macmillan.

186 Francesco Vietti

Koven, S. (2004) *Slumming. Sexual and social politics in Victorian London*. Princeton, NJ: Princeton University Press.

Lauth Bacas, J. and Kavanagh, W. (eds.) (2013) *Border encounters – Asymmetry and proximity at Europe's frontiers*. New York: Berghahn Books.

Lévi-Strauss, C. (1977) *New York in 1941. The view from afar*. New York: Basic Books.

Lin, J. (1998) *Reconstructing Chinatown: Ethnic enclave, global change*. Minneapolis, MN: University of Minnesota Press.

Low, S.M. (2011) 'Claiming space for engaged anthropology: Spatial inequality and social exclusion', *American Anthropologist*, 113(3), pp. 389–407.

Mazzara, F. (2015) 'Spaces of visibility for the migrants of Lampedusa: The counter narrative of the aesthetic discourse', *Italian Studies*, 70(4), pp. 449–464.

Nowicka, M. and Vertovec, S. (2014) 'Comparing convivialities: Dreams and realities of living-with-difference', *European Journal of Cultural Studies*, 17(4), pp. 341–356.

Ormond, M. and Vietti, F. (2022) 'Beyond multicultural "tolerance": Guided tours and guidebooks as transformative tools for civic learning', *Journal of Sustainable Tourism*, 30(2–3), pp. 533–549.

Ortner, S.B. (2016) 'Dark anthropology and its others: Theory since the eighties', *HAU: Journal of Ethnographic Theory*, 6(1), pp. 47–73.

Pastore, F. and Ponzo, I. (eds.) (2016) *Inter-group relations and migrant integration in European cities*. Dordrecht: Springer.

Rath, J. (ed.) (2007) *Tourism, ethnic diversity and the city*. New York and London: Routledge.

Riis, J. (1971) *How the other half lives. Studies among the tenements of New York*. Dover: Dover Publications.

Sennett, R. (2018) *Building and dwelling: Ethics for the city*. London: Penguin Books.

Shamir, R. (2005) 'Without borders? Notes on globalization as a mobility regime', *Sociological Theory*, 23(2), pp. 197–217.

Shaw, S., Bagwell, S. and Karmowska, J. (2004) 'Ethnoscapes as spectacle: Reimaging multicultural districts as new destinations for leisure and tourism consumption', *Urban Studies*, 41(10), pp. 1983–2000.

Sheller, M. (2018) 'Theorising mobility justice', *Tempo Social*, 30(2), pp. 17–34.

Spivak, G.C. (1990) *The post-colonial critic: Interviews, strategies, dialogues*. New York and London: Routledge.

The New York Times. (1884) 'Slumming in this town; a fashionable London mania reaches New York. Slumming parties to be the rage this winter. Good districts to visit', September 14, p. 4.

Urry, J. (2000) *Sociology beyond societies: Mobilities for the twenty-first century*. New York and London: Routledge.

Wenger, E. (1998) *Communities of practice: Learning, meaning, and identity*. New York: Cambridge University Press.

Wise, A. and Velayutham, S. (eds.) (2009) *Everyday multiculturalism*. London: Palgrave Macmillan.

Wong, B.P. and Chee-Beng, T. (eds.) (2013) *Chinatowns around the world. Gilded ghetto, ethnopolis, and cultural diaspora*. Leiden and Boston: Brill.

Zagato, L. (2015) 'The notion of 'heritage community' in the Council of Europe's faro convention. Its impact on the European legal framework' in Adell, N., Bendix, R., Bortolotto, C. and Tauschek, M. (eds.) *Between imagined communities and communities of practice. Participation, territory, and the making of heritage*. Göttingen: Universität Verlag Göttingen, pp. 141–168.

10

IN AND OUT OF BRAZIL

Overlapping Mobilities in the Capoeira Archipelago

Lauren Miller Griffith

> The old-fashioned radiators make a distinctive clang as they warm up. You have to be careful not to accidentally bump into them when you scoot back to watch the *mestre* (master) demonstrate a sequence. Snow is falling outside the windows of the old school where we train and I can hear the hipster contra-dancers who have this room next outside in the hallway. We are not in Brazil.
>
> Someone grabs a discarded car tire and strips out the wire so it can be used to string a *berimbau*, the bow-like instrument with a resonating chamber made from a gourd that controls the rhythm and pace of our play. Someone else uses a push broom to clear the dust from the floor, a simple act that is both a practical necessity and a show of dedication and belonging. The *mestre* lights some incense and prepares to sanctify the space for our *roda* (ritual game). It feels like we are in Brazil.[1]

I know what it feels like to play *capoeira*, an Afro-Brazilian martial art, in its homeland because I have been there. My *mestre* often reminded the other students of this, in fact. Having been to the northeastern state of Bahia became a badge of honor, my passport to trying more advanced moves even though I was not any more skilled than the other students who had been training alongside me for the past four or five years. Although they were the subjects of my study, in the course of studying them, I too became an apprenticeship pilgrim. Like them, I was traveling to the source of our art in order to gain knowledge, skills, and legitimacy (see Griffith, 2016; Griffith and Marion, 2018). We trained together, and we "played tourist" together, hanging out at the beach between classes, frequenting the Tuesday night street party held in the historic district, and going on the occasional excursion to nearby towns or islands. We discovered unexpected connections: Tyrell[2] and I had traveled to the same event in Atlanta a few years prior, and Bridget knew my *mestre*'s rival back in the United States because he was friends with her ex-boyfriend

DOI: 10.4324/9781003182689-11

188 Lauren Miller Griffith

whom she had met on a previous trip to Brazil. We gossiped about certain *mestres* and what they got up to when they traveled abroad to lead capoeira workshops. I learned that I could probably couchsurf anywhere in the world as long as I could find a local capoeira group since members are always willing to host a visiting *capoeirista* [practitioner of capoeira]. I had gone to Brazil expecting to understand one behavior – what I later termed apprenticeship pilgrimage – but came to appreciate that the contemporary capoeira community is characterized by a much more complex assemblage of mobilities.

Introduction

Arjun Appadurai's (1996) introduction of the concept of flows or scapes was a landmark moment in the study of globalization; however, by only having one category for the flows of people around the world, different types of mobilities were collapsed into one another. While we can look at the scholarship that grew out of this moment and see the different kinds of mobilities encompassed by the term "ethnoscape," these still tend to be discussed in isolation from one another. It is time to think about the hyphenated mobilities our cultural consultants embody. A slash (migrant/pilgrim; tourist/pilgrim; scholar/practitioner) bifurcates too completely; a hyphen is a bridge between identities, a steppingstone along a road that is not always possible to see clearly when one is walking it. One can be a pilgrim-migrant-tourist all in the same moment, and each of these identities results in a different set of lived experiences. The performance turn in tourism studies has improved somewhat the tendency to silo different types of mobilities (Uriely, 2010); however, a complete erasure of categories is almost as problematic as adhering too strictly to them. The point here is not just to show that belonging to the transnational capoeira community involves multiple forms of mobility, but to show how the innerworkings of this community demand different kinds of mobilities that overlap and intersect in theoretically significant ways.

Capoeira provides an interesting case study in which we can see how considering migration, tourism, and pilgrimage as separate phenomena is incomplete. Much of the scholarship on capoeira looks at the globalization of capoeira and the nature of capoeira as a transnational community of practice, yet focusing on the globalization of the art itself can obscure the movement of people pursuing it. I am starting from the premise that amorphous and often hard to articulate feelings about authenticity fuel various forms of mobility within the capoeira community. *Capoeiristas* around the world assiduously study the literature on capoeira, the songs, and of course the movement in an attempt at maintaining as much fidelity to its origins as possible. They reproduce islands of Brazil in their own countries, much like my group did in Indiana; however, frequent travel between the islands of this imagined archipelago and the mainland of Brazil is what keeps them connected.

The history of capoeira is hotly contested by members of the community, and debates over ownership and belonging are frequent. What right has a white woman from the United States, like myself, to lay claim to a tradition kept alive by enslaved

Africans during Brazil's colonial era? As I have argued elsewhere (Griffith, 2016), traveling to and training in the art's homeland is one way individuals lacking in traditional claims to legitimacy (e.g., race and nationality) can become more legitimate tradition bearers. Here, however, I wish to explore the different intersecting forms of mobility that characterize this social field and shape the life experiences of both students and *mestres* (masters).

Multiple Mobilities in the Transnational Social Field of Capoeira

Time and again, I was told by a cultural consultant that he or she first encountered capoeira in the film *Only the Strong* in which the main character, an ex-special forces soldier who had learned capoeira while stationed in Brazil, uses the art to rehabilitate a group of at-risk teens at his former high school in Miami. So for a significant number of *capoeiristas* in the United States, their first exposure to capoeira links the learning of capoeira with travel to Brazil. Perhaps this is art imitating life. I have yet to meet anyone who began their career as a *capoeirista* while deployed, but I have met a US *mestre* whose first exposure to capoeira was during his missionary work in Brazil. I have met students who saw it during a study abroad trip and a voluntourist whose host organization arranged a capoeira class for him and his housemates as a cultural enrichment activity. They were in Brazil for reasons other than capoeira, but their exposure to capoeira resonated deeply within them. They all pursued capoeira classes back home in the United States with Brazilian teachers, and several of them returned to Brazil later as apprenticeship pilgrims.

The desire to become a more legitimate tradition bearer drives movement from the capoeira periphery to its core in Brazil. *Capoeiristas* may undertake these trips as individuals, using whatever resources they have available to them to craft their own itinerary, or they may accompany their own teachers on a group trip that often becomes a mix of training, sightseeing, and homecoming celebration for the teacher. Movement also goes in the other direction. The demand for instruction abroad opens opportunities for Brazilian teachers to emigrate, not only because Brazil boasts a high number of skilled *capoeiristas* but also because Brazilianness remains closely tied to legitimacy in the eyes of many – if not most – prospective students. Sara Delamont et al. (2017) use the term "diasporic capoeira," as opposed to transnational or globalized, in part to recognize that it is through the movement of Brazilians themselves, not just the art, that capoeira has spread around the world. Although more and more non-Brazilians are teaching capoeira – with or without the official authorization of a Brazilian *mestre* – the greatest legitimacy has been reserved for Brazilian teachers (Delamont et al., 2010). Or at least this has been true in places like the United States (Griffith, 2016), Canada (Joseph, 2012), the United Kingdom (Delamont et al., 2010), and France (see Head and Gravina, 2012).[3]

Students from the Global North head to Brazil in search of legitimacy and teachers from Brazil head to the Global North to offer the same. Yet reality is messier than this simple two-direction model would suggest. These Brazilian teachers

190 Lauren Miller Griffith

sometimes first venture abroad on tour with a performance group, at the request of a group seeking to headline a major workshop with some star talent, or with a lover who came to Brazil on vacation. When they decide to relocate more permanently, they may make a stop in another country in the Global South before continuing on to their goal in Europe or the United States (see Contreras Islas, 2021).

Although Europe and North America are appealing final destinations because it is easier to make a living exclusively from teaching capoeira in these regions than it would be in another part of the world (González Varela, 2019), it is not always easy for Brazilian *capoeiristas* to gain entry to these markets. Aside from the high cost of air travel, particularly to Europe, a teacher's destination is in many ways dependent upon his or her personal networks. Brazilians can travel throughout South America without a visa or passport, needing only their Brazilian identity card. Travel to the United States necessitates a visa that is often difficult to obtain. The more established one is as a teacher, and the greater his or her international reputation, the easier it will be to secure the requisite travel documents. Spending time in an intermediate country such as Mexico (see González Varela, 2019) or Argentina may enable a teacher to operate in a less saturated field than what he or she would experience at home in Brazil and shore up his or her reputation before venturing further afield. If and when the teacher does leave this intermediate location, an instructional vacuum is left behind to be filled by local students who, in turn, may establish yet more travel routes as they visit Brazil to improve their own skills/legitimacy and/or invite Brazilian teachers to make guest appearances at their schools.

In the United States, there are several circumstances in which it is not possible to learn capoeira from a Brazilian teacher, even if doing so remains a tacitly held ideal. For example, when a young adult who has trained capoeira in his or her hometown moves away to pursue higher education or to take a job in a new location, it is often the case that there is no local capoeira group with which to train. Faced with the choice of discontinuing their training or leading their own group, many committed students choose the latter path. Thus, while *Brasilidade* [Brazilianness] remains an important marker of legitimacy for capoeira teachers in the United States (see Griffith, 2016), many schools are run by non-Brazilians as well.[4] In these instances, a student will typically seek the blessing of their own (Brazilian) teacher before setting up their own schools. Travel often figures prominently in how non-Brazilians progress from the rank of a student to that of an instructor. To be sure, there are some informal groups that meet and practice what aspects of capoeira they know, perhaps seeking out information via YouTube videos (Griffith, 2017) or other resources. If, however, someone wants to establish a local chapter of a larger franchise, they may be obligated to attend periodic training sessions with the head *mestre* at his primary school.

Lowen is an African American man whose capoeira group is housed in a community center in a lower-income neighborhood of a major metropolitan area. The members of this group aligned themselves with a few different organizations before finally becoming independent. At one point, the *mestre* with whom they were affiliated demanded that Lowen travel to one of his other academies monthly in order to ensure that his training was up to par and that he was qualified to teach in the *mestre*'s name. This put Lowen in the role of both pilgrim and business traveler. One of these academies was located approximately 800 miles to the east and the other nearly 2,000 miles to the west. Alternatively, they were given the option of bringing a teacher from these locations to their city on a monthly basis (and covering the traveling teacher's expenses). The head *mestre*'s philosophy aligns well with Lowen's commitment to using capoeira as a vehicle for social justice, and it is well known within this community that the teacher cultivates excellence in his students, but the price was simply too high. Lowen continues to travel within his state, periodically visiting other groups when they host events, but choosing to terminate the affiliation with this *mestre* reduced his obligation to travel and to pay travel-related costs. So while travel may facilitate the strengthening of relationships within this transnational community, travel costs sometimes lead to its fracturing.

Although the frequency with which it was demanded eventually became intolerable, Lowen's travel obligations were minor in comparison to the franchises that require a student to visit Brazil before granting him or her a teaching title. In many groups, there is an unspoken expectation that a student will make a pilgrimage to Brazil in order to experience the culture firsthand, become more fluent in Portuguese, and improve his or her skills. Some groups formalize this expectation by only awarding teacher titles at major gatherings, which just happen to take place in Brazil. Therefore, by default, someone must travel to Brazil in order to advance within the hierarchy.

Somewhat ironically, international travel may also be important for Brazilian *mestres* who desire to remain at home. If they are to make a living from teaching capoeira full-time, they must find a way to distinguish themselves from other teachers in a crowded market. One of the ways they can do this is by traveling abroad. Periodically, capoeira groups will host graduation events or workshops. These events are typically advertised within the group's region (e.g., an event in Oakland will attract people from throughout the Bay Area and perhaps the entire West Coast). Prestigious teachers are invited, and paid, to offer classes at these events. Although it is becoming more common for headlining teachers to be non-Brazilians, a great deal of energy and money is often expended on securing a Brazilian teacher's participation. Teaching at these events gives an individual visibility among foreigners who may later turn into pilgrims or who may help their training partners make decisions about which schools to seek out when visiting Brazil.

According to Delamont et al. (2017), aspiring teachers know that they will have to travel – at least within their local region – and offer classes at events in order to make a name for themselves before they can expect to have a successful career. Filling one's resume with international teaching gigs is to the Brazilian capoeira teacher what an apprenticeship pilgrimage is to the non-Brazilian student. Although they go in opposite directions, both allow an individual to move up within the art's internal hierarchy. If one performs well on these short-term trips, or if one is recruited by a pilgrim who has visited Brazil with the purpose

192 Lauren Miller Griffith

of finding a teacher (Griffith, 2016; see also Head and Gravina, 2012), this may translate into an opportunity to move abroad permanently.

In July of 2008, I attended a workshop in an upscale part of Salvador da Bahia that was hosted by a local Brazilian capoeira franchise and a woman from the United States who had spent about a year in Brazil. She was not a *capoeirista* when she first visited Brazil, but after traveling through South America with a boyfriend that was a *capoeirista*, she returned to the city of Salvador and fell in love with the art. Since she grew up speaking both English and Spanish fluently, she found it easy to pick up Portuguese. Her way of giving back to the local capoeira community was to print a small book of words and phrases that a Brazilian *capoeirista* should know if he or she wants to teach English-speaking foreigners, either by going abroad to teach students in their home countries or by staying home and teaching tourists or pilgrims. At the workshop, we practiced phrases like "keep going," "jump more," and "where does it hurt" in addition to basic conversation. Before the partner-practice began, a panel of *mestres* who had traveled abroad spoke. The word that repeatedly came up was *bacana*, which means "cool." It is cool to travel abroad, they said, but it is hard, especially if one does not know the language. They did not share many details about the things they did other than teach capoeira, but the repeated focus on how cool travel is implies that there is at least some value beyond economic rewards.

On their initial trips, these Brazilian teachers might experience and enjoy amenities that had been established for tourists like hotels and restaurants. Relocating permanently is a very different experience. Even if being paid for their work, their initial trips have more in common with tourism than migration. As a migrant, they will typically have to find their own housing and learn to run an academy, which may require them to work additional jobs on the side until they can become self-sustaining through their work teaching capoeira. Eventually, they may become successful enough to exert a magnetic pull on members within a specific community of practice, thus elevating their new city of residence so that it becomes a pilgrimage destination.

Although it happens less frequently, a Brazilian *capoeirista* might visit a friend in the United States or elsewhere randomly, without a major event on the calendar. This is yet another instance in which traditional mobility categories are inadequate for describing what is actually happening within a community. If the visitor teaches capoeira while abroad, is he/she engaging in visiting friends and relatives (VFR) tourism or traveling for work? Much/most of their stay may be spent engaging in "touristy" activities, or just enjoying the company of the person they came to visit, but teaching the occasional class gives him or her the opportunity to build an international reputation and network that can be drawn upon later in order to draw students to his/her own school in Brazil or pave the way for his/her potential emigration.

Some of the most successful *mestres* that have remained in Brazil have turned their local schools into international franchises. This creates ready-made networks for the franchise's up-and-coming Brazilian teachers to utilize when trying to build their own reputations. A franchise chapter in Paris, for instance, might invite the son of their organization's *mestre* to appear at the event, which gives the young protégé an opportunity to build his own reputation apart from that of his father. Additionally, when foreign students in one of these franchises plan to visit Brazil, it is assumed that they will build their trips around training sessions at the franchise's headquarters. Not only are the logistics easier, and they are already familiar with the organization's style, but not visiting the local group might be construed as a slight in no small part because the pilgrim would be diverting potential revenue away from the local chapter if he/she took classes elsewhere.

Experiencing the Intersections of Tourism, Apprenticeship Pilgrimage, and Migration in Brazil

I have met several *capoeirista*s from the Global North whose trajectory within the art takes a fairly predictable path, albeit one that deviates from what is considered "normal" for a young adult in the United States. Tyrell, a long-time martial artist, had a high-paying job in software design but as he became enamored with capoeira, his career took a backseat. His lunch breaks became longer and longer as he would slip out to a local park and train. Eventually, the urge to visit Brazil became so strong that he walked away from his job, his home, and his wife to pursue capoeira with a single-minded focus. He showed up on the doorstep of the academy, little more an open room on the fourth floor of a run-down office building in Salvador da Bahia, with just a rucksack. He had no idea where he was going to stay or what his time in Brazil would be like. Eventually, he took a room in the historic district and taught English under the table to support himself. I asked him how long he would stay in Brazil, and he slowly extended his arm and flipped over his hand. "Until I do this," he said, pantomiming the upturned palm of a beggar.

I have heard through the capoeira grapevine that Tyrell has finally returned to the United States but keeps a pretty low profile. His story may seem extreme but fits a pattern of intense dedication that I have witnessed multiple times. An elective leisure activity becomes so central to one's identity that he or she pursues international travel in order to satisfy a yearning for greater immersion in the activity. When that movement takes a relatively privileged person from the Global North to the Global South, where costs of living are much lower, it is easy to see how a short visit can turn into a long-term stay or even semi-permanent relocation. The pilgrim becomes a (temporary) migrant, at least until something calls him or her home.

In Tyrell's case, his ability to remain in Brazil was facilitated by finding work teaching English and translating documents. Although engaging in paid labor without a work visa is illegal, Tyrell chose to pursue it anyways because, as he explained to me, the worst that would happen would be him getting sent home and being denied reentry to Brazil for a few years. With an IT degree in hand, being sent back to one of the wealthiest and most powerful countries in the world is a far different scenario than a Central or South American migrant laborer being caught working

194 Lauren Miller Griffith

illegally in the United States; I cannot say whether Tyrell was aware of this disparity, but it did not factor into our conversations, nor did he explicitly engage with the irony of being a relatively affluent Black man and voluntarily reducing himself to a position of precarity into which many Afro-Brazilians are born and from which they will never escape.

Bridget's story is similar, though her whiteness gives her a different positionality within the capoeira community. A long-time member of the same capoeira franchise that Tyrell belonged to, she wrote her master's thesis at an Ivy League institution about capoeira. She has visited Brazil on multiple occasions. She learned Portuguese because of her interest in capoeira, as many US practitioners do, and her fluency improved with each trip she made to Brazil. Still, in my first few weeks of fieldwork in Bahia, I was awed by her confidence as she burst through the academy door. Did you miss me, she asked one of the Brazilians training there. She had gone back home to attend to some family matters, but had returned because she felt more at home in Brazil than she did back in the United States. Yet in the end, she did return to the United States and entered motherhood, a life stage that makes such dedicated training difficult.

When a *capoeirista* becomes a parent, the demands of childcare often leave little time for training, let alone traveling in pursuit of additional training opportunities. I was not yet a mother when I conducted my fieldwork in Brazil, nor can I imagine quite how having young children might have affected my ability to train capoeira and participate fully in the lives of the pilgrims who typically had ample time to relax, party, or spontaneously pursue opportunities without having to think about the desires of or consequences for anyone other than themselves. I only met one couple in Brazil who had brought their children with them on their pilgrimage. While these two *capoeiristas* were welcomed at every activity I saw them attend, they were marked as different because they could not train with the same intense focus as other pilgrims without children. Rather, they sought to balance their capoeira-related activities with excursions that the children would enjoy. Relatedly, Camile is a single mother of two with whom I trained for several years. She made a pilgrimage to Brazil at the same time that I was conducting my fieldwork. Leaving her sons at home allowed her to focus on her training while in Brazil as well as do some "touristy" things like going to beaches and a national park and enjoy a short-term romantic relationship with a local capoeirista. Yet her trip was constrained by the amount of time she felt comfortable being away from her children.

Camile still fits the parameters of my definition of apprenticeship pilgrimage – traveling to the source or major hub of a practice in order to gain skills and increase one's legitimacy/standing in the community of practice – but the duration of her trip was much shorter than those made by Tyrell and Bridget, making it more akin to tourism than temporary migration. Indeed, the difficulty of finding the "right" label for the practice in which they were engaged speaks to the need for a more complex, intersectional understanding of mobility. Despite only being in Brazil for a week and a half, Camille was enraptured by the feeling of community she shared with the local *capoeirista*s she met.

Almost any time I would walk through the historic plazas around which several capoeira academies and instrument shops are located, it was easy to spot *capoeiristas* who had only recently arrived in the city, marked as they were by newly purchased capoeira pants bearing blue, yellow, and green stripes down the side and by the maps or guidebooks they often carried. When not training, these visitors may be largely indistinguishable from other tourists, filling their time with shopping, dining out, partying at cafes or nightclubs, and enjoying the beaches. The switch from pilgrim to tourist and back again may happen in the course of a single day or it may follow the rhythm of an academy's weekly class schedule. Alternatively, it might have more to do with one's geographic location within Brazil. I met a small group of women from London on a bus who told me that they had trained hard with the chapter of their group located in Forteleza, but shied away from participating in any *rodas* (capoeira games) in Salvador because "[they] didn't want to get killed." The ease and confidence they felt among their fellow *capoeiristas* in Fortaleza did not extend to the much larger Salvador capoeira community.

Alternate Routes: Mobilities That Complicate the Apprenticeship Pilgrimage Paradigm

Bruno's story complicates the pattern of *capoeiristas* from the Global North traveling to Brazil in pursuit of training opportunities and a boost to their legitimacy. Bruno was 15 when he started studying capoeira in his hometown, just outside of São Paulo. When he was 18, he came to the United States to visit one of his sisters who lived here. So far, this is a classic example of VFR tourism. But Bruno's one-month stay stretched to six months, and then to an entire year, during which time he worked in the construction industry, thus blurring the line between VFR tourism and labor migration. It was during this year that he happened to meet and start training with a high-profile capoeira *mestre* who is Brazilian but had opened a chapter of his own teacher's school in the same city where Bruno's sister lived. This was not a branch of the school Bruno had originally started training with back in Brazil; it was a completely different style, but he "fell in love" with the capoeira being taught by this *mestre*.

Eventually, Bruno did have to return to Brazil. Because he was 18, he had to enlist in the military. In his words, he had to "go down there, enlist myself, get myself rejected, then I came back for good." He came back because of his desire to train capoeira with this particular *mestre*. "Oddly enough," he said, "it was easier for me to come to the U.S. than to move to Salvador." The city of Salvador in the Northeastern Brazilian state of Bahia is widely considered the font of capoeira, the place where it largely escaped persecution during its period of illegality and the place where the tradition's most famous *mestres* paved the way for its current popularity by opening academies. It was often described as "Mecca" by the apprenticeship pilgrim *capoeiristas*. When *capoeiristas* travel in pursuit of training opportunities or simply to experience more of the culture that gave rise to their art, this is their ideal (and idealized) destination. For Bruno, however, things were different.

196 Lauren Miller Griffith

Bruno's reference to Salvador, and the implied suggestion that it could have been a place for him to move to after getting rejected from military service, serves as confirmation that he is aware of its importance within the "folk geography" (Hamera, 2006, p. 12) of capoeira. His decision to move to the United States instead was informed by at least two factors: His sister's presence in the city where he wanted to live and the access to his *mestre* that living in this city would afford. In the United States, he worked construction jobs and in restaurants to support himself, but he also had his sister there to help him when needed. He would not have had that family support in Salvador. And while there would have been many capoeira academies from which he could have chosen in Salvador, including one that is affiliated with the very same *mestre* he wanted to study under in the United States, the magnetism of this man and his craft exerted a strong pull on Bruno. Following a family member who has previously emigrated is a predictable path, but doing so while simultaneously being an apprenticeship pilgrim is less common.

Bruno's *mestre* is himself a migrant who has become a magnet within the capoeira community. If you see him play in the *roda*, you quickly understand why. His now graying locks sprout in unruly directions and sweep the floor as he quickly turns upside down and laughs, almost maniacally, at a joke you have yet to catch on to. "We gotta get him!" another *capoeirista* remembers exclaiming the first time he saw this man play capoeira on a VHS recording, meaning he wanted to secure the *mestre*'s migration to the United States so that he could open a school locally. And get him they did. Working through a pan-African association, a small group of *capoeiristas* enticed him to move to the United States. When an unresolvable social drama resulted in him breaking away and establishing his own group, he became head of an international franchise with academies in virtually every continent. Where he goes, people will follow. Migration gave this extraordinarily charismatic man a platform from which to influence the transnational social field of capoeira, and apprenticeship pilgrims have followed him to his new location in the United States, back to Brazil for international events he hosts there, and in other locations throughout the world where he gives classes.

The martial arts provide numerous examples of migrants that are also magnets within their particular communities of practice. Within capoeira, Bruno's *mestre* is a case in point. So too is Mestre João Grande who first traveled abroad as part of Emília Biancardi's company Viva Bahia (see Höfling, 2015) but whose academy in New York City is a "must visit" location for many *capoeiristas*. This is one of the mechanisms that could theoretically result in a community's center of practice shifting from one geographic location to another over time, particularly if/as practitioners lose their attachment to the specific culture out of which the art arose. Such a shift could be threatening to those within the social field who have a personal, cultural, or financial stake in preserving the original site's centrality; however, at least within the context of US capoeira, I believe that the polarized experience of being a migrant from Latin America prompts Brazilian teachers to continue protecting the primacy of Brazil as a reference point for their students.

Migrant Teachers in Metaphoric Exile

Even though he had only had three years of experience when he arrived in the United States, Bruno received a warm welcome from the capoeira students in his new group. He attributes this at least in part to the fact that he was Brazilian. In addition to the presiding *mestre*, there was also a female student in the group who was from Brazil. Bruno brought that total to three. The US students were excited to practice their Portuguese with him, as speaking Portuguese is a helpful skill, especially for those *capoeiristas* who want to train with monolingual *mestres* and/or visit Brazil. His cultural capital was in high demand within this small enclave.

When he was not among fellow *capoeiristas*, Bruno had a completely different experience of US society. When he first arrived, he spent a year working in construction. There he got to know a lot of fellow migrants from places like El Salvador and Mexico. They embraced him, he thinks, because of the association between Brazil and soccer. As time went on, he started learning more English and sought work in restaurants. Speaking a foreign tongue was a struggle, and he often said the wrong things. He felt that they judged him because of his accent, but his first truly memorable experience with US discrimination came when he was on the metro.

The metro was almost empty that day, and he was only going a stop or two, so he sat in one of the seats by the door that was reserved for the elderly and disabled. A set of older parents with their adult daughter got on the train. The mother and daughter sat across from Bruno. There was an empty seat right next to him, but the father remained standing. They started talking about Bruno as if he was not even there, assuming "he probably doesn't know any English, that's why he's sitting there." He was upset but did not want to say anything to them because he knew it was not going to be nice and, as he said, "my parents taught me better" than to be rude to strangers. But as he walked away, he looked at them and said, in clear English, "have a nice day." He laughed a little bit with me about the looks on their faces when they realized that he did indeed speak and understand English, but it was a painful experience.

Since coming to the United States, Bruno has grown greatly as an activist and has worked as an individual and as a representative of his capoeira group to raise awareness about violations of immigrants' rights. He claims that his awareness of social justice issues stems mostly from having a daughter with a woman who is half Black, but the experiences he has had as a migrant no doubt affect his worldview as well. Several *capoeiristas* have mentioned to me how their understandings of race and racism have changed as they have moved across borders in the service of their craft. An Afro-Brazilian man will be forced to confront the system of hypodescent that dominates US thinking about race because of the color of his skin, which might be called *moreno* (brown) or *pardo* (i.e., mixed) back home but qualifies him as being Black in his new context. He may be disoriented by how people interact with him differently based on their automatic assignation of him to this category. Alternatively, a *capoeirista* who identifies with the Black movement in Brazil despite

198 Lauren Miller Griffith

having lighter skin might be frustrated when the African Americans he meets see him as Other because of his Latin American heritage and accented English. Within the capoeira academy, however, the *capoeirista*-in-exile enjoys a temporary respite from some of the stresses that accompany migration.

Sara Delamont and Neil Stephens (2008, p. 60) state that "[c]apoeira teachers all over the world have a homeland and aspire to return to it." In my own experience, Brazilian capoeira teachers in the United States often express *saudade* (nostalgic longing) for home and may seek to recreate aspects of Brazilian culture/society within the domains over which they have control (i.e., their academies). Returning to Brazil is something they may even talk about, especially when frustrated with their US students, but an actual, permanent return is unlikely for most of them and may not really be something they genuinely desire.

The Brazilian capoeira teachers Delamont and Stephens (2008, p. 60) have encountered through their research in the United Kingdom "present themselves to their students as self-exiled, nomadic Brazilians." This exile is largely metaphorical, since in most cases, there is nothing formally prohibiting them from returning to Brazil if they should so choose. Furthermore, they sometimes do return to Brazil for a few weeks or months at a time, often with small groups of their students (i.e., apprenticeship pilgrims) who wish to experience capoeira in their homeland. In those instances, the migrant capoeira teacher is simultaneously a VFR tourist and a tour guide for his or her students who are pilgrims. While there, the migrant teachers occupy an ambiguous status. In some instances, they may be welcomed home with open arms and treated like a local (e.g., being charged the local rates for classes rather than the higher, "gringo price" that foreigners are charged). In other instances, they may be snubbed, accused of having sold out, or turned their backs on their Brazilian brethren in favor of foreigners.

After the trip ends, these teachers return to being exiled. If the capoeira teacher considers him or herself to be living in exile, then the capoeira academy is not just a workplace, but a refuge, an informal embassy where the very same qualities that mark the Brazilian *capoeirista* as an outsider in society at large give him or her star status. Inside the academy, Bruno's accent is a form of distinction rather than a liability. His ambiguous ethnicity is taken as representative of Brazil's history of miscegenation rather than a problem to be solved by rival street gangs trying to figure out which side he is on.

Conclusion

Capoeira's spread beyond Brazil has both directly and indirectly ignited a frenetic criss crossing of the globe. Contreras Islas's (2021) work provides an essential corrective to the oversimplified notion of capoeira having been spread throughout the world solely through the efforts of enterprising and mobile Brazilians. New students do encounter capoeira through local presentations made by teachers who are visiting their countries or who have migrated there, but they also encounter the art through its various media representations (e.g., the film *Only the Strong*, various commercials, incorporation into public spectacles like the closing ceremony of the London Olympics, etc.) and pursue a course of self-study. Their efforts to learn capoeira are likely to eventually put them in close contact with a Brazilian representative of the art, such as when they encounter a visiting teacher at a workshop or if they go to Brazil to study under a *mestre's* close guidance.

The transnational routes that make it possible for Brazilian capoeira teachers to attain high status within their adopted countries (or at least within their schools) and that draw pilgrims from privileged nations to Brazil are collaboratively built and maintained. The initial trail may have been blazed by enterprising Brazilians who used their bodily and cultural capital to make a living through capoeira, but those pathways that connect Brazil to the rest of the world, and loci within the capoeira diaspora to one another, have been widened by a wildly diverse group of people who identify as *capoeiristas*. The twang emanating from the *berimbau* as its wire is struck calls *capoeiristas* to move, and that movement is not restricted to the *roda*. It calls *capoeiristas* from the Global North to venture to Brazil and train at the feet of local *masters*. It calls Brazilian teachers to leave their homes and make a life for themselves abroad. Whereas the former have much in common with tourists, and the journey is largely pleasurable even if it contains moments of pain (e.g., the physical pain of training and the emotional distress of culture shock), the latter arguably have a tougher road to follow. Few are lucky enough to have their paths paved with fame and generous remuneration. Most teacher-migrants will struggle and may feel as though they are living in exile but experience relief within the archipelago of capoeira schools that is maintained by the various, overlapping forms of mobility discussed here.

Notes

1   This is a narrative reconstruction of a very typical weekly activity within the academy in Indiana (United States) where I trained for approximately six years.
2   All of the personal names (e.g., Tyrell) used in this text are pseudonyms. Place names are real (e.g., Bahia).
3   Contreras Islas (2021), however, argues that capoeira's spread throughout the Global South has taken and will continue to take a different form than that seen in the Global North, which has been the focus of most studies on the globalization of capoeira. He argues that the framework of glocalization is a more productive way of thinking about the spread of capoeira, at least within these contexts, than is the idea of a capoeira diaspora. I, however, believe that glocalization can coexist with the notion of diasporic capoeira, and they need not be positioned as opposites.
4   See Delamont and Stephens (2008) for an exploration of the importance of a teacher being Brazilian in the UK capoeira market.

References

Appadurai, A. (1996) *Modernity at large: Cultural dimensions of globalization.* Minneapolis, MN: University of Minnesota Press.
Contreras Islas, D.S. (2021) 'Mexican capoeira is not diasporic! On glocalization, migration and the North-South divide', *Martial Arts Studies*, 11, pp. 57–71.

Delamont, S. and Stephens, N. (2008) 'Up on the roof: The embodied habitus of diasporic capoeira', *Cultural Sociology*, 2(1), pp. 57–74.

Delamont, S., Campos, C. and Stephens, N. (2010) 'I'm your teacher! I'm Brazilian', *Sport, Education and Society*, 15(1), pp. 103–120.

Delamont, S., Stephens, N. and Campos, C. (2017) *Embodying Brazil: An ethnography of diasporic capoeira*. New York and London: Routledge.

González Varela, S. (2019) *Capoeira, mobility, and tourism: Preserving an Afro-Brazilian tradition in a globalized world*. Lanham: Lexington Books.

Griffith, L.M. (2016) *In search of legitimacy: How outsiders become part of an Afro-Brazilian tradition*. New York: Berghahn Books.

Griffith, L.M. (2017) 'Virtually legitimate: Using disembodied media to position oneself in an embodied community', *Martial Arts Studies*, 4, pp. 36–45.

Griffith, L.M. and Marion, J.S. (2018) *Apprenticeship pilgrimage: Developing expertise through travel and training*. Lanham: Lexington Books.

Hamera, J. (2006) *Dancing communities: Performance, difference and connection in the global city*. Houndmills: Palgrave MacMillan.

Head, S. and Gravina, H. (2012) 'Blackness in movement: Identifying with capoeira Angola in and out of Brazil', *African and Black Diaspora*, 5(2), pp. 194–210.

Höfling, A.P. (2015) 'Staging capoeira, samba, maculelê, and candomblé: Viva Bahia's choreographies of Afro-Brazilian folklore for the global stage' in Albuquerque, S.J. and Bishop-Sanchez, K. (eds.) *Performing Brazil: Essays on culture, identity, and the performing arts*. Madison, WI: The University of Wisconsin Press, pp. 98–125.

Joseph, J. (2012) 'The practice of capoeira: Diasporic Black culture in Canada', *Ethnic and Racial Studies*, 35(6), pp. 1078–1095.

Uriely, N. (2010) '"Home" and "away" in VFR tourism', *Annals of Tourism Research*, 37(3), pp. 854–857.

11

INTERSECTIONS OF PROFESSIONAL MOBILITY AND TOURISM AMONG SWEDISH PHYSICIANS AND RESEARCHERS

Magnus Öhlander, Katarzyna Wolanik Boström and Helena Pettersson

We were attending a conference in Dubrovnik, Croatia. It was an important conference in our field; a good opportunity to present our research on highly skilled migration and to exchange ideas with other scholars. But a visit to the Old Town of Dubrovnik, a magnificent site listed on the UNESCO World Heritage List (and a filming location in the TV series Game of Thrones) was also a powerful incentive to come here. One of our research colleagues, who had previously lived in Dubrovnik, took us on her own city tour in which she presented both interesting facts and personal memories. We admired the scenic views, we noted historically important places and still visible traces of the recent war, while at the same time talking about the conference sessions we had just attended, recent turns in migration studies, and joint writing projects. The city walk became alternately sight-seeing, a social occasion and a scholarly conversation, in which we performed our professions while to all intents and purposes acting as many of the other "tourists" around us.

Introduction

The aim of this chapter is to highlight the intertwined and multidimensional practices of professional mobility and tourism by analyzing highly skilled professionals' reflections on their international work-related travels. As "the mobilities turn" has shown, distinctions between tourism and other forms of spatial mobility are often arbitrary and many different hybrid forms of mobility coexist (e.g., Williams and Hall, 2000; Hall, 2008; Burns and Novelli, 2008; O'Reilly, 2003; Urry and Larsen, 2011). Some examples of travelers who cannot be clearly defined along tourist/non-tourist lines are medical tourists (Connell, 2011), volunteer tourists (Schwartz, 2018), lifestyle migrants (Benson and O'Reilly, 2009; Åkerlund and Sandberg, 2015), retirement migrants (Gustafson, 2002; O'Reilly, 2003; Woube, 2014), long-distance commuters between countries (Löfgren, 2015), and business

DOI: 10.4324/9781003182689-12

202 Magnus Öhlander et al.

travelers (Willis et al., 2017; Jansson, 2016). This chapter seeks to further challenge traditional understandings of tourism by analyzing how highly skilled Swedish professionals who work for some time in another country become temporary tourists in-between mandatory job obligations, or indeed even while performing their work tasks. The professionals at the core of our research are physicians, molecular biologists, and scholars within the humanities.

Professional Spatial Mobility and Tourist Moments

Ethnologist Orvar Löfgren (2015) has discussed moving between tourism and other modes and moods of traveling. He described an experience of a leisure day before an academic conference, in a city he never visited before, as "turning into a tourist":

> As I begin to saunter aimlessly down the street, both my body and my mind are reprogrammed. I begin looking for "sights," my eyes curiously exploring buildings and city life, my movements becoming slow and uncertain. Now I am unconsciously activating both the traditional tourist gaze and gait. I am surrounded by city commuters on their way to work, yet my movements are badly synchronized with theirs; I keep bumping into people, my pace is too slow, my movements unpredictable. It is quite clear: at this moment, I am one of those tourists!
>
> *(Löfgren, 2015, p. 193)*

This kind of experience of a tourist moment was frequently described by our interviewees. However, unlike Cary's (2004) proposition of "the tourist moment" as a spontaneous instance of self-discovery, communal belonging, and a temporary fulfillment in the quest for authenticity, we propose a definition where more mundane shifts are in focus. A tourist moment may be a temporary shift from everyday routines to observing local culture, or from a professional engagement in work to a tourist gaze toward an exotic landscape. Such change of mood and gait may last for hours of just for a fleeting moment and does not need to be profoundly transformative – though it is often depicted as relaxing or enlightening.

This chapter explores the narrations of such shifts and overlaps in motifs, mindsets, moods, and gazes, and thus of the intertwined practices of professional mobility and tourism, as in our city tour in Dubrovnik. We analyze how the professionals describe practices of longer work-stays abroad or shorter visits at conferences away from home when their bodies and mindsets shifted into a different mode of the tourist gaze and gait. The tourist moments described by the interviewees varied in length; they could last for several days or entail merely a momentary change of manner and mood. The sight could be not only a typical tourist site but also a seemingly ordinary local practice that for an outsider seemed curious and exotic. As we will show, anticipation of tourist moods and moments could also impact the professionals' selection of destinations for work-related travels.[1]

Academics on work-related travels share terrain with international business travelers. For the latter, being on the move and staying abroad for longer or shorter periods is a natural part of their work (Mäkelä et al., 2015; Welch et al., 2007; Jansson, 2016). Cheryl Willis et al. (2017) argue that they have a special tourist gaze, "the business tourist gaze," as there is "an uneasy relationship of business travel as a touristic activity and with business travelers inhabiting the same space as other tourists and yet not really experiencing the same things in the same way" (p. 55). The feeling of being away from home, sometimes in "exotic" places, staying in hotels, and gaining new experiences is shared with the "traditional" tourists, but their reason for mobility is work. John Urry and Jonas Larsen (2011; see also Graburn, 1983) define tourism by contrasting it with work: "Tourism is a leisure activity which presupposes its opposite, namely regulated and organized work" (p. 3). Thus, the tourist gaze is an activity seeking and encompassing something distinct and different from the usual workspace and is "directed to features of landscape and townscape which separate them off from everyday experience," something that is "out of the ordinary" and not conventionally encountered in everyday life (p. 415). Being a tourist and practicing the specific gaze of a tourist is primarily connected to the non-work mode of life, a distinction questioned by Willis et al.'s (2017) in their study of business travelers. They state that "the binaries set up in tourism which contrast the exotic and the everyday are challenged through business travel and distinctions are increasingly blurred" (p. 52), a statement valid also for our study of mobile physicians and researchers.

Beyond recognizing, as Nelson Graburn did early on (1983), that "tourism involves for the participants a separation from normal 'instrumental' life and the business of making a living" (p. 11), Urry and Larsen (2011) argue that the tourist gaze is constructed by interpreting, giving meaning to, and making sense of what tourists have in front of their eyes. A tourist gaze needs to be learned in order to "see" and interpret the signs of "attractions" or tourist clichés. Gazing involves cognitive work of interpreting, evaluating, drawing comparisons, and making mental connections between signs and their referents (Urry and Larsen, 2011, pp. 17–18). In our studies of highly skilled mobility, we found that a "tourist moment" might relate to well-known signs and clichés but might also imply identifying the "extraordinary" amidst the "everyday" life abroad. It involved a temporary shift in how attention is directed from everyday life away from home to a (sometimes unexpected) refocusing to a different type of "gaze."

Traveling academics might have their gazes attuned to what is envisioned as typical of a place or a nation, but their tourist moments' gazes can also be aimed at the "familiar unknown" (Harris, 2014), something that feels striking and "exotic" in a seemingly shared professional environment, e.g., an extremely different dress code at a medical clinic or dining at High Table in Oxford. During their work stays abroad, the academics move around in an everyday world of signs that seem both familiar and a bit different from the ones at home. Conference centers, universities, lectures, seminars, as well as laboratories and clinics are all environments filled with activities and cultural codes that are partly well known and still in need of decoding

204 Magnus Öhlander et al.

and interpretation (cf. Kreber and Hounsell, 2014; Harris, 2014; Wolanik Boström and Öhlander, 2015). Amidst temporary "everyday life" abroad they sometimes get stricken by the "exoticness" of something in relation to their other everyday life in Sweden. In this chapter, we suggest that experiencing tourist moments as a physician or an academic away from home entails alertness not only to typical, representative tourist sights but also to sights of local "color" in everyday professional life.

In the following sections, we begin by briefly presenting the empirical material on which this chapter is based. Then we discuss how planning work visits abroad may include a tourist mode involving the decision of whether or not to travel, as well as choosing the destination. This is followed by some examples of tourist modes, including tourist gaze, and their relation to experiencing moments as a tourist or shifting to a tourist gaze when observing the "local color." We then proceed to discuss the intertwined and multidimensional practices of professional mobility and tourism.

Methodology

This chapter is empirically based on two qualitative studies exploring the practices of internationalization among highly skilled Swedish professionals in the medical field and among Swedish humanities scholars. The main data consist of ethnographic interviews with 43 medical professionals (physicians and molecular biologists) and 30 interviews with humanities scholars in history, Romance languages, and philosophy. All of the interviewees had lived most of their adult lives in Sweden.

The interviewees in the medical professions had experienced longer (a few months to several years) work periods abroad; 15 physicians and 12 molecular biologists had lived in other Global North countries (e.g., Australia, New Zeeland, United States, and Great Britain), while 16 physicians had worked on medical aid assignments in African, Asian, and South American countries. The 30 humanities scholars' stays were of varying lengths, from short visits at conferences to several years of postdocs or teachers' exchange. All of them regularly attended conferences in different parts of the world; some had collaborations with colleagues which sometimes necessitated shorter visits to other countries; some had pursued post-doctoral programs in other countries, participated in exchange teaching programs, had been guest researchers, or visited archives away from home. Contrary to the physicians and medical researchers, there was no clear-cut geography of traveling in this group.

All interviews were based on an open-ended questionnaire with a life-course perspective. The interviews focused on work life and practices of internationalization (e.g., postdoctoral programs, exchange programs, meetings, conferences, medical aid assignments), with a special emphasis on new knowledge and insights gained from working abroad for a limited time. As we conducted ethnographic interviews, we used the technique of recurrently asking the interviewees to give examples from their everyday life. In this way, the transcribed material includes the interviewees' narratives of their own everyday observations and experiences. The interviews were conducted in Swedish, digitally recorded, and transcribed. Quotations used in this chapter were translated into English with minor revisions for better readability. All names of interviewees are pseudonyms.

Although the interview guide did not contain specific questions on tourism, this theme emerged in several interviews as an aspect of moving abroad for work or an extra enticement for participating in a conference or visiting colleagues in other countries. Accounts of tourism-related experiences surfaced in questions concerning spare time, new knowledge and insights, or the general experiences of living in or visiting another country. If it was the case, follow-up questions were asked for clarification. In the chapter, we discuss the interviewees' utterances related to tourism in light of Urry's and Larsen's (2011) classic definition of tourism and tourism practice, as well as the research on the ambiguous distinction between tourism and other types of spatial mobility.

Planning Work Abroad and Anticipated Tourist Moments

Several factors influenced the participants' decisions surrounding travel and destination choices for longer or shorter stays abroad or conference attendance. Learning opportunities, career advancement, personal development, and a chance to "do some good" were usual motives but also to "see the world." As research has shown, apart from professional reasons, the appeal of different locations and an opportunity to see new places can be important factors in choosing the work location (e.g., Ackers and Gill, 2008; Doherty et al., 2011; Klekowski von Koppenfels, 2014; Öhlander et al., 2020).

The decision to work abroad and the destination choice were primarily based on professional considerations: A relevant university or laboratory, a promising cooperation with a research group, an archive containing documents not to be found online, or a hospital where one could learn a new treatment method. For doctors working for the Red Cross, Doctors Without Borders, and other international NGOs, the locale was usually based on locations in need of medical aid, but if the doctors were given a choice of several destinations for longer assignments, more "touristic" or "adventurous" factors were also taken into consideration. Other interviewees presented their motives for pursing foreign postdoctoral and exchange programs, temporary employments, conferences, and so forth at least partly in terms of tourism. Working in another country was not only about professional benefits but was also an acceptable, legitimate avenue for tourism and getting to know interesting places and cultures. In a sense, it could be seen as a form of educational tourism. In such cases, the decisions to work abroad and the destination choices were influenced by tourist longings, motivations, and rationales.

Gaining new experiences and perspectives were motivations articulated in several interviews. Maria, a medical professional who worked in the United States, said she was "curious to see a different culture and a different way of working." The molecular biologist Tina concluded that she had always been curious about how things worked in different places. Jan, a philosopher, stated that he considered it

206 Magnus Öhlander et al.

central for PhD students and researchers to gain experiences abroad – not only via the research itself but also by experiencing something new and very different, both in a seminar room and in a new city. Klara, a Romance languages scholar, said: "It is unbelievably important that everybody should live abroad for at least a year. For all Swedes to get a perspective on what is good and bad."

Previous experiences of organized tourist trips, student exchange, or other forms of traveling could be an inspiration for choosing an assignment, a postdoctoral position, or an academic exchange program. Amanda, a historian who participated in exchange programs, lived for longer periods in three different countries, and routinely attended conferences all over the world, said that she had traveled a lot in her youth and "had got a taste for it." Viktoria, a physician and researcher, chose to work for 18 months in Australia for professional reasons, but the decision to work abroad was partly inspired by the fact that "we in the family very much love traveling." And she found it to be "a good experience for children to live elsewhere. And then my husband and I had been traveling and backpacking around Australia and felt that, yes, it would be fun to try to work there."

Besides longings for new experiences as such, traveling was also connected to anticipated tourist opportunities, even if momentarily. Nora, a languages scholar, said that when she went to conferences she always tried to combine the academic aspects with seeing something more of the location:

> I always try to make time for something, like going around in the city, maybe traveling by public transport, taking a walk to the conference location, and if there is some nice museum, I try to make time for that. Or just going around one day and looking for a pair of shoes.
> [laughs].

The desire to see more of the world, to get to know other cultures, was presented as self-explanatory by all the interviewees. Implicitly, curiosity and openness were presumed to be characteristics of an educated person. Even physicians on longer medical aid assignments with the Red Cross or Doctors Without Borders, who declared the wish to make a difference in places lacking sufficient medical staff, said that they often combined their work in countries such as Kenya, India, Lebanon, Colombia, or Afghanistan with leisure trips in their free time, enabling them to become acquainted with the region. As Monika explained,

> What prompts me as well is my egoistic curiosity, I am so curious about how things truly are in different places in the world, how the culture works, how the people are. I will not stop traveling . . . well I cannot, because there are always new things that I am curious about.

She was acutely aware that being white and privileged carried implications for travel in poorer countries (also Wolanik Boström, 2018), but accepting an NGO assignment and working hard for several weeks or months in a less prosperous region was her way of justifying her tourist privilege. An aid assignment was a kind of alibi, a way of reducing some of the unfair power relations, especially in postcolonial contexts:

> But I do not think that you can go to poor countries as a tourist. On the other side, if I feel that if I can give something back then I can get it, and it is OK, it is a kind of deal. Then it feels right for me.

Peter, who had worked in India, said that working for an NGO was "obviously a brilliant way to get out in the world, as an adventure, at the same time doing something good [for the people]."

Sometimes the partner's preferences and the interests of children were taken into consideration while planning visits abroad (Ackers, 2010; Doherty et al., 2015; Wagner, 2006; Wolanik Boström et al., 2018). Safety and good schools were, naturally, of importance, but also a place was expected to be nice and offer fun and educational activities. Several interviewees expressed the need to align work and family life, thus recalling the notion of a good, fulfilling life. That is, for these interviewees, an ideal destination should foster personal development, widen one's perspectives, and enable one to see the world (Wolanik Boström et al., 2018; also Benson and O'Reilly, 2009; Åkerlund and Sandberg, 2015). Gustav, a physician and researcher who worked for a year in the United States, explained how he and his partner had discussed the choice of destination:

> We could have gone to many other places as well, but I think that where we went was obviously crucial for the partner who was supposed to stay at home. And to be honest, if we were to go to a "University of nowhere," then, of course, I do not suppose that she would be equally positive, for example the Midwest or somewhere that might not be as much fun to be when you must follow your partner and stay at home.

Gustav's observations concerning not choosing "the University of Nowhere," but rather a place that was meaningful and "fun," convey considerations that could be understood as tourist-like. His line of argument was not only built on professional concerns; it also had a touch of a tourist mode.

Considerations and practices of professional mobility are connected not only to the notion of a good life but also to imagined geographies, e.g., imaginaries of interesting places, adventures, or leisure activities. Not all professional destinations are counted as equally desirable, especially with family. The tourism imaginaries (Selwyn, 1996) included a global hierarchy of places and mental hierarchies of the West and the Rest, the cosmopolitan versus the local/national, the historical versus the modern, and so on (cf. Salazar et al., 2014; Riaño et al., 2015; Åkerlund and Sandberg, 2015; Wolanik Boström et al., 2018).

An interview with Johan offers one example of how location choice was influenced by a confluence of tourism imaginaries, longings for adventure, curiosity,

208 Magnus Öhlander et al.

and a declared desire to make a difference. Johan had worked as a clinical physician and researcher in several countries in Europe, Africa, and Australia for extended periods. His wife's work also included international mobility. A few years back, Johan and his wife had been on holiday in Kenya, and, after a couple of weeks, they started to think that they had mostly met other tourists and had not really learned anything about the country. So, they contacted a doctor at a local hospital near the Kenyan coast, and Johan was offered a job. He temporarily returned to Sweden, took some time off from his regular job, packed all the medicines and equipment he could carry, returned to the Kenyan hospital, and worked there for several weeks:

> We went on medical rounds and we operated and I was doing orthopaedics, we did major abdominal surgery, we operated on groin hernia, I cleaned hippopotamus bites and stuff like that . . . You brushed the ants away and sprayed some honey on the wound dressing and put it on. A completely different environment that was . . . it was incredibly fascinating. . . . And I think I did some good as well.

In his narrative, Johan dwelled less on the similarities of medical care, as these were probably taken for granted, and instead stressed the more unusual or "exotic" aspects of his work there, as evidenced by the reference to hippopotamus bites, ants, and honey treatments, as well as the "completely different environment." A similar fascination for and pursuit of difference was articulated by the aforementioned physician Viktor, whose memories of his medical work in Afghanistan implicitly juxtaposed "old" cultures with not-so-old Sweden:

> And the country is very fascinating, so much in it fascinated me, just to travel in this country, to be in it, in different places, and you get respect for the people, these are old cultures, old trade roads – fascinating things.

Interviewer: Did you travel?
Viktor: Yes, quite a lot. Both for work and I was also taking every opportunity to travel around to different places, in different ways. We were three doctors and we helped each other: "you can go away this week."

Some doctors on longer assignments said that they chose well-established tourist resorts for shorter vacations, just to escape the constant strain, responsibility, and visibility. Diego said that,

> Sometimes it may be really tough to be noticed all the time, you can't escape into anonymity. Many expats take flight from their workplace just to go for a vacation in Western-oriented destinations, so that you can hide among other Westerners.

Susanna and Peter, both doctors, lived for a year in India with their two young children. Although they were doing great at work, everyday life in a big town was tiresome. Experiences that seemed very exotic at the beginning – the somewhat chaotic traffic and occasionally spotting an elephant used as a vehicle on the street – eventually felt annoying or dangerous. They also felt the strain of being the constant focus of attention, as they were among the very few white foreigners in the town, and their children were often commented upon or even cuddled by strangers:

> We tried to get away on weekends, out of town, to a resort, there was a Waterland too, and it was great, it was pleasant and lots of fun. There was an elephant we got to know at the resort and it was [imitates her children] "really cool." And the kids were pretty much left in peace there, and there was a pool and you could swim.

Interviewer: Did you enjoy it as well, or just the kids?
Susanna: Absolutely! It was a real pleasure. It was a tiresome town to live in, lots of traffic, lots of exhaust, warm, and dusty, and filthy, and dogs running loose and all such things. And then, you went to such a resort and it was quiet, quiet and lovely, with a forest. Beautiful.

The well-defined tourist resort was a welcome escape, and the elephant in the resort was a tourist-oriented attraction, not a traffic-causing road obstacle on the daily commute to schools and workplaces.

Some interviewees pointed out that it was important not to be regarded as a tourist in the place where you lived. Peter said that after a time they became a part of the local environment in their town in India and avoided being treated as tourists by the local people, which entailed the risk of being duped and cheated. A similar concern was articulated by Claes, who had worked several times in Kenya, and had learned how to act in order not to be bothered on the streets of Nairobi:

> I think that when you are there for the first time, then you go slowly and you look around and such and you are unsure. But you should just go at a steady pace "yes, this is where I am heading" and you just [demonstrate] like that [that you have] a clear purpose. I know that it is not wise to stop and ask for directions, or ask what time it is, or look at a map or to have a camera. I mean it sends loads of small signals.

Claes' reflection on the semiotics of "a tourist" in Nairobi thus incorporated an awareness of behavioral cues – slower gait, uncertainty, and naïve curiosity – that, Claes noted, could easily prompt the locals to flock around an outsider. After several months in Kenya, he "no longer felt like a tourist," learned how to signal the right attitude, and felt safe, even in backstreet areas, which was an exhilarating experience for him.

210   Magnus Öhlander et al.

In sum, in this section, we have shown how the practices of professional mobility and tourism interact, in the realms of work travel motives and destination choices. Such decisions were motivated not only by professional considerations but also by longings for adventures, the need to see and learn about new places, as well as the possibility of becoming a temporary tourist while working abroad. Tourist motives, longings to see other places, and opportunities for tourist moments were articulated along with tourism imaginaries, ideas of a pause from work, and ideas of the good life in which any tourist activity could be justified (cf. Urry and Larsen, 2011).

Tourist Moments With a Shifting Gaze

As mentioned before, the medical and humanities professionals we interviewed had various experiences of spatial mobility. Most interviewees had regularly participated in international conferences, some of them had worked abroad only once, and, for some, different forms of spatial mobility had become a lifestyle. Obviously, there were also variations in tourist moments during work stays abroad, e.g., depending on the dimensions of time (the length of the stay) and space (geographical location) (cf. Hall, 2008) as well as how familiar someone was with international environments and foreign countries. Tourist moments during shorter stays at conferences were self-evident, a part of taken-for-granted benefits of travels in the everyday life of a mobile professional. Also among those who worked abroad for a month or more tourist moments became an anticipated aspect of the stay. Jan, a medical professional, who worked in Norway and the United States, pointed out that it was interesting to see a new country, and they were also interested in "experiencing something new and exciting, getting out to the countryside." Viktoria and her family took frequent trips and engaged in outdoor activities while working for two years in Australia.

Thus, professional mobility and tourism interplayed in our interviewees' everyday lives abroad. Work stays included leisure-oriented tourist activities such as excursions or just a temporary switch in one's mood during other activities. This mode of switching between being a professional and being a tourist was achieved by temporarily activating the practice of a tourist gaze (Urry and Larsen, 2011), in contrast to the "non-tourist" practices (e.g., clinical practice, research, and well-known routines). This was especially apparent in our interviews with physicians who had been on catastrophic assignments for NGO organizations where the nature of the work did not permit any typical tourist activities. For example, when Edgar started his longer aid assignment in Zimbabwe, he left a cold Swedish winter and was overwhelmed by the warmth and by catching sight of some magnificent wildlife immediately after his arrival: "The very first day I saw giraffes, the very first day! It was so strange; I came from somewhere else entirely and it was very special and pretty cool, also. Well, it was like an adventure in the middle of it all."

Sometimes, the professional gaze and the tourist gaze overlapped, as illustrated by the experiences of Camilla, a medical researcher who had undertaken longer stays in the United Kingdom and Australia:

[Learning how to] do things [in another country], as a researcher, how to do analyses or . . . how to write, how to use methodology, how to park a car, how to dress in another country . . . it was everything. Everything. The whole thing was a huge experience. How to get a boat to commute to work. . . . I mean the whole experience of being a foreigner, an immigrant in a society that is not always completely positive to people coming from other places.

For the historian Alvar, professional mobility was part of his lifestyle. He had visited places throughout the world and talked in great detail about all of his experiences, to the extent that it was hard to distinguish the historian from the tourist, as the following quote illustrates:

I have been to St. Barthélemy [the former French, then Swedish colony in the Caribbean] a few times and I've been lucky enough to get to know people there. People living on the island are French speakers and French descendants and such. There are a lot of Swedish houses left there, [but] there is no one with any Swedish historical ancestry, so to speak. But it has been important for me to also get to know [the island], . . . it is a place for the very rich, well, they're almost repulsively rich. There are some really rich Swedes there too. I've met some. But it has nothing to do with Sweden anymore. But on the other hand, it has also been very interesting to be on other poorer islands in the Caribbean to understand how they work, as well.

Another example of how the professional and tourist modes converge in a gaze was offered by Adrianna, a language scholar. She remembered her stay in Oxford as very inspiring research-wise but spoke even more excitedly about other aspects of her stay:

You know, it was magnificent! Sitting in the Bodleian Library; such a fantastic environment with both researchers and young students with their books. It is like a different world. Instead of sitting in front of your computer, though of course, you had your computer with you. But just this fantastic wall décor . . . And then, most importantly, dining in Senior Common Room. All the fellows, eating there and High Table in the evening. When all the students rise when you arrive in your black [academic gowns], well it is a bit crazy, like the Middle Ages, like Harry Potter. It is really an experience. It was fantastic to meet all the scholars from mathematics, international relations, medicine, and many of them are old, antique. Because you know, when you are a fellow at the college, you can come and eat there until you – well, until you die! Well, it is very special.

Adrianna's reminiscences were told in a fashion evocative of a tourist gaze but did not seem to contain a "pure" tourist gaze as described by Urry and Larsen (2011); rather, a kind of gaze that intertwined the practices and observations

212 Magnus Öhlander et al.

of both a professional and a tourist. Moreover, tourist sights are not limited to those listed in guidebooks. For an academic on the move, a university campus, a conference center, a seminar room, a lecture hall, old academic traditions, or something else that is not only recognizable but also exotic in appearance can constitute a tourist sight. These can be as exciting as any more typically recognized tourist sights.

The molecular biologist Marty brought up a moment of self-reflexivity and an outsider gaze in reflecting on his own situation. He had moved with his family from Sweden to the United States. His wife did not have a job lined up in the United States, so he knew she was bound to find her social interactions dependent on his research contacts there. Marty hoped she could also forge social ties of her own, outside his work environment, and he reflected on the importance of parks and outdoor facilities as meeting places for migrants. Such spaces helped create the known in the un-known environment and became especially important for his partner while they lived abroad. For her sake, they also met with other Scandinavians:

> After our stay in the United States I can, upon my return to Sweden, understand why migrants socialize together in clusters. It is easier to socialize with people in your language. And it is not strange that people want to eat the specific foods they are used to. I mean, that is what we sometimes enjoyed as well in the US. So, yes, I think I understand migrants today rather differently. Of course, it is nice to socialize in your own group and talk in your own language.

This experience may be labeled as an intersection of being a tourist and being a (temporary) migrant – albeit privileged. It is interesting to note that this enabled Marty to forge new empathies with migrants upon his return to Sweden.

For some of the NGO doctors on medical assignments, there were no clear-cut boundaries between work, everyday life in the local setting, and many unexpected tourist moments. Even everyday activities and settings could be a source of bewilderment, especially at the beginning, and contain unexpected touristic benefits – for example, admiring Kenyan countryside while being driven to remote villages to administer malaria medicines, or just sitting on a porch of the medical staff's house, looking at the jungle, sipping beer, and listening to chattering monkeys in the evening.

In these interviews, there also were examples of the "intra-tourist gaze," i.e., a gaze making distinctions between oneself and (other) tourists (Holloway et al., 2011; Schwartz, 2018). Viktor, who had worked in the Middle East and Afghanistan, said:

> There are some who backpack for a while, say 6 months, and believe that they can see the world. This, I think, is a little naive. I think that working for,

being confronted with different people, getting to know people in a different way, this has given me pretty much.

This quote illustrates Culler's (1988, p. 158) observation that "wanting to be less touristy than other tourists is part of being a tourist." The intra-tourist gaze is directed at other tourists, with a focus on "the manner in which tourists gaze each other" (Holloway et al., 2011, p. 236). It is a moral and disciplining gaze, with the power to regulate how other tourists behave. It "influences tourists' understandings about what is considered acceptable and unacceptable touring behaviors, potentially shaping the behavior of other tourists" (Holloway et al., 2011, p. 238). Similarly, some of our interviewees stressed that spending a longer time in a country while working (and being a tourist) is the best way to experience and come to know another place and its people.

Donell Holloway, Lelia Green, and David Holloway (2011, p. 239) argue that "the intra-tourist gaze is particularly evident between different generational cohorts of tourists," and Kaylan C. Schwartz (2018) analyzes how this gaze is used among volunteer tourists (see also Mostafanezhad, 2014a on hierarchies between long-term and short-term volunteers and Mostafanezhad, 2014b on marking differences between volunteers and other kinds of tourist). Our study suggests that this kind of gaze can also be found among highly skilled professionals working abroad. In fact, the presence of the intra-tourist gaze among international mobile professionals could be understood as yet another articulation of the intertwined practices of professional mobility and tourism. There is no absolute distinction between work and tourist activities while being abroad for a conference, postdoctoral program, assignment for Doctors Without Borders, or in other capacities as a highly skilled professional on assignment abroad.

To summarize, in this section, we have shown that working abroad can include tourist moments that entail shifting to a tourist gaze. These could be just a brief moment at a conference or some planned time during longer stays. For an academic abroad, the tourist gaze can be directed toward places, surroundings, traditions, social practices, and so on that both resemble and are distinct from those at home, the "familiar unknown" (Harris, 2014), and are in some cases even perceived as exotic. In some narratives, the tourist gaze and the professional gaze converge into a kind of professionals' tourist gaze.

Conclusion

The overarching aim of this chapter has been to problematize the intertwined and multidimensional practices of professional mobility and tourism. We have shown how planning work visits abroad entails tourism imaginaries and considerations of opportunities for tourism, as the notion of "a good life" includes seeing interesting places, accruing adventures, or pursuing leisure activities. If any of these experiences can be found in the overseas destination, it is a welcome complement to professional

214 Magnus Öhlander et al.

commitments and benefits. Furthermore, in our material, there are examples of how temporary work abroad, and the tourist-like experience of finding your way in an unfamiliar society, can lend new insights into the conditions and experiences of migrants, and ultimately, upon return to Sweden, these experiences can foster better empathy for not-always-welcome-"foreigners" at home. We have also offered examples of temporary "tourist moments" and "gaze shifting" in the everyday life and work as an academic abroad. Thus, tourist activities and experiences happened not only in planned forms of leisure-oriented activities on excursions but sometimes just as temporary shifts – alterations of one's mood during other undertakings. Such shifts are achieved by activating the tourist gaze (Urry and Larsen, 2011) and contrasting what one sees and experiences with non-tourist practices (e.g., clinical routines and research) or to the familiar (often referred to as things are done in Sweden). Although we have placed more emphasis on the momentarily and shifting character of tourism-related considerations and the switch to a tourist gaze, our analysis is supported by other studies that make similar observations about other categories of work travelers (e.g., Schwartz, 2018; Willis et al., 2017).

In some cases, it can be challenging to separate the practices of temporary work abroad and tourist modes and experiences, and our research confirms that the distinction between tourism and other forms of transnational mobility is sometimes arbitrary. Tourism is usually understood through the three dimensions of time, space, and type of activity as a temporary leisure activity away from home (e.g., Hall, 2008; Urry and Larsen, 2011). The international mobility of highly skilled professionals is temporary and occurs outside their home countries, but it is only to some extent a leisure activity. Or, as we have argued in this chapter, some activities, even work, can have a dimension of tourism: While working, one can experience, observe, decipher, and interpret the signs of foreign places and behaviors in a fashion akin to the leisure-oriented tourist.

In our material, tourist practices and gazes are important dimensions of the professionals' transnational mobility, but the tourist gaze is usually not deployed as an analytical perspective in studies addressing transnational professional mobility. The empirical examples offered here suggest that an analysis of highly skilled professionals' descriptions of international mobility supports the theoretical assumption that there is an ongoing interplay between different types of gazes. These can include, for instance, the tourist gaze, the intra-tourist gaze, and what might be called the gaze of highly skilled professionals. The fact that they are traveling at work as academics influences their perceptions when they momentarily shift to a tourist mode. Tourist gaze distinguishes between tourists and "locals," even if the locals are also doctors or researchers. These different types of gazes influence each other in articulations of the meanings of being a professional abroad and the meanings of "foreign" places, practices, and people.

Note

1 Some American academics playfully use the term "confer-cation" to refer to the fine line between conferences as work and as an opportunity for tourist activities.

References

Ackers, L. (2010) 'Internationalisation and equality: The contribution of short stay mobility to progression in science careers', *Recherches Sociologiques et Anthropologiques*, 41(1), pp. 83–103.

Ackers, L. and Gill, B. (2008) *Moving people and moving knowledge: Scientific mobility in an enlarging European union*. Cheltenham: Edward Elgar.

Åkerlund, U. and Sandberg, L. (2015) 'Stories of lifestyle mobility: Representing self and place in the search for the "good life"', *Social & Cultural Geography*, 16(3), pp. 351–370.

Benson, M. and O'Reilly, K. (2009) 'Migration and the search for a better way of life: A critical exploration of lifestyle migration', *Sociological Review*, 57(4), pp. 608–625.

Burns, P.M. and Novelli, M. (2008) 'Introduction' in Burns, P.M. and Novelli, M. (eds.) *Tourism and mobilities: Local-global connections*. Wallingford and Cambridge: CABI, pp. xvii–xxvi.

Cary, S.H. (2004) 'The tourist moment', *Annals of Tourism Research*, 31(1), pp. 61–77.

Connell, J. (2011) *Medical tourism*. Wallingford: CABI.

Culler, J. (1988) *Framing the sign: Criticism and its institutions*. Norman and London: University of Oklahoma Press.

Doherty, C., Patton, W. and Shield, P. (2015) *Family mobility: Reconciling career opportunities and educational strategy*. London and New York: Routledge.

Doherty, N., Dickmann, M. and Mills, T. (2011) 'Exploring the motives of company-backed and self-initiated expatriates', *The International Journal of Human Resource Management*, 22(3), pp. 595–611.

Graburn, N.H.H. (1983) 'The anthropology of tourism', *Annals of Tourism Research*, 10(1), pp. 9–33.

Gustafson, P. (2002) 'Tourism and seasonal retirement migration', *Annals of Tourism Research*, 29(4), pp. 899–918.

Hall, M.C. (2008) 'Of time and space and other things: Laws of tourism and the geographies of contemporary mobilities' in Burns, P.M. and Novelli, M. (eds.) *Tourism and mobilities: Local-global connections*. Wallingford and Cambridge: CABI, pp. 15–32.

Harris, A. (2014) 'Encountering the familiar unknown: The hidden work of adjusting medical practice between local settings', *Journal of Contemporary Ethnography*, 43(3), pp. 259–282.

Holloway, D., Green, L. and Holloway, D.A. (2011) 'The intra tourist gaze: Grey nomads and "other tourists"', *Tourist Studies*, 11(3), pp. 235–252.

Jansson, A. (2016) 'Mobile elites: Understanding the ambiguous lifeworlds of sojourners, dwellers and homecomers', *European Journal of Cultural Studies*, 19(5), pp. 421–434.

Klekowski von Koppenfels, A. (2014) *Migrants or expatriates? Americans in Europe*. New York: Palgrave Macmillan.

Kreber, C. and Hounsell, J. (2014) 'Being an international academic: A phenomenological study of academic migrants adjusting to working and living in Scotland' in Maadad, N. and Tight, M. (eds.) *Academic mobility*. Bingley: Emerald, pp. 9–33.

Löfgren, O. (2015) 'Modes and moods of mobility: Tourists and commuters', *Culture Unbound*, 7, pp. 175–195.

Mäkelä, L., De Cieri, H. and Mockaitis, A. (2015) 'International business traveler, is work always on your mind? An investigation of the relationship between sources of social support and satisfaction with work-related international travel: The moderating role of over-commitment' in Mäkelä, L. and Suutari, V. (eds.) *Work and family interface in the international career context*. New York and London: Springer, pp. 181–195.

216 Magnus Öhlander et al.

Mostafanezhad, M. (2014a) 'Volunteer tourism and the popular humanitarian gaze', *Geoforum*, 54, pp. 111–118.

Mostafanezhad, M. (2014b) 'Locating the tourist in volunteer tourism', *Current Issues in Tourism*, 17(4), pp. 381–384.

O'Reilly, K. (2003) 'When is a tourist? The articulation of tourism and migration in Spain's Costa del Sol', *Tourist Studies*, 3(3), pp. 301–317.

Öhlander, M., Wolanik Boström, K. and Pettersson, H. (2020) 'Knowledge transfer work: A case of internationally mobile medical professionals', *Nordic Journal of Migration Research*, 10(2), pp. 36–49.

Riaño, Y., Limacher, K., Aschwanden, A., Hirsig, S. and Wastl-Walter, D. (2015) 'Shaping gender inequalities: Critical moments and critical places', *Equality, Diversity and Inclusion: An International Journal*, 34(2), pp. 155–167.

Salazar, N.B., Graburn, N.H.H. and Baptista, J.A. (2014) *Tourism imaginaries: Anthropological approaches*. New York: Berghahn.

Schwartz, K.C. (2018) 'Volunteer tourism and the intratourist gaze', *Tourism Recreation Research*, 43(2), pp. 186–196.

Selwyn, T. (ed.) (1996) *The tourist image: Myths and myth making in tourism*. Chichester: Wiley.

Urry, J. and Larsen, J. (2011) *The tourist gaze 3.0*. London: Sage.

Wagner, I. (2006) 'Career coupling: Career making in the elite world of musicians and scientists', *Qualitative Sociology Review*, 2(3), pp. 26–35.

Welch, D.E., Welch, L.S. and Worm, V. (2007) 'The international business traveler: A neglected but strategic human resource', *International Journal of Human Resource Management*, 18(2), pp. 173–183.

Williams, A.M. and Hall, C.M. (2000) 'Tourism and migration: New relationships between production and consumption', *Tourism Geographies*, 2(1), pp. 5–27.

Willis, C., Ladkin, A., Jain, J. and Clayton, W. (2017) 'Present whilst absent: Home and the business tourist gaze', *Annals of Tourism Research*, 63, pp. 48–59.

Wolanik Boström, K. (2018) 'Complex professional learning: Physicians in aid organisations', *Professions and Professionalism*, 18(1), pp. 1–15.

Wolanik Boström, K. and Öhlander, M. (2015) 'Mobile physicians making sense of culture(s): On mobile everyday ethnography', *Ethnologia Europaea*, 45(1), pp. 7–24.

Wolanik Boström, K., Öhlander, M. and Pettersson, H. (2018) 'Temporary international mobility, family timing, dual career and family democracy: A case of Swedish medical professionals', *Migration Letters*, 15(1), pp. 99–111.

Woube, A. (2014) *Finding one's place: An ethnological study of belonging among Swedish migrants on the Costa del Sol in Spain*. Uppsala: Uppsala University.

12

MOBILITY THROUGH INVESTMENT

Economics, Tourism, or Lifestyle Migration?
Narratives of Chinese and Brazilian Golden
Visa Holders in Portugal

Maria de Fátima Amante and Irene Rodrigues

Introduction

This chapter aims to contribute to the enduring discussion of the conceptual boundaries between migrants and tourists (Williams and Hall, 2000) by looking at privileged mobility (Cohen et al., 2015; Croucher, 2012) and focusing on investors. The discussion draws from ongoing research on the motives, expectations, and life experiences of Chinese and Brazilian investors (and their families) holding Golden Visas (hereafter GV) in Portugal. In contrast to economic and forced mobility, the movements of relatively affluent individuals and the super-rich (one segment of privileged mobility) have only recently begun to attract researchers' attention. A burgeoning literature on privileged mobility deriving from citizenship, class, and/or cultural capital (Kunz, 2016) has gradually emerged, showcasing how studying this underexamined form of mobility offers opportunities for "better highlight[ing] the nature and implications of global inequality" (Croucher, 2012). Furthermore, studying privileged mobility can be useful in deconstructing long-held notions surrounding migration, such as the "binary divide between work and leisure," the dichotomies of "home" and "away" (Cohen et al., 2015, p. 156), and the overlapping features of various travel categories (Amit, 2007) among which we find that of tourists. Examining this phenomenon promises to overcome the typically "skewed image of migrants and immigrants as predominantly non-Western, non-White, non-elite subjects" (Kunz, 2016, p. 89). As anthropologists, from where we stand, it is also an opportunity for "studying up" (Nader, 1972; Ortner, 2010; Souleles, 2018).

Investment as an avenue for obtaining a residence permit and eventually citizenship is a strategy used by those seeking opportunities to move abroad (Rogers et al., 2015; Gamlen et al., 2019). It is also embraced by many governments seeking capital infusions (Džankić, 2018; Parker, 2017). Since the 2008 global economic

DOI: 10.4324/9781003182689-13

218 Maria de Fátima Amante and Irene Rodrigues

crisis and the post-2010 sovereign debt crisis, this strategy has become increasingly popular among European nations, especially in Southern Europe. It was adopted into Portuguese law and implemented in 2012 during the deep economic crisis that prompted the third IMF intervention in the country's 40 years of democracy. The Resident Permit for Investors (*Autorização de Residência para Investimento*), colloquially known and addressed here as the GV Program, was the first of its kind in Southern Europe and has been very successful in dramatically increasing the number of overseas investors in Lisbon (Montezuma and McGarrigle, 2019). It was part of a political strategy to overcome Portugal's shortage of foreign investment and was ultimately envisioned as a way out of the crisis. Since its inception, the GV Program has been severely criticized, both internally and externally, for its potential to produce inequality among foreigners seeking residence permits (Amante and Rodrigues, 2020) and for its acceleration of gentrification processes in Lisbon and Porto's historical quarters[1] (Mendes, 2017; Krähmer and Santangelo, 2018). The European Commission (2019) also noted its instrumental nature, promoting "residence in exchange for money" (Ampudia de Haro and Gaspar, 2019). However, the GV Program has endured, despite a huge corruption scandal in 2015 involving both state officials and real estate agents.[2]

Investors, unlike other privileged mobile groups such as students, expatriates, or retirees, have been overlooked by researchers. GV holders in Portugal have been extremely difficult to access, so published work thus far has depended almost exclusively on empirical data collected via intermediaries (Ampudia de Haro and Gaspar, 2019; Montezuma and McGarrigle, 2019). Available official statistical data (SEF 2013–2021) reveal the number of GVs granted annually, both the number of initial grants and the number of residence permits issued under the family reunification policy, as well as the grantees' nationality and type of investment (see Table 12.1).

GV holders in Portugal are mostly Chinese and Brazilian nationals. Together they represent 60.85% of all the first GVs granted between 2012 and 2021 (SEF, 2013–2018; SEF, 2019–2021), with the Chinese constituting more than half (50.4%), followed by the Brazilians, at a distant second (10.45%). These figures increase dramatically when we consider residence permits granted for GV family members (Amante and Rodrigues, 2020). By 2021, 16,615 residence

TABLE 12.1 GV grantees by country of origin, October 2012 to May 2021

Country	Number of GVs 2012–2021	
China	4,923	50.40%
Brazil	1,021	10.45%
Turkey	464	4.75%
South Africa	403	4.13%
Russia	375	3.84%
Other nationalities	2,581	26.43%
Total	9,767	100.00%

Source: SEF, 2021

permits had been granted to GV family members of all nationalities (SEF, 2021). Most GV holders channel their investments to the real estate sector (9,170 GVs out of 9,767), which is the fastest and cheapest option.

Both Chinese and Brazilians had strong migration relationships with Portugal well before the GV program, with established communities in the country. Brazilians form the largest group of migrants in Portugal, and the Chinese community is the sixth-largest immigrant group in the country (SEF, 2019). Originally, both Brazilians and Chinese arrived in Portugal as workers driven by opportunities for economic security. The Chinese began arriving in the 1980s, becoming an important community during the 1990s and 2000s (Amante and Rodrigues, 2020; Gaspar, 2017). Brazil's military dictatorship (1964–1985) produced an initial stream of political refugees in the 1980s followed by highly skilled migrants attracted by Portugal's expanding economy after its 1986 admission into the European Economic Community (Padilla, 2006; Peixoto, 2002). At the dawn of the millennium, the "proletarianization of Brazilian migration" (Padilla, 2006) kept the numbers high. More recently, before the COVID-19 pandemic, we have witnessed growing numbers of more affluent arrivals (privileged mobility) from these two nations, with the growth of student and investor mobility. Together, these have contributed to both these communities' enlargement and diversity (Amante and Rodrigues, 2020; França and Padilla, 2018). Portugal's attractiveness as a place for investment and study has been propelled by the country's increasing popularity as a tourist destination.[3]

Scholars approach the well-recognized "symbiotic relationships between tourism and migration" (Williams and Hall, 2000, p. 5) from several different perspectives. Generally, research has detailed how migration generates tourist flows (Jackson, 1990; Morrison et al., 1995), and how tourism may also generate migration flows (Monk and Alexander, 1986). This chapter highlights a slightly different approach: By examining foreign investors, we seek to discern how migration and tourism overlap in constructing the investor category. In doing so, we follow two lines of inquiry: First, since the investor is a political category, we examine how the state's strategy for promoting the country as an investment hotspot entails co-mingling economic and tourist attractions. Second, we discuss the investor category from the inside by looking at how migration and tourism intertwine as investors subjectively construct the category of "the investor."

We consider this an interesting case for exploring the blurred boundaries of migration and tourism for several reasons beyond those mentioned earlier. First, the GV program coincided with a particularly favorable moment for tourism in Portugal. In recent years, the country has received a plethora of *World Travel Awards*, with Lisbon (2018) and Porto (2017) achieving special acclaim. Perhaps not surprisingly, GV holders invested primarily in Lisbon and Porto and adjacent regions. Before the COVID-19 pandemic, we anticipated the rise in investor visa grants due to Portugal's growing attractiveness as a tourism destination (Mendes, 2017; Krähmer and Santangelo, 2018). But last year (2020), the grant totals decreased (from 1,245 in 2019 to 1,182 in 2020) and the relative number of Chinese and Brazilian

GVs also fell slightly (SEF, 2019, 2020). Accordingly, to a certain extent, mobility through investment can be conceived of as consumption-led, and therefore more closely entangled with tourism or with a specific kind of migration, namely, lifestyle migration. Thus, we explore how the Portuguese State has promoted itself using not only economics and tourism but also lifestyle imaginaries to construct the investor category.

Second, the policy does not require that grantees and their family members reside in the country to maintain their residence permits. GV holders are only required to visit Portugal annually, remaining seven days in the first year, and 14 days in subsequent years. Hence, it appears the state does not expect GV holders to become migrants. However, the predominance of real estate investment suggests that GV holders may be interested in acquiring second homes abroad to access a particular lifestyle, valuing a esthetics over (or in tandem with) economics. In short, GV holders constitute a case of lifestyle migration (Benson and O'Reilly, 2009a; Knowles and Harper, 2009; Torkington, 2012; Benson and Osbaldiston, 2014). Our approach to the concept of lifestyle derives from Pierre Bourdieu (2010) for whom different lifestyles result from relationships between economic, cultural, and social capitals, and the choices available in specific social contexts. Thus, consumption (and leisure) is associated with specific lifestyles. Social class is indeed an element of investors' actions. But, when examining investors' motives for applying for a Portuguese GV, we choose to highlight the subjective dimension, stressing how these self-articulated motivations construct the idea of lifestyle itself. For Chinese emigrants in prior eras, political and economic uncertainty at home has been cited as major push factors for pursuing a desired lifestyle elsewhere, as seen with Chinese emigration from mainland China and Hong Kong in the 1990s (Li, 2005). Our findings, however, suggest that this is not quite the case with contemporary Chinese GV holders. For upper–middle-class Brazilians, lifestyle visions were seen as more closely tied to social class and identity mobility, which are entwined with ethnic and racial identity (Robins, 2019, p. 1). However, our findings complicate other scholars' analyses of upper–middle-class Brazilians' motives for pursuing lifestyle migration. Our interviews with Chinese and Brazilian GV holders suggest that the very notion of what constitutes lifestyle migration needs to be reassessed and re-envisioned to accommodate a broader range of pursuits than is classically portrayed in the literature.

Privileged Mobility and the Investor

Privileged mobility is a very broad concept and includes various categories of mobile people whose mobility experiences do not include the hardships – economic deprivation and endangered lives – usually associated with economic and forced mobility (Rodrigues, 2013; Sayad, 2004). Investors are but one category of people who can be viewed as privileged migrants, a condition shared with highly skilled professionals, students, sojourners, retirees, and expatriates (Croucher, 2012), among others. What makes all these categories of mobile people privileged is, first, the conditions under which they move and settle in the receiving country, and second, their lifestyle in that country. Regarding the first, privileged mobile people have access to resources that can soften the migratory experience: they have time to travel, and they are either wealthy or enjoy cultural capital. These kinds of resources allow them to overcome the usual difficulties migrants experience (securing housing, jobs, schools for their children, etc.). Moreover, privilege is not only shaped by affluence but by the migrants' citizenship, as demonstrated by research on North Americans who moved to South American countries and enjoyed benefits due to their passports from powerful nations (Croucher, 2012; Benson and O'Reilly, 2009b). Thus, nationality can also play a significant role (Benson, 2013). Finally, we must attend to how the divide between privileged and "regular" migrants is subjectively constructed. That is, people categorized as privileged mobiles do not necessarily think of themselves as migrants, nor are they necessarily thought of as such by the state (Amante and Rodrigues, 2020). The literature tends to assume those engaged in privileged mobility are not working; therefore, some authors argue for a close relationship between privileged mobility and leisure, connecting this flow with categories such as lifestyle migration (Benson and O'Reilly, 2009a), amenity migration (Moss, 2006), international retirement migration (Scuzzarello, 2020), or even residential tourism (Rodriguez, 2001; McWatters, 2009).

The formal category of privileged mobility addressed in this chapter – the investor – was created in 2012 through an amendment to Portugal's 2007 Foreigner's Act. This amendment redefined the relationship between entrepreneurship, business, and migration in Portugal. More importantly, it also redefined how migration is seen, because, despite varying definitions of the concept, a persistent trait of migration is that the immigrant lives in the host country. As noted earlier, this is not mandatory for investors granted a GV in Portugal, nor for their relatives who obtain permits for family reunification. So, how do we conceptualize the investor? Is he/she an immigrant if he/she can choose not to live in the host country? Is he/she more akin to a residential tourist?[4]

To understand privileged mobility and the specific case of the investor, we conceptualize the "investor" both as a category of analysis and as a category of practice (Brubaker and Cooper, 2000; Brubaker, 2013). In doing so, we recognize that, although interdependent in some ways, the two categories do not necessarily overlap. What the state defines as a suitable applicant for a GV does not necessarily coincide with GV holders' subjective constructions.

Methodology

When we began researching privileged migration, we were aware of the challenges of "studying up" (Powdermaker, 1966). Participant observation and qualitative interviews used in classic fieldwork are not always viable when researching the powerful within our own societies (Ortner, 2010). GV holders are part of a difficult-to-access economic elite: They are not only from multiple nations, but they are also highly diverse and nationally and internationally delocalized. Unlike anthropologists studying small-scale communities via participant observation, we could not find a community of GV holders as such. The absence of a "definite community" and the challenges of accessing elites were difficulties noted by Hortense Powdermaker (1966) in her research on Hollywood power brokers, long before Laura Nader encouraged "studying up" (1972). As Powdermaker observed, these factors precluded "a constant and seemingly casual participant observation" (Powdermaker, 1966, p. 213). Given these challenges, we decided that qualitative research through interviews would be the best strategy for accessing subjective understandings.

Nader's observations that elites "don't want to be studied; it is dangerous to study the powerful; they are busy people; they are not all in one place, etc." (1972, p. 302) reverberated in our minds as we embarked on our study. For many months, we struggled to gain access to people who were granted GVs and ultimately used gatekeepers (real estate agents directly involved with high-profile real estate properties, migration lawyers, and other Chinese and Brazilian migrants living in Portugal). From the outset, we had greater access to the Chinese than to the Brazilians, as one of us had prior experience with Chinese and we both lacked Brazilian networks in Portugal.

This chapter draws on data from 18 interviews with Chinese GV holders and other Chinese migrants already established in Portugal, both workers and entrepreneurs, all involved in providing formal and informal consulting services to the Chinese interested in obtaining a GV in Portugal. The Chinese investors we interviewed came from Changsha (Hunan Province), Shanghai, and Beijing. Conversations were mainly conducted in Chinese Mandarin (with investors and family members) and some in Portuguese (through intermediaries). These interviews were hand recorded, with additional memories of the interview expanded afterward.[5] These notes were subsequently transcribed for content analysis. We gained access to our nine Brazilian interviewees (investors, their family members, and brokers) via migration lawyer offices, real estate agents, and by tracking down individuals previously interviewed in newspapers. These participants came from the States of São Paulo, Rio de Janeiro, and Bahia in Brazil.

The first interviews, conducted in 2019, occurred in participant-selected locations, either public places (e.g., cafes, restaurants, and travel agencies), their homes, or offices (for the intermediaries). Due to the COVID-19 pandemic, the 2020 interviews were conducted via online platforms (mostly WhatsApp for the Brazilians and WeChat for the Chinese). Also because of the pandemic, despite our initial plans, participant observation was not possible. During semi-structured interviews, we asked about investors' lives in their home countries, decisions to leave, opportunities associated with obtaining a GV, and prior expectations and life experiences in Portugal. We also conducted content and discursive analyses of qualitative and visual data from the AICEP-Portugal Global – Trade and Investment Agency's (hereafter AICEP) website (this is the Portuguese government's business development agency especially directed at attracting foreign investment). Finally, we drew

Mobility Through Investment   **223**

on statistical data from the Foreigner and Border's Office (hereafter SEF) to contextualize the GV policy.

Invest in Portugal! What Does the State Want?

Over the past 13 years, the Portuguese government has embraced different strategies to enhance foreign investments, beginning in 2009 with the Non-Habitual Residents Program. This program offered tax incentives for foreign investors.[6] In 2012, the state launched the GV Program to stimulate Third Country Nationals' (TCN) investment in the real estate sector which was in deep crisis at the time. This program established various investment options: in exchange for a residence permit, interested TCNs could invest either a minimum of half a million euros in real estate, make capital transfers of at least one million euros to Portuguese banks, or create a business with at least 30 employees.[7] In addition, in 2007, the Portuguese governmental agency AICEP was reconfigured as a front desk for investment in Portugal, charged with providing support services, counseling, and contacts for companies involved in investment processes. Beyond providing information about investment and trade in Portugal, the agency's website is dedicated to persuading individuals and corporate businesses to invest in Portugal.

Our discourse analysis of this website[8] revealed five rationales aimed at drawing foreign investors to Portugal, namely: (1) economic; (2) human resources; (3) innovation and technology; (4) geographic, historical, and cultural; and (5) tourist attractions.[9] For this chapter, we concentrate on the last two rationales, which highlight the intersecting terrain between tourism, migration, and elite investor mobility. On the site, geographic, historical, cultural, and touristic allure comprise almost as many reasons offered to entice potential foreign investors as the economic set alone. Although these geographical, historical, and cultural rationales are presented separately on the site, they comprise important tourist assets and the state combines them to present an image of Portugal as a "globally positioned" and "connected country" (expressions used in the promotional film), both in the past and today. Accordingly, the AICEP website highlights information such as the average temperature at noon in summer and winter and the many tourism awards received by the country's primary cities (e.g., Best European Country to Visit, Best City in the World to Invest, and Best Place in the World to Enjoy Retirement). These tourist and economic "facts" are all spotlighted in the film as reasons to invest.

In the AICEP's promotional film, economics, innovation and technology, and manpower indicators are enfolded with touristic and cultural images and data about Portugal. The video opens with three young adults on a sailboat off the coast of Lisbon. As potentially attractive economic facts are presented, images of science, technology, and innovation are merged with tourist images of Praça do Comércio and Lisbon's riverside. The film concludes with tourism and travel indicators and returns to the image of the three young adults on the sailboat berthing at Lisbon's Parque das Nações dock, which is situated in an attractive, modern living and working zone. In this way, by combining economy and tourism to draw investors, this governmental agency targets not only economic investors in general but also tourism, leisure, and residential investment, in particular.

Recognizing the impossibility of competing with powerful economies in the contest for overseas investors, the government employs certain internationally widespread stereotyped images of Portugal. These tropes of Portugal as a tourist destination of sun, sea, and leisure become valuable assets for attracting foreign investors. In the next section, we draw on our interviews with GV investors, their family members, and intermediaries to analyze how these kinds of images of Portugal have figured into their decisions to invest in Portugal.

Migration or Tourism? or Both? Investors' Narratives

Some studies have stressed economic performance as a key motivation for GV investments in Portugal, associating foreign investment (and the need to expatriate capital) with the urban tourist boom and the growth of tourist amenities. Historical ties between the investors' countries and Portugal are also considered relevant (Montezuma and McGarrigle, 2019). Finding an economic "safe haven" is reported as one reason for investing in real estate. According to some (Montezuma and McGarrigle, 2019), this is the primary objective for many Chinese and Turkish investors in Portugal. From our research with Chinese investors, the properties purchased are either left vacant or rented to co-nationals or others for residential purposes: They do not appear to be rented to tourists.[10]

Since the GV is an investment visa, one would expect that GV seekers would highlight economic investment as a primary motivation. However, the Chinese GV holders and their family members we interviewed do not mention capital investment or China's real estate market pressures as the key motivations driving their GV applications. As noted earlier, most Chinese GV applicants and holders in Portugal tend to apply for family reunification, thus increasing the incoming flow beyond that of the GV holders alone. This practice in tandem with our interviews suggests that the main motivations for moving are family-related (Amante and Rodrigues, 2020). As Xi, a male Chinese real-estate agent residing in Lisbon stated: "Many investors leave their children with grandparents in Portugal and spend most of their time in China taking care of their businesses." The literature suggests education and economic investment as the primary reasons for this permit's appeal in Portugal and elsewhere (Montezuma and McGarrigle, 2019; Ampudia de Haro and Gaspar, 2019; Robertson and Rogers, 2017). The Chinese GV intermediaries we interviewed indicated that Chinese families were leaving China for numerous reasons: To escape pollution, pursue better educational and social environments for their children, and avoid rising housing costs that were pushing middle-class residents of larger Chinese cities into outlying regions. Some Chinese GV holders and their family members confirmed that concerns about family health and education were strong motivations (and a Chinese real estate agent reported that many GV holders were coming from China's most polluted cities). As Huang, a male Chinese GV holder explained,

Mobility Through Investment **225**

This desire to go abroad started when our second son was five years old and got a very serious respiratory illness. It was coincident with a period of high pollution levels in Beijing, so we wanted to get out and go to a healthier place.

Similarly, Zhang, the wife of a Chinese GV holder told us,

We decided to leave China because of the environment (the pollution), but it was mainly due to our son's education. . . . He was suffering great anxiety due to the rankings pressure – Chinese children suffer very much.

The intense social pressure to be successful was also noted as one of the causes driving emigration from China in previous migratory flows to Portugal, long before the GV policy (Rodrigues, 2013). Literature on migration and social reproduction in China has noted the growing importance of higher education certificates from prestigious "Western" universities in the accumulation of social capital among the Chinese middle class (Waters, 2006; Tsang, 2013). To overcome the intense competition Chinese students face when entering Chinese universities, many parents choose to send their children abroad, where they can enjoy less stressful lives: Chinese GV-holding parents living in Portugal feel their children need not spend as many hours studying to succeed. Likewise, one of the informal intermediaries interviewed said that her acquaintance's Chinese parents and grandparents were considering applying for a GV and buying a house in Portugal to enable them to send their children there in the future. Although the children were still very young, concerns over their future education were the main motivation for the investment. In short, for the Chinese mainlanders we interviewed, the investment opportunity is not the primary motivation for applying to the GV Program: Education opportunities and family health are the reasons that most stood out.

The topic of leaving China for political and economic reasons is very sensitive among mainland Chinese. Although not a reason volunteered by investors and family members themselves, it is difficult to ignore these reasons when discussing Chinese GV holders' rationales for leaving China. Significantly, the Portuguese GV program has aroused great interest among Hong Kong Chinese for overtly political and economic reasons.[11] Rising fears of instability have emerged since the recent approval of the national security law in Hong Kong and Macau, which reduces the autonomy of these areas from China (activating laws approved during the 1997 transfer of Hong Kong's sovereignty and the 1999 transfer of Macau's sovereignty). This may be prompting increasing numbers of Chinese GV holders to move to Portugal, as occurred with the Chinese relocating to Canada in the late 1990s (Li, 2005). During our fieldwork, we heard of several Hong Kong GV holders who do not reside in Portugal. It seems possible that although some Hong Kong GV holders are not currently residing in Portugal, possessing a GV may offer a kind of insurance should they need to leave Hong Kong for political reasons.

Some of our interviewees mentioned intentions to leave China, but not specific desires to target Portugal. Rather, these Chinese GV holders were interested

226 Maria de Fátima Amante and Irene Rodrigues

in living in Canada, the United States, and Italy. Thus, Portugal was not the first choice, but the second available option. As Wang, the Chinese wife of a GV holder, articulated,

> We came because our only son wanted to move to the United States, though we could not make it. Then the emigration agency we had consulted to go to the US advised us to consider Portugal. We had no previous relations with Portugal, we came for a visit and decided to apply. . . . I feel very comfortable in Portugal, the education is good, my son is very content, and he also has the opportunity to experience other things compatible with a European lifestyle.

And Huang, a male Chinese GV holder, detailed,

> At first, we applied for Canada, but the process was too long, they asked for many documents and, in the end, we didn't make it. It was rejected. Then, in 2013, the emigration agency told us about the possibility of Portugal. We didn't know anything about Portugal, I knew Ronaldo and I knew it was next to Spain. So, I searched for information. Then, I realized that it was a European Union country and that it was part of the Schengen Agreement, and that it would be good for traveling and even doing business. I sought information from the League of Chinese in Europe and Portugal. I wanted to know if it was good for children and what the weather was like. Then they told me that the summer was long and hot and that children got much less sick than in China because the winter is shorter and milder. So, we thought it would be a good idea to come and see, and we liked it. The emigration agency [in China] took care of everything for us: they took care of the house business, all the paperwork of the purchase, the visa, as well as the school enrollment for our children.

The GV holders and their family members we interviewed all came from large cities in China – Beijing, Shanghai, and Changsha (in Hunan Province). They were middle-class families, professionals, or businesspeople with ambitions to live outside China, but without many of the resources – including language skills – that would enable them to enter the United States or Canada, traditionally the most desired destinations for Chinese pursuing life abroad. They all came to Portugal as families, with children and even grandparents. Those with ongoing business ventures in China faced family separations, with some members in China and others in Portugal. However, such separations may be transitory, since many Chinese GV holders, once in Portugal, start looking for local business opportunities. Others, professionals working for private companies in China, pursued professional jobs upon arrival in Portugal. However, none mentioned professional ambitions as a motivation for applying for the GV. One GV grantee, Huang, said he and his wife were enjoying living in Portugal so much that they decided to enlarge the family with a third child. Their interest in Portugal began while they were still residing in China and were introduced to Portugal by immigration agencies that partnered with real estate companies in Portugal. We also heard of others who were more informally introduced to Portugal (without immigration agencies), by Chinese individuals who had been commissioned by Portuguese real estate agencies to attract GV clients. In fact, the Chinese community in Portugal was very excited about the program back in 2013, and many Chinese migrants plunged into the real estate sector, viewing drumming up Chinese GV applicants as an attractive business opportunity (Amante and Rodrigues, 2020; Gaspar, 2019).

Not all Chinese families invest in real estate before relocating to Portugal. For some families maintaining businesses in China, the investment comes after residing in Portugal. Nevertheless, the real estate investment is what opens the door for them to consider acquiring a GV and a longer-term relationship with Portugal. Cui, the wife of a Chinese GV holder explained,

> I came to Portugal with my mother and my teenage son only, while my husband stayed in China looking after our businesses. After traveling in Europe, I decided that I wanted to live here. Though Portugal was not my first choice – I preferred Italy – we are pleased with our choice.

For GV holders, at least initially, Portugal's advantage is not so much its intrinsic appeal, but rather its geopolitical position in Europe.[12] For Chinese GV holders, Portugal's location in Europe and its association with the Schengen Agreement offer possibilities for both business and tourism. Some Chinese GV holders explore Portugal as tourists, often with an eye for potential investments, treating Portugal as a point of departure for tourism in Europe. As Cui, the already quoted wife of a Chinese GV holder explained,

> I had already traveled to Europe for tourism, to Italy, and I liked it very much. After that, I thought about coming to Europe and I found the opportunity in Portugal. In the meantime, since our arrival, I have already traveled with my mother and son to various European countries for tourism.

In contrast to the Chinese investors, Portugal offers a slightly different kind of "safe haven" for Brazilian investors. Research data collected by Joaquim Montezuma and Jennifer McGarrigle highlighted that "this group is primarily seeking a safe investment setting and a relocation option to exit Brazil rather than high returns" (2019, p. 14). Our empirical data, gathered through interviews with Brazilians' GVs, revealed a financially diverse group of people with desires to invest in Portugal and particular lifestyles there once settled. In this group, we find people who are not only extremely wealthy but also members of the upper-middle class, with enough money in the Brazilian banking system to acquire Portuguese GVs, which they use to avoid the delays generally associated with the country's highly bureaucratic migration process.

228 Maria de Fátima Amante and Irene Rodrigues

Brazil's recent political turmoil, the corruption scandal that impeached Dilma Rousseff, Temer's conservative government, and the election of right-wing nationalist Jair Bolsonaro figure into Brazilian investors' desires to leave the country. As Sandra, a Brazilian female GV holder in her early 40s recalled,

> Five years ago, when I came [to Portugal], the Golden Visa was a good resource. Since then, it has changed a lot . . . But I feel that, back then, the people coming were older than me, with more money . . . That group went a lot to Cascais[13]. In the last two years, more people of my own age are coming, with a similar lifestyle, that is not having a lot of money but wanting to have a different life. Five years ago, when I came, it was at the time of Dilma's impeachment, which I was totally against. Those [supporting the impeachment] are precisely the group of people who now voted for Bolsonaro. It's a right-wing group of people, who five years ago were running away.

Both political and economic motivations can be inferred from our interviewee's words. The super-rich she refers to as "older right-wing Brazilians" (who arrived during or immediately after Dilma's impeachment) were not confident about the Brazilian economy and sought a "safe haven" for investments. Those who arrived more recently, upper-middle-class Brazilians like Sandra, are escaping a conservative government and allude to political factors as primary reasons for leaving.

Why did they choose Portugal? More often than not, in contrast to the Chinese migrants, scholars cite "lifestyle orientations, historical factors, as well as shared linguistic and cultural terrain" (Montezuma and McGarrigle, 2019, p. 14) as important factors. Although we concur that there is a cultural connection, it is worth noting that

> Portugal has never featured in the Brazilian imagination as a developed "First World" country. Instead, Brazilians share a general sense of superiority vis-a-vis the Portuguese, who are the butt of many derogatory jokes in Brazil and whose country was perceived as the 'backwater' of Europe.
> *(Torresan, 2011, p. 235)*

So, beyond the cultural factors cited in the literature, for the upper-middle-class Brazilian GV holders, Portugal's appeal lies in its low investment threshold compared to other potential destinations: The financial investment requirement for a Portuguese GV is more manageable than the financial thresholds required by other European countries with immigrant investor programs (Amante and Rodrigues, 2020).[14]

In contrast to the Chinese migrants, Brazilian elites' interest in Portugal, the "option to exit Brazil" (Montezuma and McGarrigle, 2019), is closely related to the search for a more carefree lifestyle and a better quality of life for themselves and their families. Notwithstanding the unavoidable economic dimension of investment migration, Brazilian GV holders might be better defined as lifestyle migrants

Mobility Through Investment **229**

because they are "relatively affluent individuals of all ages, moving either part-time or full-time to places that, for various reasons, signify, for the migrant, a better quality of life" (Benson and Reilly, 2018, p. 609). Unlike "regular" migrants who also seek better lives and class mobility via far-flung jobs (Torresan, 2011), Brazilian GV holders interviewed envision a better quality of life in tandem with a change of scenery not necessarily related to career prospects. Rather, the object is to realize an improved lifestyle for themselves and their families unencumbered by the constraints they face at home in Brazil.

The desire for a more relaxed quality of life is reflected in comments concerning security and professional competition. Security is ubiquitous in the narratives of Brazilian immigrants in general (Schrooten et al., 2016), and the terms also pepper the narratives of the Brazilian GV holders and their family members as we discovered in our interviews. The anthropological work on violence in Brazil is extensive, and security concerns are a pervasive element of urban life in many Brazilian cities (e.g., Larkins, 2015; Penglase, 2011; Scheper-Hughes, 2006; Wacquant, 2003). As Löic Wacquant observes, "Brazilian society remains characterized by vertiginous social disparities and mass poverty, which together feed the inexorable growth of criminal violence that has become the main scourge of the big cities" (Wacquant, 2003, p. 199). Ben Penglase's argument that "urban violence provides Brazilians with a 'map' which they can use to interpret their daily lives and organize their social practices" (2011, p. 431) is also noteworthy. Penglase's observations hint at a link between perceptions of urban insecurity and the drive to emigrate (Adorno, 2002; Pinho, 2014). In a 2017 media interview about the new wave of Brazilian immigrants arriving in Portugal, the Brazilian Deputy Consul General highlighted the link between wealth and security in Brazil and the decision to leave the country, declaring that "they come in search of a more peaceful and secure life . . . even though they have money they could not enjoy it due to the violence and the Brazilian political crisis. . . . Here, they don't need cars with bulletproof glass windows."[15]

These Brazilian GV holders were critical of Brazil's urban violence and insecurity, fueled by poverty and social inequality (Wacquant, 2003; Penglase, 2011). Débora, a Brazilian GV holder, stated that

> The banality of violence in Brazil is absurd . . . For us, Brazilians, especially for those from the urban areas, like Rio de Janeiro or São Paulo, security is really an issue . . . I lived in Copacabana. My office was located right in the city center, a safe place, one might think. However, when I left work at night, the sidewalk in front of the building transformed into a dormitory for homeless people, beggars. It bothered me a lot and I started to think that I couldn't live in Brazil anymore. So, you see, the best place in Brazil doesn't even compare to the worst place here in Portugal.

The individuals we interviewed repeatedly highlighted personal traumatic experiences as triggering their urgent desires to leave Brazil and prompting their decisions to apply for GVs. They expected that life in Portugal would foster a safer lifestyle and a more relaxed future. This is even more significant in the narratives of people with children. Sandra, a teacher and a mother, observed that

> Many people are very afraid. Like my husband, his ex-mother-in-law was murdered, and since then he has been unable to live as he used to . . . living in Rio changed a lot after that fact. So, security is not something I deny, we have this . . . I was robbed at gunpoint once, but I don't know . . . it didn't scare me. That was not what brought me here but living here I recognize that it's much more peaceful, and being a mother, I imagined my children walking alone to school. I wouldn't do that in Brazil.

In a similar vein, Wilson, a male GV holder, commented,

> We and our daughters have been in Portugal since 2015. In these four years, we adapted to a calmer life. We still live in a private condominium and next year our daughters will leave private school to attend a public school . . . can you imagine? That would be impossible back home.

Brazilian GV holders view Portugal as offering a better quality of life, which encompasses a less competitive environment in school and at the workplace, as compared to what they experienced in Brazil. As Débora observed,

> In Brazil, there are many people. For every job you want to get, there are millions of candidates. You have to be the first, the best, in everything. We are used to it. The level of competition in Brazil is higher . . . So, those who came here are sharks, not golden fish.

Investors are part of a "new flow of Brazilians" coming to Portugal (França and Padilla, 2018). They are highly skilled, a characteristic shared with previous flows (França and Padilla, 2018; Torresan, 2011; Pinho, 2014). Although their privileged economic status enables them to apply for a GV, they are not rich enough to cease working while in Portugal. All our interviewees are professionally active people and enjoy successful careers in the arts, finance, media, or advertising. Some continue their line of work while others embraced a completely different professional path.

Despite the often-negative stereotypes of Portugal mentioned earlier (Torresan, 2011) and in keeping with Montezuma and McGarrigle's (2019) observations, we find among our interviewees those for whom language, historical links, and shared cultural terrain were intrinsic to their decisions to invest and ultimately live in Portugal. This is not necessarily due to the past colonial relationship between Portugal and Brazil but rather for more pragmatic reasons. For some of our interviewees, it was a matter of choosing the easiest destination possible, in terms of adaptation to a new social, cultural, and linguistic environment. Moreover, familiarity with other

Brazilians living in Portugal and an imagined cultural proximity attracted them. As Vitória, a female GV holder from São Paulo, noted,

> When I decided to come here, as I was moving with my family, the language and climate were the things that mattered the most. I speak English, but my husband, my daughter, and my mother speak only Portuguese, so . . . this was important when I decided to come to Portugal. Also, in Germany, England, or France, in these countries they don't have the joy of life, there is greater civility there, and everything works better . . . Maybe that is why we Brazilian are the way we are, we were colonized by the Portuguese.

For Brazilian elites, moving to Lisbon is not quite the same as moving to Europe, despite Portugal's European identity. Brazilians, especially the wealthy ones, consider Europe not as a geopolitical concept but as embodying a certain lifestyle commonly associated with northwest Europe, including France. However, for economic and linguistic reasons, Brazilian elites see their possibilities of living in Europe as limited to Portugal. Nevertheless, we found our interviewees referring to Portugal as presenting several advantages which are relevant for our discussion of GV holders and the blurred boundaries between migration and tourism. Particularly, but not exclusively, retired investors were engaged in consuming the Portuguese past through regular travel and visits to the country's hinterlands or by living in Lisbon's historic neighborhoods: These pursuits directly link these Brazilian residents to tourism and a more consumption-driven form of migration. Karen O'Reilly (2003) argues that migration and tourism, which are often considered separately, need to be brought together within research so that we can develop a better understanding of the interrelations between these two types of movement. Among the Brazilian GV holders, some of our interviewees' initial encounters with Portugal were as tourists. As Brazilian citizens do not need a visa to enter Portuguese territory for short periods, some came as tourists, stayed for several weeks, and explored possibilities for relocation. Ultimately, they visited real estate agents and lawyers' offices to help them embark on the process of moving to Portugal. In some cases, starting as tourists they became tourism promoters, investing in travel agencies. Others work as consulting agents, assisting co-nationals wanting to obtain Portuguese GVs. In either case, we can find here the "symbiotic relationships between tourism and migration" that Allan M. Williams and C. Michael Hall (2000, p. 7) refer to, namely through a "tourism entrepreneurial migration [which] may constitute a special case of both lifestyle seeking migration and labour migration" (Williams and Hall, 2002, p. 31) with individuals being, in the case of Brazilian GV holders, first motivated by "quality of life considerations" (Williams and Hall, 2002, p. 31).

On a different level, for many Brazilians, the relationship between investment and tourism emerges from a perceived advantage of Portugal's relatively central location, which is often understood more as a place from which they can travel rather than as a place in which to live. In this way, for many, it is primarily a

232 Maria de Fátima Amante and Irene Rodrigues

European base that maximizes travel possibilities. Sandra, a female GV holder, explained to us that,

> Portugal is the size of Piaui,[16] for us everything is close, it's all a matter of reference . . . traveling two and a half hours, and being there, far away . . . I think Portugal has a lot of cool places, it has a lot to offer despite being small, it has so many travel possibilities. And I don't know whether travel is cultural in Brazil. There is an advantage, a Brazilian with higher purchasing power, living in Portugal, makes it easier because it's in the center, so we can travel a lot. . . . Traveling from Portugal is a lot easier than from Brazil. My parents bought an apartment here as a way to get their residence permit. They travel a lot. It is great for them! Sometimes they come from Brazil and stay in Lisbon for long periods; when my daughter was born, they were supposed to stay for a year to help me, but during that period they also booked "a thousand" trips to Europe.

When speaking Portuguese and having Portugal as their departure point, Brazilians usually talk about traveling "to Europe," instead of traveling around or in Europe, thus expressing their perceptions of Portugal's location: A place that allows them to spend more time as tourists, both in the country of residence (Portugal) and abroad (Europe and elsewhere). So, in a certain way, for Brazilian GV holders, investment allows them a path not only to migration but also to tourism.

Conclusions

In this chapter, we examined the case of GV holders as an avenue for highlighting the blurred boundaries between investment, migration, and tourism. By exploring the political reasoning behind a specific policy that created a category and an opportunity for mobility, we found a diverse array of motives for applying for GVs among Chinese and Brazilian investors extending beyond the realm of economic investment.

Chinese and Brazilians have very different historical and cultural ties with Portugal. However, by centering on motivations underlying GV applications, we unearthed striking commonalities. Among the similarities, we found that both Chinese and Brazilians in Portugal expressed strong desires to exit their home countries and abandon certain lifestyles. The desired lifestyle is not so much for what Portugal offers but rather centers on the fact that Portugal does not suffer from the problems pushing them away from their home countries. The GV offers the opportunity to transform that dimension of their lives. However, in both cases, Portugal is generally not the first option but rather the most viable, when compared to different constraints that both groups face entering and/or living in North America or other European countries. Nevertheless, in both cases, Portugal's location is perceived as advantageous for travel to other European countries or continents. The very different spatial scale that both Brazilians and Chinese use when thinking about their home countries and Portugal tends to drive their maximization of travel possibilities and therefore consumption-led mobility.

In this sense, the search for a better, less stressful European lifestyle seems to exceed the desire to expatriate capital. In the Chinese case, for the mainland Chinese GV holders effectively living in Portugal, the opportunity to enjoy a certain educational atmosphere and a cleaner environment supersede economic concerns. Hence, the idea that many Chinese invest in Lisbon to expatriate capital (Montezuma and McGarrigle, 2019) still needs further research. From the narratives of the GV holders – both Chinese and Brazilians – we may conclude that they are more interested in moving to change their lives than in investing their capital (although clearly capital investment is part of the picture). In fact, these people live in Portugal, many work there as well, and they are looking for a better quality of life for themselves and their families. Thus, their motivations and practices greatly resemble those of migrants.

Besides these common aspects, there are also some differences between the two cases. Although both China and Brazil have long historical, colonial, and migratory ties with Portugal, the language and cultural proximity between Portugal and Brazil is much stronger and influences the Brazilian imaginary of Portugal. In contrast, for the Chinese, despite the Portuguese presence in Macau from the 16th to the end of the 20th century, no distinctive imaginary of Portugal was produced. The country remained largely unknown to most Chinese. Another contrast lies in primary motivations for leaving. While in the Chinese case, families verbalize worries about educational competition and pollution but do not explicitly mention political or economic fears (possibly due to caution), in the Brazilian case, families are very vocal about the banalization of violence and the political and economic instability.

Tourism was a common theme in both the state's narrative and investors' narratives. The Portuguese state's narrative of the attractiveness of investment in Portugal not only encompasses economic, cultural, and geographical aspects but also highlights a tourist lifestyle that resonates with the motivations and expectations of the GV holders who seek a new lifestyle rather than simply a place in which to invest economically. In fact, the Portuguese state largely promotes the country through tourist postcards, even though the main goal is to attract foreign investment. It is quite interesting to note that in the case of the GV, the Portuguese state requires residence in the country for just 14 days per year, meaning that the state does not expect investors to have an interest in living in the country. However, for our interviewees, residence in the country was revealed as more important than the capital investment itself. The country's touristic attractiveness makes it a viable candidate for relocation not only by offering a more relaxed lifestyle but also for its location in Europe and thus the possibility of easy travel to tourist destinations in Europe. In several interviews with GV real estate investors, we found yet another connection with tourism: Tourist activities and investments come after living in Portugal, boosting their economic integration in the country.

Our data deconstruct certain stereotypical images of foreign investors held by the Portuguese state and public: The conception of them as super-rich and absent from the country. On the contrary, the investors' experiences we encountered defy conceptions of the investor as an entirely economic category and instead locate the investor in the blurred and intersectional territory of migration and tourism. Like migrants, they seek opportunities to leave their countries of origin to pursue a better quality of life. This does not exempt them from having professional lives, though they also share a tourist ethos in the sense that they choose a country that promises travel opportunities they did not have before. For this reason, we suggest that the GV investors in Portugal are more lifestyle investors than capital investors, as they are more interested in shifting how they and their families live than in maximizing or hiding their capital.

Notes

1 In February 2021, the Portuguese government published new legislation on the GV Program (DR 14/2021) announcing changes starting in January 2022. The key amendment is the exclusion of all mainland coastal areas, namely, Lisbon, Porto, and the Algarve, as real estate investment areas eligible for GV. The archipelagos of Madeira and Azores remain eligible.
2 Elsewhere, we have discussed this policy as a "governmental technology" constituting part of a neoliberal political project (Amante and Rodrigues, 2020; see also Rose and Miller, 1992).
3 One reason for this is Portugal's increased presence in international media (see www.jornaldenegocios.pt/empresas/media/detalhe/destino-portugal-bate-recorde-de-referencias-na-imprensa-estrangeira).
4 The category of tourist is also complex, and its conceptualizations are debated (see, e.g., McCabe, 2005; O'Reilly, 2003).
5 Chinese interviewees stated they preferred not to be taped. We experienced this previously in our long-term fieldwork with Chinese migrants in Portugal. This is not necessarily for political reasons: It is linked to self-protectiveness vis á vis strangers and non-Chinese (see Rodrigues, 2012).
6 Decree-Law n. ° 249/2009, September 23. https://dre.pt/application/file/a/157238304.
7 A 2015 amendment lowered this requirement to ten people.
8 See http://portugalglobal.pt/PT/Paginas/Index.aspx.
9 We examined the 2020 website's promotional film (images, text, and audio information) as well as written incentives for investing.
10 In the Chinese case, rentals to co-nationals include short-term rentals to Chinese students in Portugal and Chinese workers. During the COVID-19 pandemic, GV holders' houses were also used by other Chinese to quarantine.
11 See, e.g., www.scmp.com/business/article/3022507/portugals-golden-visa-program-swamped-inquiries-hongkongers-seeking.
12 Additionally, as previous research on GV Programs indicates (Amante and Rodrigues, 2020), the Portuguese GV Program – as compared to similar programs in other European countries – is less expensive and more flexible in terms of working status and family reunification.
13 Cascais is a fishing village near Lisbon, associated with economic and social elites.
14 Compared to other nations' Immigrant Investment Programs, Portugal' GV is a relatively straightforward, low-cost option, requiring a real estate investment of half a million euros. This contrasts favorably with the United Kingdom's program, where the minimum investment is one million pounds, and with France, which requires a minimum investment of €10 million in industrial or commercial assets and job creation.
15 http://miraonline.pt/elite-brasileira-traz-novos-negocios-para-portugal/.
16 A Brazilian state with a small area compared to others.

References

Adorno, S. (2002) 'Exclusão socioeconómica e violência urbana', *Sociologias*, 8, pp. 84–135.

Amante, M.F. and Rodrigues, I. (2020) 'Mobility regimes and the crisis: The changing face of Chinese migration due to the Portuguese golden visa policy', *Journal of Ethnic and Migration Studies*, 47(17), pp. 4081–4099.

Amit, V. (ed.) (2007) *Going first class: New approaches to privileged travel and movement.* New York: Berghahn Books.

Ampudia de Haro, F. and Gaspar, S. (2019) 'Visados dorados para inversores en España y Portugal: residencia a cambio de dinero', *Arbor*, 195(791). Available at: https://doi.org/10.3989/arbor.2019.791n1008.

Benson, M. (2013) 'Postcoloniality and privilege in new lifestyle flows: The case of North Americans in Panama', *Mobilities*, 8(3), pp. 313–30.

Benson, M. and O'Reilly, K. (2009a) 'Migration and the search for a better way of life: A critical exploration of lifestyle migration', *The Sociological Review*, 57(4), pp. 608–625.

Benson, M. and O'Reilly, K. (eds.) (2009b) *Lifestyle migration: Expectations, aspirations and experiences.* Farnham: Ashgate.

Benson, M. and O'Reilly, K. (2018) *Lifestyle migration and colonial traces in Malaysia and Panama.* London: Palgrave McMillan.

Benson, M. and Osbaldiston, N. (eds.) (2014) *Understanding lifestyle migration: Theoretical approaches to migration and the quest for a better way of life.* London: Palgrave Macmillan.

Bourdieu, P. (2010) *Distinction. A social critique of the judgement of taste.* London: Routledge.

Brubaker, R. (2013) 'Categories of analysis and categories of practice: A note on the study of Muslims in European countries of immigration', *Ethnic and Racial Studies*, 36(1), pp. 1–8.

Brubaker, R. and Cooper, F. (2000) 'Beyond identity', *Theory and Society*, 29, pp. 1–47.

Cohen, S., Duncan, T. and Thulemark, M. (2015) 'Lifestyle mobilities: The crossroads of travel, leisure and migration', *Mobilities*, 10(1), pp. 155–172.

Croucher, S. (2012) 'Privileged mobility in an age of globality', *Societies*, 2, pp. 1–13.

Džankić, J. (2018) 'Immigrant investor programs in the European Union (EU)', *Journal of Contemporary European Studies*, 26(1), pp. 64–80.

European Commission (2019) *Investor citizenship and residence schemes in the European Union.* Available at: https://eur-lex.europa.eu/legal-content/EN/ALL/?uri=COM:2019:0012:FIN.

França, T. and Padilla, B. (2018) 'Imigração brasileira para Portugal: entre o surgimento e a construção mediática de uma nova vaga', *Cadernos de Estudos Sociais*, 33(2). Available at: https://core.ac.uk/download/pdf/302960634.pdf.

Gamlen, A., Kutarna, C. and Monk, A. (2019) 'Citizenship as sovereign wealth: Re-thinking investor immigration', *Global Policy*, 10(4), pp. 527–541.

Gaspar, S. (2017) 'Chinese migration to Portugal. Trends and perspectives', *Journal of Chinese Overseas*, 13(1), pp. 48–69.

Gaspar, S. (2019) 'Chinese descendants' professional pathways: Moving to new businesses?', *Portuguese Journal of Social Science*, 18(1), pp. 91–108.

Jackson, R.T. (1990) 'VFR tourism: Is it underestimated?', *Journal of Tourism Studies*, 1(2), pp. 10–17.

Knowles, C. and Harper, D. (2009) *Hong Kong: Migrant lives, landscapes and journeys.* Chicago, IL: University of Chicago Press.

Krähmer, K. and Santangelo, M. (2018) 'Gentrification without gentrifiers? Tourism and real estate investment in Lisbon', *Sociabilidades Urbanas – Revista de Antropologia e Sociologia*, 2(6), pp. 151–165.

Kunz, S. (2016) 'Privileged mobilities: Locating the expatriate in migration scholarship', *Geography Compass*, 10(3), pp. 89–101.

Larkins, E. (2015) *The spectacular favela: Violence in modern Brazil.* Berkeley, CA: University of California Press.

Li, P.S. (2005) 'The rise and fall of Chinese immigration to Canada: Newcomers from Hong Kong special administrative region of China and mainland China, 1980–2000', *International Migration*, 43(3), pp. 9–34.

McCabe, S. (2005) 'Who is a tourist?' A critical review', *Tourism Studies*, 5(1), pp. 85–106.

McWatters, M. (2009) *Residential tourism. (De)constructing paradise.* Bristol: Channel View Publications.

Mendes, L. (2017) 'Gentrificação turística em Lisboa: neoliberalismo, financeirização e urbanismo austeritário em tempos de pós-crise capitalista 2008–2009', *Cadernos Metrópole*, 19(39), pp. 479–512.

Monk, J. and Alexander, C. (1986) 'Free port fallout: Gender, employment and migration on Margarita Island', *Annals of Tourism Research*, 13, pp. 393–413.

Montezuma, J. and McGarrigle, J. (2019) 'What motivates international homebuyers? Investor to lifestyle 'migrants' in a tourist city', *Tourism Geographies*, 21(2), pp. 214–234.

Morrison, A.M., Hsieh, S. and O'Leary, J.T. (1995) 'Segmenting the visiting friends and relatives' market by holiday activity participation', *Journal of Tourism Studies*, 6(1), pp. 48–63.

Moss, L. (2006) *The amenity migrants.* Oxfordshire: CAB Institute.

Nader, L. (1972) 'Up the Anthropologist: Perspectives gained from studying up'. Available at: https://eric.ed.gov/?id=ED065375.

O'Reilly, K. (2003) 'When is a tourist? The articulation of tourism and migration in Spain's Costa del Sol', *Tourism Studies*, 3(3), pp. 301–317.

Ortner, S.B. (2010) 'Access: Reflections on studying up in Hollywood', *Ethnography*, 11(2), pp. 211–233.

Padilla, B. (2006) 'Brazilian migration to Portugal: Social networks and ethnic solidarity', *CIES e-Working Papers.* Available at: https://repositorio.iscte-iul.pt/bitstream/10071/175/4/CIES-WP12_Padilla_.pdf.

Parker, O. (2017) 'Commercializing citizenship in crisis EU: The case of immigrant investor programs', *Journal of Common Market Studies*, 55(2), pp. 332–384.

Peixoto, J. (2002) 'Strong markets, weak states: The case of recent foreign immigration in Portugal', *Journal of Ethnic and Migration Studies*, 28(3), pp. 483–497.

Penglase, R.B. (2011) 'Lost bullets: Fetishes of urban violence in Rio de Janeiro, Brazil', *Anthropological Quarterly*, 84(2), pp. 411–438.

Pinho, F. (2014) *Transformações na emigração brasileira para Portugal. De profissionais a trabalhadores.* Lisbon: ACM-IP.

Powdermaker, H. (1966) *Stranger and friend. The way of an anthropologist.* New York: W.W. Norton & Company.

Robertson, S. and Rogers, D. (2017) 'Education, real estate, immigration: Brokerage assemblages and Asian mobilities', *Journal of Ethnic and Migration Studies*, 43(14), pp. 2393–2407.

Robins, D. (2019) 'Lifestyle migration from the Global South to the Global North: Individualism, social class, and freedom in a centre of "superdiversity"', *Popul Space Place*, 25. Available at: https://doi.org/10.1002/psp.2236.

Rodrigues, I. (2012) 'Ser laowai: o estrangeiro antropólogo e o estrangeiro para os migrantes chineses entre Portugal e a China', *Etnográfica*, 16(3), pp. 547–567.

Rodrigues, I. (2013) *Flows of fortune: The economy of Chinese migration to Portugal.* PhD thesis. Lisbon: University of Lisbon.

Rodriguez, V. (2001) 'Tourism as a recruiting post for retirement migration', *Tourism Geographies*, 3(1), pp. 52–63.

Rogers, D., Lee, C.L. and Yan, D. (2015) 'The politics of foreign investment in Australian housing: Chinese investors, translocal sales agents and local resistance', *Housing Studies*, 30(5), pp. 730–748.

Rose, N. and Miller, P. (1992) 'Political power beyond the state: Problematics of government', *BJS*, 43(2), pp. 173–205.

Sayad, A. (2004) *The suffering of the immigrant*. Cambridge, MA and Malden, MA: Polity Press.

Scheper-Hughes, N. (2006) *Dangerous and endangered youth: Social structures and determinants of violence*. London: Routledge.

Schrooten, M., Salazar, N. and Dias, G. (2016) 'Living in mobility: Trajectories of Brazilians in Belgium and the UK', *Journal of Ethnic and Migration Studies*, 42(7), pp. 1199–1215.

Scuzzarello, S. (2020) 'Practicing privilege. How settling in Thailand enables older Western migrants to enact privilege over local people', *Journal of Ethnic and Migration Studies*, 46(8), pp. 1606–1628.

SEF (2013–2018) 'Relatório de Imigração, Fronteiras e Asilo (RIFA)'. Oeiras: Serviço de Estrangeiros e Fronteiras. Available at: https://sefstat.sef.pt/forms/Home.aspx

SEF (2019) 'Autorização de Residência para Atividade de Investimento (ARI)'. Oeiras: Serviço de Estrangeiros e Fronteiras. Available at: https://www.sef.pt/pt/pages/conteudo-detalhe.aspx?nID=93

SEF (2020) 'Autorização de Residência para Atividade de Investimento (ARI)'. Oeiras: Serviço de Estrangeiros e Fronteiras. Available at: https://www.sef.pt/pt/pages/conteudo-detalhe.aspx?nID=93

SEF (2021) 'Autorização de Residência para Atividade de Investimento (ARI)'. Oeiras: Serviço de Estrangeiros e Fronteiras. Available at: https://www.sef.pt/pt/pages/conteudo-detalhe.aspx?nID=93

Souleles, D. (2018) 'How to study people who do not want to be studied: Practical reflections on studying up', *PoLAR: Political and Legal Anthropology Review*, 41(1), pp. 51–68.

Torkington, K. (2012) 'Place and lifestyle migration: The discursive construction of 'glocal' place-identity', *Mobilities*, 7(1), pp. 71–92.

Torresan, A. (2011) 'Strange bedfellows: Brazilian immigrants negotiating friendship in Lisbon', *Ethnos*, 76(2), pp. 233–253.

Tsang, E.Y. (2013) 'The quest for higher education by the Chinese middle class: Retrenching social mobility', *Higher Education*, 66, pp. 653–668.

Wacquant, L. (2003) 'Toward a dictatorship over the poor? Notes on the penalization of poverty in Brazil', *Punishment & Society*, 5(2), pp. 197–205.

Waters, J.L. (2006) 'Geographies of cultural capital: Education, international migration and family strategies between Hong Kong and Canada', *Transactions of the Institute of British Geographers*, 31, pp. 179–192.

Williams, A. and Hall, M.C. (2000) 'Tourism and migration: New relationships between production and consumption', *Tourism Geographies*, 2(1), pp. 5–27.

Williams, A.M. and Hall, C.M. (2002) 'Tourism, migration, circulation and mobility. The contingencies of time and place' in Hall, C.M. and Williams, A.M. (eds.) *Tourism and migration. New relationships between production and consumption*. Dordrecht: Springer, pp. 1–52.

13

PANDEMIC POSTSCRIPT

Tourism, Migration, and Exile

Stephanie Malia Hom

In late February 2020, more than 2,000 passengers boarded the luxurious Grand Princess cruise ship in San Francisco and set sail to the Hawaiian Islands and the Mexican Riviera. Two weeks later, the ship had transformed into a symbol of "America's fear of the coronavirus," returning with infected passengers and an outbreak the scope of which was unknown and uncontrolled (Fuller et al., 2020). It circled for days outside the Golden Gate Bridge until finally permitted to disembark its passengers and crew in Oakland, much to the chagrin of local residents who protested this act as the "continuation of the unjust dumping of environmental hazards" in the city (Goffard, 2020).

In just the span of two weeks, tourists who had set out to enjoy a cruise vacation had transformed into "environmental hazards." They had become stigmatized as carriers of a contagion that threatened to upend both social relations and everyday life. On this rapid shift from being a tourist to being perceived as a disease carrier, Grand Princess passenger Cheri Harris noted, "It made me feel like I was abandoned." She added, "You are an inconvenience now – you are unimportant" (Goffard, 2020). Another passenger, Denise Stoneham said, "It just makes me angry that people are putting a label on us." She added, "We're human beings, we want to come home. We're not an infestation that's coming to their city" (Fuller et al., 2020).

Social anxieties and fears were projected onto these tourists–turned–carriers, because, according to Priscilla Wald, the figure of the carrier embodies the danger of microbial invasion, i.e., they are believed to be threats to life itself (Wald, 2008, p. 10). These fears are often signified by words like "invasion," "contagion," "contamination," or as Stoneham noted, "infestation." To assuage this fear, the Grand Princess was isolated in port and its passengers quarantined, not unlike the practices established by the plague ships and lazarettos of 15th-century Venice. It was this forced immobilization that seemed to bother the passengers most, according to

DOI: 10.4324/9781003182689-14

their statements to local news outlets and social media posts. Passengers recalled the feeling of being in limbo, of being stuck (both on the ship and in their staterooms), of waiting, and of not knowing what was going to happen. "Floating around was so stressful," said passenger Cookie Clark (Fuller et al., 2020).

The vocabularies of limbo, attenuated space-time, waiting, and not knowing are all too familiar to those who study or work in the field of migration and exile. They are terms that are lived every day by the tens of millions of people who have been forcibly displaced throughout the world.[1] Much scholarship has been dedicated to the temporality of migration and refugeehood, and the precarity it exacerbates in waiting zones, transit centers, informal settlements, refugee camps, and the like; however, anthropologist Michel Agier put it best when he described it as living in the "intolerable paradox of being held in a waiting zone with no possibility of exit" (Agier, 2011, p. 51).

The passengers on the Grand Princess were held in a waiting zone, but as tourists, they were guaranteed an exit. Although their ability to move by choice – the defining feature of being a tourist – was erased almost instantly when they were labeled as carriers, it nevertheless facilitated their access to communicative mobilities, like cell phones and social media, which helped these passengers successfully navigate this particular waiting zone. More than a year later, some passengers have continued to exercise their privilege: making their voices heard in class-action lawsuits against the cruise line and in follow-up media stories about the trauma of their quarantine.

***

The swift re-categorization of cruise ship tourists into carriers of disease, and the weighty affective consequences that came with it, is but one example of the many ways in which the COVID-19 pandemic has reshuffled understandings of subjectivity linked to tourism, migration, and exile. This re-classification underscores the point made convincingly by all the chapters in this volume: tourism, migration, and exile are interdependent mobilities. Divisions between them are artificially imposed, often created by top-down state policies, and reified by scholarship itself. Rather, the lines between subject positions such as tourist, migrant, and refugee are blurred and ever-evolving; for instance, one can be a refugee and a tourist at the same time as in the case of Sahrawi teenagers in Spain (see Reis in this volume). Likewise, Cubans living abroad as migrants, or even as political exiles, return to Cuba on holiday and find themselves occupying a liminal space between host and guest (see Simoni in this volume). So, too, are the power differentials related to these mobilities always shifting. For example, one can exist precariously for decades "in a state of uncertain displacement" as a temporary migrant in Panama, but then make a brief, celebratory return as a tourist to the Antilles (see Guerrón Montero in this volume). The point is, as Kathleen M. Adams and Natalia Bloch make in their introduction, transcending the categorical boundaries of tourism, migration, and exile illuminates new ways of conceptualizing the relationships between those who move by choice, like tourists, and those who are moved by force, like refugees, as well as all other movements in between.

240 Stephanie Malia Hom

The pandemic has thrown into sharp relief how quickly all of these relationships can change. Seemingly overnight, immobility, rather than mobility, became the locus of privilege. Those who could work remotely purchased goods online, got food by takeout or delivery, and attended school virtually, among other things – people who possess what John Urry calls "network capital" – could shelter safely away from the virus (Urry, 2007, pp. 194–203). On the other hand, those whose jobs were deemed "essential" were mobilized to the front lines of the pandemic, especially in food and agriculture. In the United States, 100% of farmworkers were classified as essential, compared to just 30% of health care workers, and they took on the additional risk of being exposed to the virus under already hazardous working conditions (McNicholas and Poydock, 2020). In California, where the majority of the state's 800,000 farmworkers are economic migrants from Mexico, this group was disproportionately affected by COVID-19, according to a study by the University of California Berkeley School of Public Health (Eskenazi et al., 2020). Not only did farmworkers have a higher positivity rate, but they also worried that any time lost from work due to getting sick would affect their ability to support their families, and especially, to send remittances (Eskenazi et al., 2020, pp. 19–20). For California farmworkers in the pandemic, mobility became a burden that cost both lives and livelihoods, a demonstration of the virus's grossly unequal impact on traditionally disadvantaged socioeconomic communities.

This postscript focuses attention on how the pandemic demands we think in paradox about mobilities, and how it opens up new avenues of critical inquiry for the relationships between tourism, migration, and exile. Several chapters in this volume briefly remarked on the pandemic's repercussions. For instance, it caused a complete shutdown of tourism activities such as migrant-led tours in Italy (see Vietti in this volume), imposed new forms of immobility on marriage migration between Cuba and Denmark (see Fernandez in this volume), and produced a novel form of touristic quarantine known as the "Phuket Sandbox" in Thailand (see Butratana, Trupp, and Husa in this volume). As a result of the pandemic, the categories of tourist, migrant, and exile have also been modified in new ways related to one's COVID status: fully or partially vaccinated, unvaccinated, boosted, infected, recovered, tested, and so on. In many cases, to be a tourist now, one must demonstrate proof of vaccination or a negative COVID test before boarding a plane or entering or exiting a foreign country. Under pandemic conditions, any tourist is a potential carrier, a threat that must be protected against vis à vis the exposition of medical knowledge during travel.

The Privilege of Choice

The privilege once ascribed to mobility, as belonging to the elite class of globals who move seamlessly across borders and cultures (Elliott and Urry, 2010), including investors in Portugal (see Amante and Rodrigues in this volume) and Swedish academics and physicians (see Öhlander, Wolanik Boström, and Pettersson in this volume) is no longer entirely the case. Instead, the pandemic has created a paradox in which mobility and immobility have become the terrain of privilege, and at the same time, they have also become the terrain of inequality and injustice (Adey et al., 2021). What matters in the face of COVID is having the choice to immobilize at home and the choice to move outside it.

By way of example, tourism as an industry fell precipitously at the beginning of the pandemic, with international arrivals down more than 70%, according to the UN World Tourism Organization.[2] Yet luxury leisure tourism has boomed as the world's wealthiest class profited from the crisis. Some billionaires saw their wealth more than double since 2020 (Brady, 2022). Sales of private jets and personalized flight services have soared during the pandemic as did long-term bookings of luxury hotels (Block, 2022; Presser, 2020). For this elite class, choosing to be mobile has always come with the built-in safeguards of moving in and through protected spaces, sheltered by private transportation and secluded accommodations, but even more so during the pandemic. They have become what Noel Salazar (2020) has called "kinetic élites." Having the choice to be mobile or to remain immobile has become the marker of privilege under pandemic conditions.

At the beginning of the pandemic, many tourists experienced the shock of not being able to exercise this privilege of choice when the world went on lockdown, closing off borders and shutting down air travel. News reports detailed the plight of hundreds of thousands of international tourists who had become "stuck" abroad.[3] Embassies and consulates mobilized *en masse* to repatriate their tourist citizens with charter flights and other forms of transportation. For American tourists overseas, however, there was little guidance or action from the US government (then under the Trump administration) on how to return home. Some ended up staying for weeks, even months, in a foreign country at their own expense, often worrying that their money and medications would run out (Wilson, 2020). "It's super frustrating not hearing anything from your own government," said Elizabeth Eden, an American tourist stranded in Morocco at the time. "I feel completely abandoned" (Mzezewa, 2020). "And we're just waiting," added Lauren Davenport, another American tourist there (Mzezewa, 2020).

Tourists in these situations repeatedly used words like being "stuck," "stranded," "abandoned," "trapped," "lost," and "imprisoned," i.e., they engaged the vocabularies of forced immobilization that commonly characterize migrants' experiences of becoming immured in what Ruben Andersson has called the illegality industry (Andersson, 2014, pp. 15–16). These tourists' narratives of waiting and abandonment also recall migrants' claims of suspended time once the state labels them as "illegal." Indeed, state control over movement often centers on the control of time (see Fernandez; Rydzewski in this volume). The power dimensions of time are acutely felt, adds Hans Lucht (2011) in his study of Ghanaian migrants in Italy. His interviewees all expressed feelings of being stuck, and he writes, "when time is either arbitrarily wasted or simply negated, [it] is a form of nontime, a testimony to one's social insignificance, a time that does not unfold in connection with any aim or expectation but marks the end of the possible" (Lucht, 2011, p. 73). In this example of American tourists "stuck" overseas at the start of the pandemic, many

242 Stephanie Malia Hom

grew frustrated (and sometimes indignant) about having to wait and "waste time," while the US government did nothing to help them. Framed in the context of Lucht's observations, their resentments seemed to cover over a fear of being socially insignificant, and at the same time, the shock of having their privilege of choice – to move or not move – ignored by the state. Put another way, these tourists were re-situated by the state into the subjective position that many migrants, refugees, and asylum seekers find themselves in (neglected by the state), and in this way, they unwittingly experienced the affective consequences of that repositioning.

Contrast this belief in the freedom of mobility among tourists against the afore-mentioned migrant farmworkers in California who feared that staying at home during the pandemic would threaten their jobs and hinder their ability to send remittances, and the terrain of inequality and injustice becomes apparent. Whereas luxury tourists have the resources to exist in a prolonged state of leisure during the pandemic – thus transforming the liminal state of ritual and play described by Nelson Graburn as a key feature of modern tourism into the practice of their everyday lives (Graburn, 1983, 2017) – farmworkers have been thrust further to the margins, further into a precarious state of liminality. For these migrants in the United States, seemingly no choice existed between staying at home or going to work. They were deemed "essential" by the state and therefore obligated to mobilize, whether they might be ill or not. Elsewhere, however, migrant farmworkers, like those in Italy, decided to mobilize in a different way. They protested against exploitative labor practices, degraded living conditions, and the Italian state's increasingly restrictive policies toward migration. They went on strike multiple times during the pandemic, advocating not only for better working conditions but also the very right to have rights (Corrado and Palumbo, 2021, p. 156).

A fruitful avenue of future research, then, might examine the circumstances under which elite classes, like luxury tourists, and those already existing on the margins, like migrant farmworkers, "deploy" or "activate" mobility or immobility, and what ethical consequences those actions might hold. Who benefits and how? What instruments are used to exercise this mobility-power? What is the effective fallout? How might variegated mobilities reaffirm or call into question established hierarchies of social order? What will having the privilege of choice to move or not mean beyond the pandemic? How might we envision new dimensions of mobility justice?

Biopolitics, Contagion, and Immunity

While this novel coronavirus exacerbated already existing mobility-generated disparities, such as those outlined with great care by Mimi Sheller in her work on mobility justice (Sheller, 2018, pp. 20–44), it also inserted matters of biopolitics at the forefront of tourism, migration, and exile. If we consider biopolitics the sphere by which politics intervenes in biological life, government-issued vaccine cards, for example, might be understood as marking state control of corporeal borders, and, since they are increasingly mandated for travel, state control of political borders as well. The cards also signify one's access to health care, and at the same time, the inequity of vaccine distribution wherein the world's wealthiest countries accumulated surpluses while the world's poorest struggled to secure vaccines.

In countries where the COVID-19 vaccine was not widely available, expats from wealthier countries, like the retirement migrants in Thailand and the residents of American-Vietnamese descent living in Vietnam (see Butratana, Trupp, and Husa as well as Bui respectively in this volume), debated returning home to get their shots. News reports in the summer of 2021 also profiled "vaccine tourists" who spent thousands of dollars to travel to countries where COVID-19 vaccines were more readily available in order to get inoculated. Some tour companies even offered coronavirus vaccine getaways, i.e., package tours that combined a holiday with vaccination. For example, the Norwegian tour company, World Visitor, offered a four-day package to Moscow to receive the Russian-made Sputnik vaccine.[4] Or, visitors to Italy could take a day trip to the Republic of San Marino where they could get vaccines and booster shots for a small fee.[5] While health and medical tourism have been studied for decades (Connell, 2011; Gatrell, 2011), COVID vaccine tourism accelerates the speed and the scale of the practice.[6] Instead of spending weeks recuperating after a surgery, for instance, vaccine tourists are in and out of a clinic within a matter of days, or sometimes even hours, as with the case of San Marino. It also reinforces mobility-generated inequalities by sustaining the privilege of those who have the choice to travel and who can buy access to vaccines. In short, vaccine tourism turns health inequity into a precondition of mobility and assimilates it into the practices of sociocultural differentiation innate to tourism (MacCannell, 1999, pp. 39–56).

With the pandemic, too, the most common form of tourism – visiting friends and relatives (VFR) – has been reframed as a biopolitical quandary in that visiting one's family has the potential to become a matter of life and death. A trip to see an elderly grandparent, for example, could turn deadly if an infected relative unknowingly transmits the virus to them. In fact, media stories about intergenerational COVID transmission abounded early on in the pandemic; often, these were stories with happy beginnings of family gatherings at holidays or vacations, and tragic endings of infection, isolation, and death.[7] As a result of the pandemic, popular VFR activities, like weddings, have been recast as dangerous super-spreader events that hold the potential for mass casualties. For example, a small wedding held in rural Maine in August 2020 resulted in an outbreak of 147 COVID cases, seven hospitalizations, and seven deaths. A study of the outbreak noted that there was little social distancing or mask usage among the friends and relatives who attended the wedding (Mahale et al., 2020). The celebration of a couple's new life together had instead become the source of illness and death.

Any traveler can be a potential disease carrier, i.e., a threat to life; however, VFR tourists can be seen to threaten the lives of those closest to them. One trip or one visit by an infected relative has the potential to decimate families, if not entire kinship networks. In this way, VFR tourism raises the fundamental questions of biopolitics: What is the value of life? Who or what has the power to value (or

244 Stephanie Malia Hom

not value) life? With VFR especially, COVID has put us in the position to have to constantly re-evaluate the question of whose life holds value. For instance, is preserving a grandparent's life more important than a trip to visit them? But what if that grandparent was suffering from the isolation of the pandemic, and a visit would enhance their quality of life? Is the risk to their proper life acceptable?

Those questions, of course, assume the privilege of choice to move or not. For many, like refugees and asylum seekers, mobility is born of necessity and there is little choice. In fact, theirs might be considered hypermobility perforce as a result of having to navigate constantly in and through closed routes and roadblocks as well as changing bureaucratic rules (see Rydzewski in this volume). Still for others, though, there exists a grey zone whereby there is no privilege of choice in one situation, but yet in another one that choice exists. Returning to the example of migrant farmworkers in California, who, labeled as "essential" workers, had little choice but to mobilize and go to work during the pandemic. Yet some of those workers also made the choice to undertake seasonal return trips to Mexico to visit friends and relatives. Still others, such as those in Imperial County, California, commute daily between Mexico and the United States (Keeney et al., 2022) complicating the categories of "tourist" and "migrant" in such a way as to almost render them immaterial. Put another way, migrant farmworkers in California "transgress mobility categories" (Bloch, 2020) and challenge daily the conceptual boundaries between these subject positions.

Similar to the way that the virus has challenged the limits of the physical body, so, too, the pandemic has challenged the borders of the body politic (Agier, 2020). The pandemic forced the issue of public health to become "the pivot around which the entire economic, administrative, and political affairs of the state revolved" (Esposito, 2011, p. 137). For Roberto Esposito, a philosopher who builds on Michel Foucault's idea of biopolitics, the preservation of life – of the individual body and of the collective body politic – defines our contemporary existence. Life exists as the object of political care. For him, this care and preservation hinge on the concept of *immunitas*. He uses the Latin word, *immunitas*, to describe both the action of immunization and the state of immunity, which reproduce "in controlled form that which is meant to protect us from" (Esposito, 2011, p. 8). For example, in medicine, immunity is often conferred by a vaccine made from an inactive part of a virus, which is then injected into a physical body to protect it from a whole active virus.[8] Or in law, immunity involves testifying and admitting to a lesser crime in exchange for a lighter sentence, which protects the self from the risk of harsher punishment.

Migrants, refugees, and asylum seekers are often cast as threats to the body politic, i.e., risks to the nation-state's body of citizens, and the viral metaphors deployed against them (i.e., contagion, contamination, infestation) can be seen as an immunitary response. Equating migrants with viruses dehumanizes them, and more importantly, it also devalues their life, for viruses exist in a grey zone between living and nonliving (Villareal, 2008). Ongoing devaluation and dehumanization lead to what Giorgio Agamben has called "bare life," a condition that migration

Pandemic Postscript **245**

scholars have well documented among migrants and refugees (Agamben, 1998; Diken and Laustsen, 2005). "Bare life" became spatialized in the form of the concentration camp in the past (Agamben, 1999), and, in our present day, in places like migrant detention centers (Hom, 2019, pp. 81–82).

Although she was not a migrant, Denise Stoneham, the cruise ship passenger cited earlier in this essay, reacted intuitively against the immunitary response that attempted to re-categorize tourists as disease carriers. By exclaiming her humanity (we're human beings, we want to come home) and protesting vehemently against viral metaphor (we're not an infestation that's coming to their city), Stoneham resisted the attempt to dehumanize her and thus devalue her life. Because she was a tourist who had access to communicative mobilities like cell phones and email, her voice was heard by no less than *The New York Times*, whereas so many other migrants in the midst of the pandemic had no recourse but to remain silent and thus vulnerable to the conditions that pushed them closer to the edges of "bare life." Put another way, while the pandemic has blurred the categorical bounds between tourists and migrants, it has also reified their distinctions, especially when framed in the context of immunitary response.

When viewed through a biopolitical lens, the pandemic brings into focus new questions about the relationship between mobility and immunity that are ripe for future exploration. How do intersecting medical and legal immunities unevenly affect those who move by choice and those who are moved by force? How are power relations changed? Under what circumstances are borders transgressed and reified simultaneously? How might viral metaphors, like the "invasions" of tourists and migrants, represent an immunitary response by the state? How might that reaction reshape questions about the value of life and who or what determines that value?

Conclusion: New Imaginaries?

What has distinguished the COVID-19 pandemic from previous others has been the rise of a corresponding infodemic that has hampered public health efforts to mitigate COVID-19, particularly in the United States. The ongoing deluge of mis- and disinformation has literally cost lives. The World Health Organization estimates that within the first three months of the pandemic, more than 6,000 people were hospitalized worldwide of which at least 800 died, owing to falsehoods, rumors, and conspiracy theories circulated about COVID-19.[9] The death toll has only risen since then.

The powerful imaginaries conjured by mis- and disinformation have been directly tied to people taking dangerous actions that have led to injury and even death, such as drinking bleach to kill the virus or refusing the vaccine based on rumors that it would implant a microchip used for tracking and surveillance (Islam et al., 2020; Hartman et al., 2021; Nguyen, 2020). These pandemic imaginaries function to reinforce shared worldviews, like the belief that COVID is a hoax, as well as to catalyze collective action, like anti-vaccine protests. Often, pandemic mis- and disinformation has offered up the idea of an Other as the source of contagion – be it "the government," "China," or "migrants." In doing so, it has strengthened feelings of belonging to an in-group (i.e., anti-vaxxers) by hardening divisions between "us" versus "them."

Since pandemic imaginaries both challenge and make meaning and thus give shape to worldviews, they can be seen as having much in common with tourism imaginaries (Salazar and Graburn, 2014; Gravari-Barbas and Graburn, 2016). Noel Salazar's definition of tourism imaginaries as "socially transmitted representational assemblages that interact with people's personal imaginings and are used as meaning-making and world-shaping devices" (Salazar, 2012, p. 864) can be applied easily to the imaginaries that proliferated during the COVID-19 pandemic. Just as tourism is a practice of "difference projection and vehicle for Othering par excellence" (Hollinshead, 1998, p. 121) so, too, has the infodemic increased marginalization and violence against people perceived to be Others. By way of an example, the documented rise in hate crimes across the United States against migrants and specific ethnic groups, like Asian-Americans, demonstrates how mis- and disinformation about COVID-19 (i.e., migrants as disease carriers) not only alienates people but also leads to violence against them as well as loss of life (James and Hanson, 2021).

Imaginaries also broker heavily in images. Understood broadly as cultural representations, images – which might be anything from Inuit soapstone carvings (Graburn, 1976) to capoeira films (see Griffith in this volume) to artwork by Banksy in Bethlehem (see Isaac in this volume) – have the power to generate an effect. And effective force influences behavior: inspiring some to buy Inuit carvings as souvenirs, others to travel to Brazil to learn capoeira, and still others to tour Palestinian refugee camps in the West Bank, for instance. Images and imaginaries are thus intertwined, and together, create a representational apparatus that mediates identity with all its attendant political and spiritual aims. For example, tourism imaginaries help blur the lines between hosts and guests, as both negotiate the self-images produced for and consumed by one another (Adams, 2006; Chio, 2014; Salazar, 2009). In migration, too, encounters with the imaginary of illegality trigger people to reconceive of themselves as "illegal." They come to accept a new identity as "illegal immigrants" *ex post facto*, i.e., after long-term exposure to the imaginary of illegality and the day-to-day reality of coping with mobility-generated inequality (Andersson, 2014, pp. 107–108). If imaginaries serve to forge identities, as they do in tourism and migration, what happens to that process when it is thrust into the crucible of the pandemic?

New questions thus emerge: How might we conceive of a pandemic imaginary and what images might constitute its representational apparatus? What happens when that new imaginary intersects with others, such as those linked to tourism, migration, and exile? How might it change the already indeterminate boundaries between subjective categories as well as create new ones (i.e., tourist carrier)? What new borders might emerge from a pandemic imaginary, especially concerning identity, mobility, and life and death? What are the ethical consequences of those

Pandemic Postscript **247**

new borders? What moral responses are necessary to best navigate such boundaries in the pandemic's wake?

It is likely that this pandemic imaginary will give rise to images that will challenge and make meaning, shape worldviews, and create and even concretize differences in new and unforeseen ways. They will entreat us to hold in tension paradoxical sites and sights, which may be unsettling at times, and at others, hopeful. Unsettling like the tourists on the Grand Princess cruise ship confined at the port because they were considered "environmental hazards." Or, the hundreds of weather-worn migrants adrift in the Mediterranean Sea rescued by Maltese authorities and imprisoned on ill-equipped tourist "pleasure boats" for more than a month under the aegis of quarantine (Baldacchino, 2021). Or, hotels like the Park Hotel in Melbourne, Australia, where tourists who tested positive for COVID were held alongside the dozens of asylum seekers brought to shore for medical treatment from offshore detention centers on islands like Nauru where they had been held without due process for years (Zhuang and Cave, 2022).

Yet there are hopeful sights, too, however fleeting they might be. Sights like the clear air and blue skies over polluted cities like Delhi owing to a lockdown-induced drop in emissions (Kotnala et al., 2020). Or, the dolphins that returned briefly to swim in Venice's Grand Canal thanks to decreased boat traffic during quarantine (Buckley, 2021). Or, the new means created to connect us with one another, whether singing collectively on balconies or video calls with family and friends. In this way, the pandemic has provided us with an opportunity for reflection, and if we so choose, a chance for recalibration among ourselves and the world we live in. It just might be the catalyst for imagining a future centered on communal rather than categorical bounds. The privilege of choice is ours. If we take it, we just might learn to live in symbiosis with one another, and together, tread more softly on this planetary biome that is our collective home.

Notes

1   As of February 2022, UNHCR estimates more than 82.4 million people are forcibly displaced worldwide. www.unhcr.org/en-us/figures-at-a-glance.html (accessed February 13, 2022).
2   The UN World Tourism Organization maintains an "International Tourism and COVID-19 Dashboard" with statistics related to the impact of COVID on the global tourism industry. www.unwto.org/international-tourism-and-covid-19 (accessed February 13, 2022).
3   For a representative example of news stories about tourists "stranded" abroad by coronavirus immediately after the worldwide lockdown in early 2020, see Feng, 2020; Logue, 2020; Mzezewa, 2020; and Murray, 2020. These stories also echo those of tourists who were "stranded" abroad due to natural disasters like the 2004 Indian Ocean tsunami and the 2010 eruption of the Eyjafjallajökull volcano that disrupted international travel for weeks, if not months. Exploring the parallels between the coronavirus pandemic and these natural disasters could be fruitful in revealing new conceptual ties between tourism and emergency.
4   For details, visit the tour company's website: www.worldvisitor.com/2_short_trips_moscow (accessed February 13, 2022).

248 Stephanie Malia Hom

5   The Republic of San Marino maintains a webpage for vaccine tourists: www.visitsan-marino.com/pub1/VisitSM/contenuto/Vivi/Turismo_vaccinale.html (accessed February 13, 2022).
6   What we consider health and wellness tourism today is clearly linked with the origins of tourism. Practices such as "taking the waters" and traveling to milder climates for health reasons date back to as early as the Roman empire. Pilgrims often traveled to sacred sites, like Lourdes or Chimayo, in search of cures for ailments. By the late 18th and early 19th century, as modern mass tourism expanded its reach, spa tourism in places like Blackpool and Nice had already emerged as a popular practice. On this, see Connell (2011, pp. 12–22) and Hom (2015, pp. 130–131).
7   For two examples of stories of family gatherings resulting in coronavirus tragedy, see Meyer (2021) and Tulley (2020). An upcoming special issue of the journal *Tourism and Hospitality* will explore VFR tourism in a post-Covid world: www.mdpi.com/journal/tourismhosp/special_issues/Visiting_Friends_Relatives_COVID.
8   The advent of mRNA vaccines that do not use a deactivated portion of the virus like those created by Pfizer-BioNTech and Moderna against SARS-CoV-2 may complicate Esposito's theory of *immunitas*.
9   By May 2020, the problem of mis- and disinformation related to COVID-19 had become so damaging that the World Health Organization (WHO) launched a "Stop the Spread" public health campaign with the aim of limiting false information. On this, see www.who.int/news-room/feature-stories/detail/fighting-misinformation-in-the-time-of-covid-19-one-click-at-a-time (accessed February 13, 2022).

References

Adams, K. (2006) *Art as politics: Re-crafting identities, tourism, and power in Tana Toraja, Indonesia.* Honolulu, HI: University of Hawai'i Press.
Adey, P., Hannam, K., Sheller, M. and Tyfield, D. (2021) 'Pandemic (Im)mobilities', *Mobilities*, 16(1), pp. 1–19.
Agamben, G. (1998) *Homo sacer: Sovereign power and bare life.* Stanford: Stanford University Press.
Agamben, G. (1999) *Remnants of Auschwitz: The witness and the archive.* Stanford: Stanford University Press.
Agier, M. (2011) *Managing the undesirables: Refugee camps and humanitarian government.* Cambridge: Polity Press.
Agier, M. (2020) 'Borders of the pandemic: Against epistemological nationalism'. Paper presented at the Virtual Workshop: Migration and Borders in the Age of the Pandemic. University of the Aegean. Available at: https://summer-schools.aegean.gr/MigBord2021/Virtual-Workshop.
Andersson, R. (2014) *Illegality Inc.: Clandestine migration and the business of bordering Europe.* Berkeley, CA: University of California Press.
Baldacchino, G. (2021) 'Forced immobility: Undocumented migrants, boats, Brussels, and islands', *Transfers*, 11(1), pp. 76–91.
Bloch, N. (2020) 'Beyond a sedentary other and a mobile tourist: Transgressing mobility categories in the informal tourism sector in India', *Critique of Anthropology*, 40(2), pp. 218–237.
Block, F. (2022) 'Private jet travel soared in 2021', *Barron's*, 25 January. Available at: www.barrons.com/articles/private-jet-travel-soared-in-2021-01643152417.
Brady, E. (2022) 'World's 10 richest men got richer during the pandemic, worth combined $1.5 trillion: report', *Newsweek*, 17 January. Available at: www.newsweek.com/worlds-10-richest-men-got-richer-during-pandemic-worth-combined-15-trillion-report-1670126.

Buckley, J. (2021) 'These dolphins took a day trip up Venice's Grand Canal', *CNN*, 23 March. Available at: www.cnn.com/travel/article/venice-canal-dolphins/index.html.

Chio, J. (2014) *A landscape of travel: The work of tourism in rural ethnic China*. Washington, DC: University of Washington Press.

Connell, J. (2011) *Medical tourism*. Wallingford: CABI.

Corrado, A. and Palumbo, L. (2021) 'Essential farmworkers and the pandemic crisis: Migrant labour conditions, and legal and political responses in Italy' in Trianafyllidou, A. (ed.) *Migration and pandemics: Spaces of solidarity and spaces of exception*. New York: Springer, pp. 145–166.

Diken, B. and Laustsen, C.B. (2005) *The culture of exception: Sociology facing the camp*. New York and London: Routledge.

Elliott, A. and Urry, J. (2010) *Mobile lives*. York and London: Routledge.

Eskenazi, B., Mora, A.M., Lewnard, J., Cuevas, M. and Nkowcha, O. (2020) *Prevalence and predictors of Sars-COV-2 infection among farmworkers in Monterey County, California. Summary report*. Berkeley, CA: UC Berkeley School of Public Health.

Esposito, R. (2011) *Immunitas: The protection and negation of life*. Cambridge: Polity Press.

Feng, L. (2020) 'Coronavirus lockdown leaves international tourists stranded in Australia', *ABC News Daily*, 19 May. Available at: www.abc.net.au/news/2020-05-20/coronavirus-lockdown-leaves-tourists-stranded-in-australia/12265658.

Fuller, T., Eligon, J. and Gross, J. (2020) 'Cruise ship, floating symbol of America's fear of coronavirus docks in Oakland', *The New York Times*, 9 March. Available at: www.nytimes.com/2020/03/09/us/coronavirus-cruise-ship-oakland-grand-princess.html

Gatrell, A. (2011) *Mobilities and health*. Farnham: Ashgate.

Goffard, C. (2020) 'We called it voyage of the damned': Days of despair on the Grand Princess', *The Los Angeles Times*, 23 December. Available at: www.latimes.com/california/story/2020-12-23/covid-19-spread-despair-grand-princess.

Graburn, N. (ed.) (1976) *Ethnic and tourist arts: Cultural expressions from the fourth world*. Berkeley, CA: University of California Press.

Graburn, N. (1983) 'The anthropology of tourism', *Annals of Tourism Research*, 10, pp. 9–33.

Graburn, N. (2017) 'Key figure of mobility: The tourist', *Social Anthropology*, 25(1), pp. 83–96.

Gravari-Barbas, M. and Graburn, N. (eds.) (2016) *Tourism imaginaries at the disciplinary crossroads: Place, practice, media*. New York and London: Routledge.

Hartman, T., Marshall, M., Stocks, T., McKay, R., Bennett, K., Butter, S., Miller, J., Hyland, P., Levita, L., Martinez, A., Mason, L., McBride, O., Murphy, J., Shevlin, M., Vallières, F. and Bentall, R. (2021) 'Different conspiracy theories have different psychological and social determinants: Comparison of three theories about the origins of the Covid-19 virus in a representative sample of the UK population', *Frontiers in Political Science*, 3, pp. 1–17.

Hollinshead, K. (1998) 'Tourism, hybridity, and ambiguity: The relevance of Bhabha's 'third space' cultures', *Journal of Leisure Research*, 30(1), pp. 121–156.

Hom, S.M. (2015) *The beautiful country: Tourism and the impossible state of destination Italy*. Toronto: University of Toronto Press.

Hom, S.M. (2019) *Empire's mobius strip: Historical echoes in Italy's crisis of migration and detention*. New York: Cornell University Press.

Islam, M.S., Sarkar, T., Khan, S.H., Kamal, A-H., Hasan, S.M., Kabir, A., Yeasmin, D., Islam, M., Chowdhury, K., Anwar, K., Chughtai, A. and Seale, H. (2020) 'Covid-19-related infodemic and its impact on public health: A global social media analysis', *The American Journal of Tropical Medicine and Hygiene*, 104(4), pp. 1621–1629.

James, N. and Hanson, E. (2021) 'Reported increase in hate crimes against Asian Americans', *Congressional Research Service*. Available at: https://crsreports.congress.gov/product/pdf/IN/IN11622

Keeney, A., Quandt, A., Villaseñor, M., Flores, D. and Flores, Jr., L. (2022) 'Occupational stressors and access to Covid-19 resources among commuting and residential Hispanic/Latino farmworkers in a U.S.-Mexico border region', *International Journal of Environmental Research and Public Health*, 19(763). Available at: www.mdpi.com/1660-4601/19/2/763

Kotnala, G., Mandal, T.K., Sharma, S.K. and Kotnala, R.K. (2020) 'Emergence of blue sky over Delhi due to coronavirus disease (Covid-19) lockdown implications', *Aerosol Science and Engineering*, 4(3), pp. 228–238.

Logue, J. (2020) '"We are abandoned": These tourists stranded in the U.S. because of coronavirus want to go home', *NBC News*, 14 May. Available at: www.nbcnews.com/news/latino/we-are-abandoned-these-tourists-stranded-u-s-because-coronavirus-n1206386.

Lucht, H. (2011) *Darkness before daybreak: African migrants living on the margins in southern Italy today*. Berkeley, CA: University of California Press.

MacCannell, D. (1999) *The tourist: A new theory of the leisure class*. Berkeley, CA: University of California Press.

Mahale, P., Rothfuss, C., Bly, S., Kelly, M., Bennett, S., Huston, S. and Robinson, S. (2020) 'Multiple Covid-19 outbreaks linked to a wedding reception in rural Maine – August 7-September 14, 2020', *Morbidity and Mortality Weekly Report*, 69(45), pp. 1686–1690.

McNicholas, C. and Poydock, M. (2020) 'Who are essential workers? A comprehensive look at their wages, demographics, and unionization rates', *Economics Policy Institute*, 19 May. Available at: www.epi.org/blog/who-are-essential-workers-a-comprehensive-look-at-their-wages-demographics-and-unionization-rates/

Meyer, A. (2021) '"I tried to barter with God": Family ravaged by Covid after gathering', *KXAN NBC News*, 8 August. Available at: www.kxan.com/news/i-tried-to-barter-with-god-family-ravaged-by-covid-after-gathering/

Murray, T. (2020) 'Tourists stranded across Europe as Covid-19 lockdowns kick in', *Euronews*, 16 March. Available at: www.euronews.com/2020/03/16/tourists-stranded-across-europe-as-covid-19-lockdowns-kick-in.

Mzezewa, T. (2020) 'Americans stranded abroad: "I feel completely abandoned"', *The New York Times*, 18 March. Available at: www.nytimes.com/2020/03/18/travel/coronavirus-americans-stranded.html

Nguyen, A. and Catalan-Matamoros, D. (2020) 'Digital mis/disinformation and public engagement with health and science controversies: Fresh perspectives from Covid-19', *Media and Communication*, 8(2), pp. 323–328.

Presser, B. (2020) 'Luxury hotels become home for some rich folks looking for a Covid haven', *The Los Angeles Times*, 3 September. Available at: www.latimes.com/business/story/2020-09-03/pandemic-luxury-hotels-become-home

Salazar, N. (2009) 'Imaged or imagined? Cultural representations and the "tourismification" of peoples and places', *Cahiers d'Études Africaines*, 49(193–194), pp. 49–71.

Salazar, N. (2012) 'Tourism imaginaries: A conceptual approach', *Annals of Tourism Research*, 39(2), pp. 863–882.

Salazar, N. (2020) *Covid-19, mobilities, and futures. 2020 John Urry Memorial Lecture with T. Cresswell and M. Sheller*. Center for Mobilities Research, Lancaster University. Available at: www.lancaster.ac.uk/cemore/4566-2/.

Salazar, N. and Graburn, N. (eds.) (2014) *Tourism imaginaries, anthropological approaches*. New York and Oxford: Berghahn Books.

Sheller, M. (2018) *Mobility justice: The politics of movement in an age of extremes*. London: Verso.

Tulley, T. (2020) 'Coronavirus ravages 7 members of a single New Jersey family, killing 4', *The New York Times*, 18 March. Available at: www.nytimes.com/2020/03/18/nyregion/new-jersey-family-coronavirus.html.

Urry, J. (2007) *Mobilities*. Cambridge: Polity Press.

Villareal, L. (2008) 'Are viruses alive?', *Scientific American*. Available at: www.scientificamerican.com/article/are-viruses-alive-2004/.

Wald, P. (2008) *Contagious: Cultures, carriers, and the outbreak narrative*. Durham, NC: Duke University Press.

Wilson, C. (2020) 'Coronavirus: Brits stranded abroad due to the virus', *BBC News*, 27 March. Available at: www.bbc.com/news/uk-52053325.

Zhuang, Y. and Cave, D. (2022) 'At an Australian hotel, Djokovic is not the only cause of controversy', *The New York Times*, 8 January. Available at: www.nytimes.com/2022/01/08/world/asia/australia-djokovic-refugees-hotel.html.

INDEX

activist 3, 64, 109, 100, 112, 133, 134, 134, 139, 140, 141, 144, 146, 198
Afro-Antillean 18, 130–144
age of migration 31, 134, 174
Algiers 79–81
amenity migration 8, 150–151, 221; *see also* retirement, migration
amistad interesada 51–52
apprenticeship: pilgrim 187–188, 189, 191, 195–196, 198; pilgrimage 188, 191, 193–196
asylum seekers 3, 6, 10, 17, 112–126, 242, 244, 247
Austria 150, 158–165
authenticity 46, 114, 120, 183, 188–189, 202
autonomy of migrations 132–134, 136–144

Balkan route 16, 17, 112–126
Banksy 100, 102–103, 107, 246; *see also* solidarity, art
belonging 16, 32, 35, 45–55
Bethlehem 94–109, 246
bi-national: couples 43; lifestyle 42; relationship 35–36
biopolitics 20, 242–245
Border Free Association 114–115, 116
Brazil 187–199, 218, 222, 227–230, 232, 233, 246
business traveller 3, 6, 191, 203

capoeira 4, 18–19, 187–199, 246
Caribbean 131–132, 137, 142, 143, 144

casa particular 37–38, 39
Chinese 67, 134, 136, 170, 174, 217–222, 224–228, 232–234
chronos 34–35, 42; *see also kairos*
citizenship 34, 35, 42, 63, 64, 65, 69, 70, 133, 143, 174, 182, 217, 221
class mobility 229
closed society 178–179; *see also* open city
colonial 178; approaches 123; era 189; relationship 230; -style displays 173; ties 233
community of practice 176–177, 188, 192, 194–195, 196
consumption-related mobilities 7, 8, 18, 151
COVID-19 19–20, 31, 43, 63, 72–73, 82, 141, 153, 164–165, 183, 219, 222, 239–247
cross-border: marriage 154, 161; marriage migration 18, 153, 160; migration 148–149; visits 159, 164
cruise ship 238–239, 245, 247; *see also* Grand Princess
Cuba 16, 31–43, 45–55, 84, 85, 87, 131, 239–240
Cuban: –Danish couples 16, 32–43; lifestyle 45; -ness 48–50, 52–54

Denmark 31–43, 81, 176, 240
deportation 16, 62, 63–65, 68
deportees 17, 61, 64, 65
diaspora 4, 9, 13, 17, 18, 47, 61, 62, 68, 70–71, 72, 73, 102, 136–138, 142–143, 148, 199

Index 253

discrimination 48, 50, 178, 197
displaced person 2, 20n5, 79
diversionary tourists 124; *see also*
  volunteer, tourism
domestic tourism 183–184

Eastern European Outreach 117
economic migrant 17, 47, 62, 70, 80,
  87–88, 89–90, 116, 240
educational mobility 9, 17, 20, 79, 90; *see
  also* student, mobility
emotional exile 69–73
environmental hazards 238, 247
essential workers 20, 244
ethnoscape 172, 188
EU border regime 17, 124, 125, 126
exemplary victims 123
exile 1–20, 32, 36–37, 46, 60, 61–63, 66,
  67–73, 78–79, 81–86, 89–90, 94–95,
  104, 108–109, 120, 139, 171–172, 173,
  174, 175, 197–198, 199, 238–240,
  242–243, 246
exiled tourist 67–69
expats 13, 17, 60–73, 155–157, 208, 243
experience of mobility 131, 141

family reunification 32, 34, 36, 42, 152,
  218, 221, 224
folk geography 196
forced: migration 6, 15, 64, 132, 143, 144;
  returns 63–69
Fresh Response 115, 117

generosity 50
global borderland 66
Golden Visa (GV) holders 19, 217–234
Grand Princess 19, 238–239, 247; *see also*
  cruise ship

heritage 10, 13, 14, 15, 18, 79, 97,
  170–184, 198, 201
highly skilled: migrants 219; professionals
  19, 201, 213–214, 220–221
Holidays in Peace program 1, 79, 80–81
horizontal solidarity movements 114
humanitarian 6, 10, 14, 65, 83, 85,
  112–114, 117, 120–125; *see also*
  volunteerism
humanitarianism 114, 122

imaginaries: pandemic 245–246; tourism
  19, 207–208, 210, 213, 246
immigration 1, 35, 39, 47, 149, 152,
  160–161, 173–174, 227

immobility 43, 61, 132–133, 240–242;
  vulnerable 125–126
immobilization 112, 238–239
immunity 242–245
indigenous 1–2, 46, 135–136, 142,
  173, 178
integration 33, 150, 233
investor mobility 219, 223

Jamaica 130–144
jineterismo 50–52; *see also amistad interesada*

kairos 34–35, 42; *see also chronos*

labor migration 7, 9, 150, 153, 195
LGBT+ 72
lifestyle: migrants 18, 19, 135–136,
  138–139, 141–144, 151, 201–202,
  228–229; migration 8, 133, 138, 151,
  217–234; *see also* consumption-related
  mobilities
limbo 19, 69, 239; *see also* liminality
liminality 72, 242; *see also* limbo

marriage: migrants 20, 148, 150, 153, 159,
  162–163, 164–165; migration 8, 14,
  18, 37, 148–150, 152–154, 158–161,
  163–164, 240
migrant Teachers 197–198
Migrantour 18, 170–184
mobility: justice 20, 173–175, 242; regimes
  6–7, 12, 149, 172
motivation 104–108, 205–210, 220,
  224–226
multiculturalism 18, 135–136, 137, 174

nation-building 17, 84–85, 134–136, 144
neoliberal capitalism 121, 133–134
new mobilities paradigm 7, 133
nomadism 4, 79, 134, 143
nomads 78; cosmopolitan 3; digital 4, 8;
  global 133, 143

open city 179; *see also* closed society

Palestine 94–109
Panama 130–144, 239
permanent resident 69, 71, 139, 141, 152;
  see also permit, resident
permit: reside abroad (PRE) 37; residence
  217, 218–220, 223, 232
politics of mobility 132, 134
Portugal 6, 16, 19, 176, 179, 217–234,
  240–241

254 Index

postcolonial: context 207; disparities 8; theorist 177

Preševo 114–124

privileged mobility 19, 125–126, 217, 220–221

privilege of choice 240–242, 244, 247

public pedagogy 181–183

refugee 2–3, 5, 6, 7, 11–13, 16, 17, 18, 60–73, 79–90, 94–109, 112–126, 143, 170–171, 177, 239, 244, 246

refugeehood 6, 79, 94, 105–106, 109, 239

relationship: cross-cultural 150; mobile 16, 32

relocation 138, 193, 227, 231, 233

repatriated 17, 61–62, 63, 64, 73

residency 16, 34–35, 36, 37, 40, 41–42, 43

responsible tourism 182

retirement: migrant 8, 148–149, 150–152, 154–158, 163–164, 201, 243; migration 3, 6, 8, 18, 148–165, 221; see also amenity migration

returnees 16, 46, 50, 52–53, 55, 70; Cuban 48, 51; diasporic 63, 69; forced 62; mobility 16; Vietnamese 63, 65–67; voluntary 17, 63

return migrants 3, 8, 9, 16, 15, 49–50

roots tourism 3, 9, 18, 142

securitization 21, 34, 124; see also biopolitics

security 19, 63, 67, 121, 131, 158, 161, 219, 225, 229–230

segregation Wall 97–99, 102–109

senior: citizen migration 151; migration 148, 149; see also retirement, migration

Serbia 17, 112–126

sex tourism 153–154, 156

slumming 173–175

social justice 114, 191, 197; see also mobility, justice

solidarity 55, 80, 90, 95, 112, 125; act 10; activism 113; art 102; association 82; groups 124; movement 114, 118, 126; network 108; partnership 85; program 81; tourism 10, 16–17, 83, 90; tours 3, 13, 18; travel 182

Spain 8, 12, 16, 17, 33, 47–48, 56, 78–90, 121, 124, 126, 134, 136, 157, 176, 226, 239

spatial mobility 2, 20, 46, 148, 151, 164, 201, 202–203, 205, 210

stateless person 79, 90

strategic essentialism 177–178

student: migration 78–90; mobility 16, 79–80, 88, 89

subaltern 10, 17

Subotica 114–115, 117

Sweden 36, 142, 204, 208, 211–212, 214

temporality 16, 31–43, 89, 239

temporary migrant 18, 130–144, 239

Thai: migrants 150, 158–159, 164; mobilities 150; population 158–159; – Western marriages 154

Thailand 10, 16, 18, 69, 148–165, 240, 243

tourism hotspots 155, 164

tourist moment 202–204, 205, 210–214

transformative encounters 18, 173

transnational 3, 18, 53, 65, 78, 79, 80–82, 84, 90, 115, 118, 124, 126, 132, 137–138, 150, 164, 172, 188, 189, 199; education model 80, 85; marriages 153; migration 153; mobility 80, 83, 89–90, 214; solidarity-based activism 13; social field 189–193

trauma 64, 72, 239

traveling: cultures 172; dwelling 18–19, 142, 174

Turin 170–171, 176, 182–183

undocumented: migrants 1–2, 12–13, 18; migration 11; person 139

vaccine: getaways 243; tourists 243

Vietnamese 17, 60–73, 152, 154; American 61–73, 154, 243; postwar exile 61

violence 7, 19, 65, 159, 229–230, 233, 246

visa: family 41; investment 224; investor 219–220; student 39, 43, 63; tourist 41, 139, 160; Schengen visa 164; work 122, 193–194

visiting friends and relatives tourism (VFR) 3, 6, 7, 14–15, 16–17, 18–19, 40–41, 69, 140, 148–149, 154, 162–163, 164–165, 192, 195, 198, 243–244

volunteer: tourism 17, 113–114, 120–125; tourists 3, 114, 120–125, 201, 213; see also voluntourism

volunteerism 112

voluntourism 10, 70, 113–114, 120

Printed in the United States
by Baker & Taylor Publisher Services